WHERE ELSE BUT THE STREETS

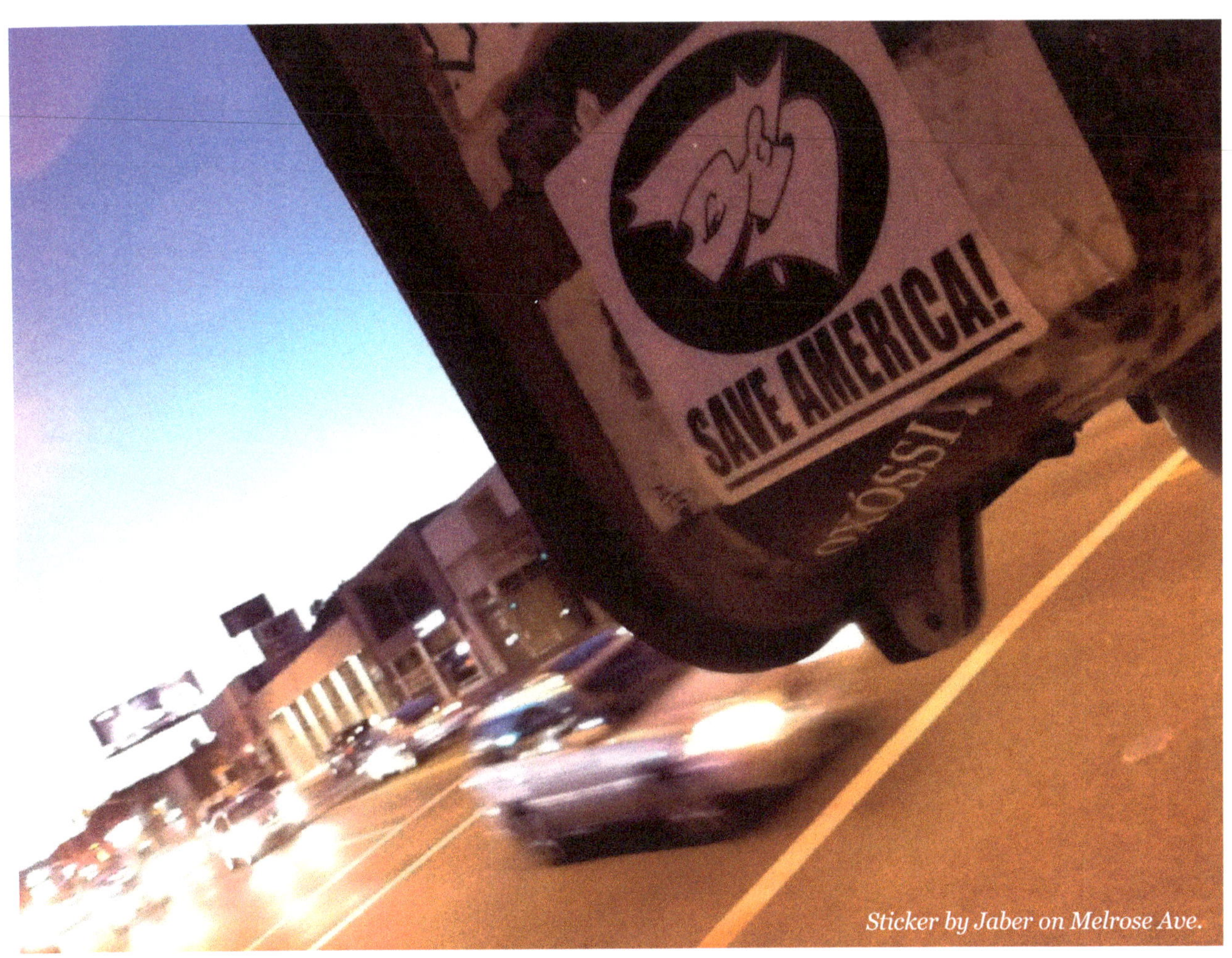

Sticker by Jaber on Melrose Ave.

WHERE ELSE BUT THE STREETS

A STREET ART DOSSIER

BY JOHN WELLINGTON ENNIS

ROTHCO PRESS • LOS ANGELES, CALIFORNIA

Check out Pay2Play.TV for videos, solutions, screenings, swag.

Visit WhereElseButTheStreets.com for updates, events, more.

ROTHCOPRESS

Published by
Rothco Press
8033 West Sunset Blvd.
P.O. Box 1022
Los Angeles, CA 90046

Cover design by John Wellington Ennis
Cover images by John Wellington Ennis

Photography by John Wellington Ennis
Artwork by credited artists

Portions of this book were previously published as *Where Else But the Streets* by John Wellington Ennis, Copyright © 2014 by John Wellington Ennis.

Rothco Press is a division of Over Easy Media Inc.

ISBN: 978-1-941519-97-4
Electronic ISBN: 978-1-941519-49-3

Revised Edition

For Tara

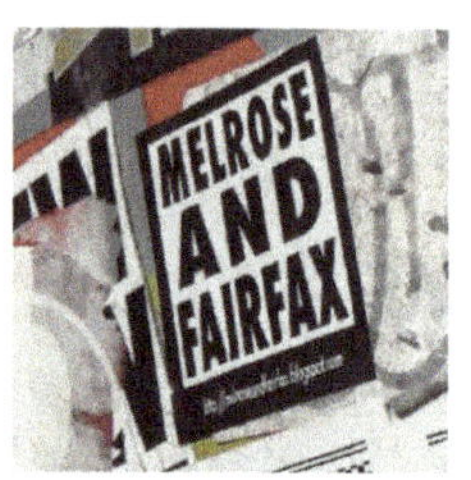

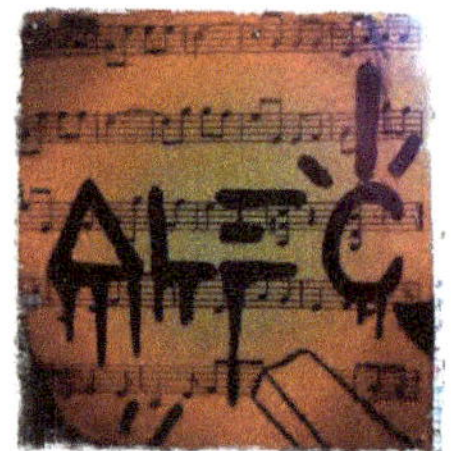
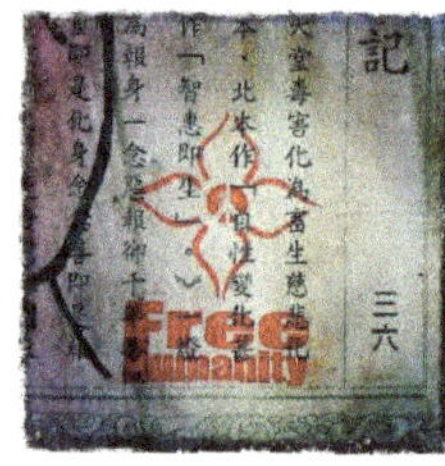
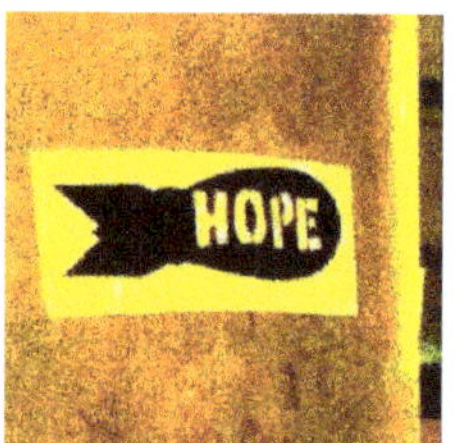

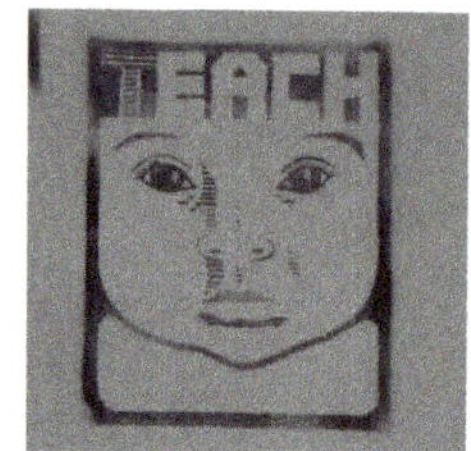

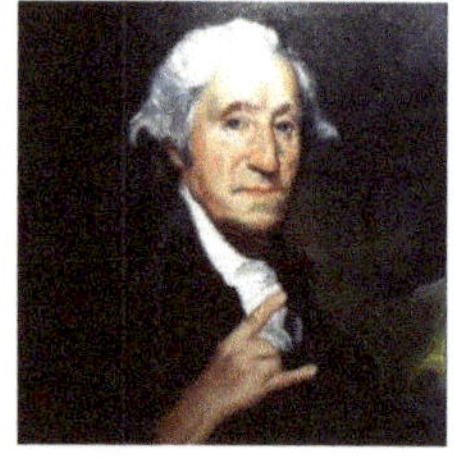
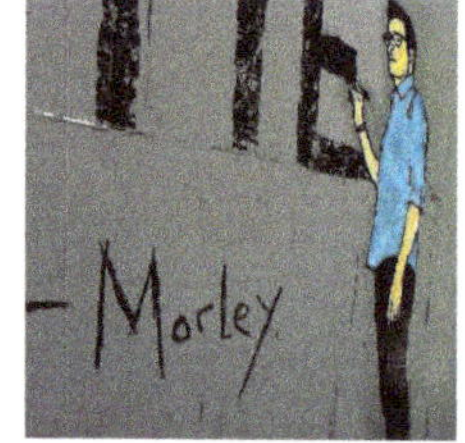

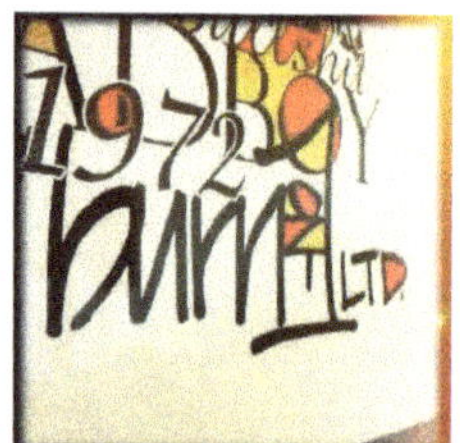

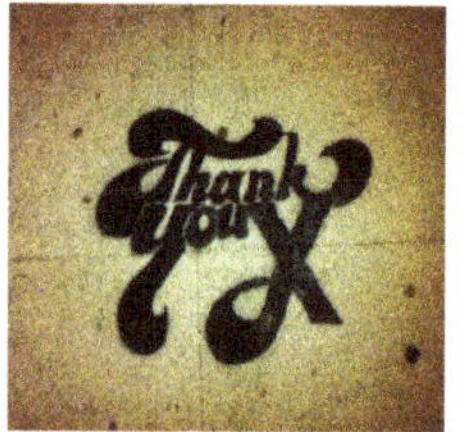

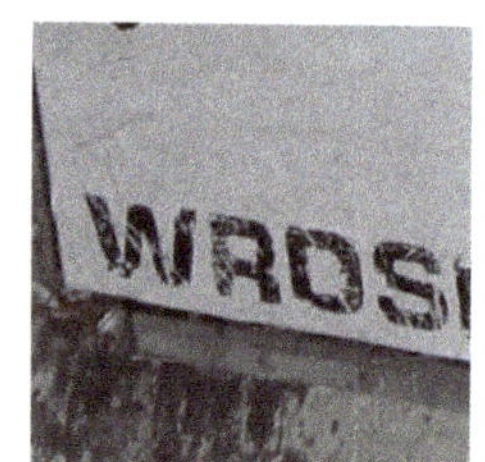
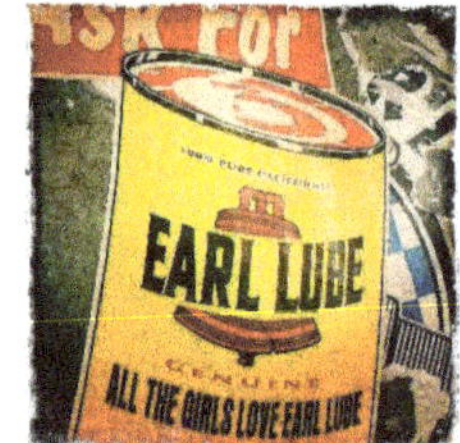

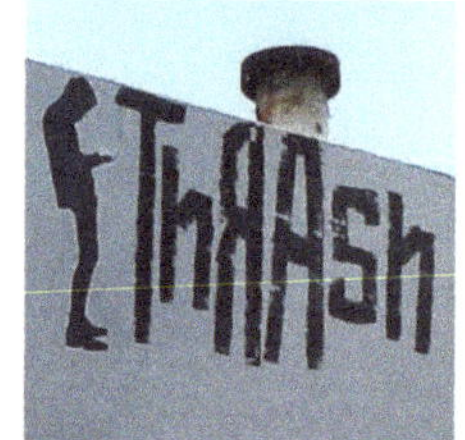
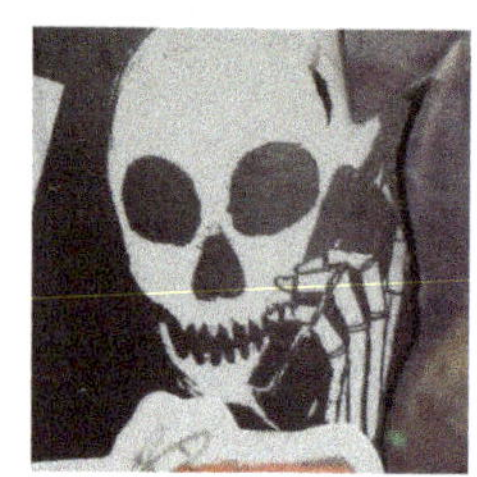
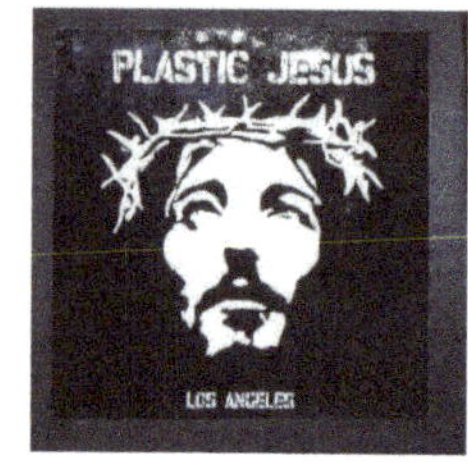

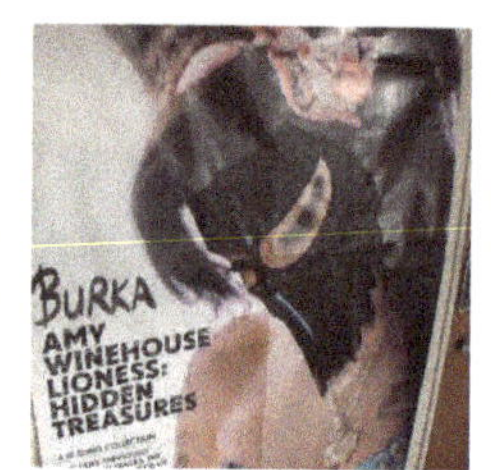

TABLE OF CONTENTS

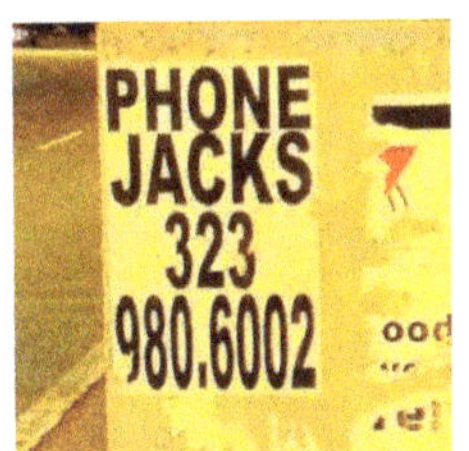
PHONE
JACKS
323
980.6002
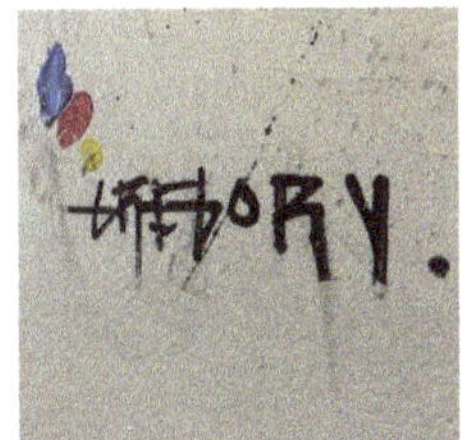
GREGORY.
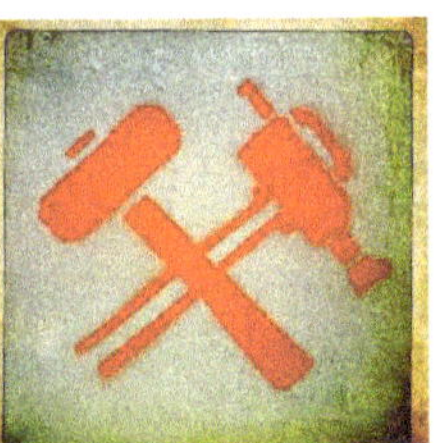
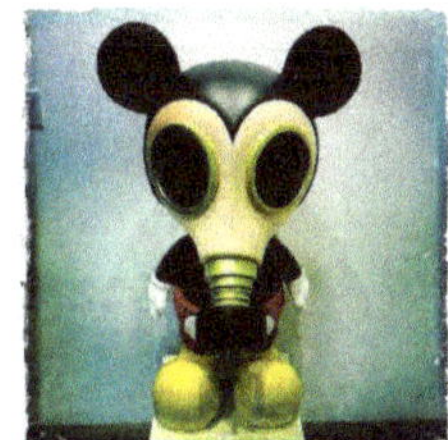
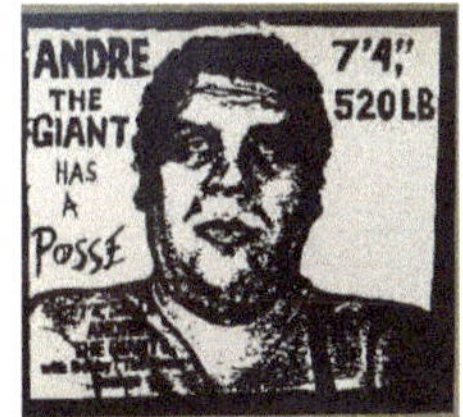
ANDRE
THE
GIANT
HAS
A
POSSE
7'4"
520LB
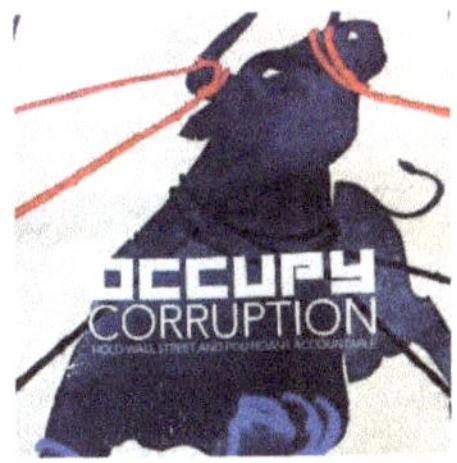
OCCUPY
CORRUPTION
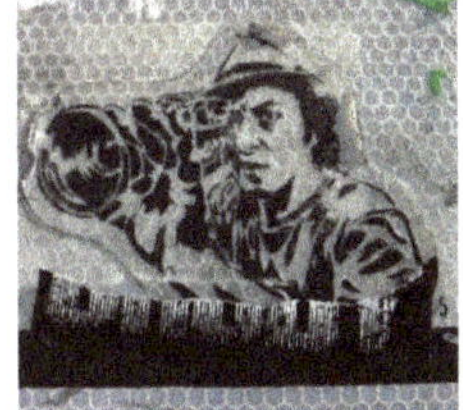
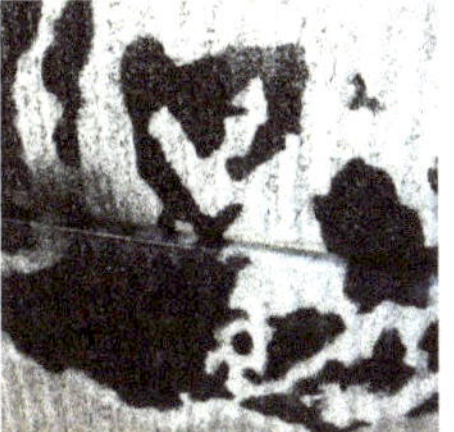
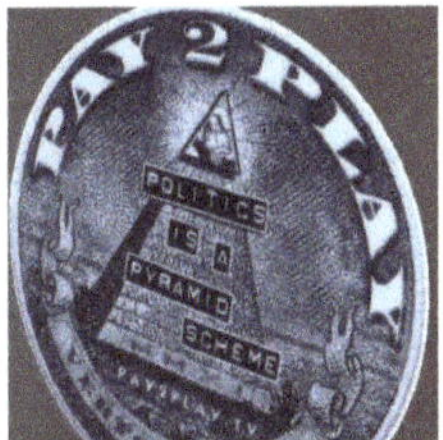
PAY 2 PLAY
POLITICS
IS A
PYRAMID
SCHEME
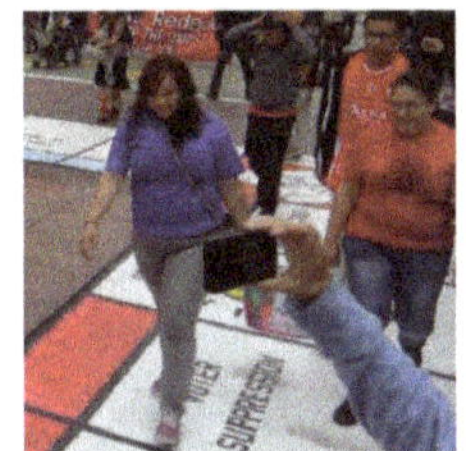
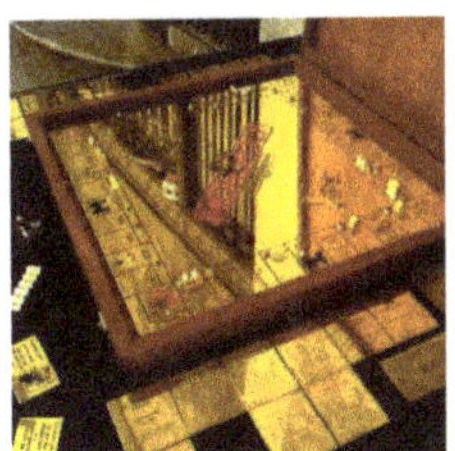
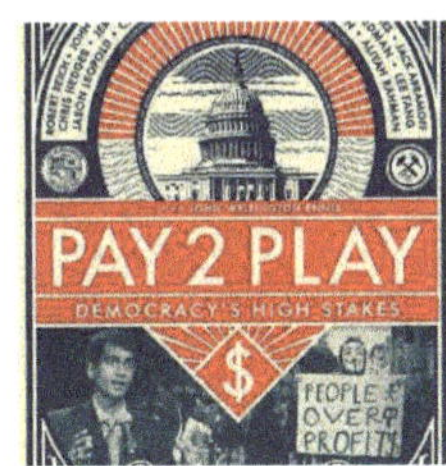
PAY 2 PLAY
DEMOCRACY'S HIGH STAKES
$
PEOPLE
OVER
PROFIT
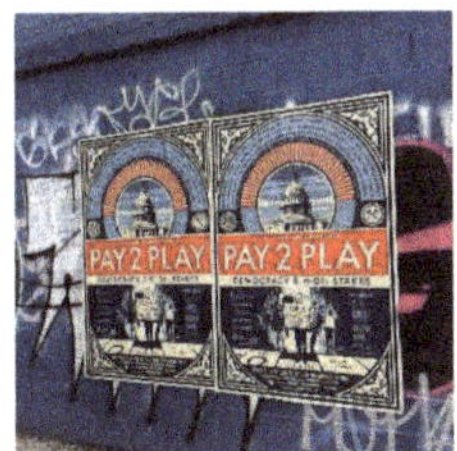
PAY 2 PLAY
PAY 2 PLAY
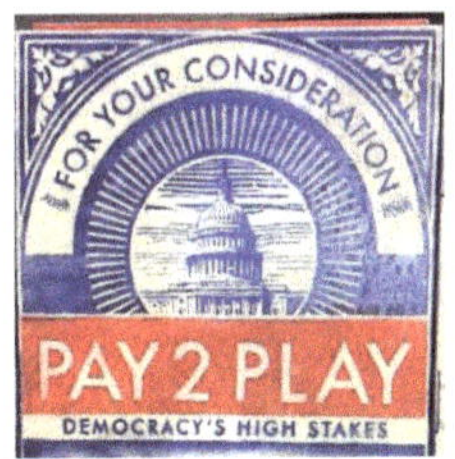
FOR YOUR CONSIDERATION
PAY 2 PLAY
DEMOCRACY'S HIGH STAKES
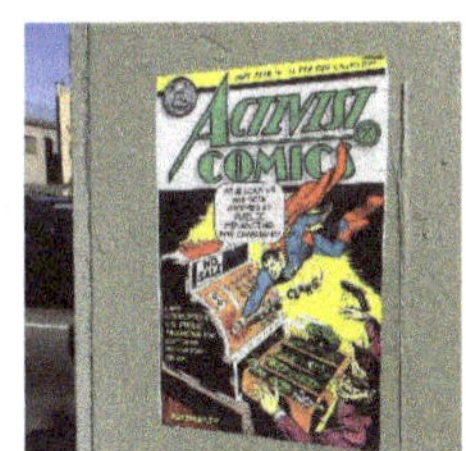
ACTIVIST
COMICS

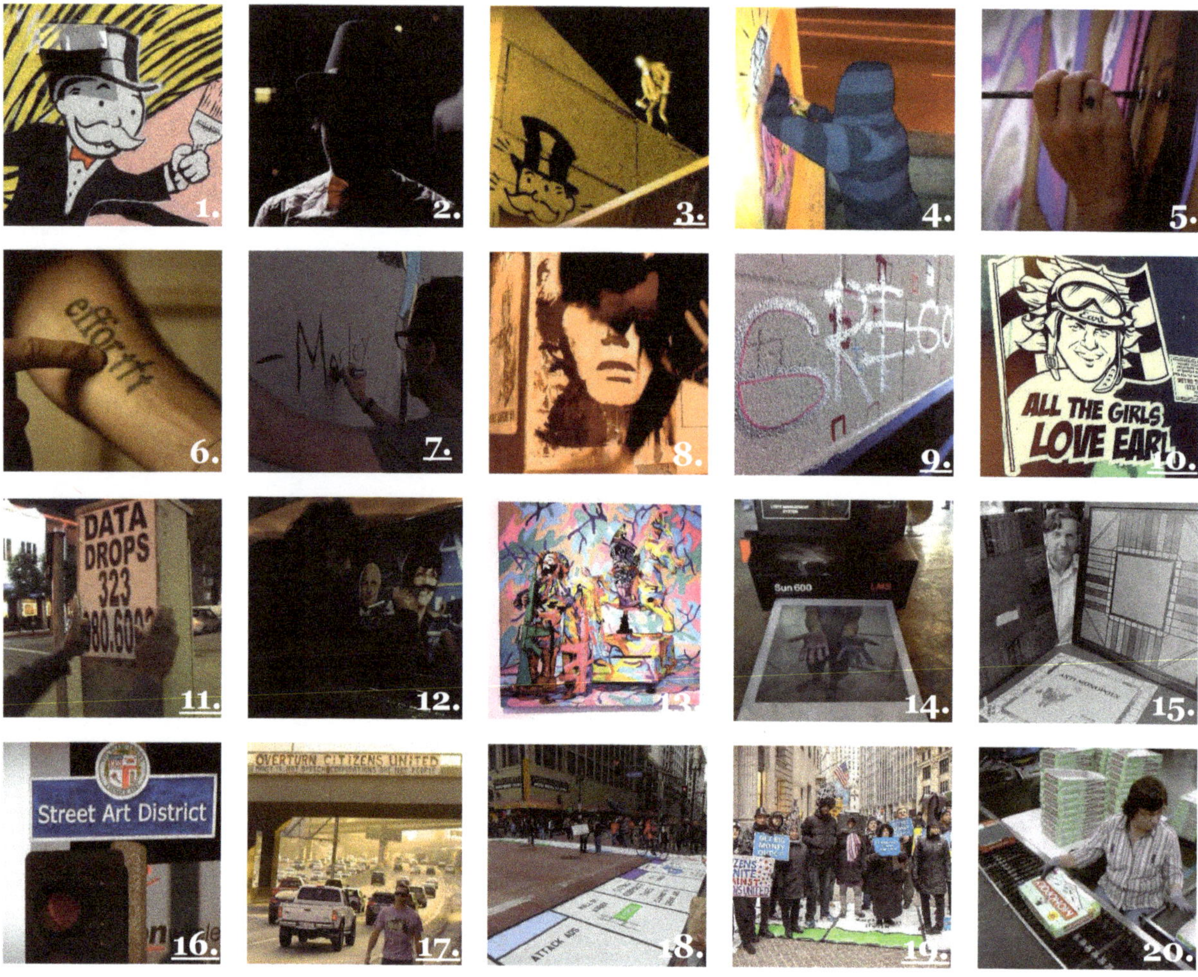

VIDEO CONTENT

1. Who is Alec Monopoly? (3:56)
2. Alec Monopoly NYC 2010 (3:54)
3. Alec Monopoly, Graffiti Zorro (3:34)*
4. Free Humanity: Diamond in the Lotus (3:15)
5. LydiaEmily: The Tattooed Artist Lady (2:41)
6. Teachr: Teaching Peace (2:53)
7. Morley: Making a Mockery of Street Art (3:19)*
8. Thank You X: Los Angeles (2:28)
9. Gregory Siff: Timelapse (2:18)*
10. All The Girls Love Earl (2:45)*
11. Phone Jacks (3:56)*
12: Sabo: Unsavory Agent (2:41)
13: Ron English: Godfather of Street Art (4:08)
14: Mr. Brainwash: Art Show 2011 (6:30)
15: The Secret History of Monopoly (4:48)
16: The PSA Crew (2:39)*
17: Overturn *Citizens United* banner drop (3:18)*
18. May Day 2012 (3:45)
19. P2P at the NYSE (2:14)*
20: The Opening of *PAY 2 PLAY* (8:18)

*(*Video plays online for music licensing purposes.)*

INTRODUCTION

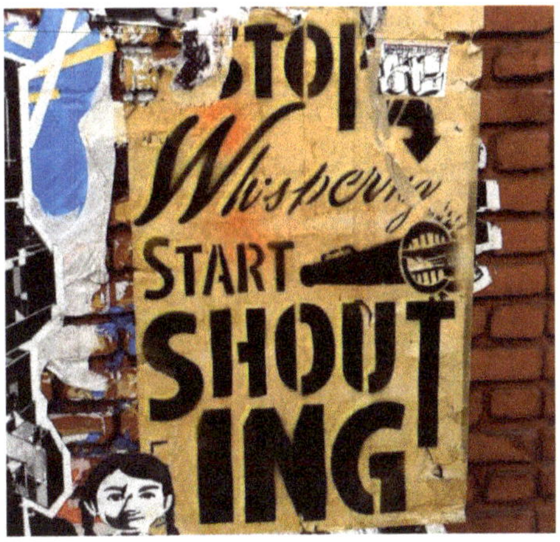

"Stop Whispering, Start Shouting" by Leba on Traction St. in Downtown L.A.

Outdoor signage has proliferated since there was enough public foot traffic to warrant advertisement to travelers. Artwork traces back to the walls of early cave dwellers. Marking territory goes back to the beginning of dogs. That is to say, displaying artwork in public to express oneself is not new, and delineating the genealogy of graffiti into street art is the province of academics, old schoolers, and the truly obsessed.

This book is about a very specific window of time in street art, really just a sliver in the larger timeline of the city of Los Angeles. These are the same roads traveled by Native Americans thousands of years ago, built upon by settlers under Mexican rule hundreds of years ago, populated with Jewish Orthodox families and Russian émigrés under *glasnost* decades ago.

This is the story of what it was like to go down Melrose Avenue, a main drag of cafés and fashion boutiques, and see hand-crafted art decorating the street from La Brea to Fairfax, updated daily by artists hungry to be seen. There have always been several street art regulars getting up around the city at any given time. But from 2010 to 2012, there were dozens, and they were making art for everybody. Melrose, as well as its alleys and side streets, looked like a summer arts camp. Increasingly creative displays inspired others to step up their game and encouraged even more to give it a shot.

People started noticing and sharing pictures, even taking street artwork home and hanging it on their own walls. A blog sprung up dedicated to the area's art explosion, *Melrose & Fairfax*, which brought international followers to this art scene, and became one of the top street art blogs in the country, if not the world. This local recognition encouraged struggling artists, validating the most obscure of creative scrawls, feeding ambitions of decorating the entire city and creating a community of commenters, supporters, and fierce critics worthy of NFL fandom. This reached a crescendo in 2011, a peak year for street art in Los Angeles.

While Tahrir Square in Cairo raged in protest, the Arab Spring was felt on the streets of LA, itself a home for many Middle Eastern immigrants and their descendants. A common realization had been reached, particularly among young people: *If they can do that there, we can do something here.* In the U.S., massive protests in blistering cold Wisconsin against their governor added to the fervor to take to the streets.

In February, the British street artist Banksy came to Los Angeles for the Academy Awards, where his film *Exit Through the Gift Shop* had been nominated for Best Documentary. The anonymous stencil artist was suddenly everywhere—ubiquitous in culture and then abruptly dropping bold new pieces all over the city. Banksy created quite a tizzy in a town that does not get too star-struck.

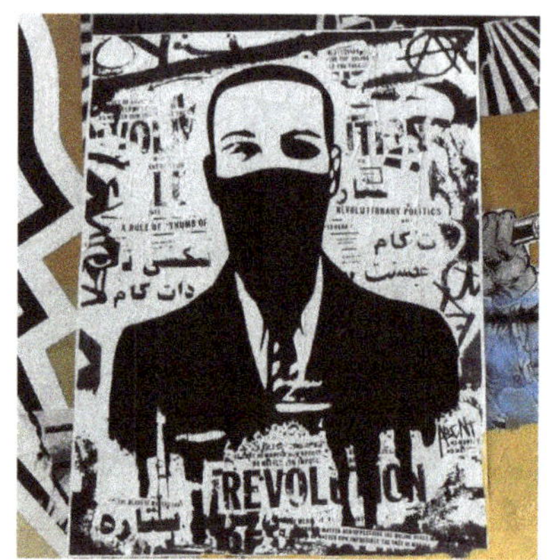

Street art reflective of Middle East tumult by Abcnt, on Melrose.

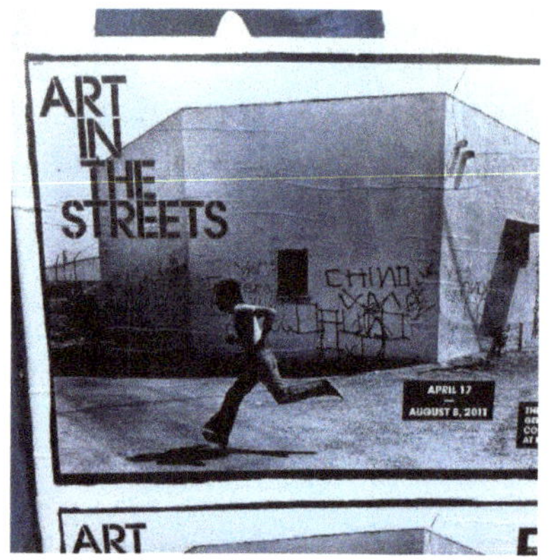

MOCA's "Art in the Streets" exhibit brought major street artists to L.A.

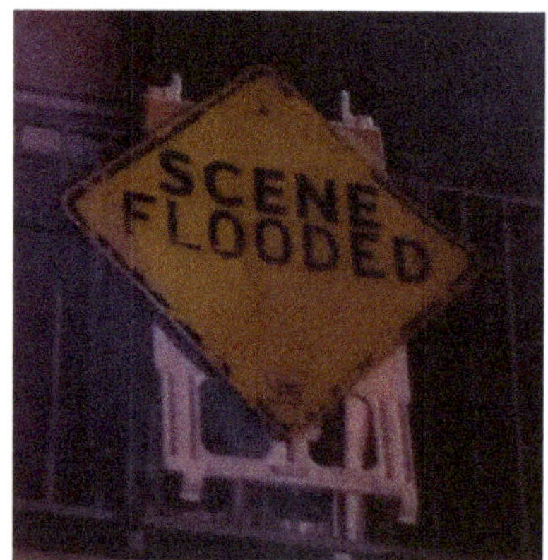

As street art exploded in summer of 2011, this sign was hoisted over Melrose: "SCENE FLOODED"

In June, Los Angeles' Museum of Contemporary Art held a first-of-its-kind street art retrospective, "Art in the Streets," a sprawling installation featuring legends of the genre, attracting artists from around the world to get up on the streets while in town. Banksy even sponsored Mondays to be free to the public. The exhibiton was the highest-attended art show in MOCA's history.

In October, Mr. Brainwash's open house was dubbed "the Street Art Woodstock" by *Melrose & Fairfax*, as he opened the doors of a sprawling warehouse in the middle of Hollywood to any and all artists to decorate, in advance of his own show at the end of December, which was set to top the one that made him famous in *Exit*.

This open call for sanctioned street art allowed artists that would never venture onto the streets to see their work displayed, while introducing active street artists to each other who otherwise would not meet, since they put up their artwork alone at night in fear of getting caught. These introductions spawned countless collaborations.

And then, Occupy Wall Street happened. When a bunch of demonstrators camped out in New York's Financial District, their call for accountability of Wall Street executives spread like wildfire. Soon, their numbers had swelled to thousands. Before long, supportive demonstrations and Occupy encampments had sprung up in cities all over the country—even around the globe.

Support for the Occupy phenomenon was reflected in the streets of Los Angeles, well beyond Occupy L.A. downtown at City Hall, and not just in the areas where street art typically proliferated. Mirroring the widespread uprising that reached across factions, "We Are the 99%" posters, signs, and stickers popped up all over the city. When people take to the streets, they can't always stay, so leaving up artwork or messages for your cause is akin to leaving your protest sign protesting without you.

Through all of this, there was a thriving community daring to share in a time when digital imagery is so ubiquitous; handmade expression was surprisingly refreshing—and fun. It was thus inevitable that the LAPD would have to crack down, as you will read about from the artists herein.

There isn't enough space in this book to do justice to all the artists active at that time. That's why there are the streets, as big as you can go. This is a collection of interviews conducted over this period for my documentary *PAY 2 PLAY,* a film about the difference one person's voice can make. This is not a coffee table book of erudite art.

This is a street art dossier.

ALEC MONOPOLY

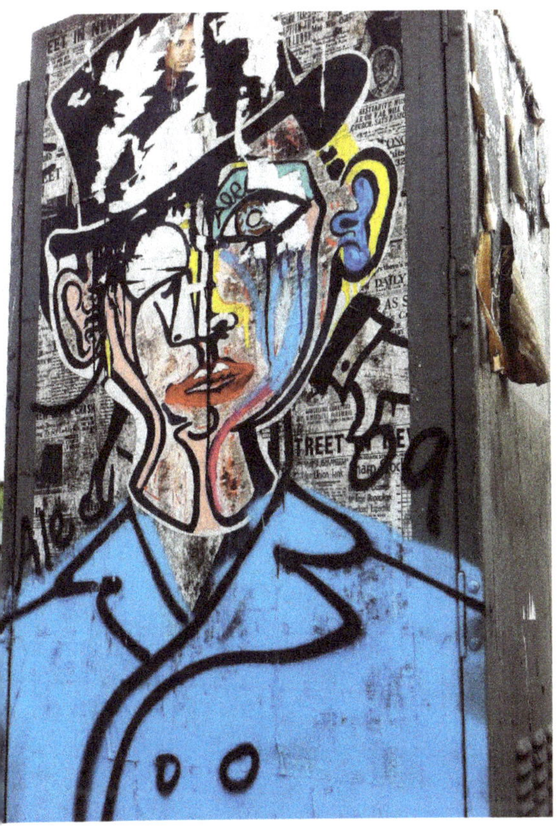

Alec's "Picasso Monopoly Man" on Third St.

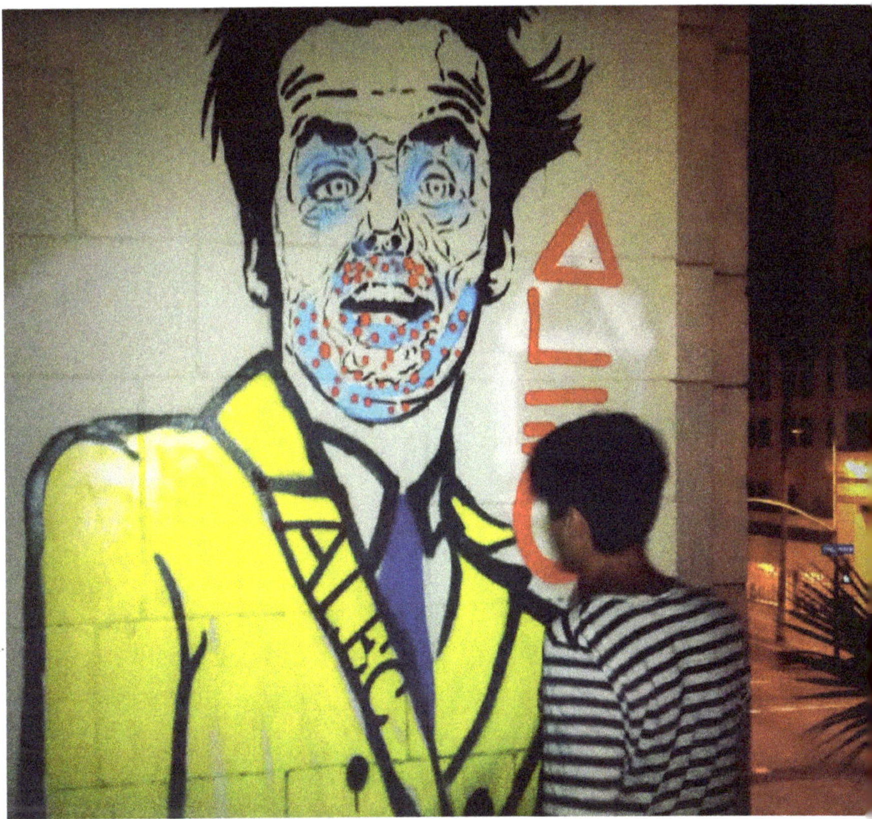

Alec paints Jack Nicholson in Lakers colors over Hollywood Blvd.

My street art odyssey began inauspiciously. Driving around Los Angeles in early 2010, I noticed a Monopoly Man adorning traffic boxes and light posts. This struck me, because at the time I was immersed in investigating the secret history of Monopoly for my documentary. I decided I had to track down whoever was behind it, to find out if they were driven by the same thoughts as I— that our beloved childhood game Monopoly taught us some insidious lessons that have come to fruition today. It took a while, but eventually Alec agreed to be interviewed, albeit in silhouette.

The resulting short doc I posted, "Who is Alec Monopoly?" allowed the anonymous artist to share his inspirations: "For me, the Monopoly Man, he is that corporate guy... Corporations run America. They run all the imagery you see outside, so I wanted to throw it back out there using art." Putting a story to the splattered images of Jack Nicholson and Bob Dylan intrigued art collectors who had spotted Alec's street art in Los Angeles or New York. Then, things started to take off for Alec very quickly.

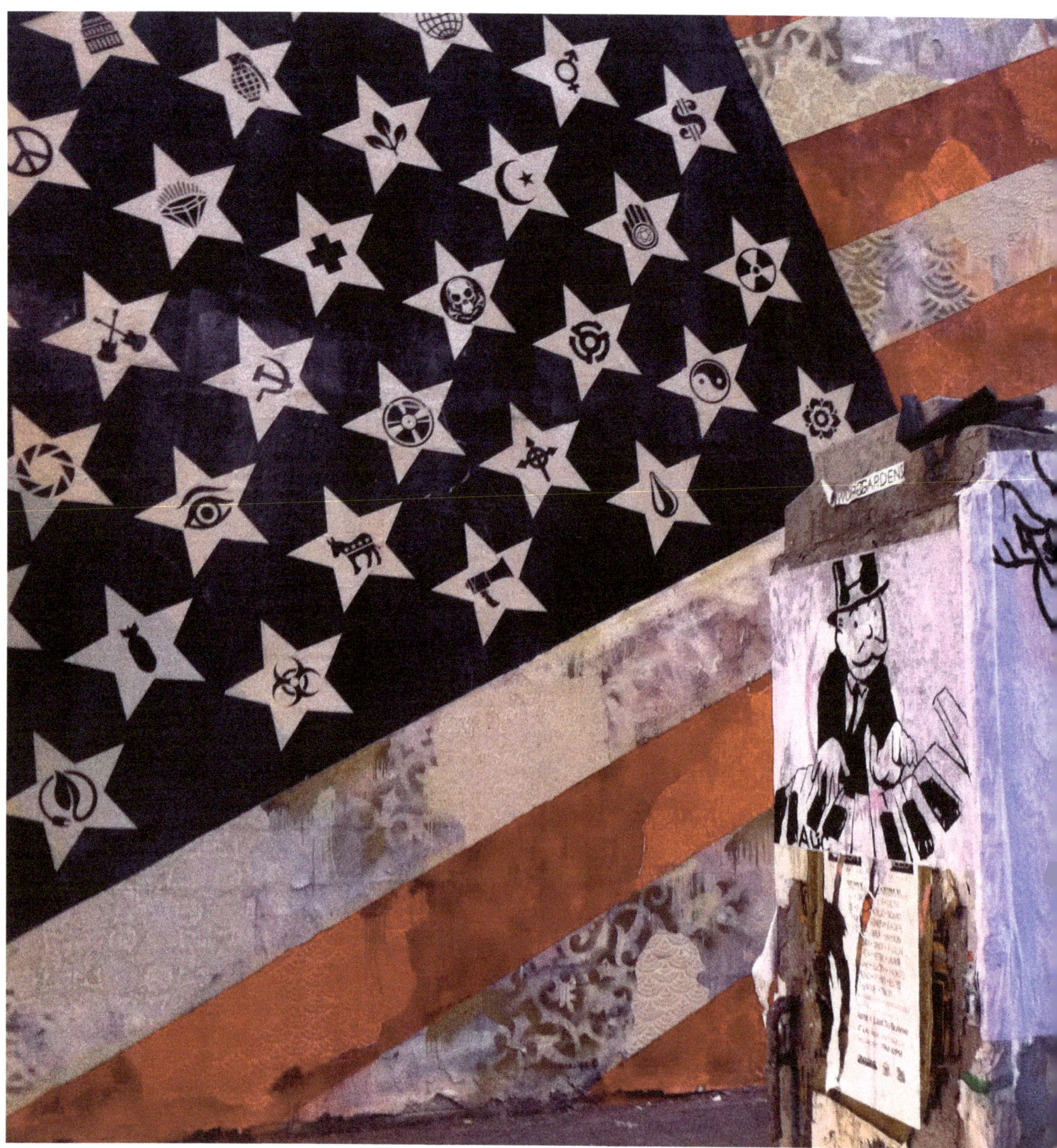

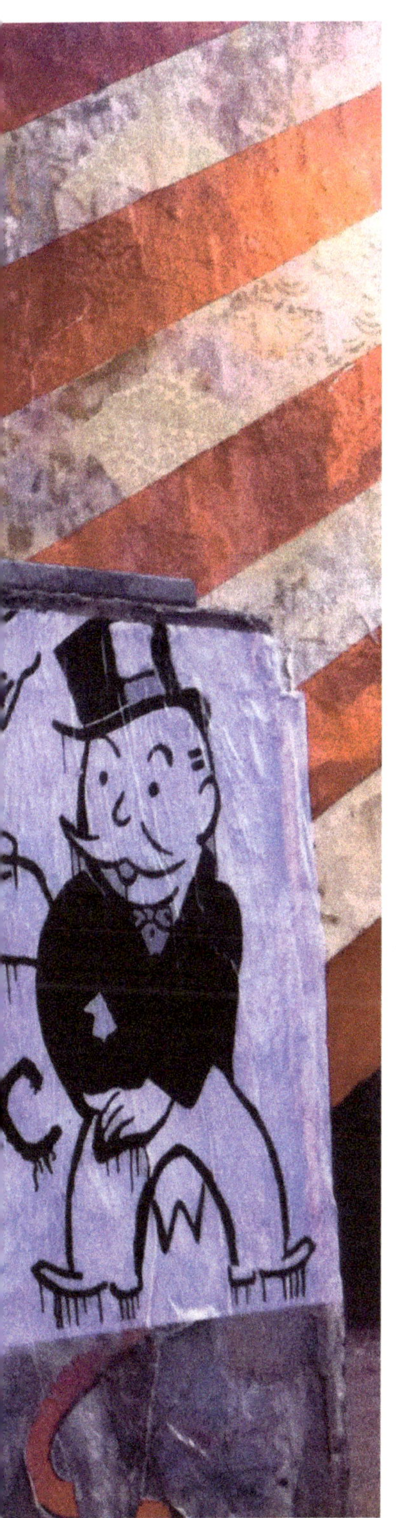

This wall on Melrose and Ogden in Hollywood, across from Fairfax High School, was the apex for street art. Murals a half-block long would be put up by artists when they had a major show, book, or tour coming out. It was known as the Barracuda Wall.

The traffic light cabinet box directly in front of the mural would become a daily battleground for up and coming artists, sticker crews, and taggers vying for placement in front of Barracuda, a training gym. Eventually it was under regular police surveillance because of its popularity.

Here, Alec Monopoly posters ride on the box, still wet from wheat paste in the early morning hours. These are from Alec's earliest posters, a modified Monopoly Man. Alec and Free Humanity dominated the street art scene in 2009-2011 in large part because Free had a hookup from a guy at a Fed Ex Kinko's copy shop who gave them tons of free copies of their art, until he got fired.

The mural is the American flag re-imagined by Shepard Fairey, a.k.a. OBEY. On the box in front of this mural, Alec wrote "To Shep."

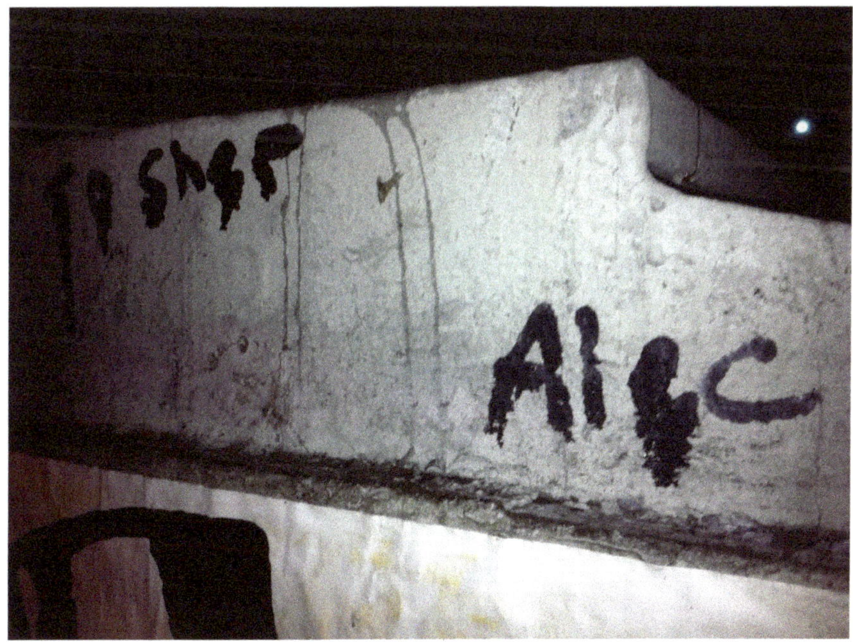

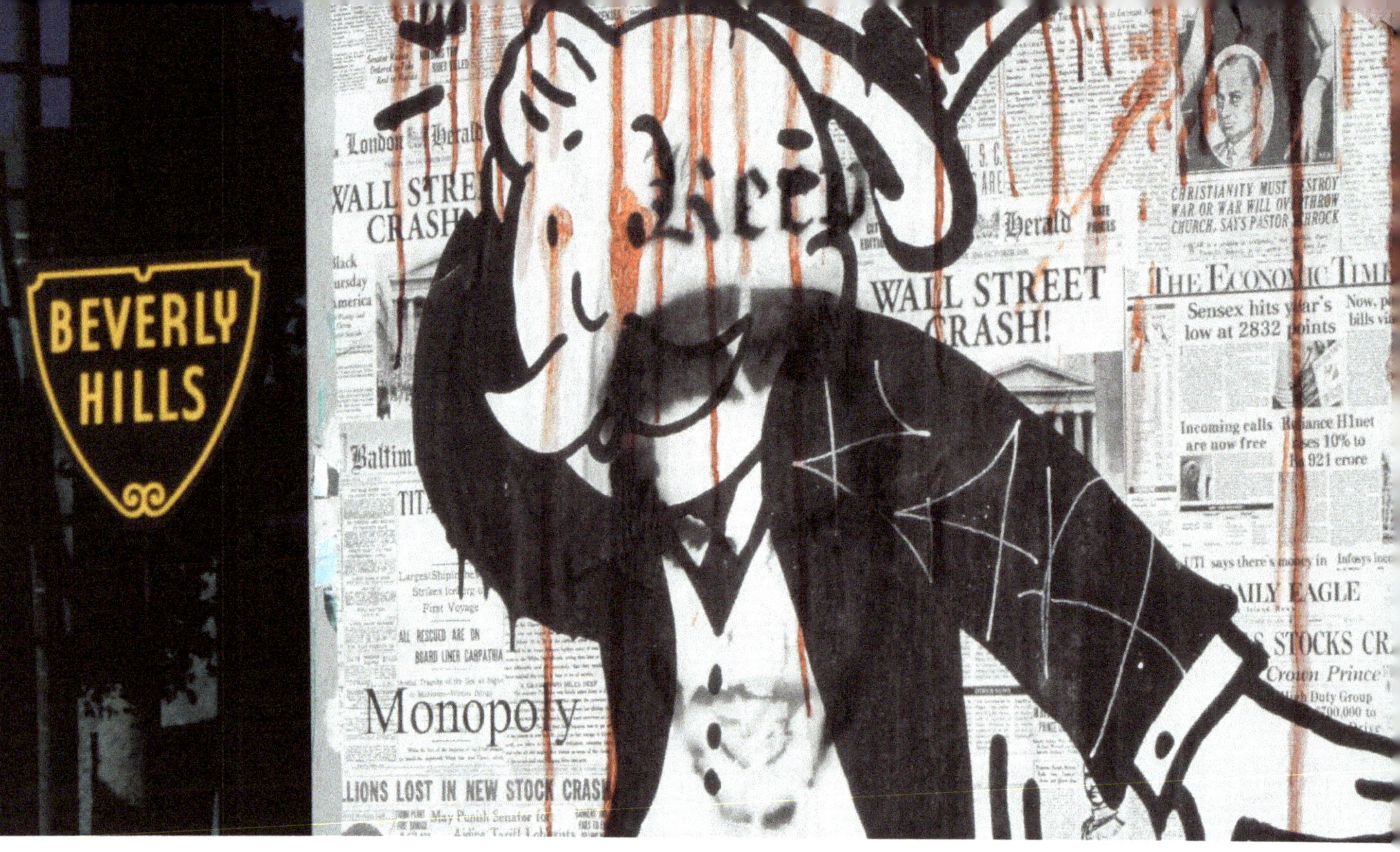

Alec's Monopoly Man on Little Santa Monica: "In Beverly Hills, for some reason, my pieces stay up."

At once, a New York collector ordered a body of paintings by Alec, so many they needed to be painted locally in New York. Excited by the opportunity to spend time on detailed versions of his street art images and create new pop art designs, Alec planned to exhibit his paintings in a vacant Chelsea storefront so others could see them.

I was covering a congressional race for my documentary, when late at night I got a text in my Cincinnati hotel room from a number I did not recognize. It was Alec, on a pre-paid booster phone. He needed help.

ALEC: "So when I first got to New York, I was in the studio working every day productively, painting away. I had some time to go out onto the streets and do some work. I'm not gonna say what pieces I did or where, but I was successful in getting up a lot of work. And one of the ways of measuring your success in street art is the authorities—if the authorities are after you and coming to get you, you know you're doing something right.

"So it was a Saturday, and I was meeting with the collector who was buying the majority of the show, he was actually the building owner as well. So we were meeting in the studio and these two suspicious-looking guys come in. I'd actually left the front door open. And these two guys just walked right in, and they were asking about information on the show, and they were asking who the artist was. And immediately I knew they were police, because one of them was short and chubby and had a mustache, which is, you know, a dead giveaway for a cop... And he had handcuffs on his belt.

"So immediately my heart started racing. I was scared. They left, and I actually, like ran out of the studio. I told him like, 'I'll see you later. We gotta go.' And I just ran out through the trash chute. Got out of there. So, after I left, I called the front desk, the concierge, and he let me know that he was... well he said, 'Now there's five cops out there and they're taking pictures and peeping into the cracks in the tape in your studio,' and 'you better not come back around here, because they are looking for you.'

"So after that I was extremely alarmed. And it was funny, I was actually in Soho with my friend, we were just at the studio together and I was just kinda hiding out, and these two girls came up to me out of nowhere, and they said, 'Oh, my god, you're Alec the artist!'

"And immediately I became sketched out, I was like looking around, like, they were like trying to, like, they were gonna arrest me or something. But they were just two young art students, and they were, like, big fans of my work, and they actually lived across the street from my studio—above one floor. So they could see into my studio where it was taped up; they could see over the tape. So they had actually seen everything that was going on in the studio, and they knew what I looked like.

"They were actually telling me one night—it was kinda funny—that I stripped out of my clothes into my boxers, because I didn't wanna mess up my nice, like, outfit or whatever I had on. And they saw me painting in my boxers, and we were laughing about that. But they actually became my counter surveillance to the police. And if I hadn't met those two girls... It was ironic that I met them the day that the two police came in. So after that I had eyes on the building throughout the rest of the show.

"I was working for about a week up until then, and I didn't first start getting suspicious that my phone was tapped until I called the lookout, actually, and I called her, and I said, 'Is the coast clear? I'm coming in now.' So I was walking up, and as we're on the phone she says, 'No, no, don't come. Don't come in. The cops are... They're out front. They're in an undercover car.' And I was already up in front of the studio, and I saw for myself that they were out there. So I quickly walked into the hotel, and as I walked in, the concierge was saying, 'Get out of here. Get out of here. They're out front!'

"So I run out the back, and I start running down 21st St. And as I'm on 21st St., I give the hotel desk a call again. I go, 'Are they still there? What's going on?' He goes, 'Yeah, they're here. Now there's uniformed police. It's undercovers and uniforms. Get outta here!' And then he said, 'Wait. What? Now they know you're on 21st St.' So when I heard that, I was on 21st St. I just started running.

"Man, I was so lucky that this cab just rolled up with its light on, and I just hopped in and got outta there. Now that was probably the closest they came to them actually getting me. And then after that, it was just a game of cat and mouse where the lookout would see them—the cops were literally waiting outside my studio to arrest me, and I would be inside working.

"And I would know where they were because I could call the girls from across the street, and they would tell me exactly where the officers were. And she would say, 'Hey, he's walking out of the car.'

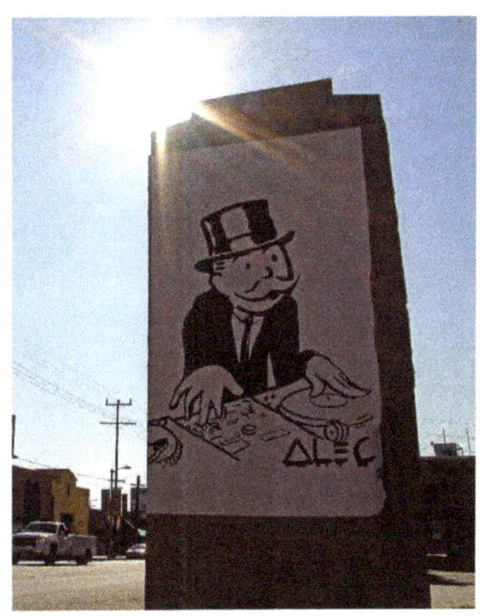

DJ Monopoly Man on Third St., LA.

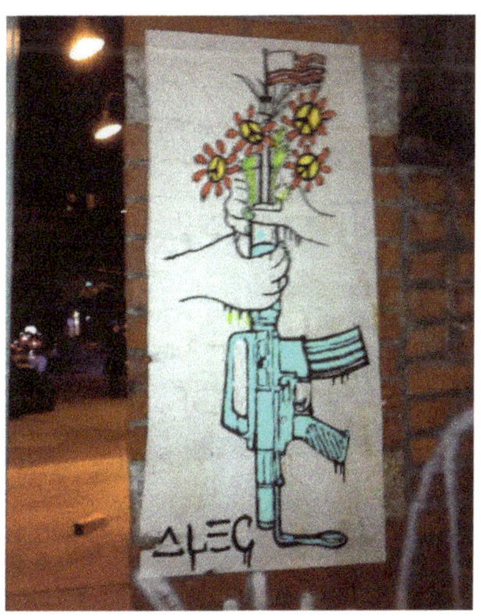

Guns & Roses in East Village, NYC.

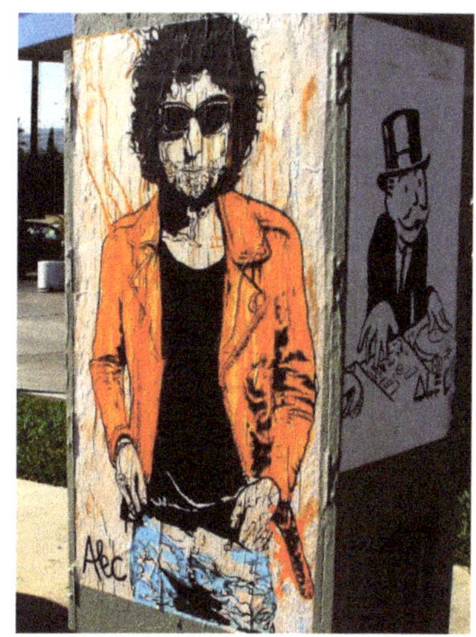

Bob Dylan on Third St., LA.

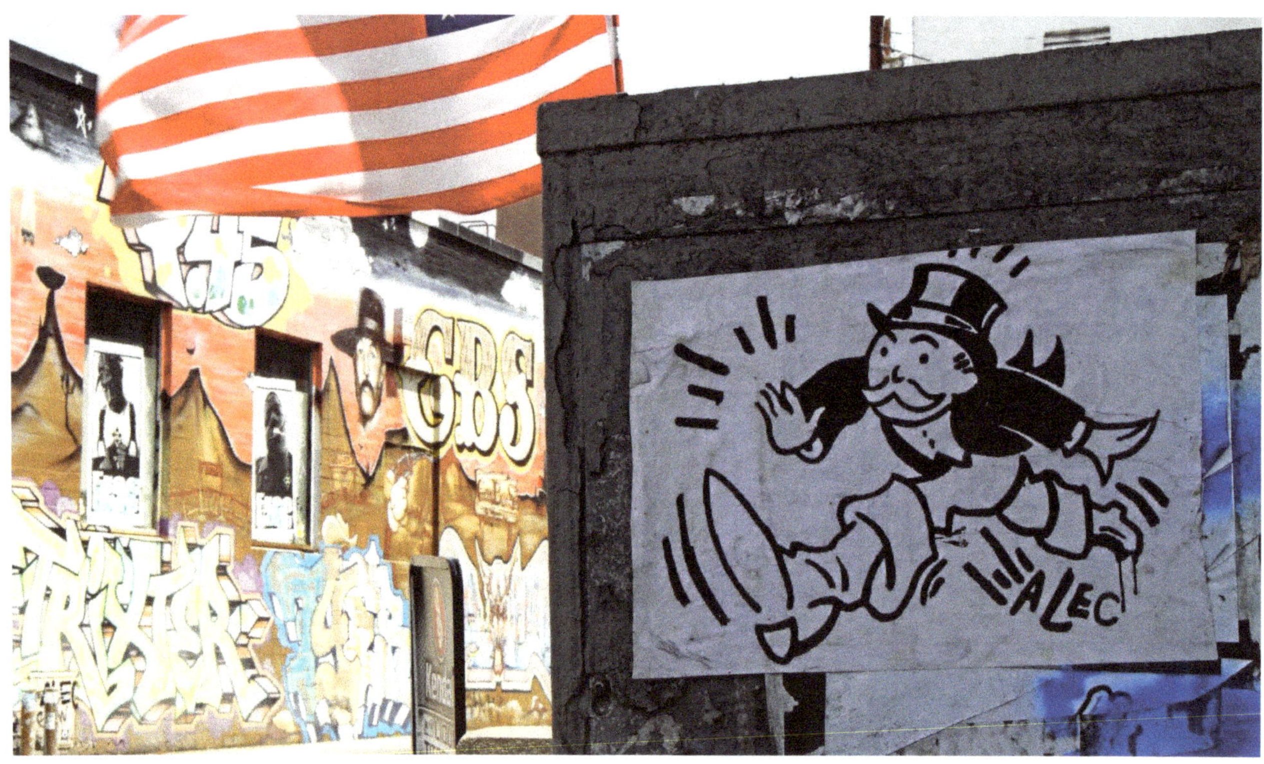

ABOVE: Mr. Monopoly running, with Free Humanity's Biggie and Tupac on the wall in the background. On La Brea & Melrose. BELOW: An uncommissioned mural on Sunset Blvd. by Alec, which was quickly covered up. OPPOSITE: Alec puts finishing touches on a huge DJ Monopoly Man painted on sheet music for his first solo art show in NYC, 2010.

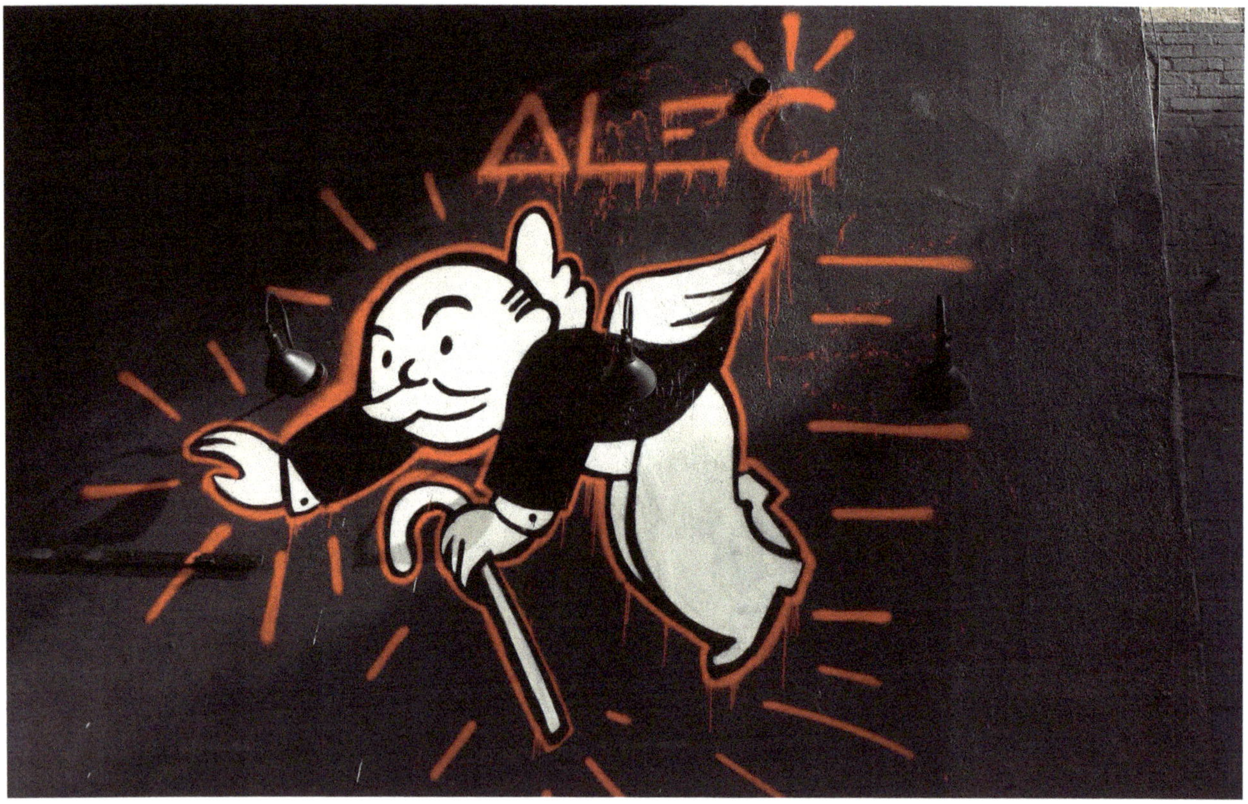

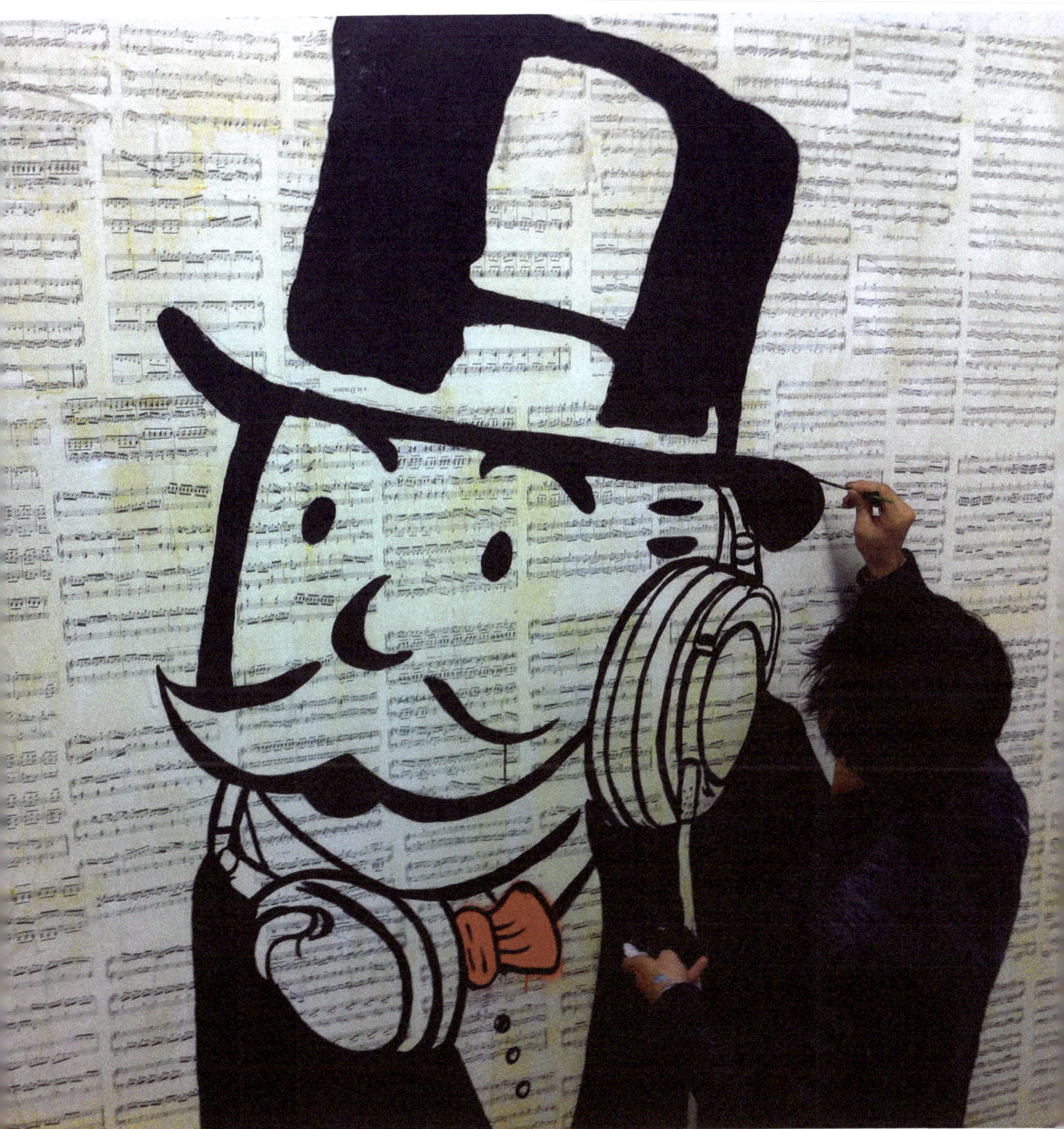

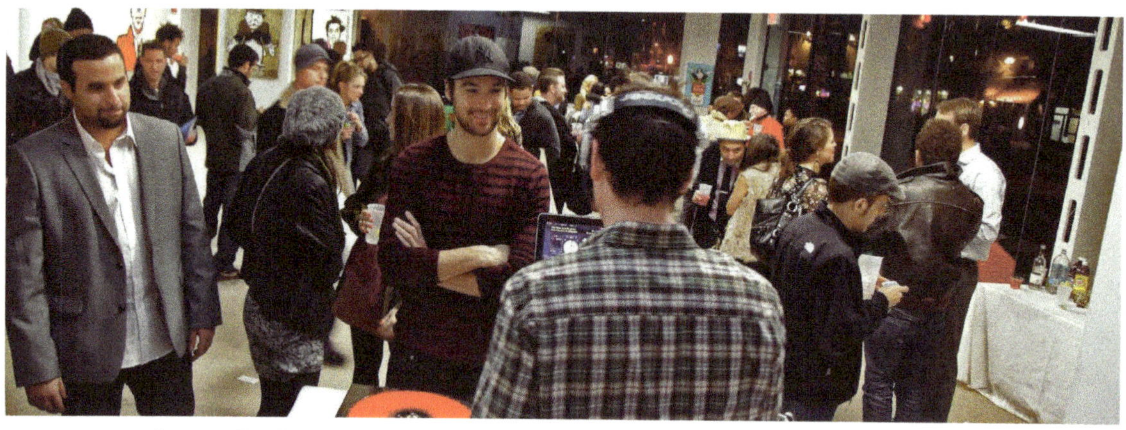

ABOVE: To throw off police, Alec announced the opening night reception for his exhibit. Then he threw the real party the night before. OPPOSITE: Alec's art show and video. (Photos by Andrew Einhorn)

'He's right by the studio door. Don't leave now.' But then he would go back in the car to meet with the other guy, and they'd be like, 'Alright, the coast is clear. You have five seconds. Run!' And I would run out of the studio and get outta there.

"So it was really hairy that last week up until the show. It was really sketchy. And you know being in New York... I really couldn't even enjoy New York City because I was so paranoid, literally looking over my shoulder everywhere I went for police officers and undercovers. It was just... I just wanted to get out of New York, to tell you the truth. I couldn't stand being there one more minute."

In New York, I helped Alec move canvases and hang his art show, since he had been painting in basement hallways and was afraid of coming by his own studio space. We then shot a new video for visitors to his art show: another silhouetted interview where Alec explained his travails with the NYPD. The video played on a loop in the storefront window, which included shots of the NYPD staking out that same storefront waiting for Alec.

By that time, Alec had left town and was back in L.A. But local street artists took note: Alec had made it, and showed it was possible to go from Melrose to Manhattan. And if you could make it there, you could make it anywhere.

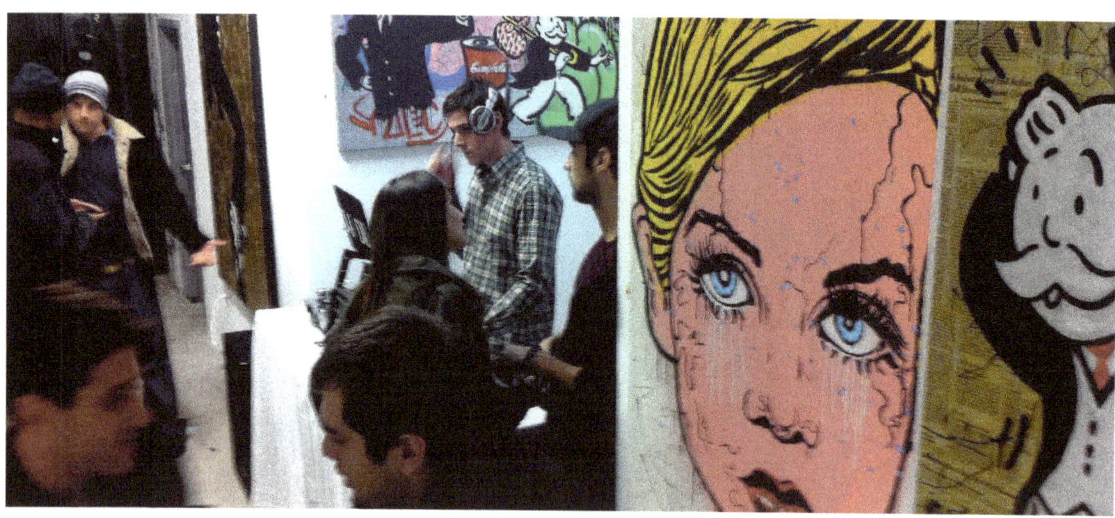

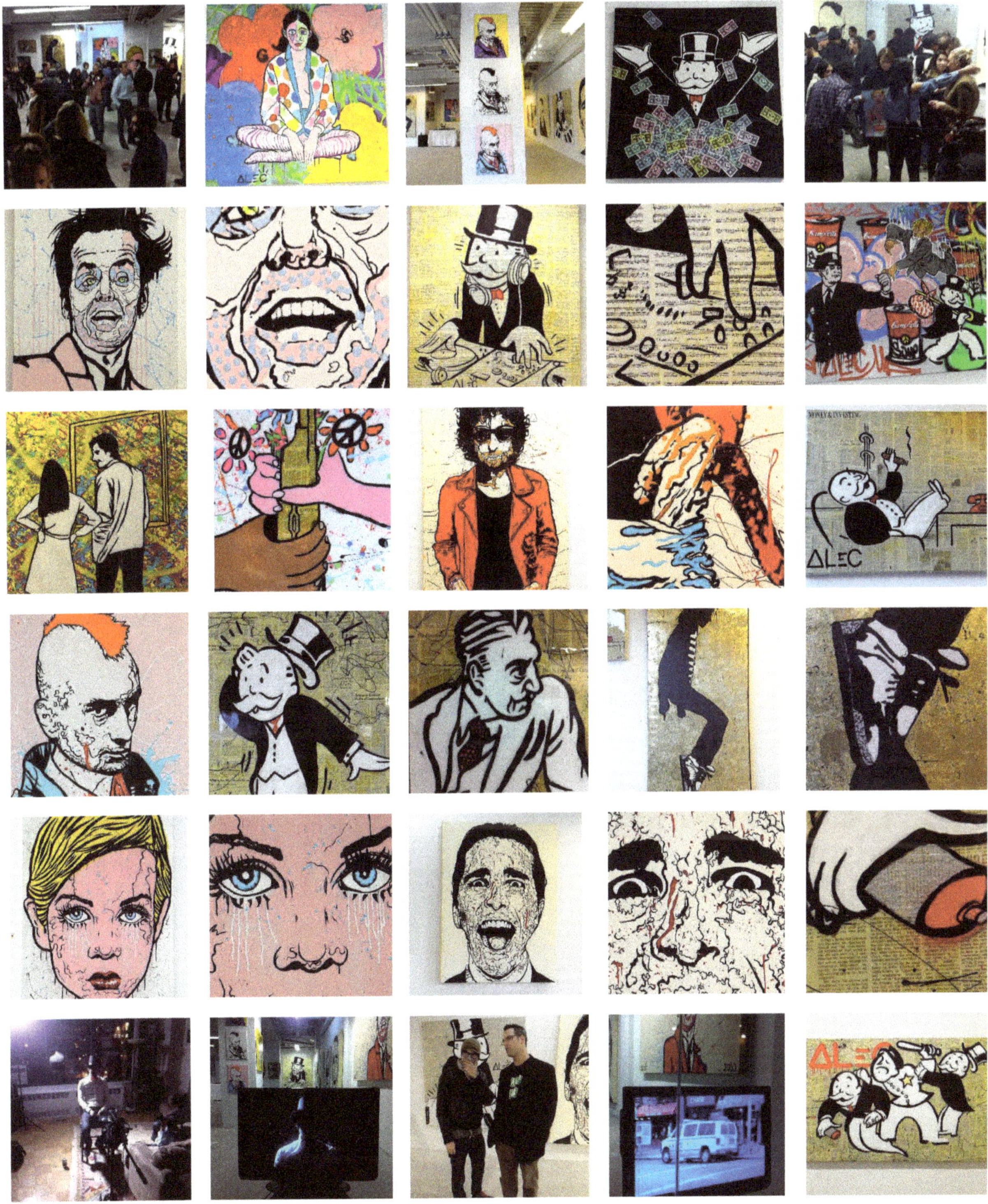
ΔLEC

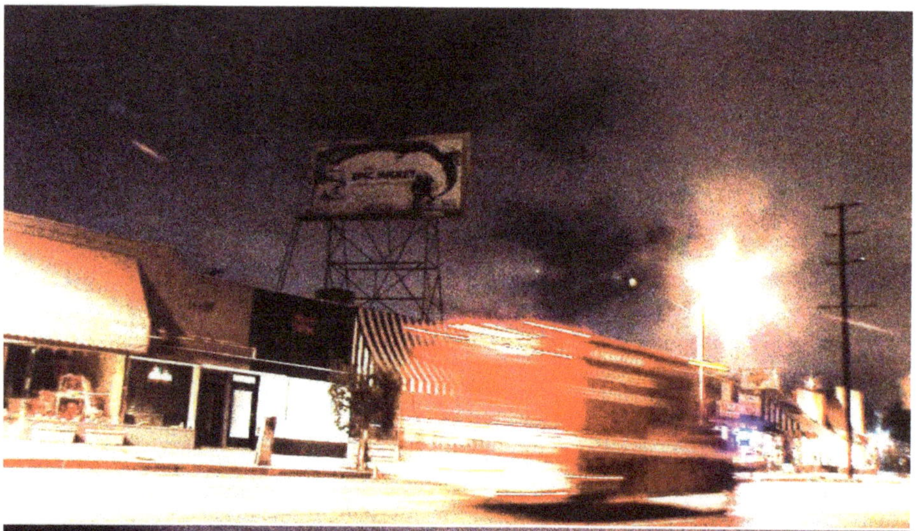

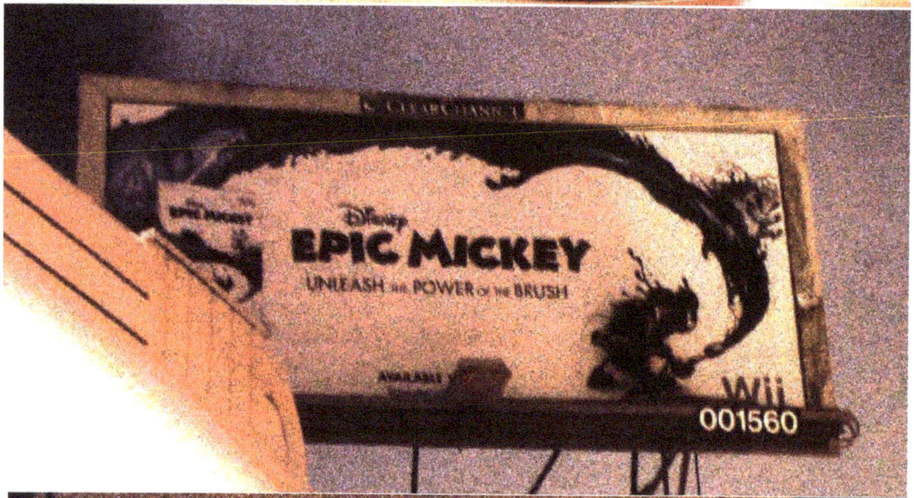

Disney
EPIC MICKEY
UNLEASH THE POWER OF THE BRUSH
Wii
001560

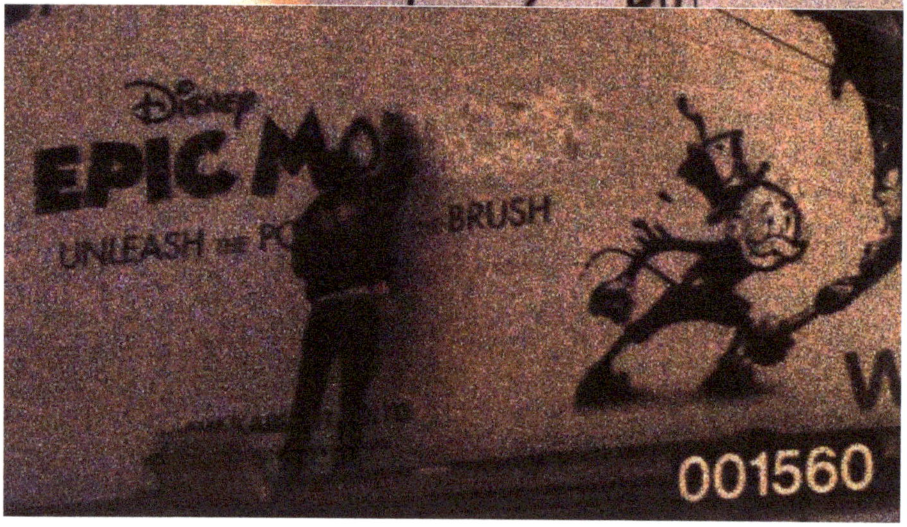

Disney
EPIC
UNLEASH THE
BRUSH
001560

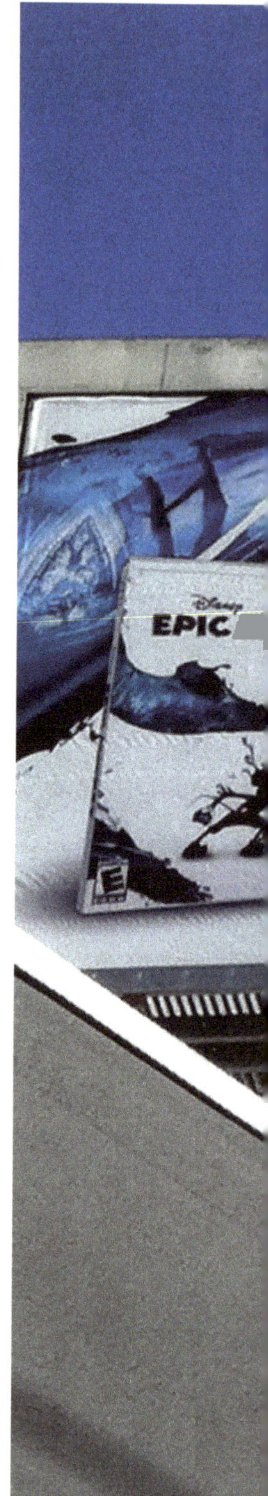
Disney
EPIC

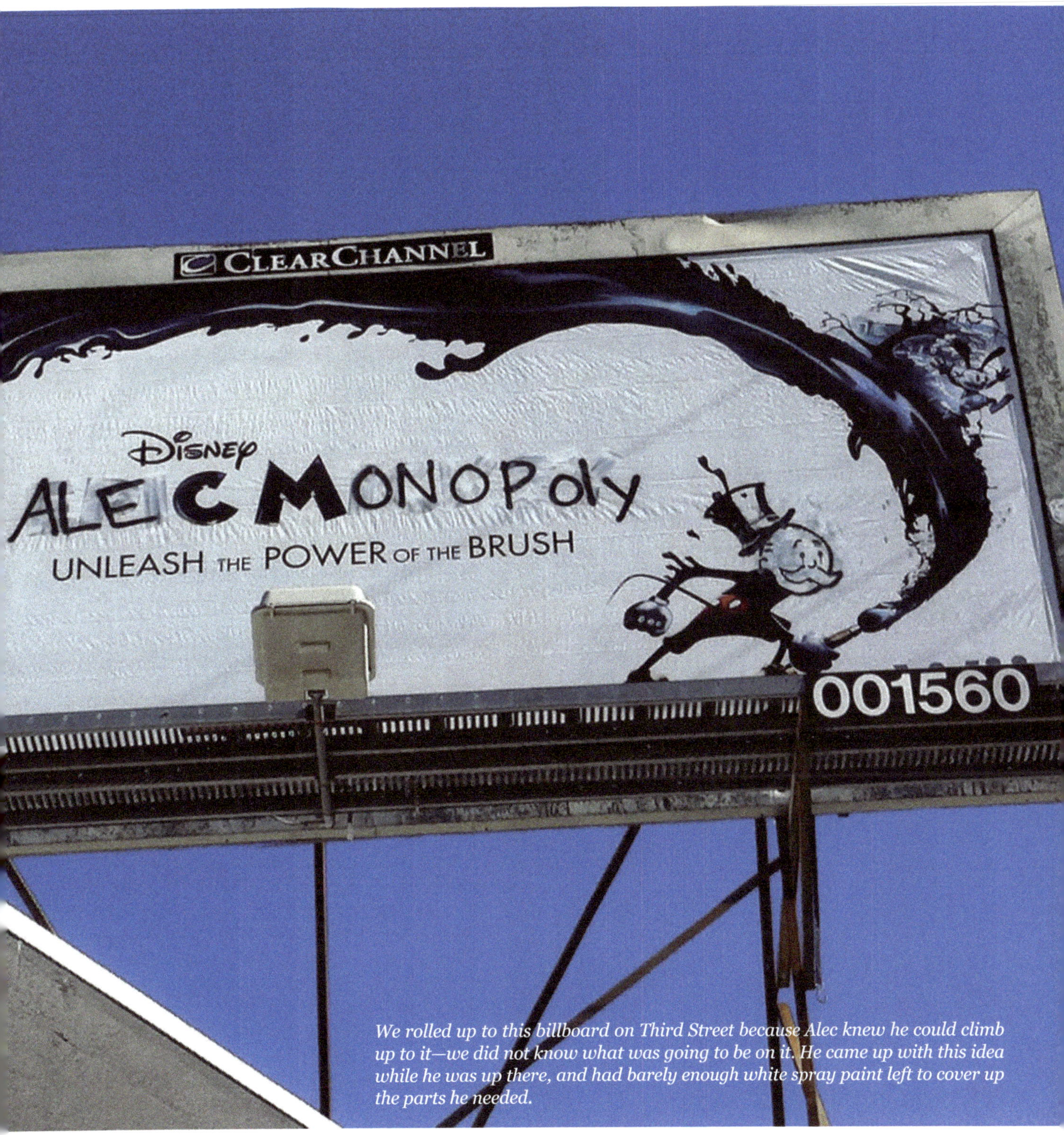

We rolled up to this billboard on Third Street because Alec knew he could climb up to it—we did not know what was going to be on it. He came up with this idea while he was up there, and had barely enough white spray paint left to cover up the parts he needed.

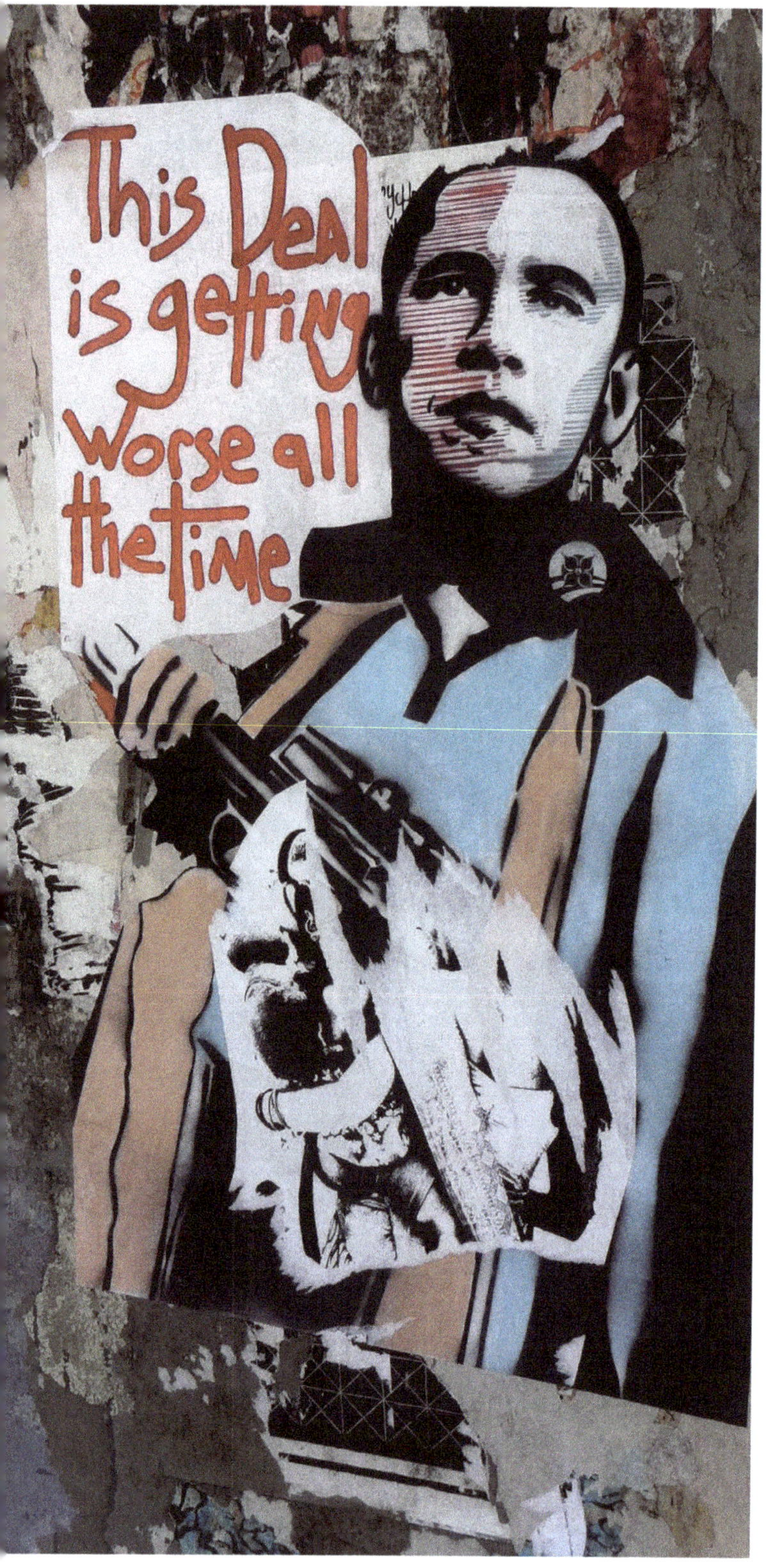

"This deal is getting worse all the time"—LandObama

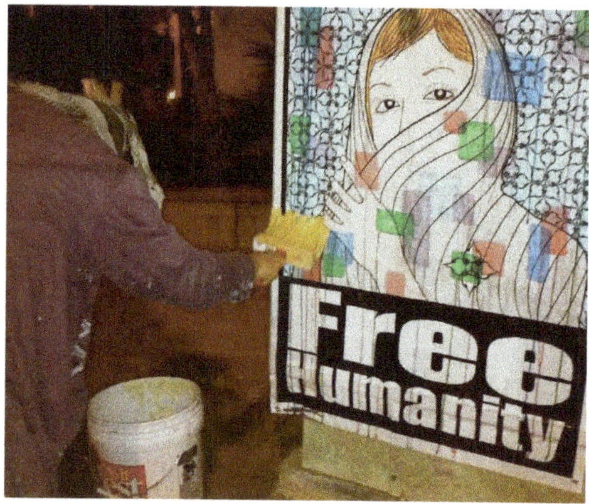

FREE HUMANITY

Soon, Alec was abroad, preparing shows in London, Morocco, and elsewhere. I was curious about another street artist whose work was as prevalent as Alec, but more expressly political: Free Humanity.

When I first reached out to him, he checked with Alec to vouch for me, who gladly did. Free also kept a concertedly low profile, preferring anonymity and living off the grid, well outside the city, far from the Hollywood streets he skulked at night.

FREE HUMANITY: "I don't think I've ever been part of society. I think growing up in America, there's not much for the youth. This generation doesn't have much. And we're all looking for something—something good, something meaningful to do, something worthwhile. And I guess I've been trying to do that my whole life, and I guess the easiest way to do it was put my art up illegally to represent my perspective. And I think it's changed my life and hopefully made people think about something, whatever it be, or maybe make them smile hopefully. I think that's very—most important.

"Basically what I'm trying to do is steal back the humanity that's been stolen from social manipulation and plant positive seeds through art and consciousness."

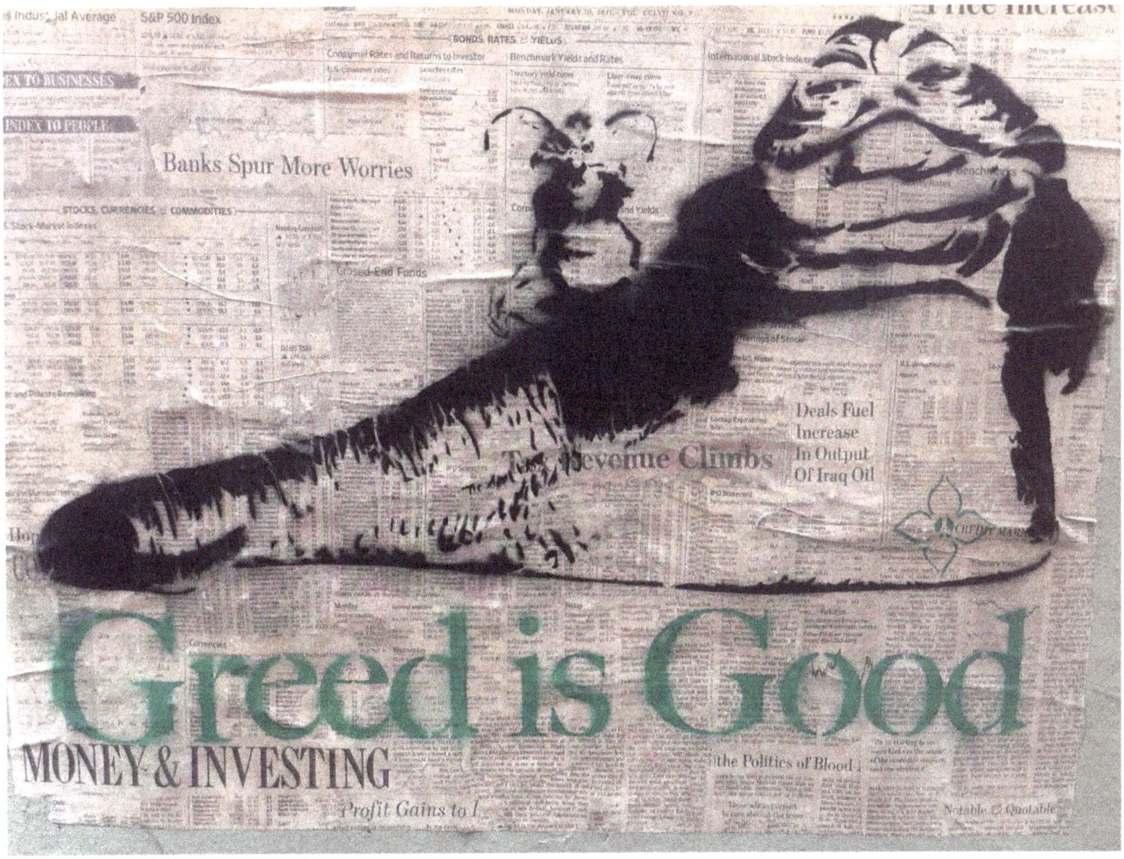

"Greed is Good" stencil of Jabba the Hutt on Wall Street Journal newsprint, on Melrose.

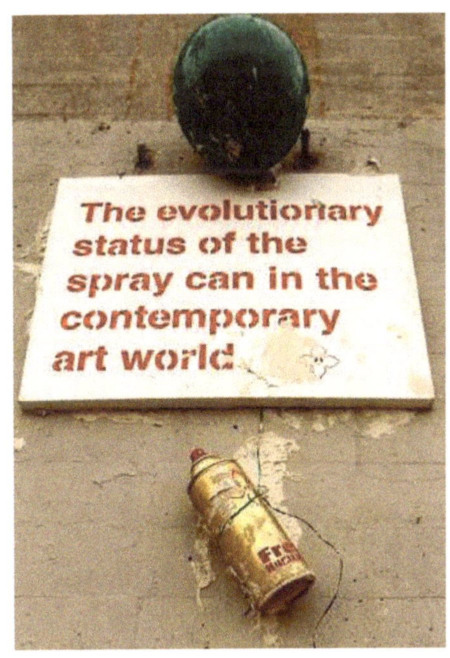

Mounted on the wall of MOCA during the street art exhibition. (Photo by Listak)

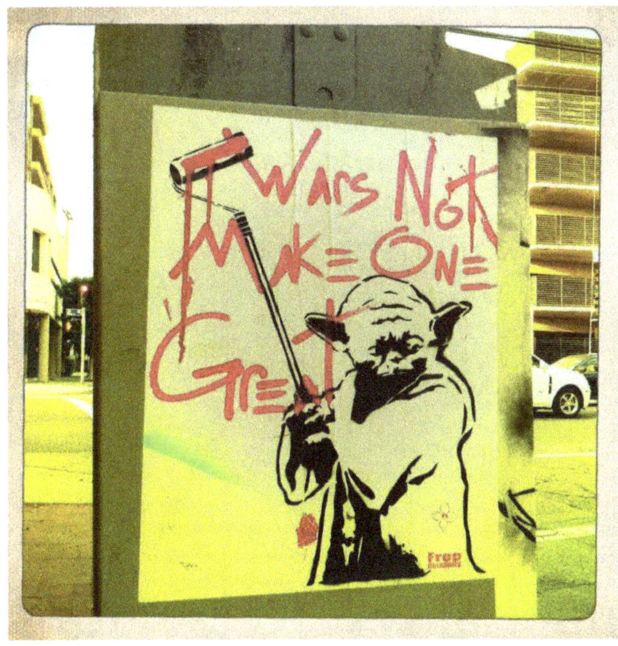

"Wars Not Make One Great" — On Beverly Blvd.

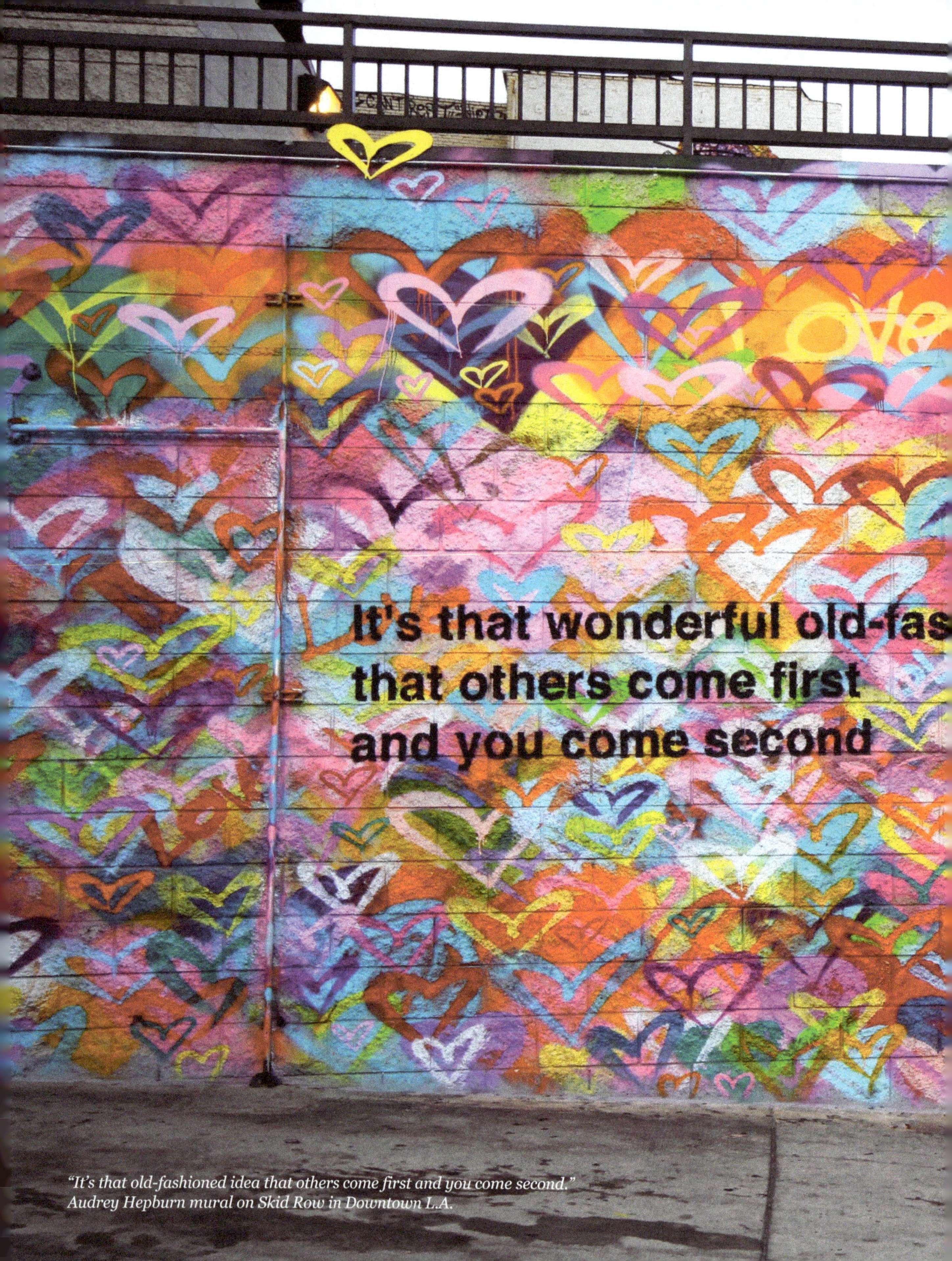

"It's that old-fashioned idea that others come first and you come second."
Audrey Hepburn mural on Skid Row in Downtown L.A.

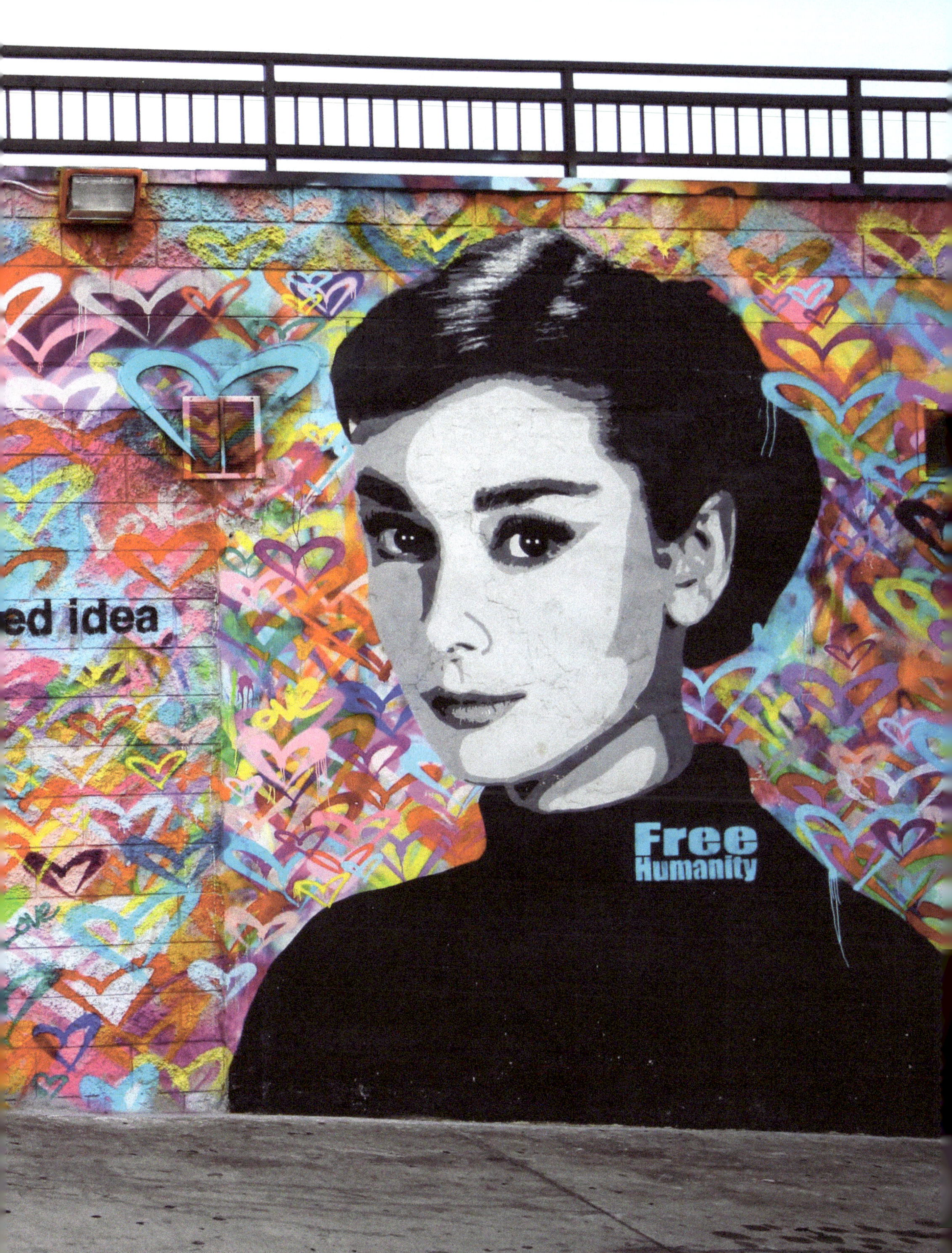
ed idea
Free
Humanity

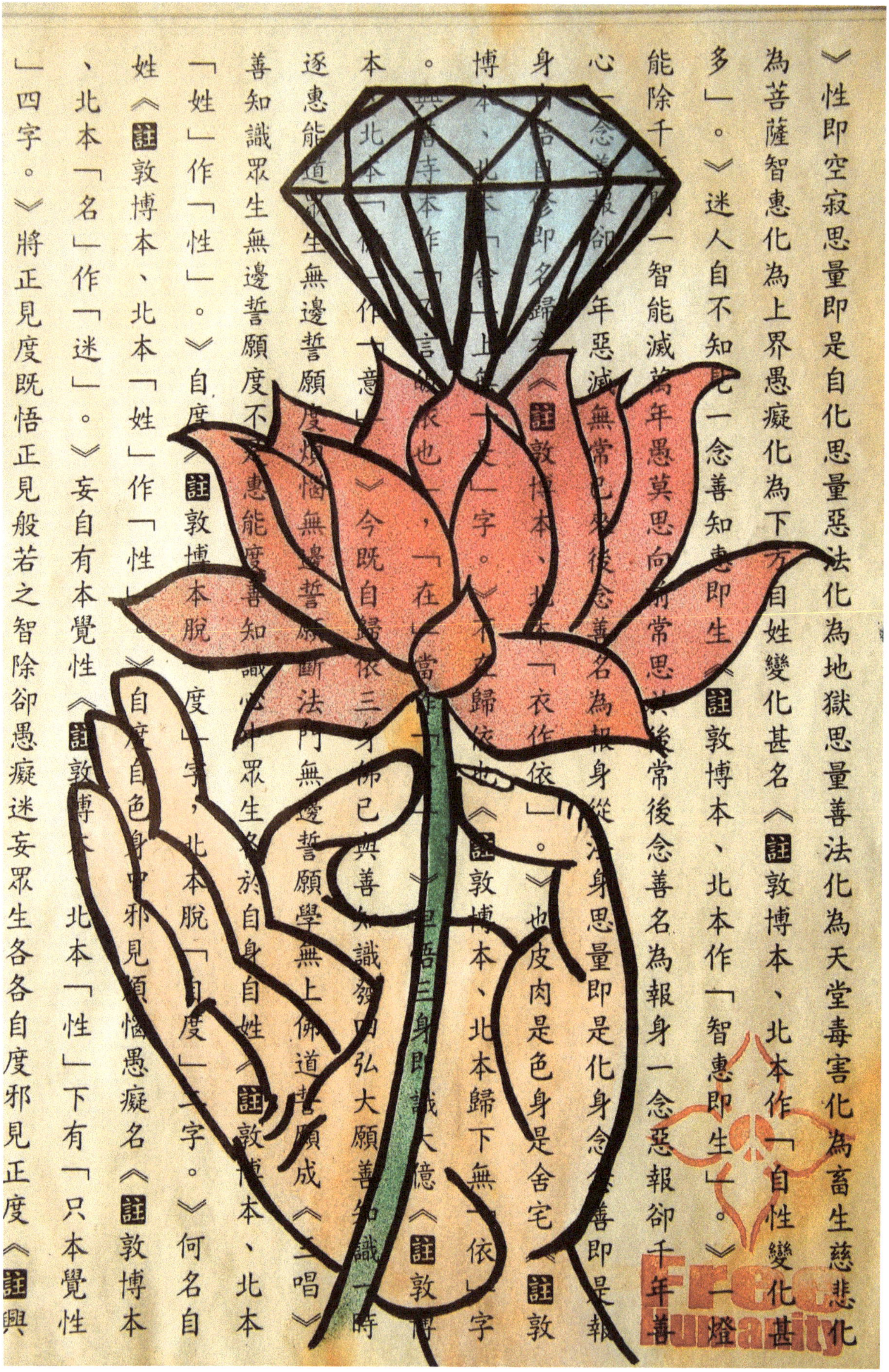

》性即空寂思量即是自化思量惡法化為地獄思量善法化為天堂毒害化為畜生慈悲化為菩薩智惠化為上界愚癡化為下方自姓變化甚名《註敦博本、北本作「自性變化甚多」。》迷人自不知見一念善知惠即生《註敦博本、北本作「智惠即生」。》一燈能除千年闇一智能滅萬年愚莫思向前常思於後常後念善名為報身一念惡報卻千年善心一念善報卻千年惡滅無常已來後念善名為報身從法身思量即是化身念念善即是報身自悟自修即名歸依《註敦博本、北本「衣作依」。》也皮肉是色身是舍宅《註敦博本、北本「含」上有「是」字。》不在歸依也《註敦博本、北本歸下無「依」字。興聖寺本作「不言歸衣也」，「在」當作「[illegible]」。》但悟三身即識大億《註敦博本、北本「億」作「意」。》今既自歸依三身佛已與善知識發四弘大願善知識一時逐惠能道眾生無邊誓願度煩惱無邊誓願斷法門無邊誓願學無上佛道誓願成《三唱》善知識眾生無邊誓願度不是惠能度善知識心中眾生各於自身自姓《註敦博本、北本「姓」作「性」。》自度《註敦博本脫「度」字，北本脫「自度」二字。》何名自姓《註敦博本、北本「姓」作「性」。》自度自色身中邪見煩惱愚癡名《註敦博本、北本「名」作「迷」。》妄自有本覺性《註敦博本、北本「性」下有「只本覺性」四字。》將正見度既悟正見般若之智除卻愚癡迷妄眾生各各自度邪見正度《註興

Free Humanity

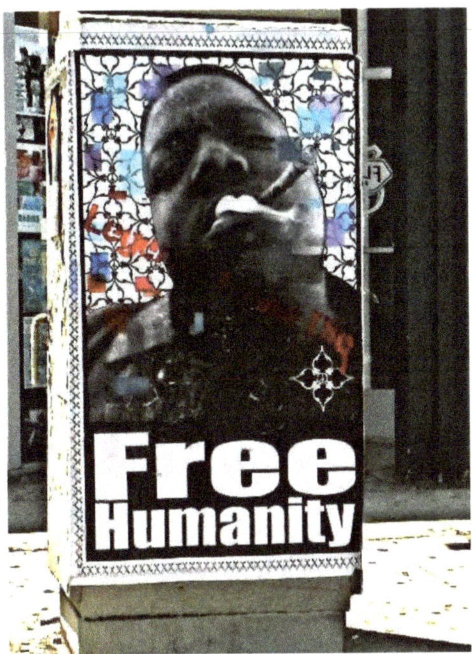

"Legends Never Die" — Notorious B.I.G. art on Melrose.

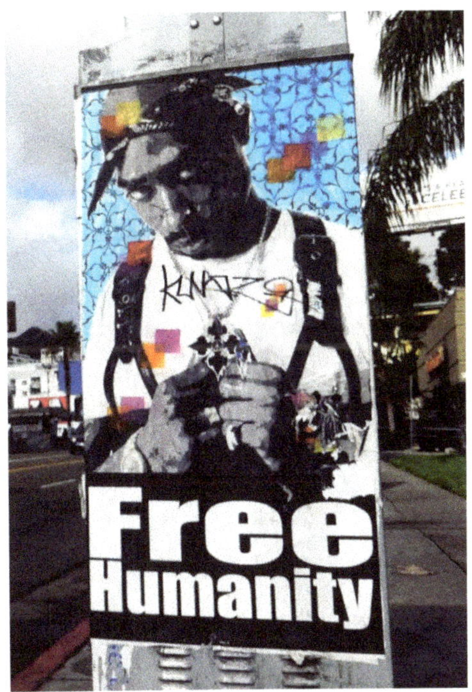

ABOVE: Tupac Shakur on La Brea at Sunset Blvd. OPPOSITE: Diamond in the Lotus printed on Japanese prayer sheet.

"Should street art be considered a crime? I think that goes back to almost this age-old question, like who owns the public space? Who's to say that a corporation that has millions of dollars can take over the skies, take over the skylines... And let's say if you try to put up a piece of art you might go to jail for what you feel might be beautifying the city.

"The public space has been turned into a corporate advertising canvas. So you have these millionaire marketers that get paid millions of dollars to try to make people feel insecure that they need to buy a certain car, look a certain way, have a certain pair of shoes in order to fit into society.

"Street artists are trying to plant a certain seed out in society that isn't there at the moment with art, and seizing the opportunity of doing it illegally—even though they might get arrested, even though they might be thrown in jail—to share a message with the public that isn't out there at the moment. And I think putting your art on the streets is key. It's the biggest gallery in the world.

"So you can work your ass off for years, trying to get in some gallery, trying to get permission to try to get some legal wall but nothing gets the job done quicker than just going out and doing it yourself without permission and just doing it illegally.

"Humanity has gone back and forth throughout time, but I believe we definitely lost an aspect of society... and that is the human aspect. I think the concept itself—'free humanity'—just to put out in society as a word is a concept that people don't think about in this time. Where people speak about 'Free Tibet' or 'Free Iran' or any country... I think it's important to understand that we're all suffering through these oppressions in life. And to me, that is what Free Humanity is."

Before long, I got a call from Free. He was on the lam. LAPD Detectives from Major Crimes Unit were out for him ever since a piece of his street art caused an unintended bomb scare downtown. The local TV news had even covered it. The cops had harrassed his ex-girlfriend at her work and threatened to deport her. Free was taking no chances. While he dropped out of the scene for a few months, I decided to reach out to more artists, wary of the risks.

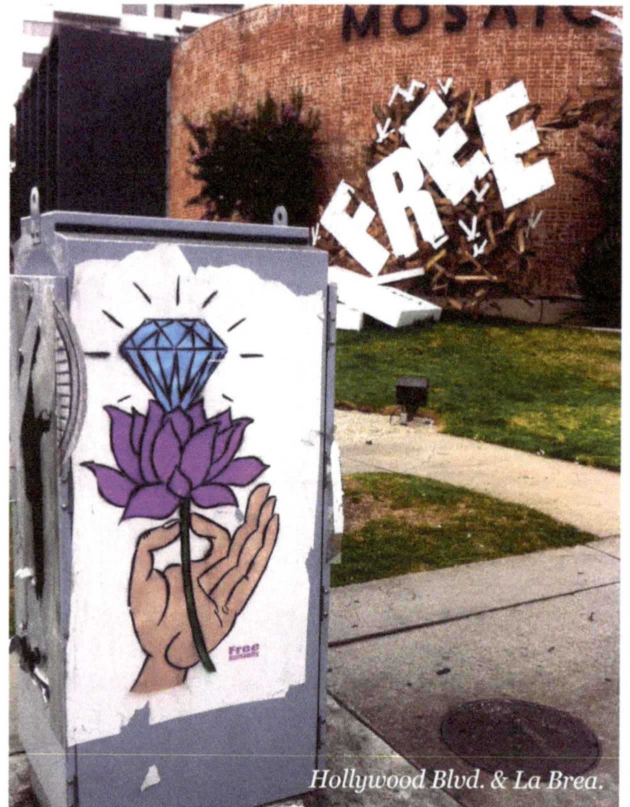

Hollywood Blvd. & La Brea.

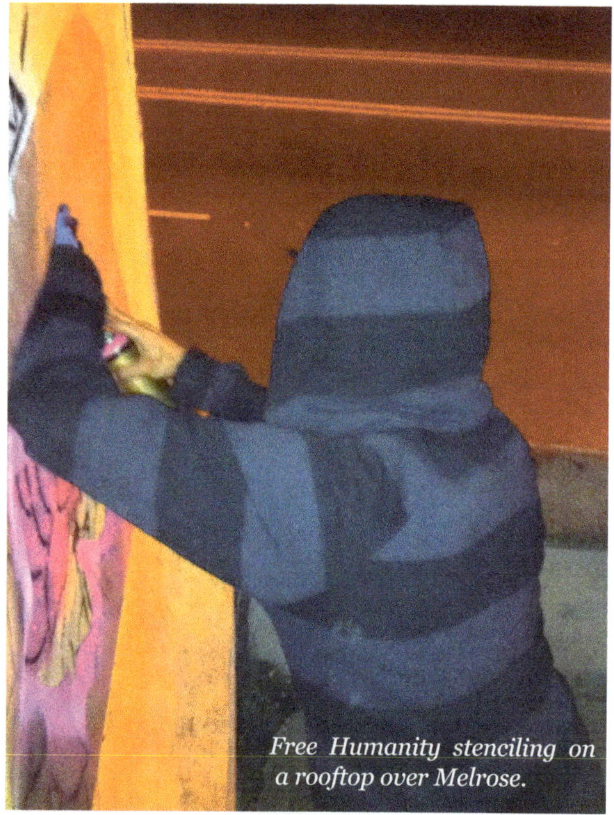
Free Humanity stenciling on a rooftop over Melrose.

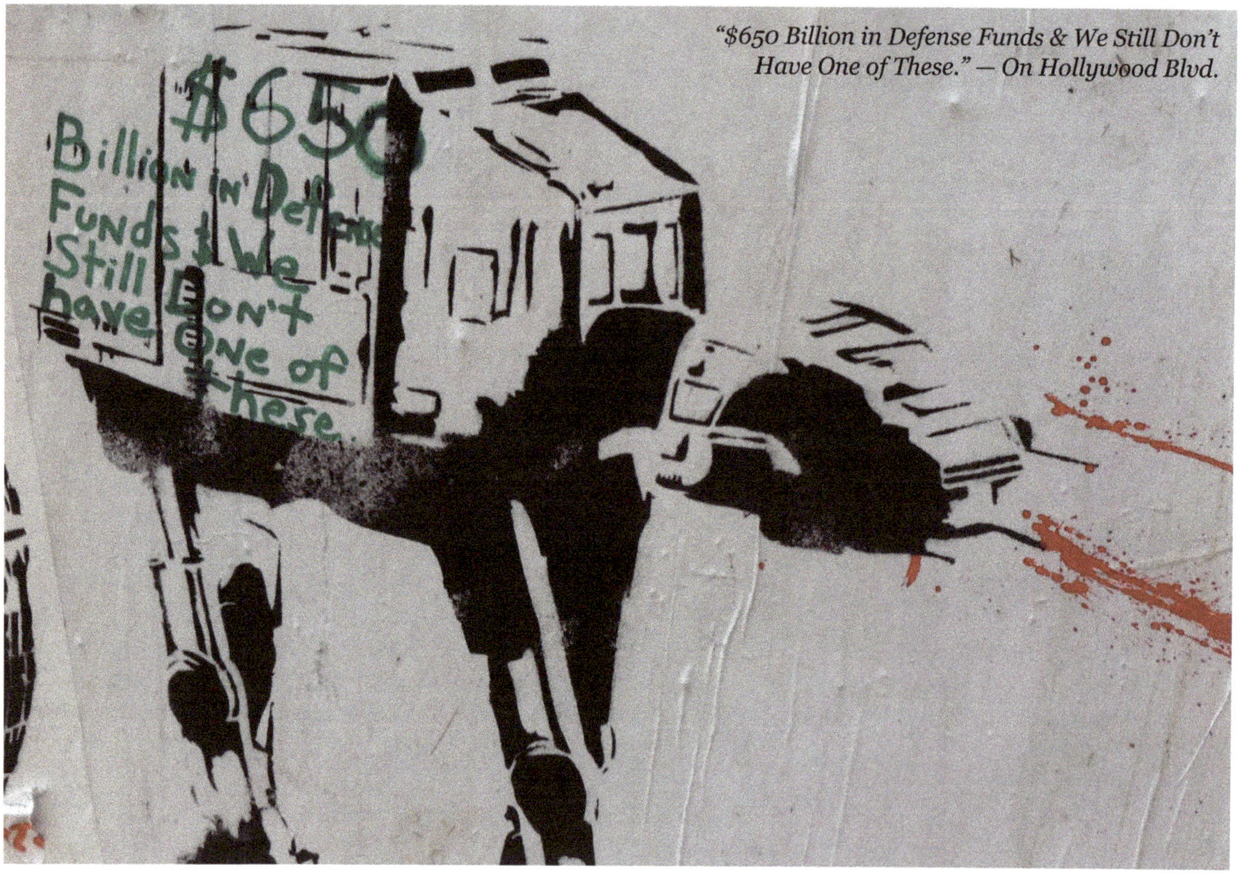

"$650 Billion in Defense Funds & We Still Don't Have One of These." — On Hollywood Blvd.

LYDIAEMILY

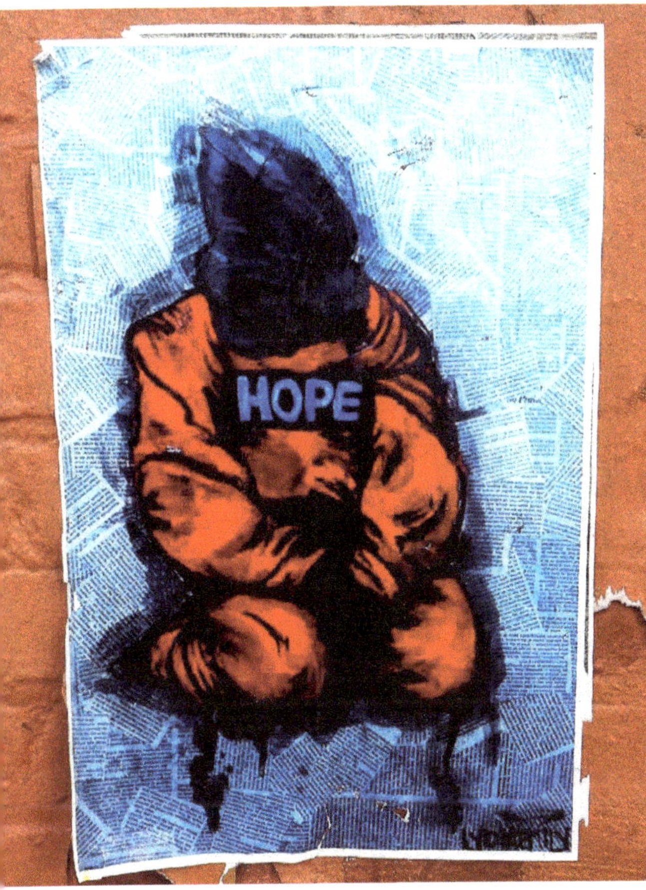

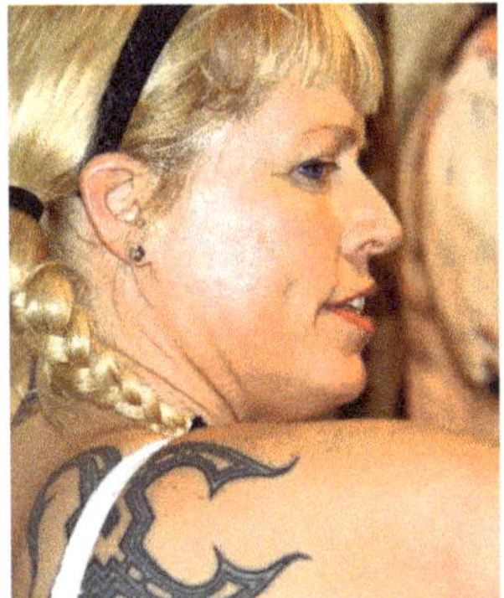

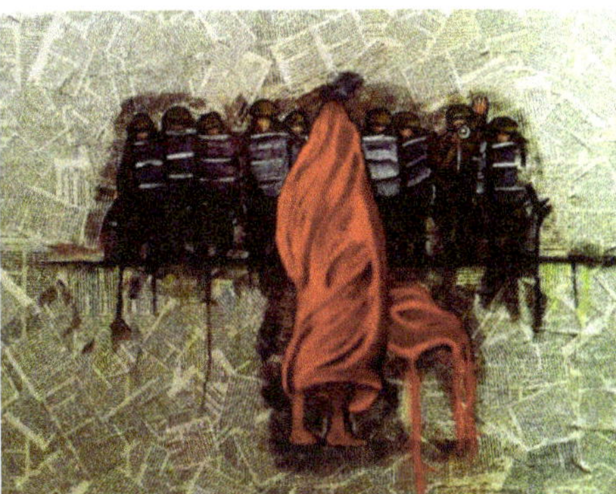

CLOCKWISE FROM LEFT: "HOPE" prisoner off Melrose; artist LydiaEmily; some of her Tibetan resistance-themed artwork; Julian Assange, "The Truth May Not Set You Free," on La Brea.

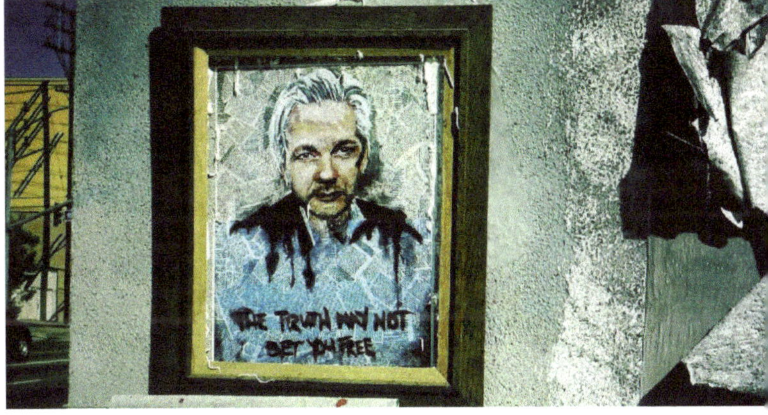

"I was a fine art painter for a really long time. And I did portraits, I did people's kids, I did people that I loved, I did other painters, and I did my political stuff on the side. And all my friends who were fine artists, who were in big galleries, kept saying, 'Don't do the political art. Nobody's gonna buy it. Nobody wants to see it. Nobody wants a picture of Mahmoud Ahmadinejad in their living room. Nobody wants to be told how to feel. And nobody wants to feel stupid.'

"That was the big problem with political art is that you put out a message and automatically some of the viewers feel like you're talking down to them. Like you're saying you're not educated, your beliefs aren't smart. Here's this painting of Obama and you just voted for Obama, so I'm saying as the artist that, 'You're uneducated. You're not academic enough to understand what's really going on.' And that's why people believe it didn't sell well."

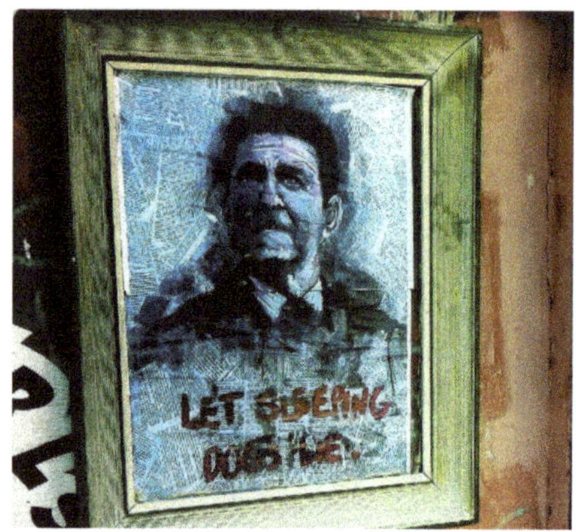

Ronald Reagan portrait off Melrose, framed: "Let Sleeping Dogs Lie."

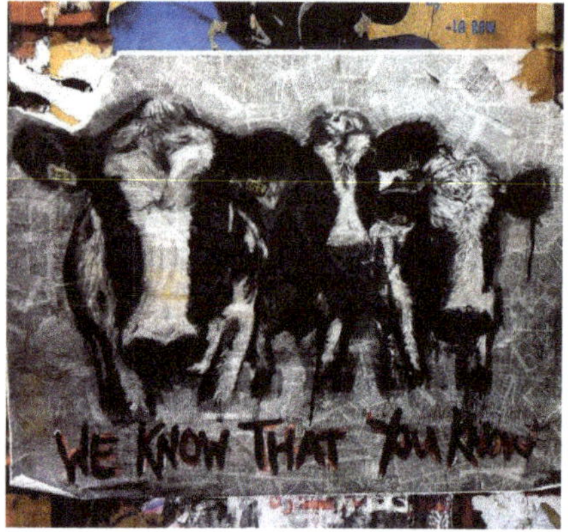

"We Know That You Know" — Factory farm cows on Traction Street Wall.

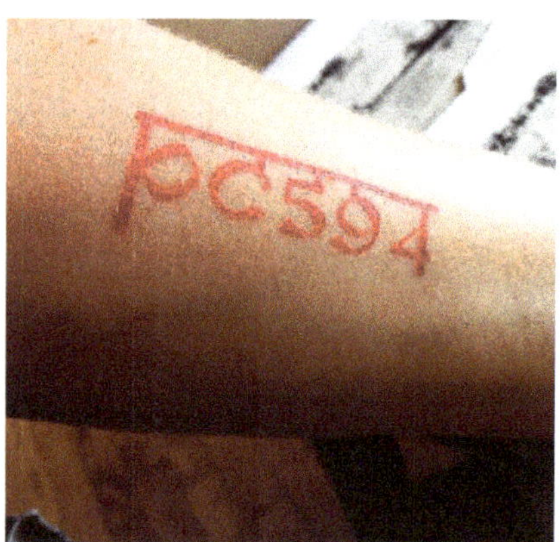

After her arrest, LydiaEmily got the LAPD citation number for vandalism tattooed on her arm: Penal Code 594.

"So, I made my little political pieces off to the side, and I'd make little flyers, and I would hang them up in cafes. I would just walk up with little, you know... that's what I mean by the stuff I've been putting up. I would just take little push pins, and I would to go to La Luz de Jésus Gallery or any place that had these big corkboards out front, and I would put up my little political posters.

"I wasn't out pasting, I wasn't like hitting Hollywood or the Valley or anything like that. I was just putting up my little teeny, tiny—I don't know, I guess they were like leaflets or pamphlets. And then I would continue to try and paint portraits of people's kids or things like that to get into galleries. And then, I did get into galleries. And it didn't sell. And I thought, 'What am I killing myself for, making these portraits to try and be respected as a fine art painter when I want to do the political stuff and no one's buying the fancy stuff anyways?'

"And then I got a recipe for wheat paste from some friends of mine who did that, and I just started doing it more legitimately. More like on walls... and I started doing it more like on walls and boxes and things like that about, I don't know, two years ago. Now I only do political pieces. And what's weird is the galleries that rejected me before for doing political pieces now want the political pieces.

"I ended up in court because I was... you know, coffee is an awesome drug. And I have this assistant, and she was helping me paint posters, and then she left, and we had a whole pot of coffee, and it was three o'clock in the morning and coffee was like... Coffee I think is like beer when you're in a bar, it's always, 'See that girl, she's pretty...' Coffee is the same way. It was all, 'You're not going to get caught. It's three o'clock in the morning. You don't have a scout. Go out, man. You know, whatever.' And I was all, 'Yeah, coffee, you're *right*.'

"And the first place I hit—I went to Beverly and Rossmore, like totally nice neighborhood, right across the street from a golf course, and it was dumb, it was totally dumb. And I started to take apart the bottom of the bus bench. I was pulling out the bottom of the bus bench.

"And they just rolled up on me. What am I... what am I going to do? Like I had a bucket of paste, and I'm holding the bottom of this bus bench, and... I like, I wasn't going to try and run, I just was like...

"But they handcuffed me, and I sat on my hands for an hour and a half. And they confiscated all my posters, confiscated all my friends' posters that I've been collecting, took all my stuff, went through my phone, which I now know is illegal."

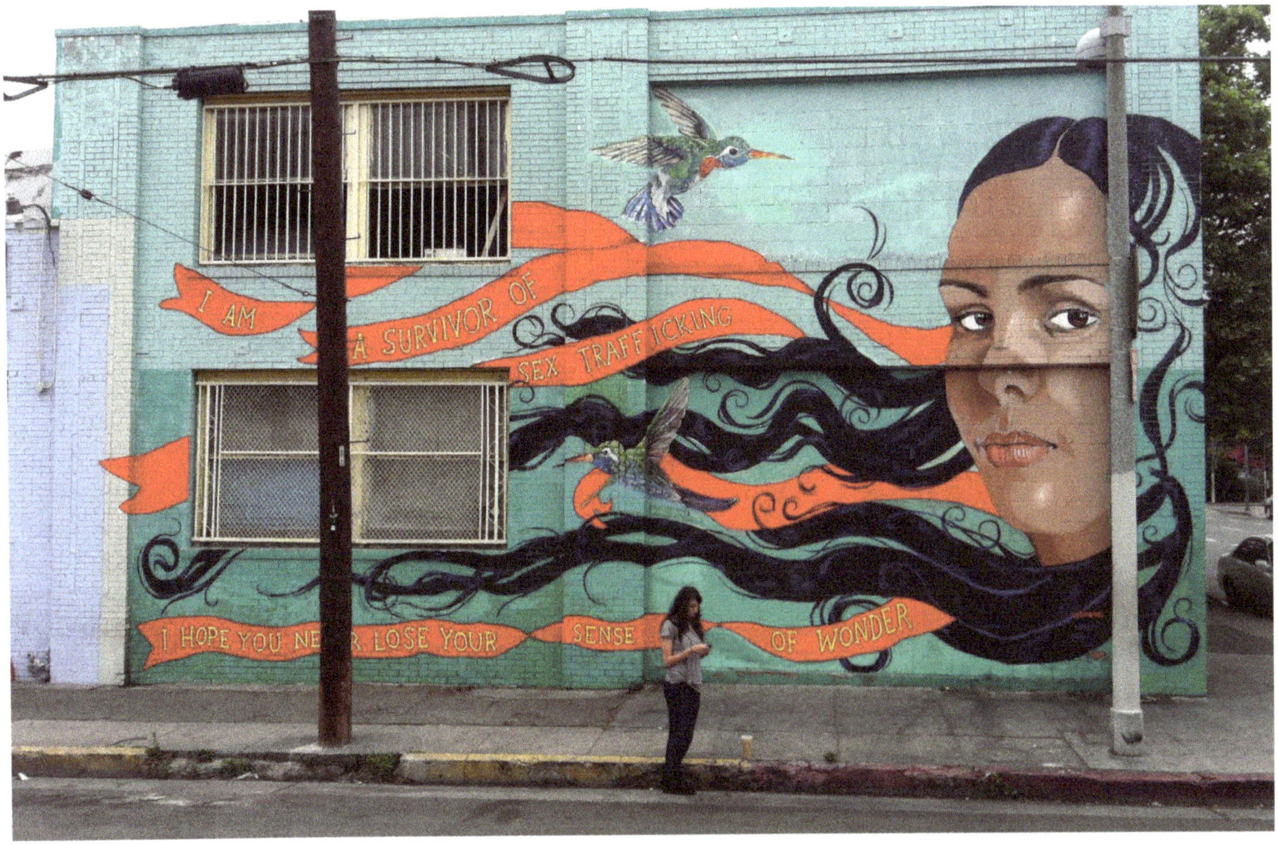

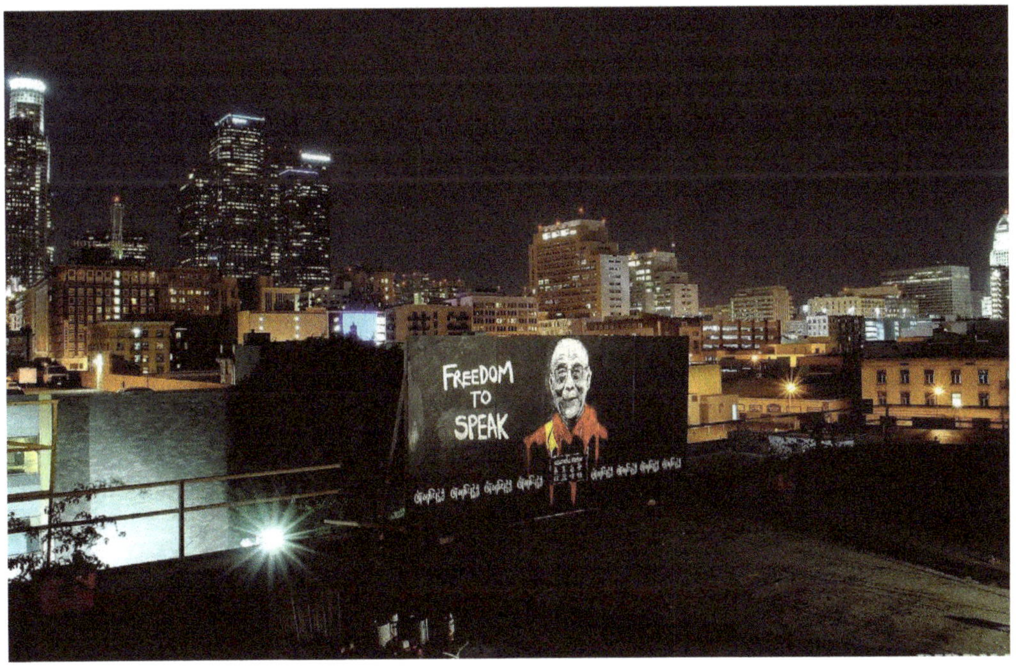

ABOVE: Mural dedicated to Jessica, survivor of sex trafficking, in East L.A.

RIGHT: Mural of Dalai Lama, "Freedom to Speak," dedicated to Tibeten freedom, on a rooftop wall in Downtown L.A. LydiaEmily started her own charity to create a Tibetan buddhist school for girls, The Karma Underground.

Photos by Birdman, Birdman Photography.

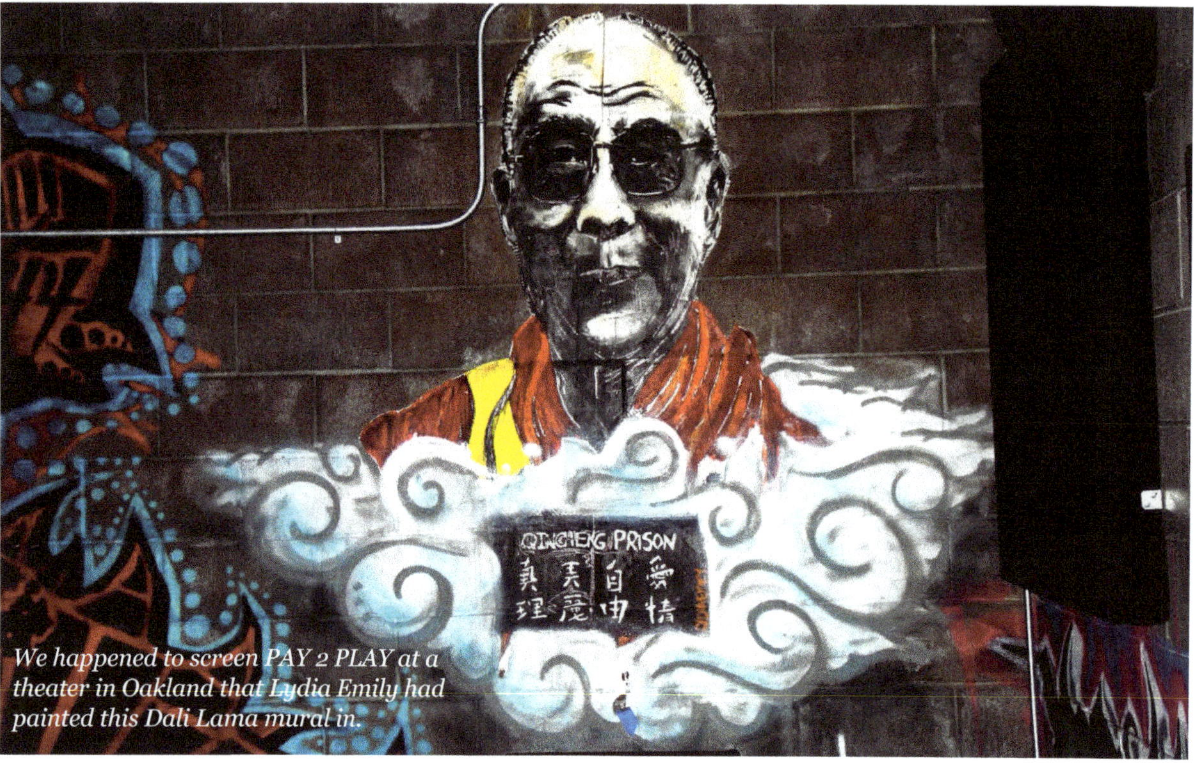

We happened to screen PAY 2 PLAY at a theater in Oakland that Lydia Emily had painted this Dali Lama mural in.

"After an hour and a half, they let me go. I mean they gave me a citation, but they were like, okay, we're done, you can go. And I said, 'Cool.'

"And I took my citation, and I went home. And it was about five o'clock in the morning. And at about eight o'clock in the morning, an unmarked police car came to the house and delivered me a nice file of everything I've done, from San Francisco to Mexico, black and white photos of every single... I mean of pieces I forgot, places where I did not even recognize the corner...They even had some of those little...um, ones I was telling you about like when I would go and put up little paper with little push pins. They even had pictures of some of those.

"And so they had black and white pictures of everything I had done, and all they needed to do was catch me doing it once. And then they were able to give me this file and each page had a little, like, yellow tab that said, you know, 'Two hundred fiftydollar fine,' 'seventy-five dollar fine,' 'government property,' 'private property,' you know, and then the whole stack added up to $3,200 dollars.

"My probation is three years. It's called summary probation. It's kind of like... my lawyer described it as probation 'light.' It's not like 'hard' probation. It's probation 'light.' I can't make any money off of any piece that has been on the street. I can't profit.

"The reason I didn't lie in court is because, I mean I had this opportunity when I got popped to go to court and say, 'I didn't do this.' That's all I had to say when I talked to the ACLU and my lawyer who's not with the ACLU—they're two separate entities—but they said all you have to do is say you didn't do it. There's no picture of you doing it. It's all you have to do is say you didn't do it. All the charges will be dropped. Your felony would be brought down to maybe a misdemeanor if you're lucky. And I just... I couldn't do it. Because I have this stack of letters from people who are living in countries that are... like... I don't even know how to articulate it... really... they believe in me. And I show my face, and I say my real name, and I believe in my rights."

TEACHR

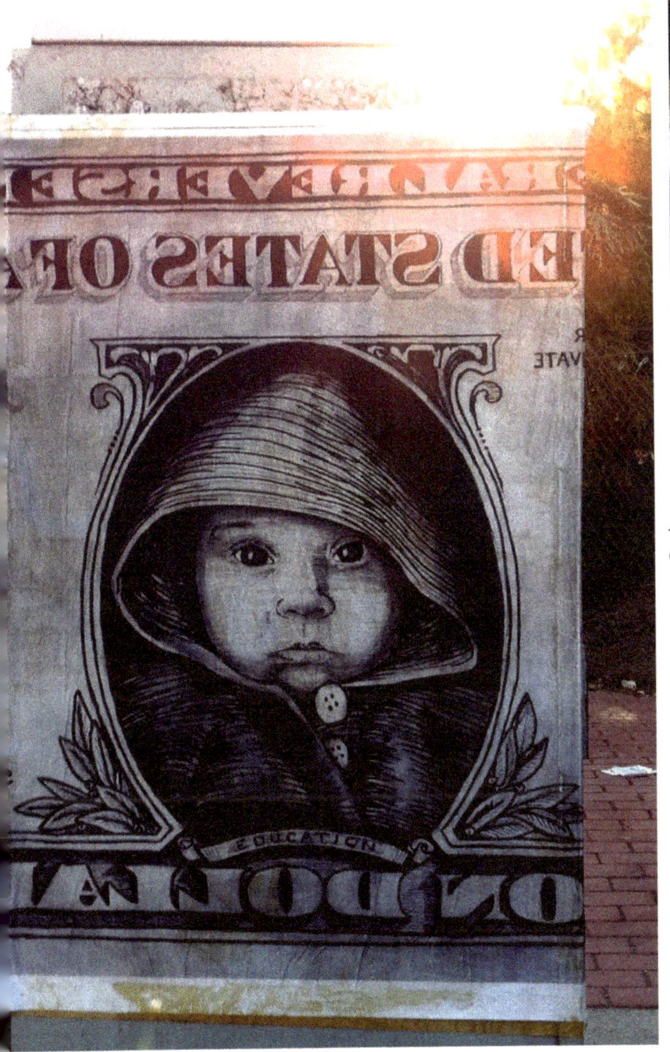

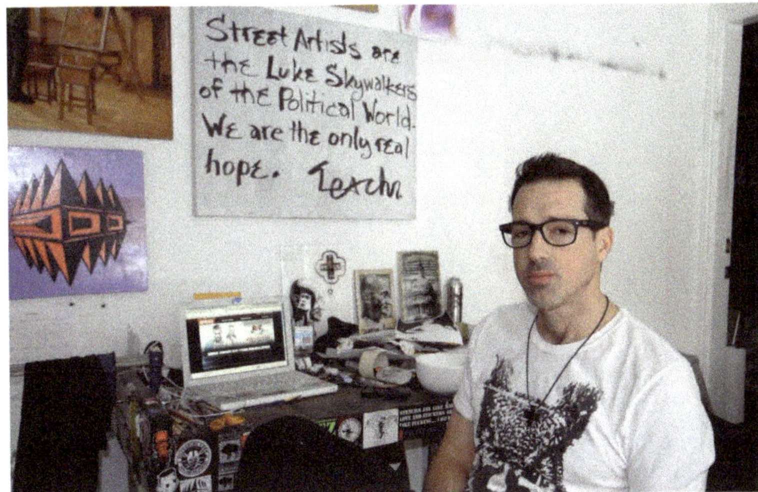

LEFT: "Education Dollar" on Moorpark. ABOVE: Keith Biele, a.k.a. Teachr. BELOW: JFK stencil on La Brea.

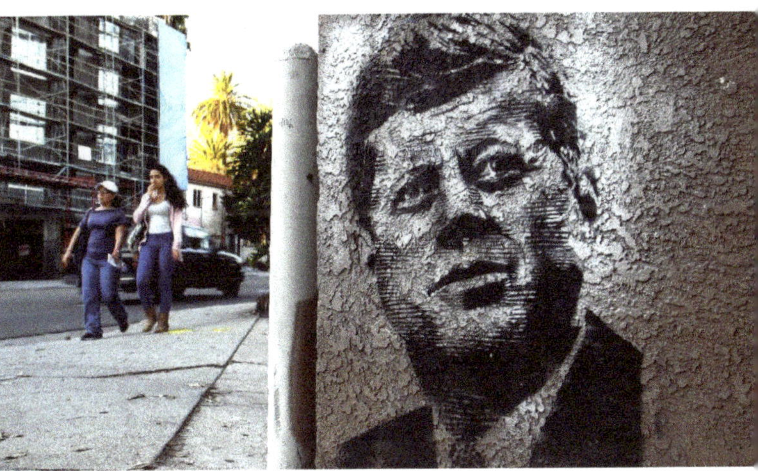

"I've wanted to do street art, actually, for quite a few years. I started seeing some of Shepard Fairey's pieces, and then I became aware of Banksy, and actually when I saw the movie, *Exit Through the Gift Shop*, that was just like a manual, like a how-to manual, you know?

"And having my children, too. I'd been doing commission paintings for many years and that doesn't give you any residual income. And since I need to start saving for their future and their education, I needed to start to get into a gallery, and it's hard; it's very difficult to get into a gallery these days.

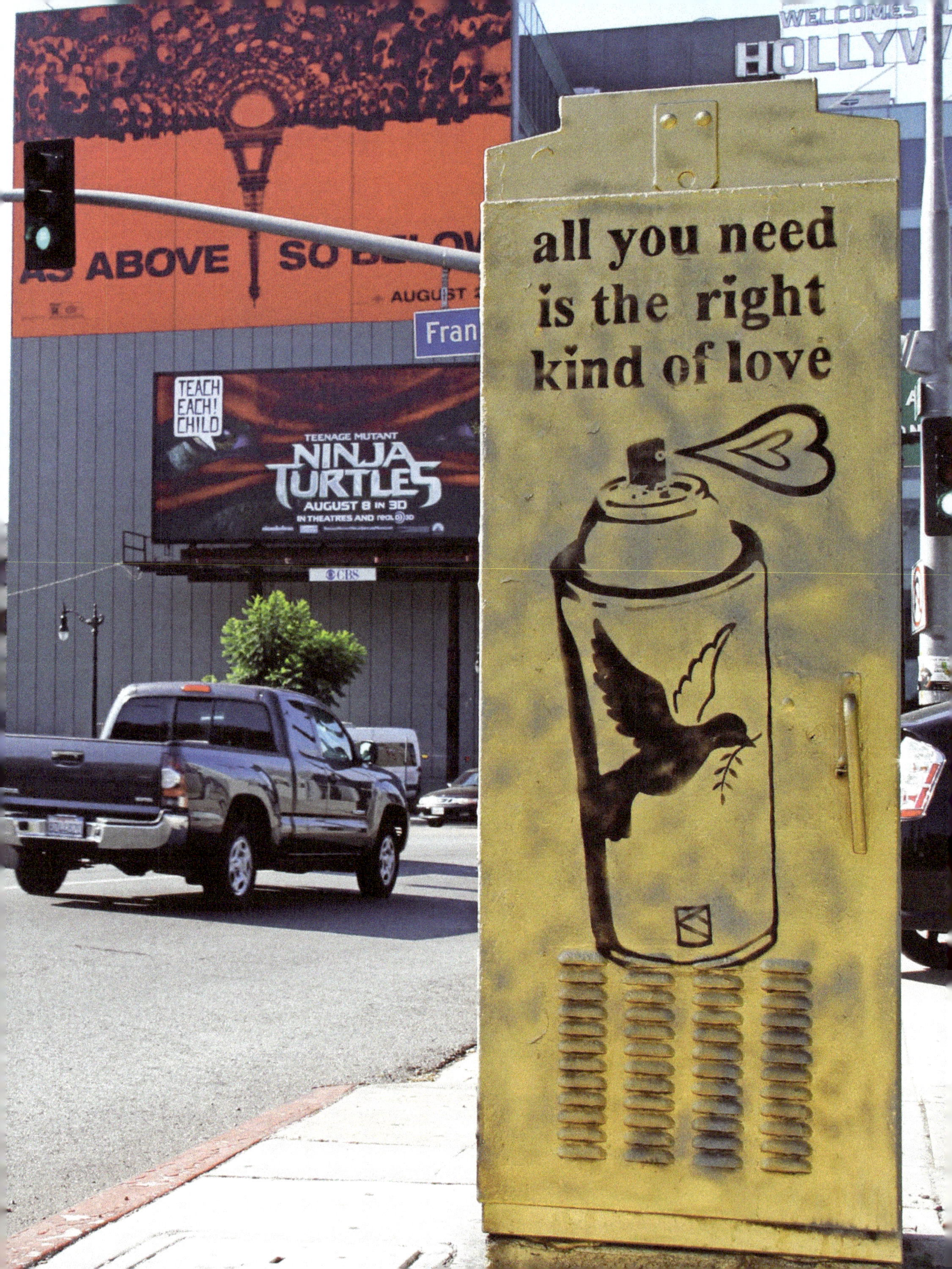

WELCOMES
HOLLYW
AS ABOVE
SO BE
AUGUST
Fran
TEACH EACH! CHILD
TEENAGE MUTANT NINJA TURTLES
AUGUST 8 IN 3D
IN THEATRES AND
CBS
all you need
is the right
kind of love

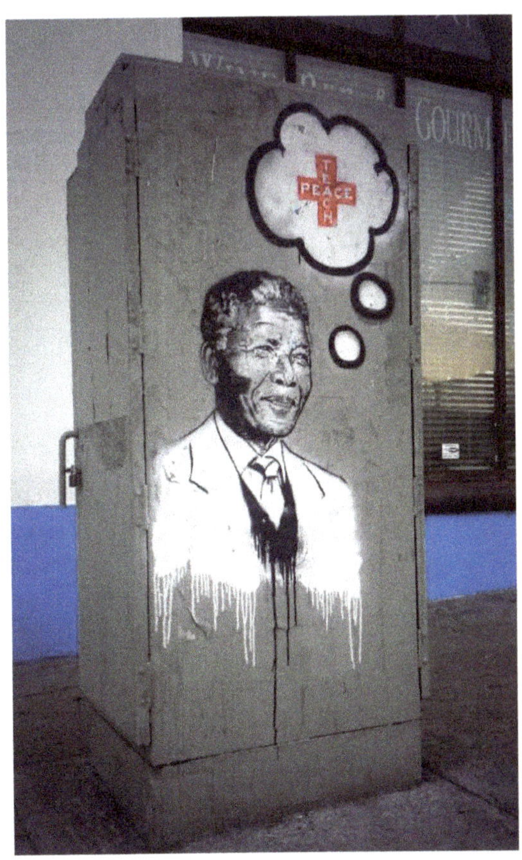

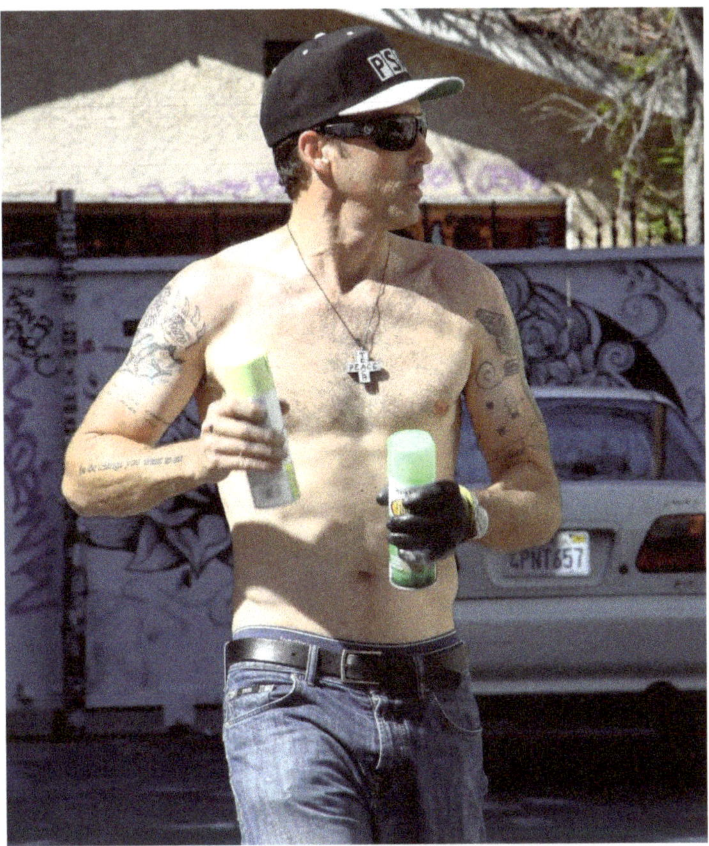

ABOVE: Nelson Mandela tribute stencil, off Sunset; Teachr at work on Melrose.

RIGHT: A Robin Williams tribute stencil on the Sunset Strip, across from the Laugh Factory.

OPPOSITE: "All you need is the right kind of love" stenciled over gold paint, at Highland and Franklin, the entryway to Hollywood. Note the billboard in the background that has "TEACH EACH CHILD" pasted up by Teachr. Some of his billboard takeovers have stayed up surprisingly long here in this heavily marketed intersection.

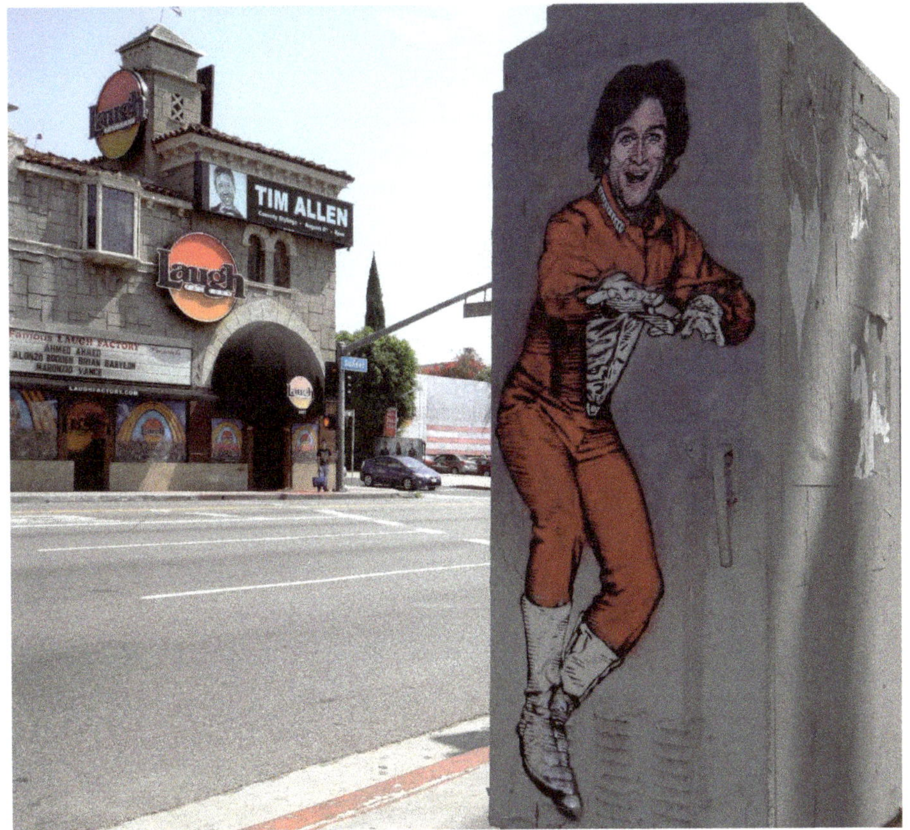

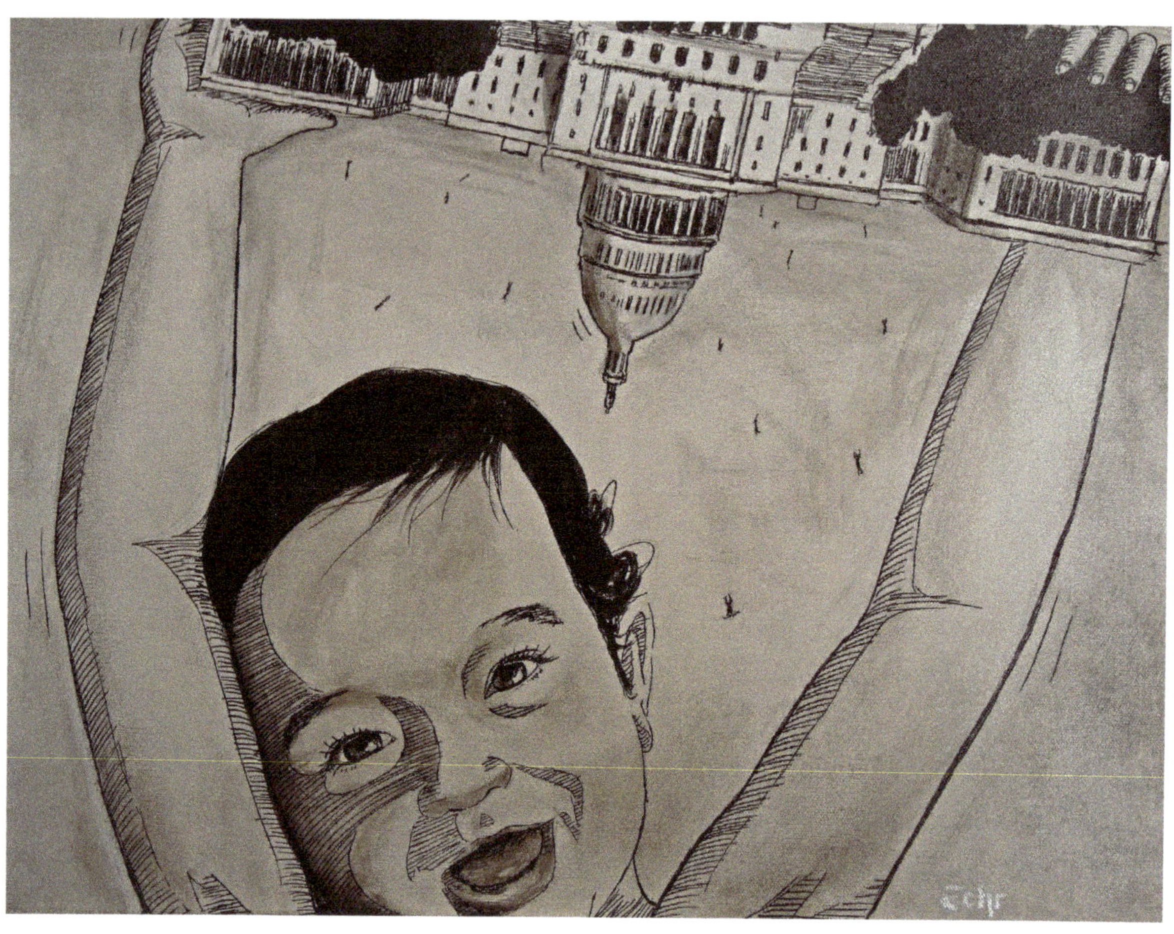

"Capitol Hill Shake Up" on canvas.

"And so I thought, 'You know what? If you want to reach more people, put your stuff on the street.' And since at that time, the most current thing that I wanted to address was the cuts in the education budget, that's why I started with the original image of my daughter's face, and it says 'TEACH EACH.' And then from there, it just kind of developed into other things.

"I was hitting some signs in Sunset Plaza and a security guard saw me and called the cops. And they said they normally didn't reply to something like that, but the guy used to be a deputy and so they had to come quickly. And by the time they got to me, I was further down the street, and two cop cars pulled up on each side, and they had their guns pulled and everything.

"It's funny because, I always thought, you know, I was prepared for that moment to come, that I would have something cool to say, you know, whatever? *[Laughs]* But when it happens—oh man, I feel like a little five-year-old boy who's, you know, doing something up a tree he shouldn't, or something like that. But when I, you know, I told them what I was doing, they're like, 'What?'

"They cuffed me, stuffed me, took me down to where the security guard was so he ID'ed me, and then he went and showed them the sign I had just done, the stencil that said 'TEACH EACH CHILD,' and I wish you could have seen their postures, the cops walking over there, you know, and look at this sign and just like... *[Shrugs]*

"They come back over and were like, 'Why were you doing that?' I'm like, 'Well, do you agree that the cuts in the education budget are pretty ridiculous?' And they're like, 'Yeah.' And I was like, 'Well, sometimes you have to have drastic measures to reach things, like this.'

"And they're like, 'Don't you have a look-out or anything?!'"

KAÏ

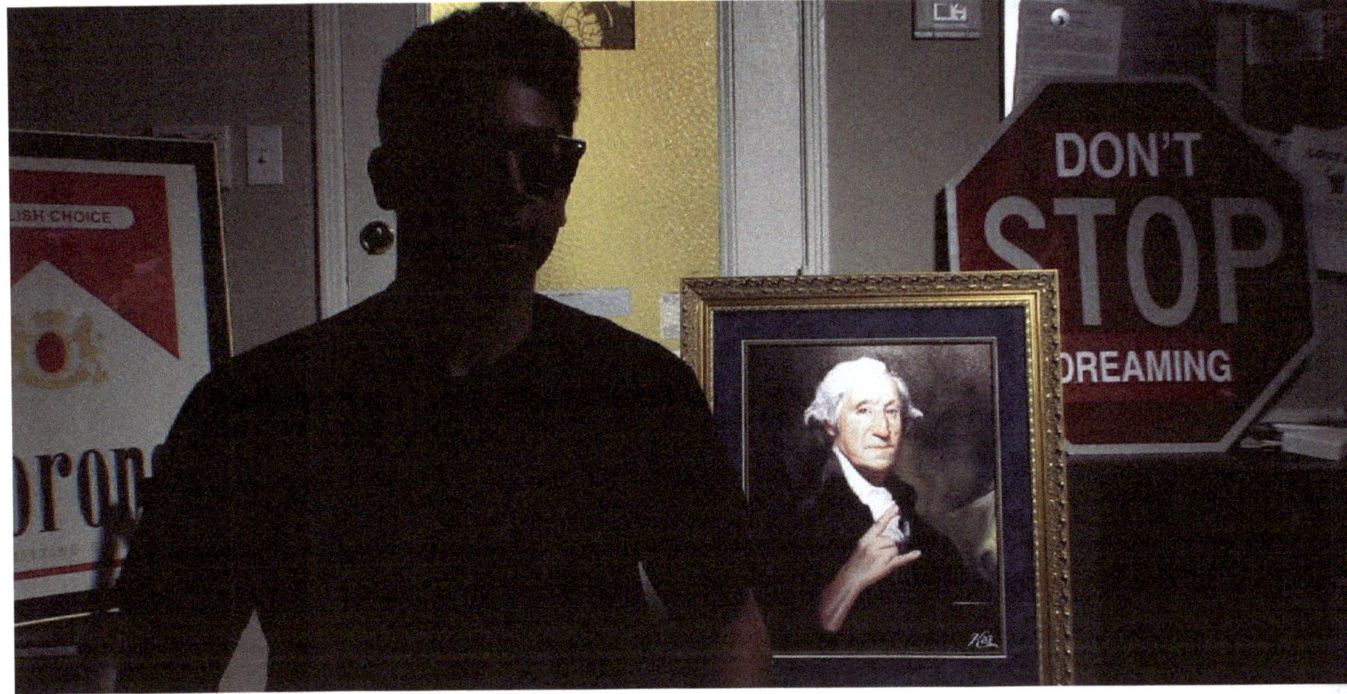

"Most people view street art as a form of destruction. However, art is my personal method of fighting the mainstream and societal norms, as well as my way of relaying important messages to the general public. I grew up during a time when street art was booming, and this trend had a very strong effect on me. To me, it felt like a statement against propaganda and manipulative advertisements.

"The juxtaposition of street art and heavily photoshopped ads is, to the average eye, jarring. In my opinion, the contrast between the two emphasizes the purpose of street art—to create an environment of fresh air for consumers.

"I chose this path because I want to affect people while doing something about which I am very passionate. Street art is seen by practically everyone and often influences its viewers quietly but strongly.

"Not only does it serve as a respite from advertisements put out by major companies, but it also gives us a break from the everyday habits and rituals that bore us without us even noticing. When new street art pops up, the average businessperson, mother, student, etc. gets to look at something new on their slow drive home through rush hour.

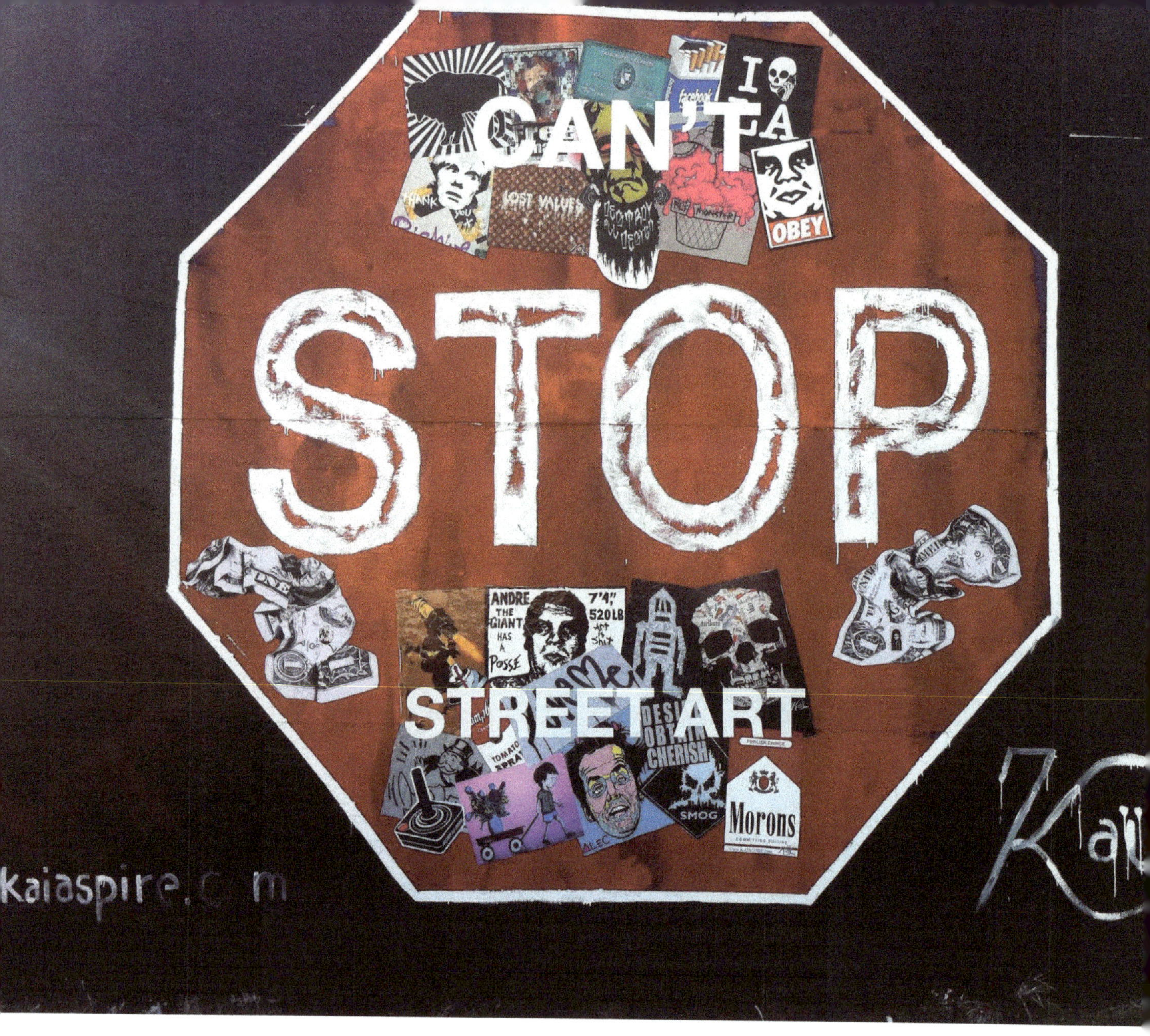

"Just because tax dollars go towards dull paint jobs on phone booths and the like, that does not mean that we should become accustomed to colors that don't excite us. This form of art is my favorite above all others because street artists typically remain anonymous. This allows people who appreciate the art to make the message personal, rather than focus on who created it and why.

"Before I put new artwork on the street, I do two things: First, I scan the area for policemen and/or city officials. In the past, I have had some very close encounters. Trust me—they are not fun, which takes away from the thrill of it all.

"Second, I consider whether my art will affect the neighborhood in which I'm putting it up. It is very important to feel that the work I'm going to put up will be noticed by those who pass by. If I am going to spend my time and money on something that ends up being ignored, what's the point?

"I don't see street art as a gift to the public, but rather as a freshly-planted seed in that it has the potential to spark new ideas and perspectives. If my artwork gets the viewer to really think even for just a moment, then the seed has been successfully planted. If the viewers consider it further, the the plant starts to grow and so on. My job is simply to plant the seed. Street art is one of the most effective ways to communicate with people, because we don't have to go looking for it. In a way, it comes looking for us."

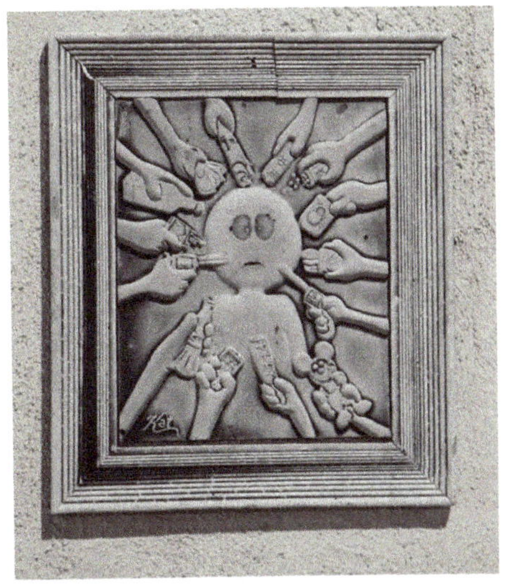

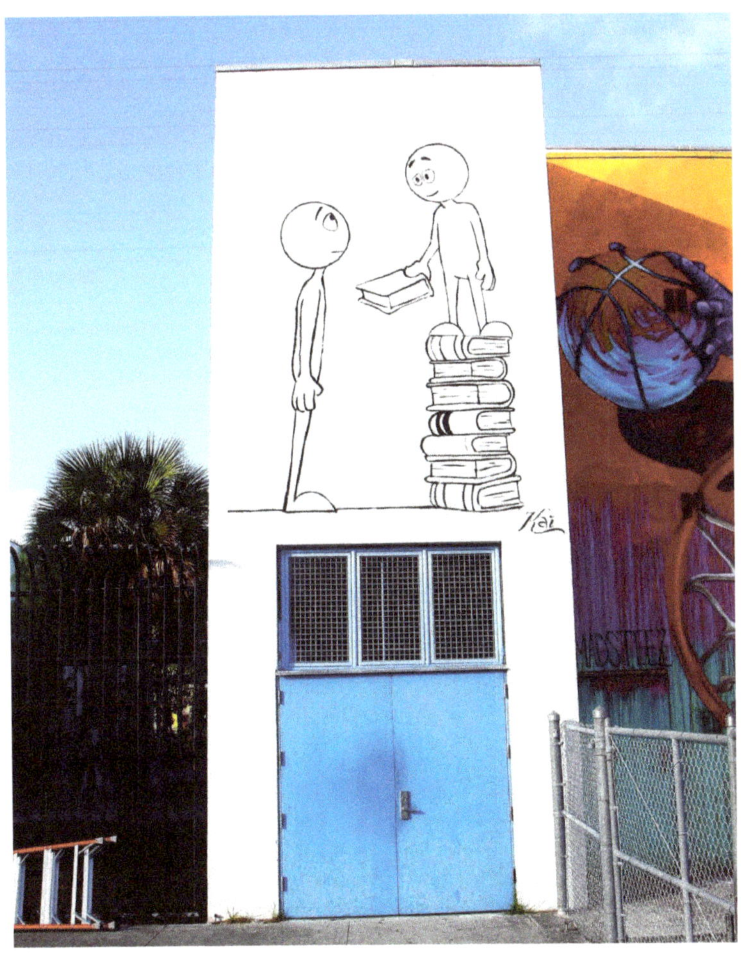

ABOVE: "Grow With Books" mural on a school. LEFT: Framed mounted 3D piece. BELOW: Kaï painting on a rooftop on Melrose. (Photos by Nobody Photography) OPPOSITE: "Can't STOP Street Art" mural on Melrose & Spaulding, with homages to other artists.

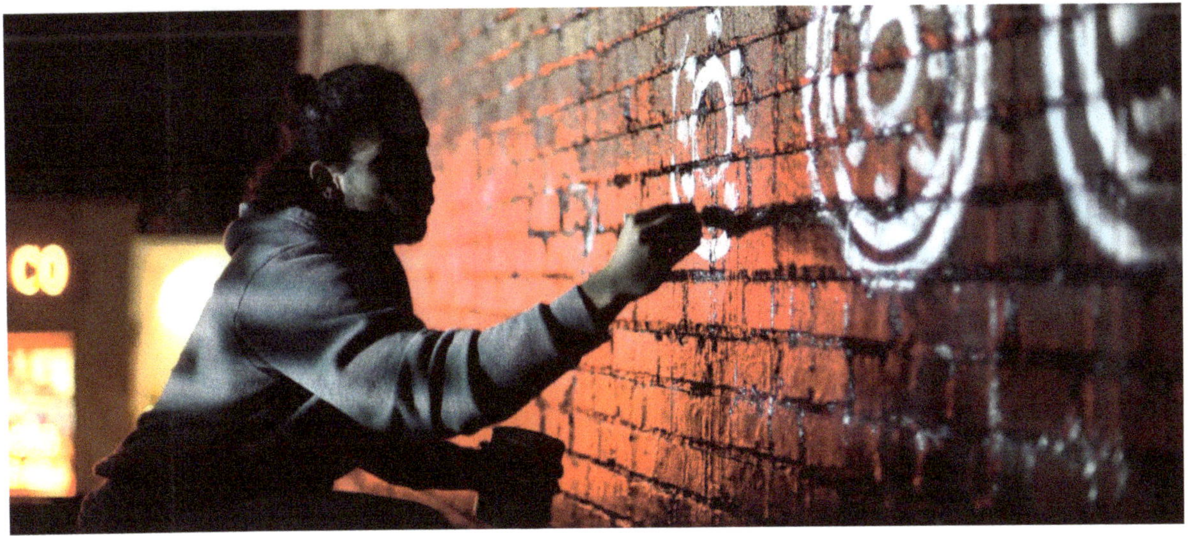

MORLEY

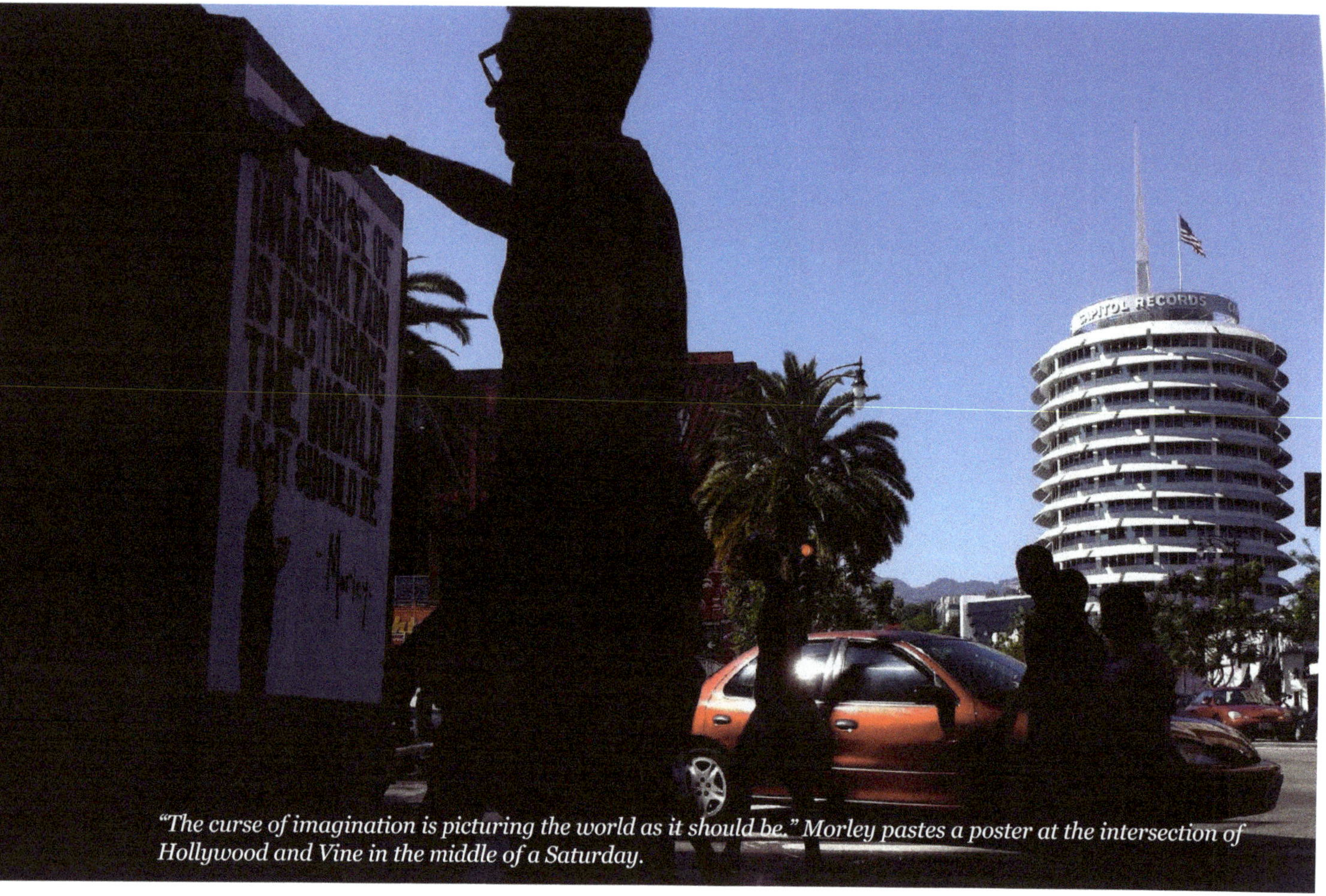

"The curse of imagination is picturing the world as it should be." Morley pastes a poster at the intersection of Hollywood and Vine in the middle of a Saturday.

Morley is the antithesis of street artists in Los Angeles. Where traditional taggers obscure their name in scrawl only readable to their own, Morley prints big messages with large capital letters. Where most find it cool to be cryptic, Morley shares his wit in complete sentences. Where many street artists prefer anonymity or an empowered alter-ego, Morley includes a plain drawing of his unglamorous self writing each ironic aphorism. His humor veers from self-deprecating to sly; his insight ranges from soul searching to silly.

Morley is so un-street art, he walks around in broad daylight plastering his posters up at the busiest intersections.

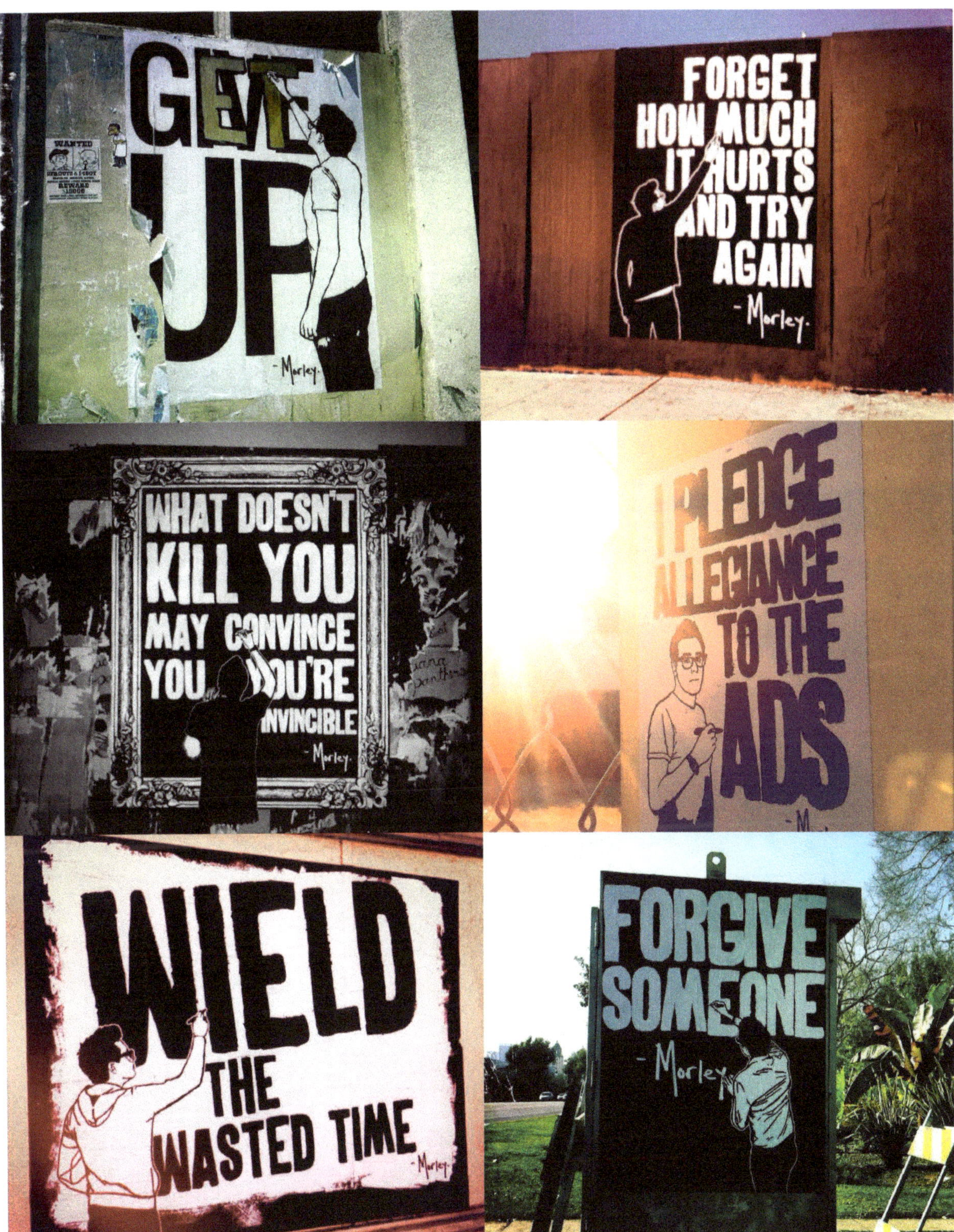
WANTED
REWARD
GET
UP
- Morley.
FORGET
HOW MUCH
IT HURTS
AND TRY
AGAIN
- Morley.
WHAT DOESN'T
KILL YOU
MAY CONVINCE
YOU YOU'RE
INVINCIBLE
- Morley.
I PLEDGE
ALLEGIANCE
TO THE
ADS
WIELD
THE
WASTED TIME
- Morley.
FORGIVE
SOMEONE
- Morley

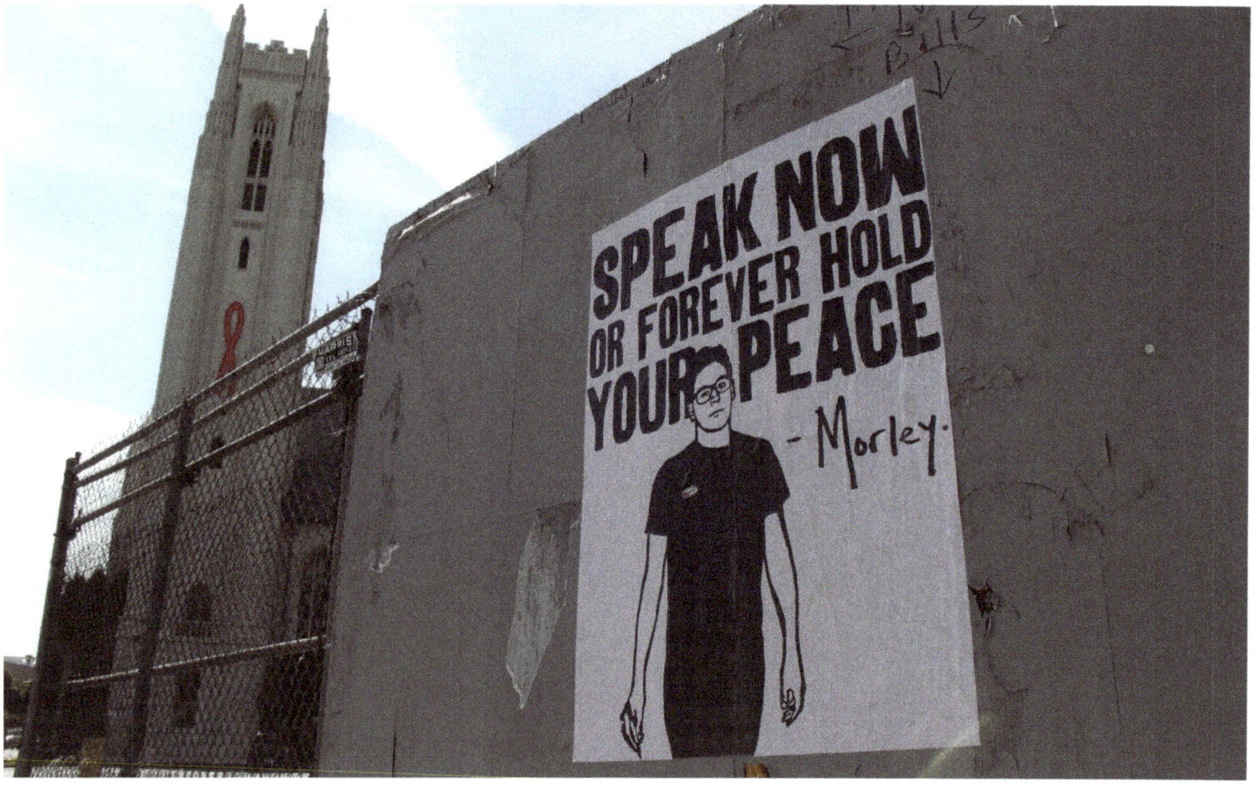

Morley's poster seen in PAY 2 PLAY, "Speak Now or Forever Hold Your Peace," with Morley's likeliness sporting an "I VOTED" sticker, because voting is a vital act of using your voice. On Highland at Franklin in Hollywood.

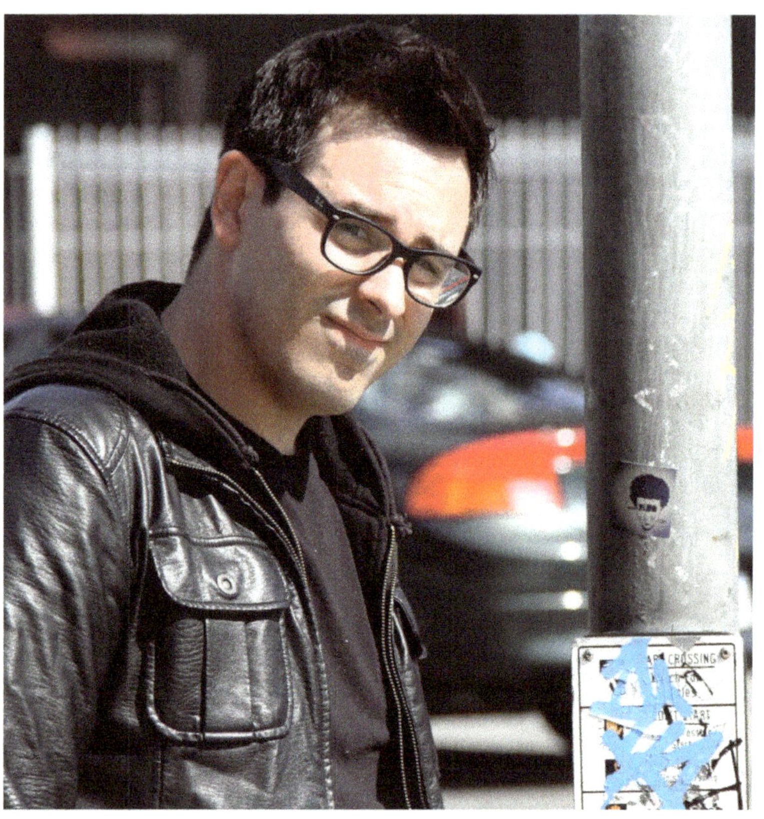

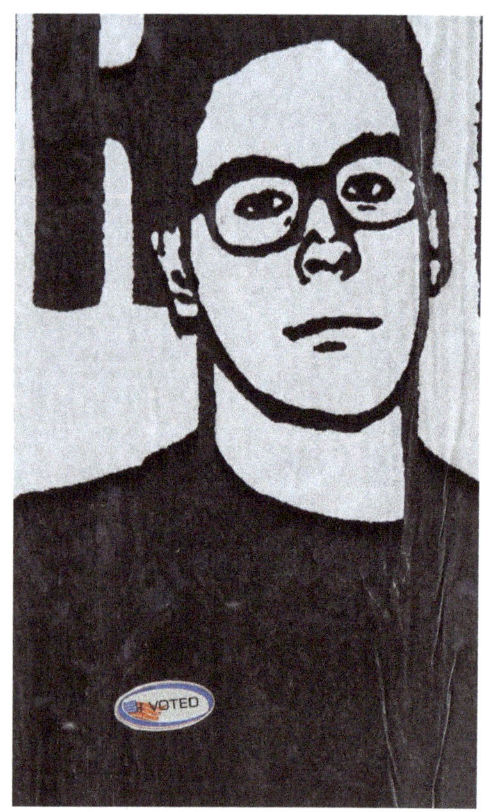

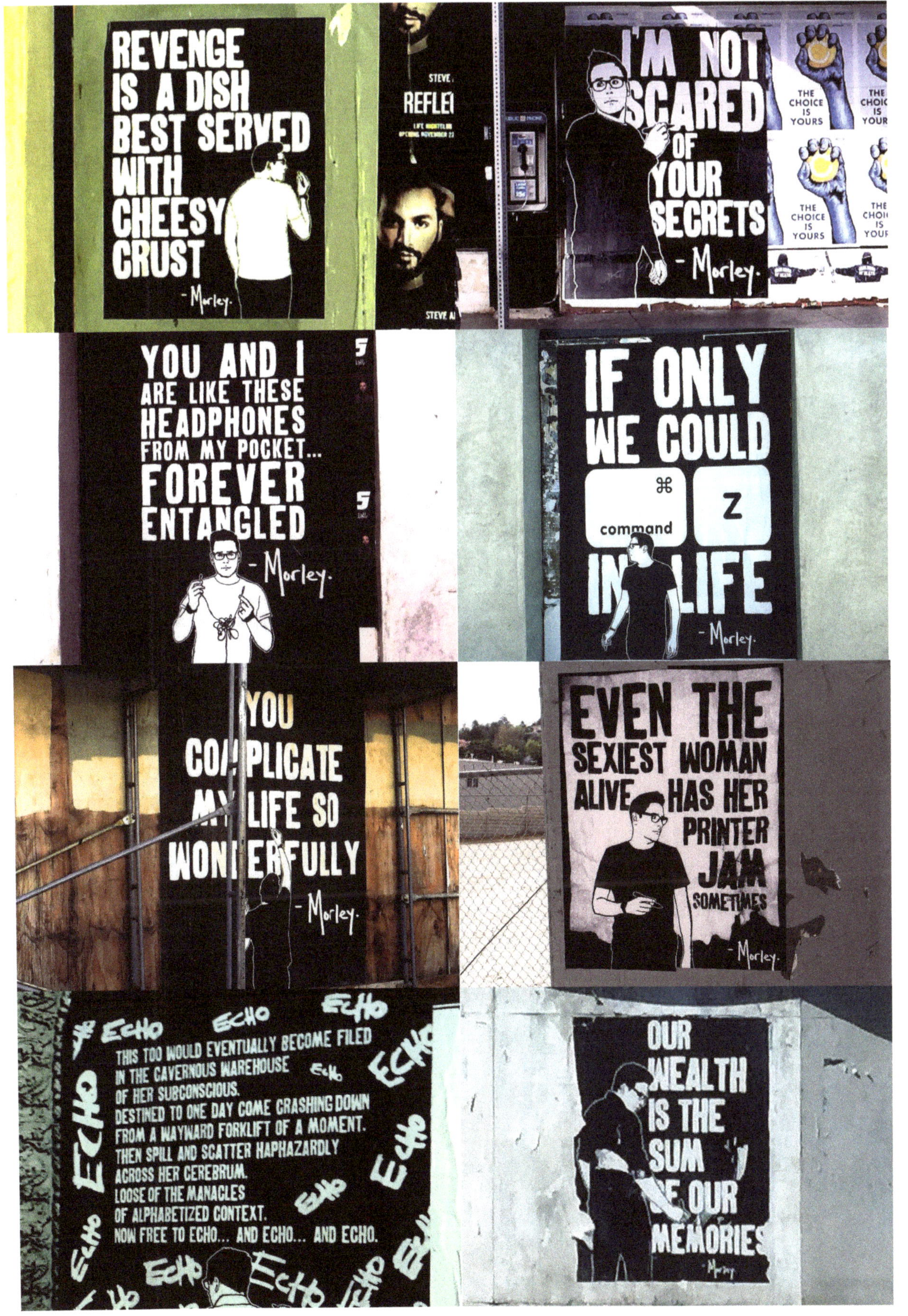
REVENGE IS A DISH BEST SERVED WITH CHEESY CRUST
- Morley.
I'M NOT SCARED OF YOUR SECRETS
- Morley.
THE CHOICE IS YOURS
YOU AND I ARE LIKE THESE HEADPHONES FROM MY POCKET... FOREVER ENTANGLED
- Morley.
IF ONLY WE COULD
⌘
command
Z
IN LIFE
- Morley.
YOU COMPLICATE MY LIFE SO WONDERFULLY
- Morley.
EVEN THE SEXIEST WOMAN ALIVE HAS HER PRINTER JAM SOMETIMES
- Morley.
ECHO
THIS TOO WOULD EVENTUALLY BECOME FILED
IN THE CAVERNOUS WAREHOUSE
OF HER SUBCONSCIOUS.
DESTINED TO ONE DAY COME CRASHING DOWN
FROM A WAYWARD FORKLIFT OF A MOMENT.
THEN SPILL AND SCATTER HAPHAZARDLY
ACROSS HER CEREBRUM.
LOOSE OF THE MANACLES
OF ALPHABETIZED CONTEXT.
NOW FREE TO ECHO... AND ECHO... AND ECHO.
OUR WEALTH IS THE SUM OF OUR MEMORIES
- Morley

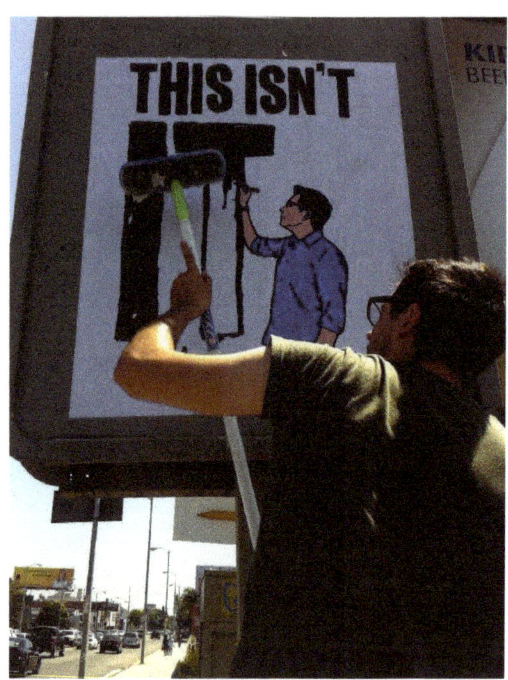

Morley's "This Isn't It" on Vermont.

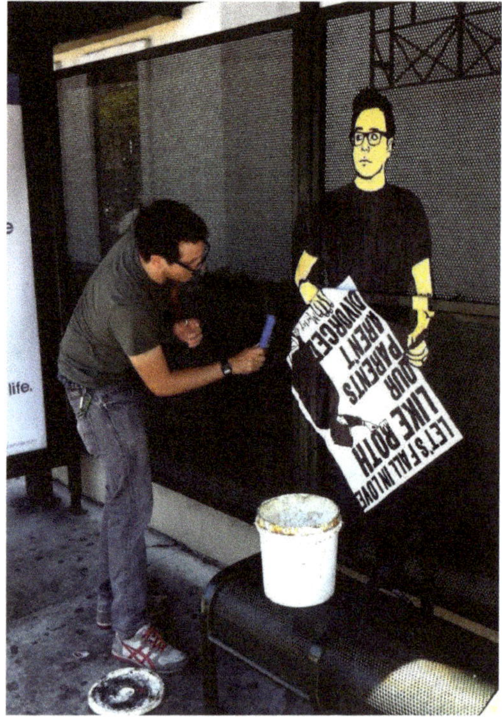

Morley's "Let's Fall in Love Like Both Our Parents Aren't Divorced" on Santa Monica Boulevard bus shelter.

Morley is tattooed, like most street artists, though his forearm sports a cross, proclaiming his Christianity (coincidentally, Teachr's does, too). Having grown up misbehaving in Catholic School, the parts with Jesus teaching tolerance, forgiveness, and unconditional love apparently stuck with him. That spirit of redemption seems to be a driving theme in his aphorisms as well as his approach to street art.

MORLEY: "Because I put my stuff up during the day, I tend to be more, just a little bit more aware about what kinda stuff I'm putting my posters on, because I don't think police care. I mean, I've had a number of cops drive by while I'm working; I'm pretty sure that they don't see me as being much of a threat. Especially compared to the people that you know, the gang taggers, that kinda thing—those are things police are looking out for.

"One of the things that our, my, generation is faced with is just an incredible lack of hope—feeling hopeless and feeling like there's just... it'll never get better, it's only going to get worse, progressively over time get worse, and I think that, for me in my art, one of the things I try to do is bring a little bit of the hope that I feel and express it to the world, you know? Whether it's a statement like, 'I promise you you're not just a waitress,' to me, speaks to the person who's living out here and dreaming and thinking, 'Is that all I am? I came out here to be an actress, or I came out here to be, you know, whatever, but all I'm doing is being a waitress.'

"And so, to me, I feel like a statement like that speaks to, and attempts to give, that person hope, and to recognize 'You're more than just a waitress; you're more than just your job; you're more than just a temp,' you know? And I think the goal is to just bring a smile to someone's face, you know...

"I think that it's really easy living in Los Angeles, or living in any major city, for that matter, to get lost, you know, and feel sort of just like a face in the crowd, or an anonymous person walking along, surrounded by people, surrounded by all these images of perfection and stuff. I think that every once in a while if you can capture, if you find something that you feel is speaking to you, not just speaking to you as a consumer, but speaking to you as a person, I think is something that could do some good in this world. And that's sort of my main goal."

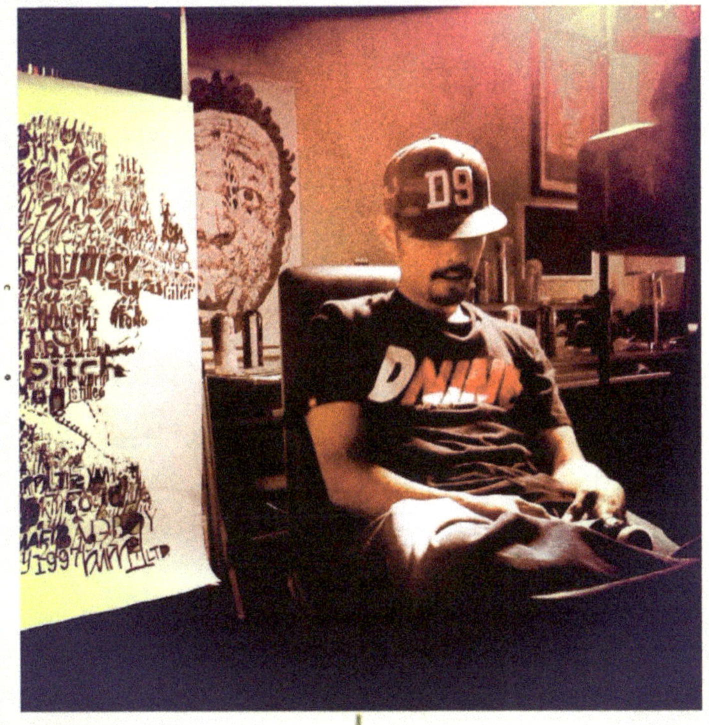

"We didn't really have much money so I would, you know, go out and make money for myself to be able to pay for my own shit. Without having to ask my parents for any money... G rides (steal cars), burglaries, fights, shit like that, nothing too serious.

"It was fun, back in the day, having money. So, yeah, it was, it was fun, but you know, like, as you get older, you don't wanna... go to jail. *[Laughs]* Or fuckin' have bad karma, basically.

"I stopped doing that 'cause you don't want to be fucking with other people that don't fuck with you, you know? That you don't have to be, you know, doing wrong towards. Or ending up having to go to jail, so, yeah, I'm done with that.

"Like, I used to get a lot of, like, adrenaline rushes doing, you know, stupid shit. But like, I see the street art thing as kinda like—it's not as big an adrenaline rush, it's still a good rush to be out there, in the street, you know, putting up your stuff."

LEFT: Notorious B.I.G. portrait posted for the 15th anniversary of his death, at the intersection where he was killed, Fairfax & Wilshire.

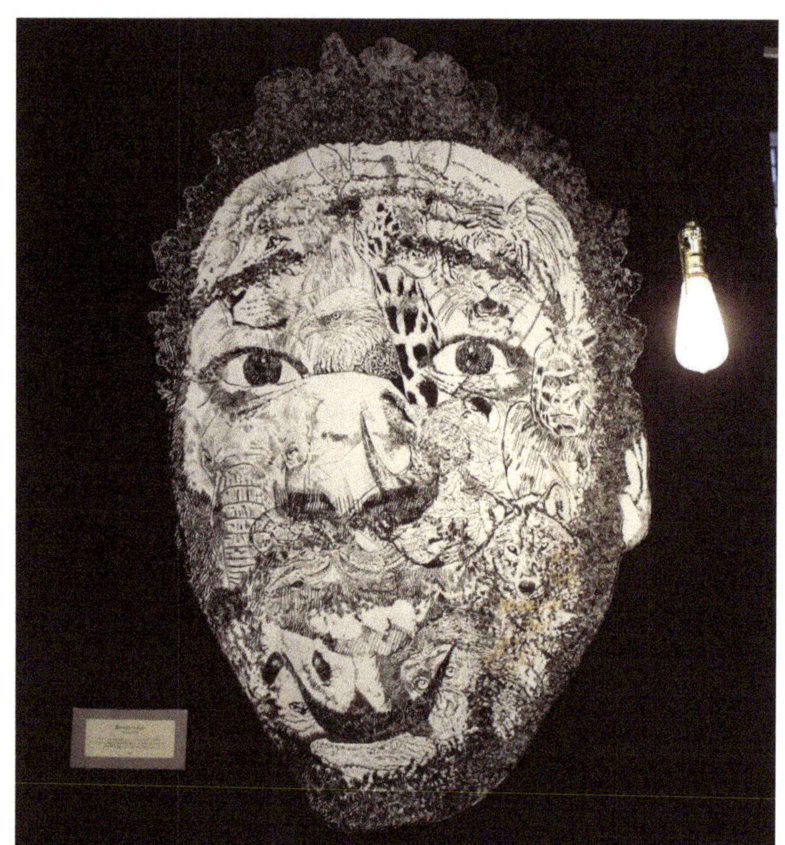

THIS PAGE: Burn One's tribute to Ol' Dirty Bastard, "Brooklyn Zoo," featuring a menagerie detailed in ODB's visage. BELOW: Burn One cutting out a paste of Tokey the Bear. OPPOSITE PAGE: Poster for musician/street artist Bankrupt Slut; Tyler the Creator drawing with images embedded such as microphones, fornication, skateboards, and an inhaler, because Tyler is asthmatic.

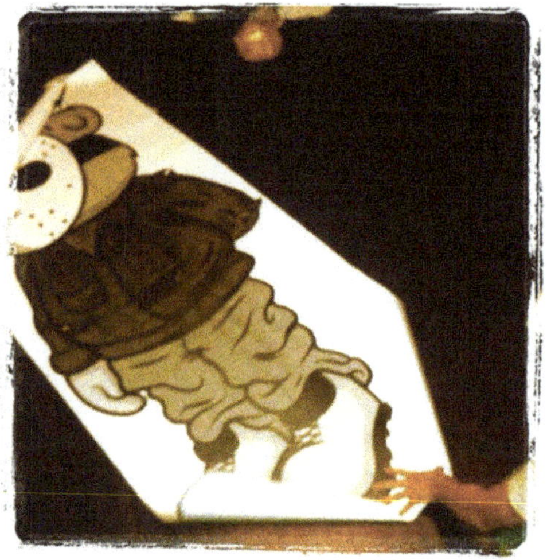

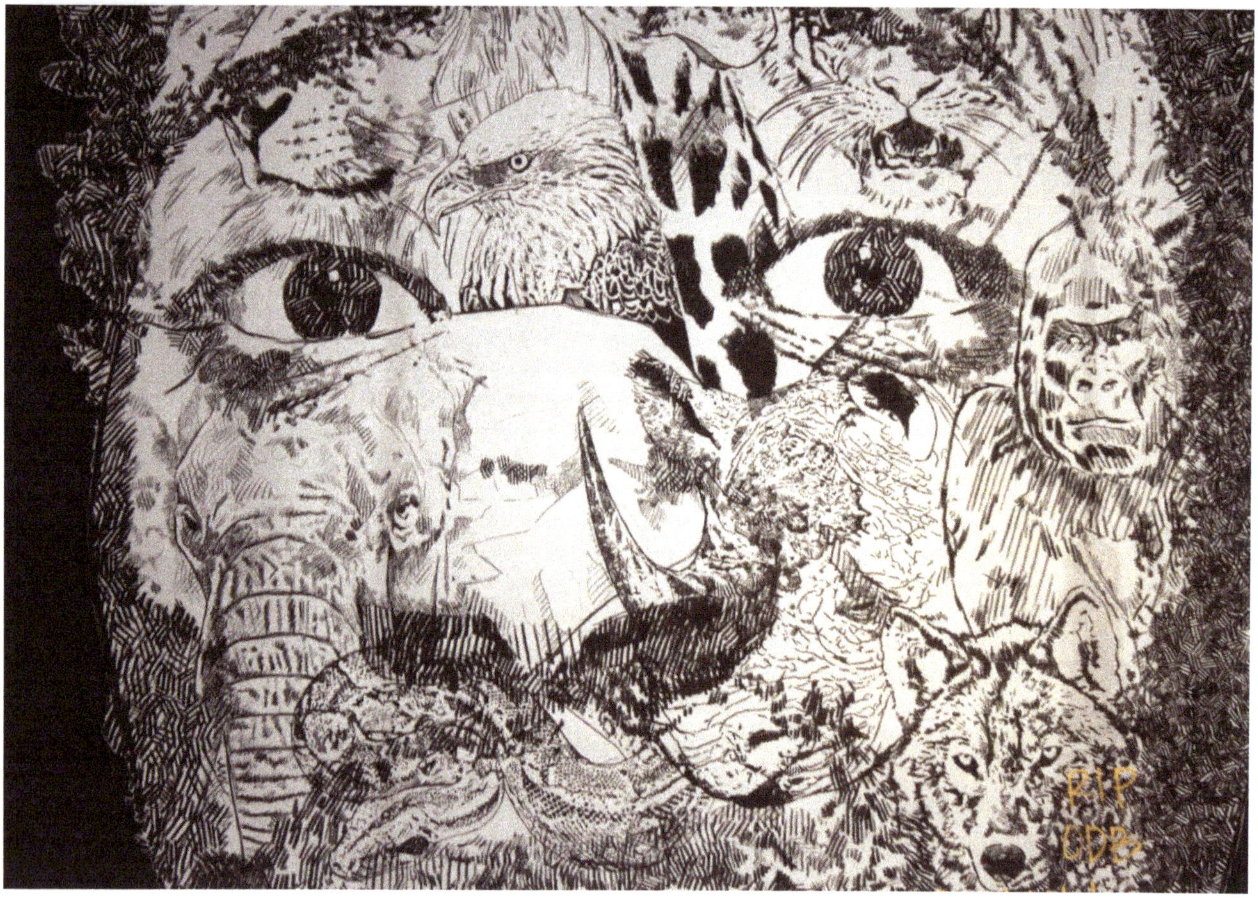

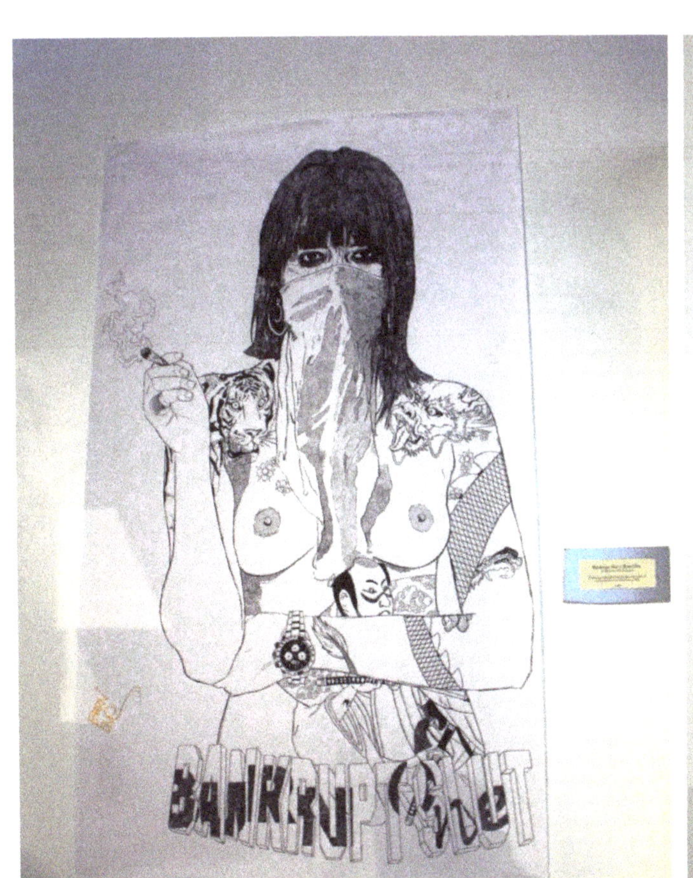

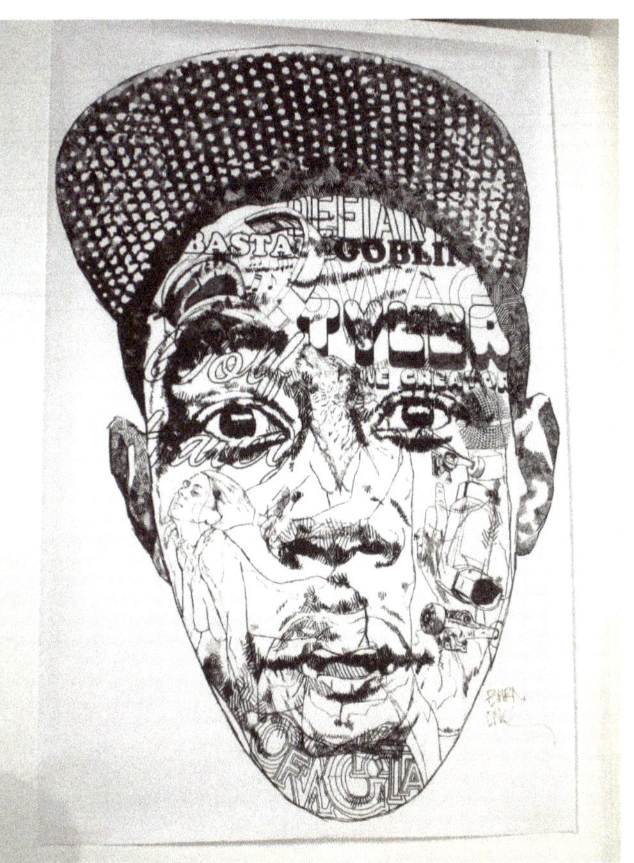

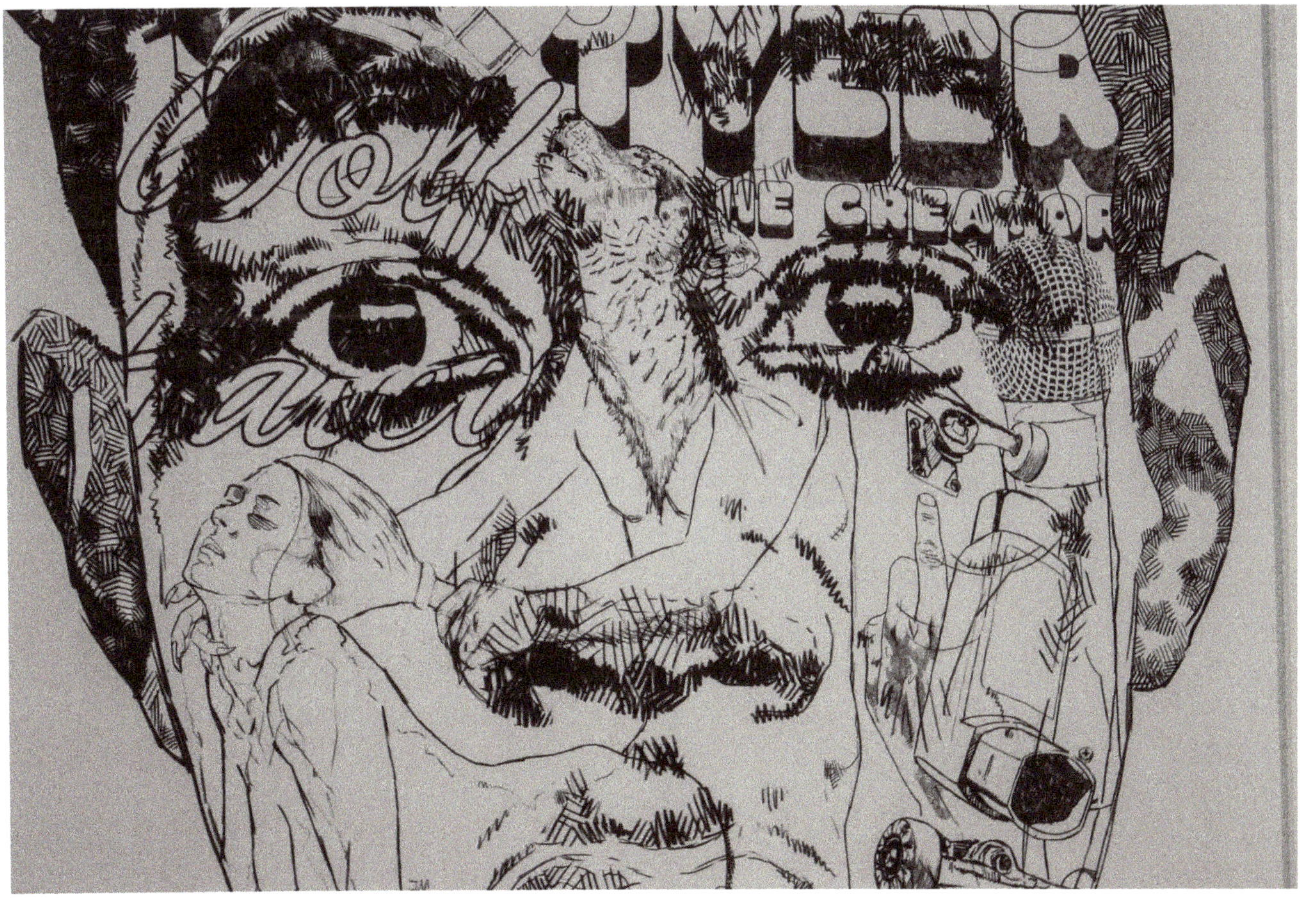

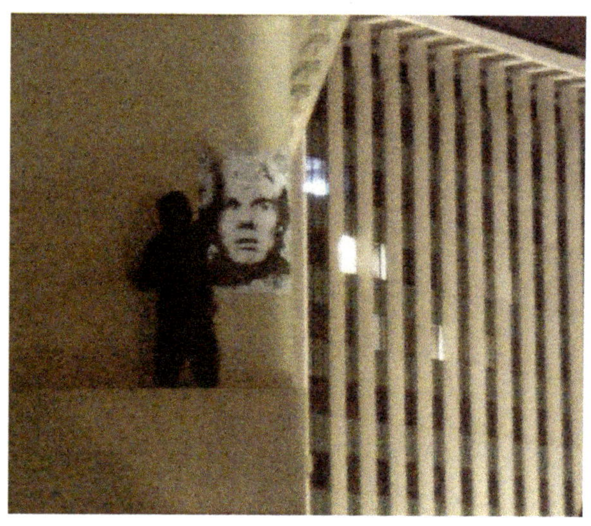

THANK YOU X

Much of today's street art is reflective of Andy Warhol's signature style of celebrity iconography, stenciled composites, and above all, repetition of imagery. It is no wonder that Warhol's ideas, sixties images, and commercial success have inspired young artists to take to the streets. So it is both intuitively astute and perfectly logical to see Andy Warhol's stenciled visage appear across Los Angeles signed simply, "Thank You, X."

TOP: Thank You X gets up atop Beverly Hills office buildings. RIGHT: Mural in Downtown L.A. BELOW: Thank You X poster on Third Street.

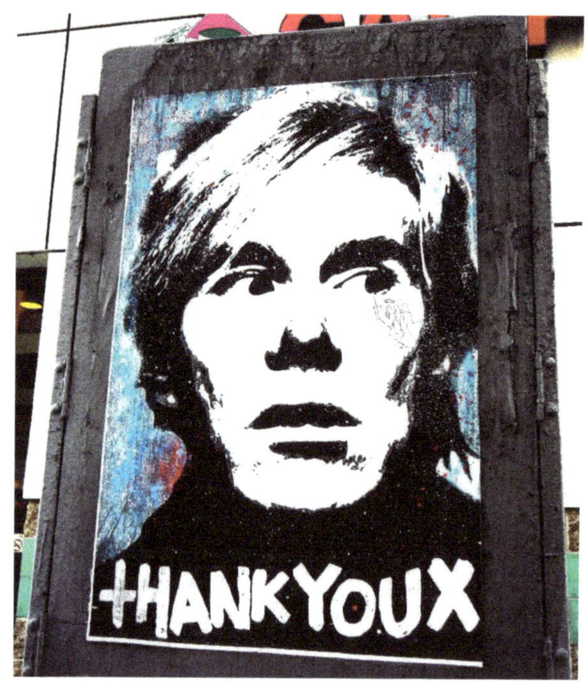

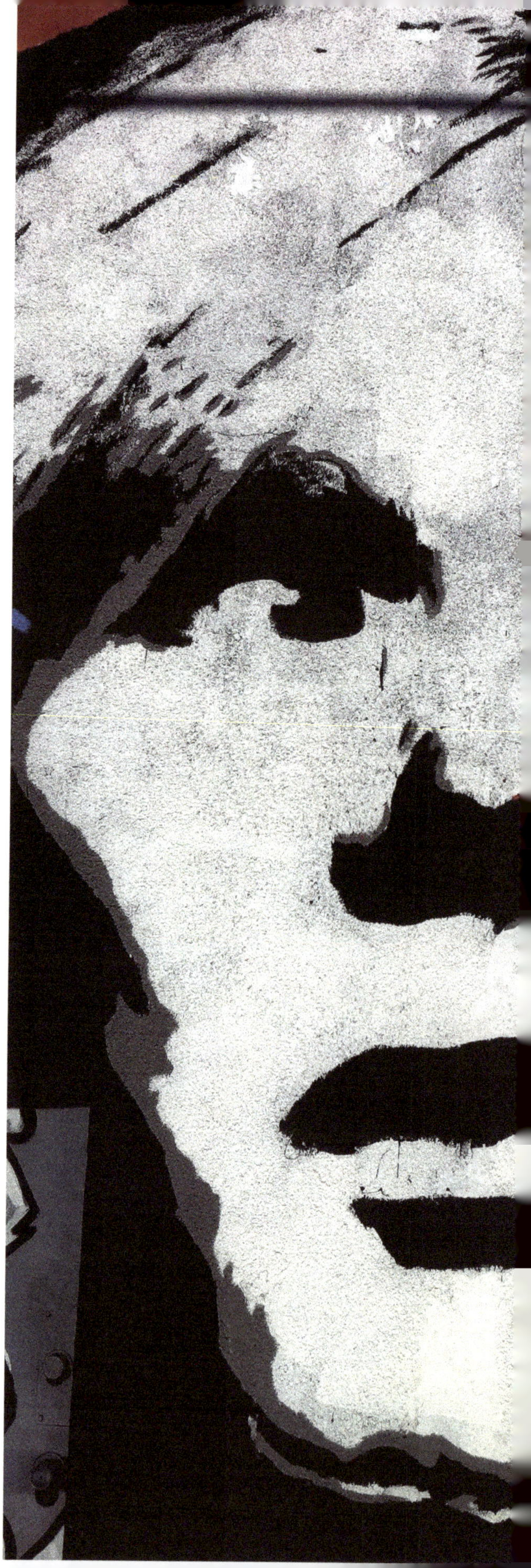

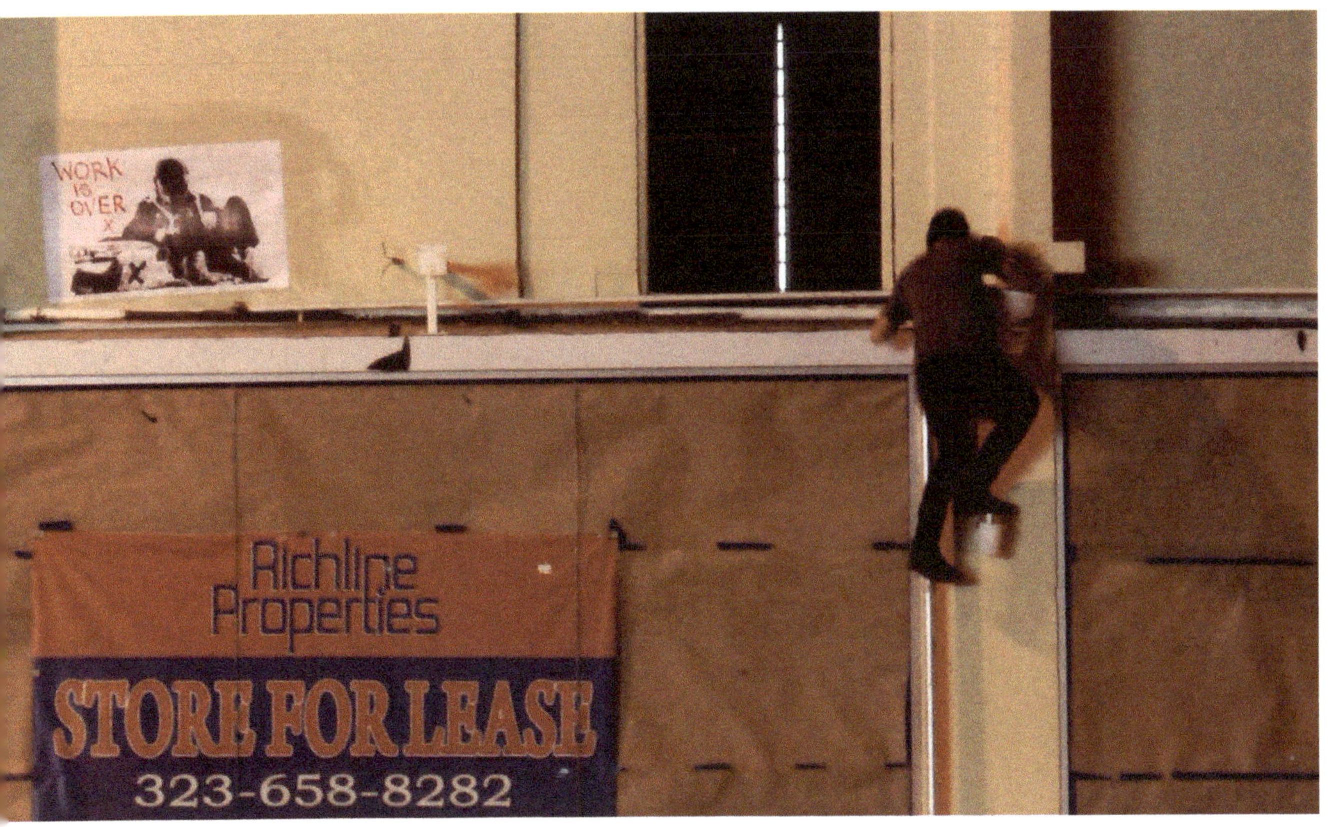

Thank You X scaling down a storefront after pasting a Daft Punk poster, "Work is Over," on La Brea.

Thank You X intended his moniker to simply be "X," the penultimate pseudonym of an anonymous artist. But as curious fans might not be able to Google "X" at their workplace without fear of reprisal, "Thank You X" has stuck as his *nom de guerre*. The image of Warhol used in X's pieces is from a lesser-known photo taken by an assistant of Warhol's to build his portfolio. The casual, unguarded spontaneity in this head shot of Andy looking away suggests a genuine appreciation of a subject whose mind is often elsewhere.

And it is a similar appreciation that drives Thank You X to convey his gratitude for the trails blazed by Warhol, an accomplished artist in an array of disciplines. Perhaps as much as his oft-quoted "15 minutes of fame" and classic colorful stencils that defined Pop Art, Warhol's enduring contribution to our multimedia culture today is his defiance of labels or limits to his artwork.

Many still debate the artistry or innovation in replicating Campell's Soup labels, painting famous people in funny colors, or filling a gallery with silver balloons. Nevertheless, Warhol's energy and aesthetic still connects, and is actively inspiring young artists today.

Thank You X has made his mark not just by his Warhol homage, accented with flourishes of paint, but by his preternatural ability to hit higher-up spots of the Los Angeles landscape. Posting one's artwork alongside a stand-alone piece of strategically placed street art (known as "spot-jacking") is no small feat to achieve with some of Thank You X's pieces. The art of climbing can be appreciated by street artists regardless of the piece. The higher up the piece, the greater the visibility and longevity. Some posters (with good paste) can ride for over a year and become part of the city scenery. That's what happened with X's Daft Punk poster, above.

WRDSMTH

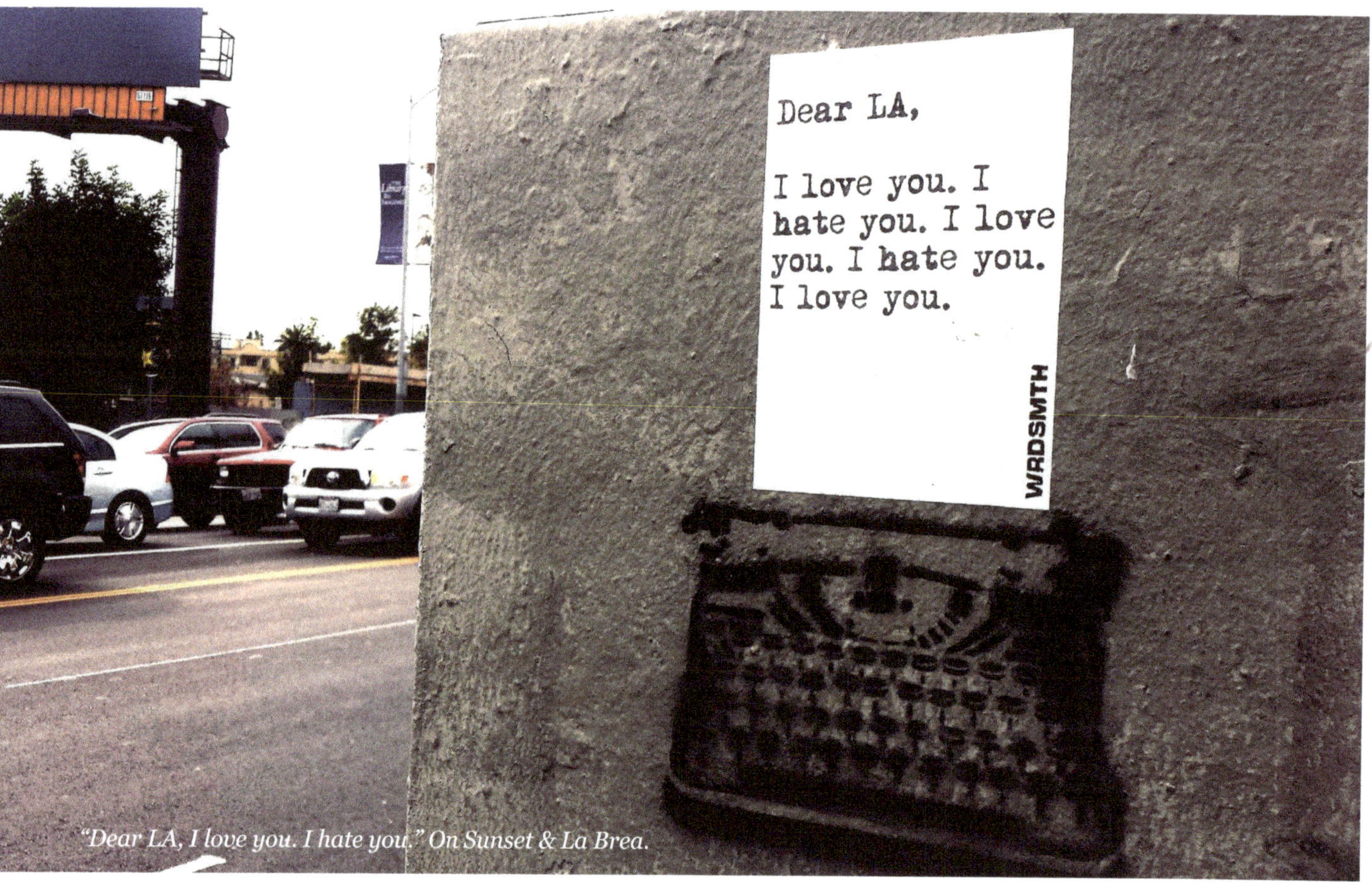

"Dear LA, I love you. I hate you." On Sunset & La Brea.

What made you start doing street art?

I am a writer—always have been. I enjoyed a very creative year in 2013, but that meant I was sitting in front of my computer all day most days. Toward the latter part of the year, I realized I need an active hobby that got me away from the computer at times. However, I did not want it to be something like photography, something that distracted from my first love. Faced with that conundrum, I contemplated doing some street art, something obviously word-based given my background. As I pondered, the idea for WRDSMTH formed and when I confirmed that no one had done anything similar to my idea before, I decided to run with it.

How did you decide upon your look?

The moment I decided to do something word-based, the image of an old school typewriter came to mind. At first I thought I'd just do stickers—white slaps with a black typewriter and black words floating above it in the white. When I happened upon the idea to paint the typewriter via a stencil and then wheatpaste the page coming out of it, I got so excited about the concept, I think I made it reality inside of a week.

What was it like going out at night in Hollywood after having envisioned "Hollywood the movie place" all your life?

It was great. That initial fix and constant adrenaline rush fuels the fire. However, night time didn't work for me. L.A. is still active and you can't see or be prepared for surprises around every corner. So early on I started to hit the streets in the AM—like 4/5 AM when the city is still asleep and pin-drop quiet. Working in Hollywood was great because so many of my initial messages were directed at all those individuals "doing time in Hollywood"—the countless actors, writers, musicians, dancers, and artists that move here to chase the dream. I went out of my way to talk to them and tell them things I wished people would have told me when I first moved here. My messages broadened early on, though, when I realized it wasn't just about the people "doing time in Hollywood," but people "doing time anywhere." Everyone has a dream of some kind and I think the bulk of my messages speak to that.

Did WRDSMTH become a character to you, or still feel like yourself?

It's me, but it's definitely a bolder and more confident version of me. It's also one of the reasons I embrace my anonymity. The mystery of "who's going out at all hours to post these inspirational, romantic, and funny messages around town?" definitely adds to the aura and the mystique.

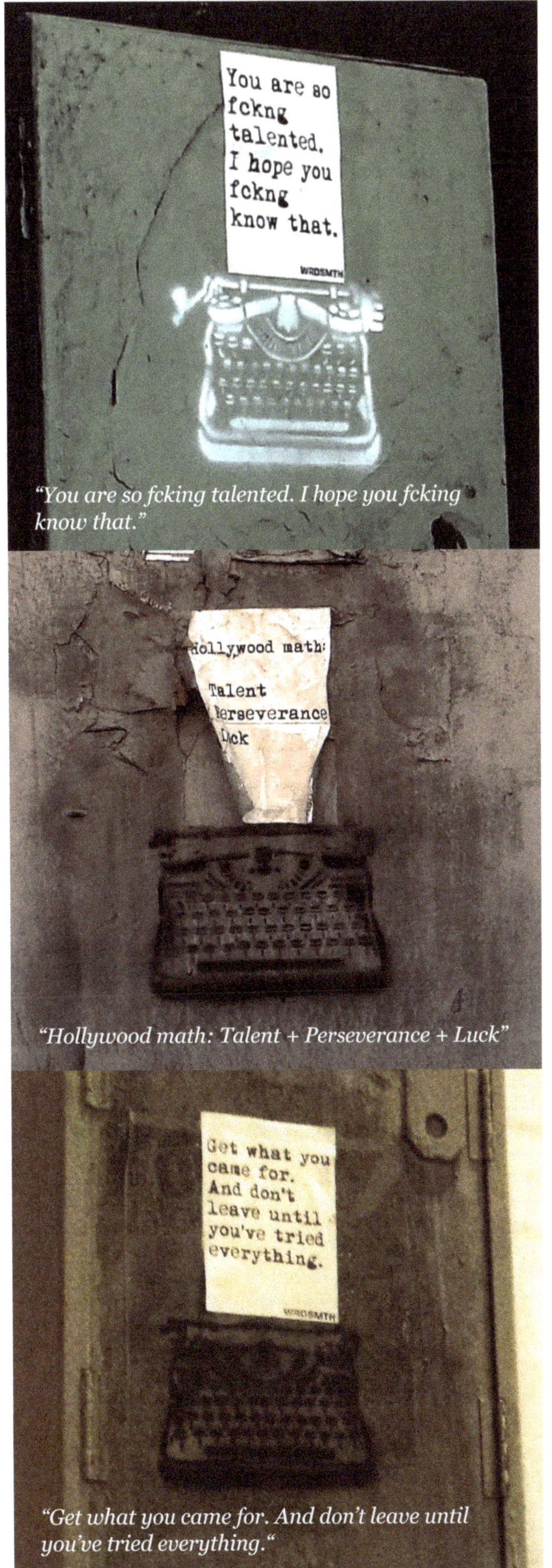

"You are so fcking talented. I hope you fcking know that."

"Hollywood math: Talent + Perseverance + Luck"

"Get what you came for. And don't leave until you've tried everything."

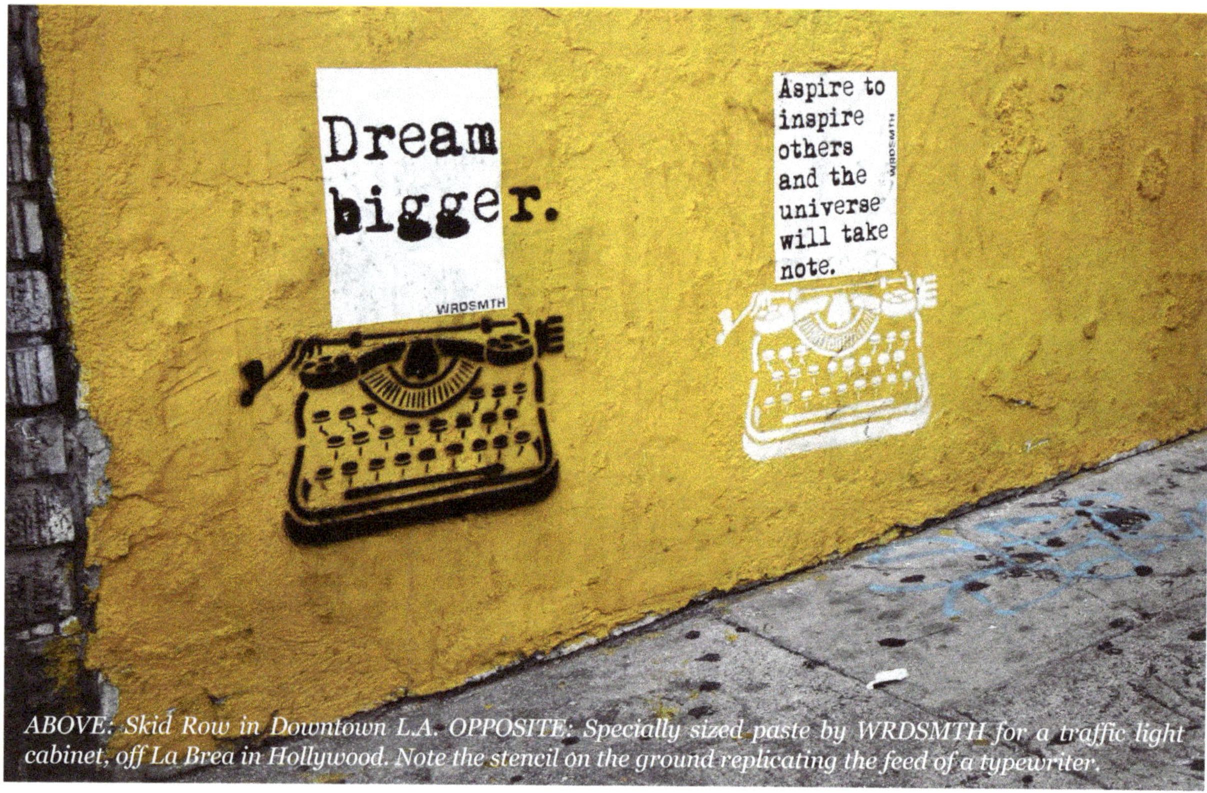

ABOVE: Skid Row in Downtown L.A. OPPOSITE: Specially sized paste by WRDSMTH for a traffic light cabinet, off La Brea in Hollywood. Note the stencil on the ground replicating the feed of a typewriter.

How has WRDSMTH evolved since you started?

I've been active for almost two years now and have evolved in many ways. My messages have changed to speak to a wider audience. The look and size of the typewriter has obviously evolved. And my techniques have evolved. I always say that I never considered myself an artist of the paint/brush variety before I started WRDSMTHing—however now I think the art has met up with the writing and the shared experience is evident in the work. At least I hope it is.

What kind of message are you looking to spread?

I do three types of "WRD"s—inspiration/motivation, romantic, and funny (I think I'm funny). I just aim to affect people. If someone happens upon one of my pieces and I can make them smile or laugh or ponder their place in the world, I think I have done my job. Overall, I'm very positive in my work. And my signature has kind of become, "Aspire to inspire others and the universe will take note."

What has the reaction been to your work?

The reaction has been nothing short of amazing. I started this whole endeavor for me, but the fact that my WRDs are resonating with such a wide audience makes me smile every single day. I am getting read on a daily basis all over the world, and for a writer, that is living the dream.

Have you had run-ins with police?

I had my very first run-in about a year and a half after starting up. I was more nervous than I expected, but the officers were cool. They even calmed me down and said, "Don't worry, we actually like your stuff." That was pretty cool. Granted others might not be so supportive. I'm conscious of that and I am always as careful as I can be to avoid any surprises when I am working.

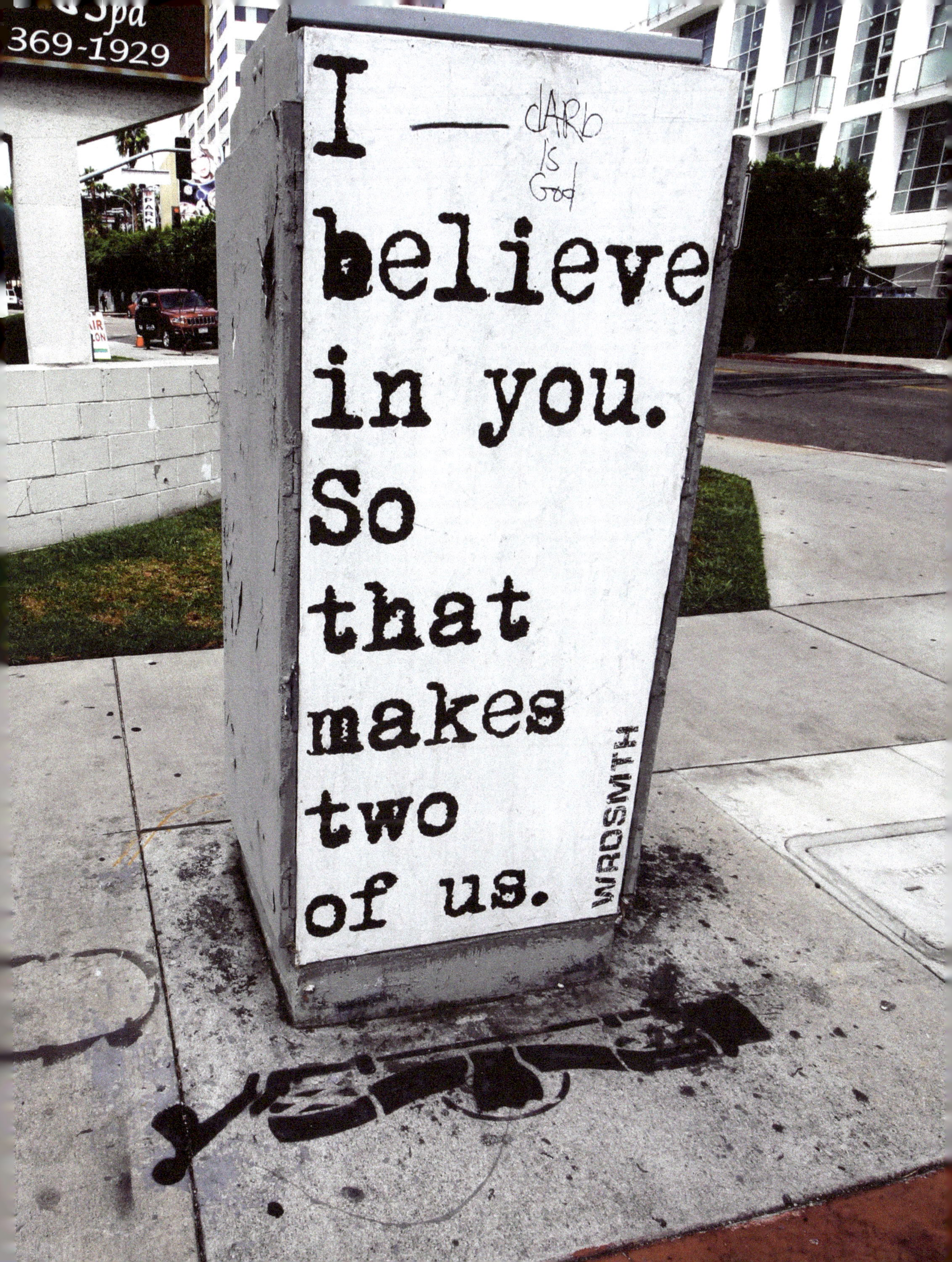
Spa
369-1929
I ___ believe in you.
So that makes two of us.
WRDSMTH

ALL THE GIRLS LOVE EARL

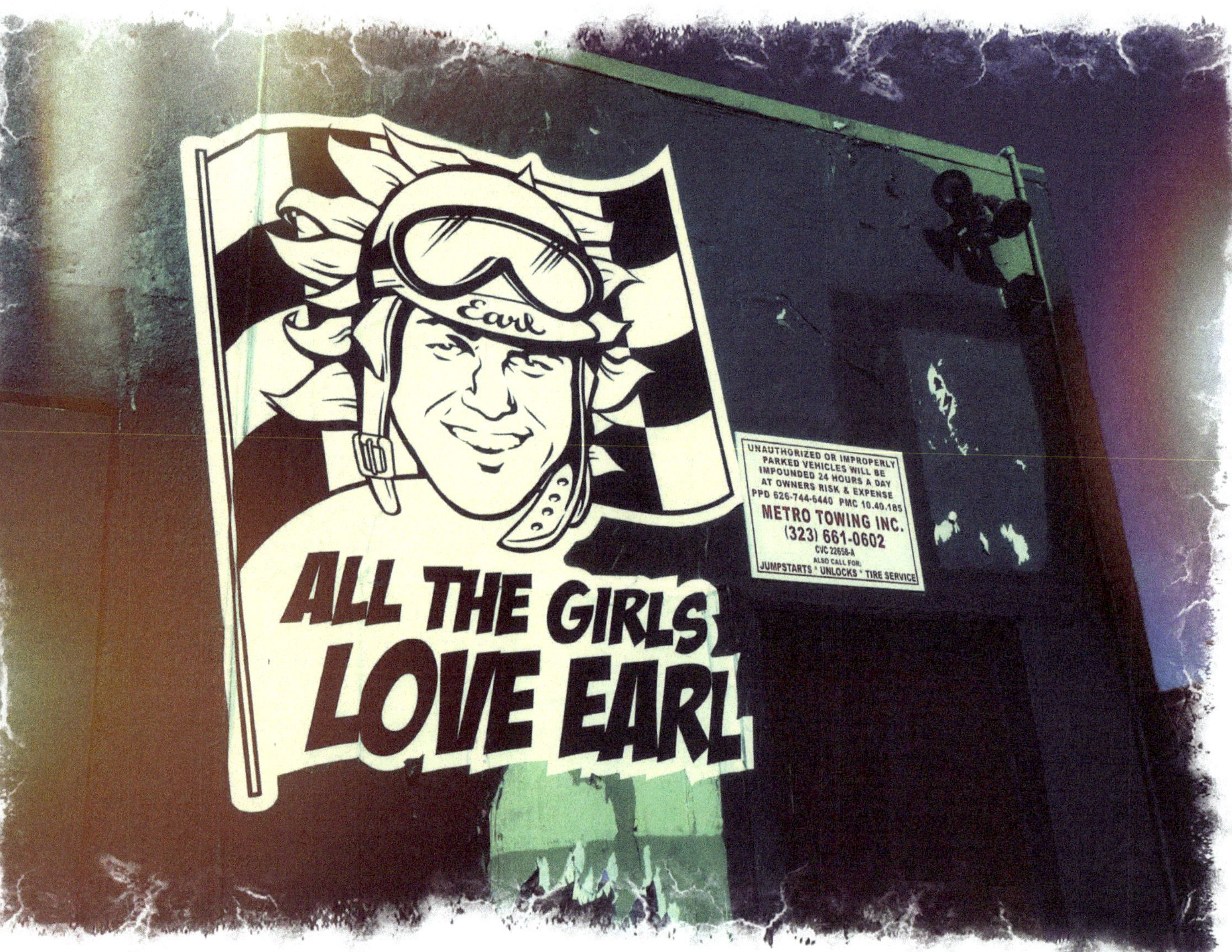

Earl Lee is a celebrity race car driver, known for his ubiquity and reclusiveness, a man of mystery, because if one thing is for certain, it is that All The Girls Love Earl. His vintage visage has been appearing around Hollywood for years, both on and off screen, and his signature style stands out from other street artists. I sought to interview Earl, but was told that his press inquiries are handled by his lube company's janitor, Bubba.

What do you do for Earl?

I worked for Earl's father and have known Earl since he was a wee lad. I have always worked as the janitor at Earl Lube Industries. What better person to know all the ins & outs and gossip of the company than the lowly, inconspicuous janitor?

Does Earl revel in the limelight or is he more of a recluse?

Earl is a little bit of both. He is illustrious in the fact that he is world famous yet he does not seek fame. People may get the perception that he is elusive only in the fact that he takes all the adulation with a grain of salt. It is not his motivation and he's not the kind of guy to waste a bunch of words, especially to speak about himself. He innately knows how to deal with all the fame. He is an adrenaline junky... always thinking of the next race, the next trophy. The same with the admiration from all the women... it is a biproduct of the life he leads. He loves women and loves to entertain them but while they are all thinking of church bells and wedding rings, all he's thinking about is the next competition or movie roll.

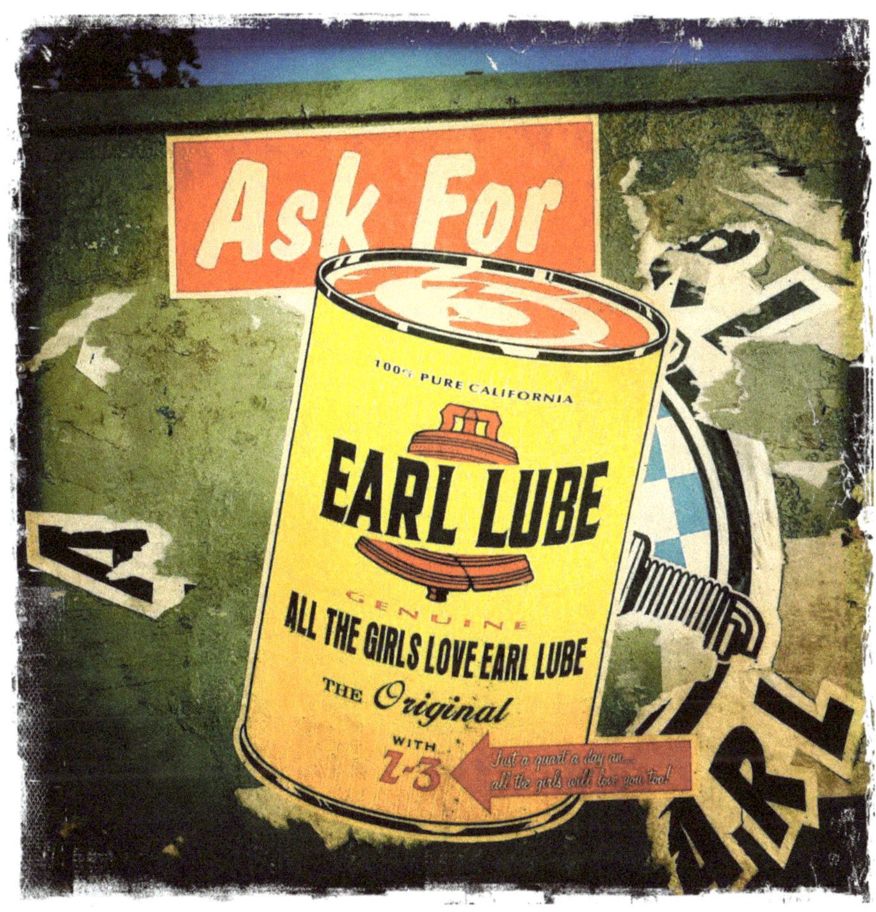

What made you start doing street art?

I'm always careful to say that it was Shepard Fairey's work ethic and proliferation that was the original inspiration to get Earl up on the streets. While I do enjoy his artwork I don't think he's really had much aesthetic influence on Earl's art. I did spend several years on the street with one of "his guys" and in that sense I understand how he thinks and I am a student of his methods... i.e., where to get up, what to put up in a particular spot, how long is that spot likely to ride and how many people are going to see it. In this game it's all about the risk and reward factor.

Who does the wheat pasting? Earl himself, or you, Bubba?

Earl is too busy living the story... it takes someone like Bubba to chronicle and tell the story, whether on the street or in other forms. From humble beginnings Bubba has become a professional grade wheat paster. So much so that he has developed the minty-fresh, Earl Lube-branded street paste now used by many of the "local legend" pasters in the So-Cal area.

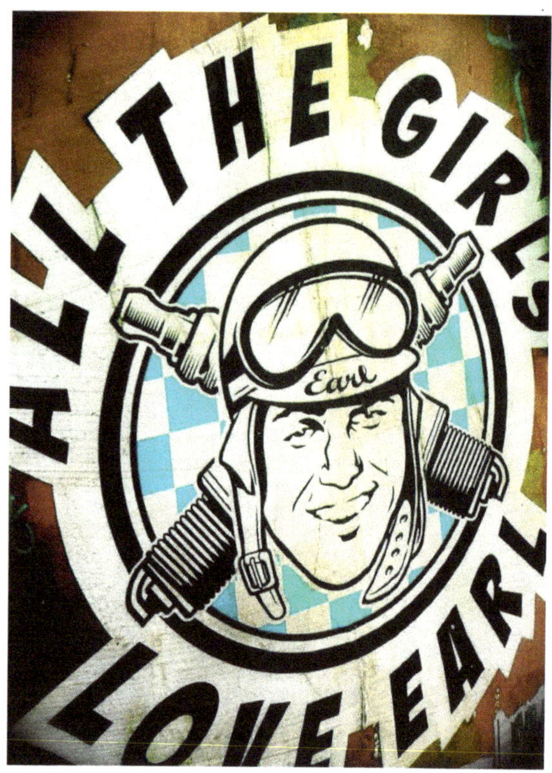

What does Earl drive?

So Earl has this huge airplane hangar at the old Santa Monica airport filled with every conceivable go fast plane, train, automobile, motorcycle, boat, and whatever toy you can think of. He owns all the normal hot rods, customs and such you'd expect any California guy to own and he can have his pick of any of these, any day... but more days than not you're going to see him cruising around in his ole Fifties beater Chevy pick-up truck. That's good enough for him. However, lately, if he's going for a blast up the coast to Santa Barbara or Pebble Beach, he might roll out his Koenigsegg Regera of Pagani Zonda.

What is Earl like when he is racing?

When he puts on his helmet, everybody notices the change on his face... he in now all business. Earl sets quick time on his first lap out... even on cold tires. He brings it back into the pits and tells Bubba to turn the wick up even more. When they line up for the main event, Earl likes nothing more than serious competition and he'll race any man clean, but if you try to put a foot peg, wheel or rooster tail on Earl you better watch your ass. Earl is a 'win it or wear it' kind of guy. He always puts on a good show for the fans. Earl does not win every time but no one can remember the last time he didn't. In the winner's circle the crowd goes wild... Earl kisses the trophy girl/s and all the other women are jealous. It's party time in Earl's pits. When the track owner turns off the lights the party moves outside to the parking lot. Whatever those dudes are smoking behind the race car trailers... don't go over there. Of course the trophy girl and two of her friends... go home with Earl.

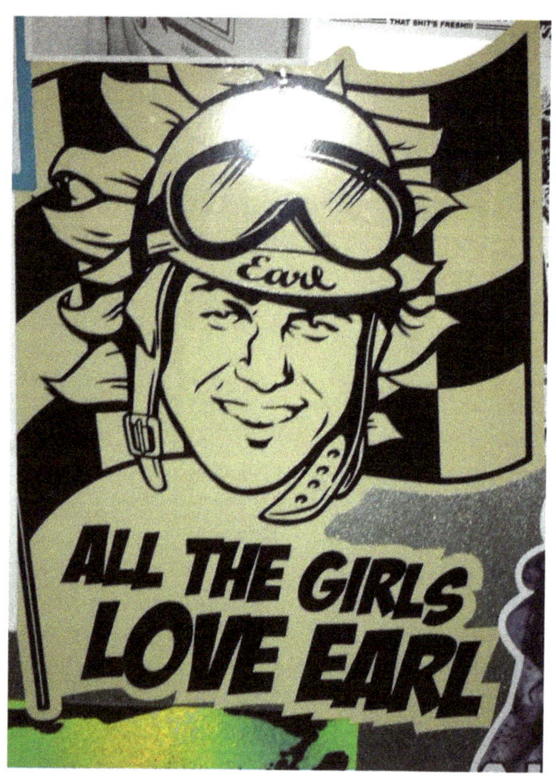

What is Earl's artistic outlook on life?

Art should move you... or stop you in your tracks.

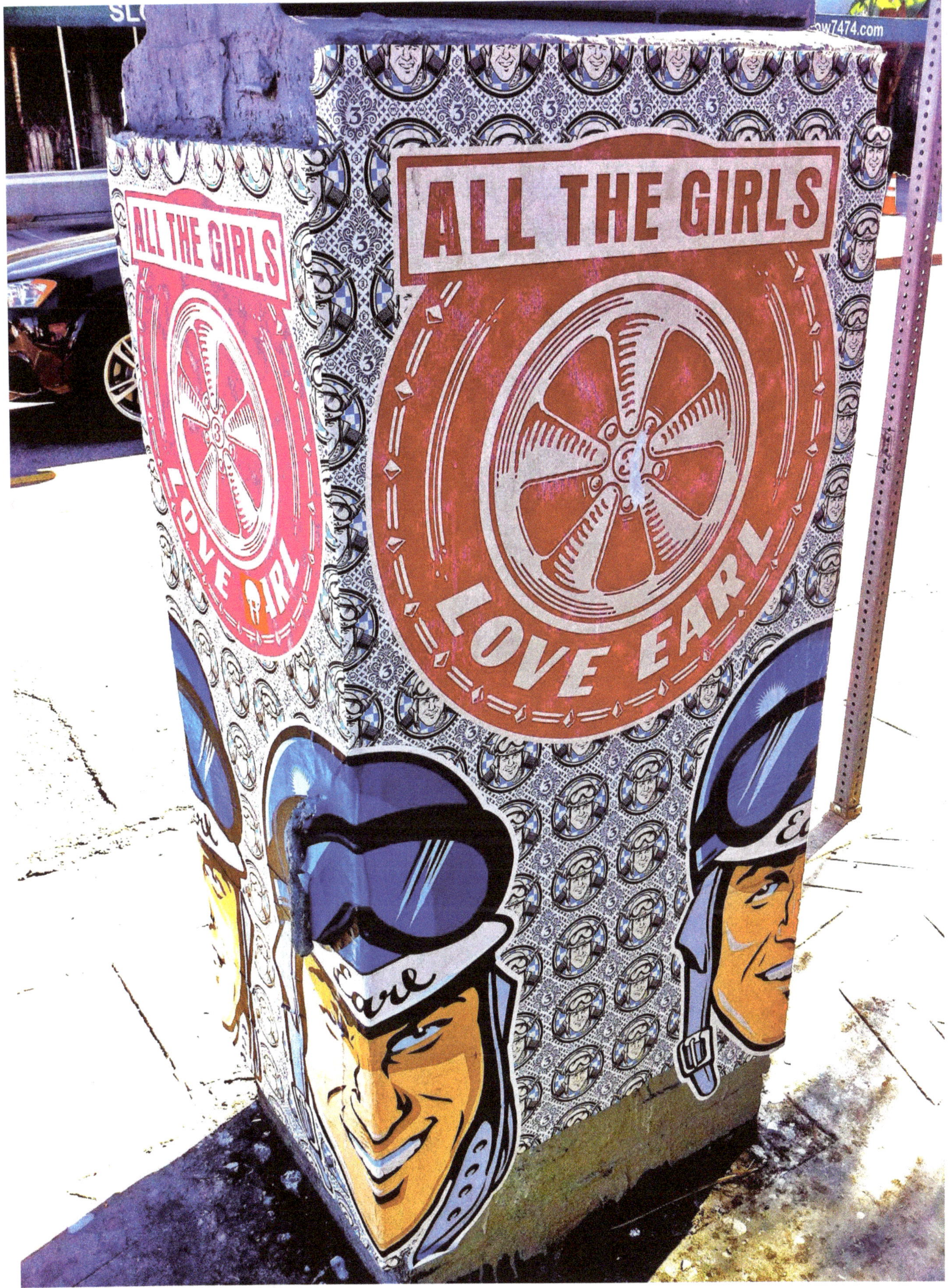
ALL THE GIRLS
LOVE EARL
ALL THE GIRLS
LOVE EARL
Earl

THRASHBIRD

What made you start doing street art?

I felt an imperative need to communicate with people on a grander scale.

What impact are you hoping to have?

I want to encourage people to act and incite them to question things around them.

How has your work evolved?

My work evolves as I evolve.

What is Hollywood like at the middle of the night?

Hollywood, at midnight, is like no other place I've ever been—it is deeply unsettling and appropriately bleak.

When you put up a bunch of posters saying Vote Romney, would it be fair for others to think you are a Romney supporter?

I mean, I used the images of clearly recognizable Pop Culture villains alongside the phrase "Vote Romney"... so no, I don't think it would be fair.

Have you had run-ins with the police?

Yes. Although, I don't worry as much about cops as I do your "Good Samaritan Gary," or

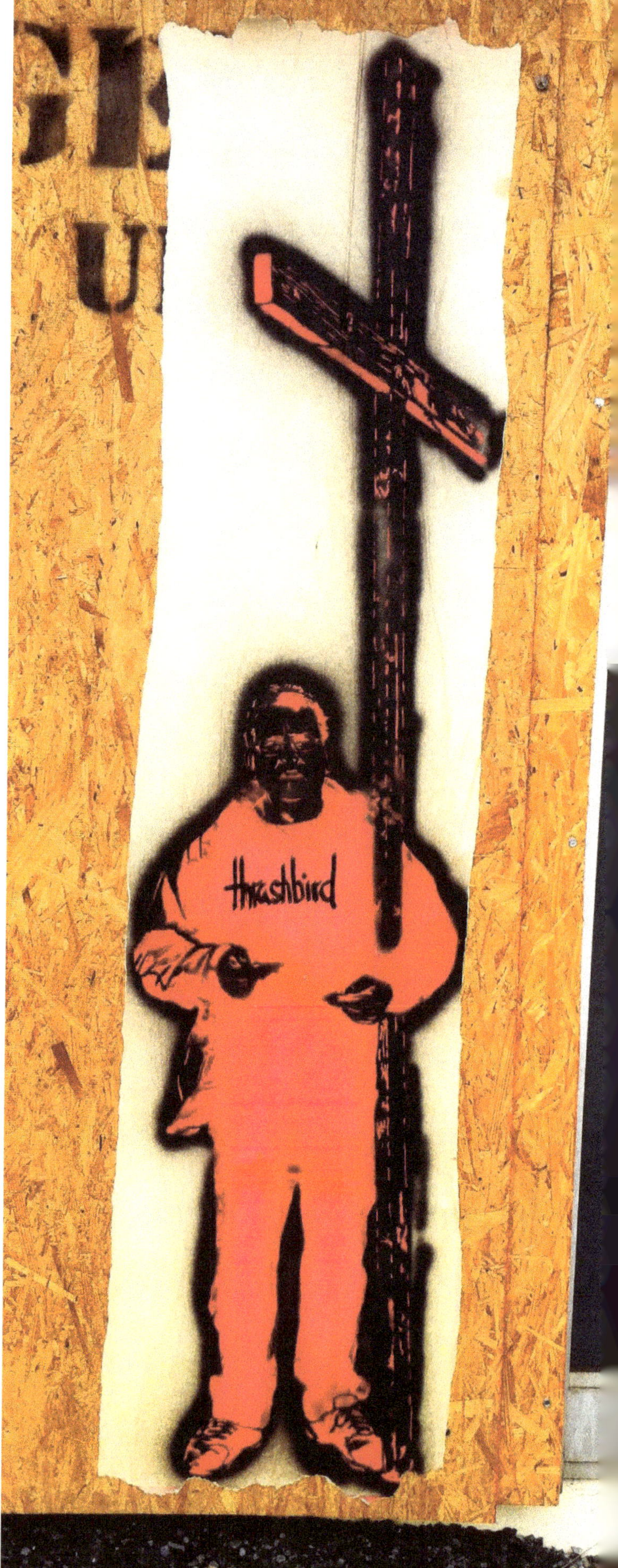

your "Crimebusting Vigilante Chad." That's who you have to look out for. Fuck those people.

How do you get high up for your art?

Magic. Stay High.

What ails us as a society?

Money/Individualism.

What has been the reaction to your artwork?

It runs the gamut of the emotional scale. That's the exciting part for me. People get emotional about it.

Just who do you think you are?

Clearly, I'm a genius.

What did you want to be when you grew up?

The first thing I can remember was wanting to be a Major League Baseball Player... but then again the answer to this question depends on when you consider one to have "grown up." In my head, I still have a lot I want to accomplish and achieve before I grow up.

Why "Thrashbird"?

Because I thought of it and you didn't.

What accomplishment are you most proud of?

The rare times I'm not selfish and self-obsessed.

What would you like to accomplish?

More of that "doing things for others" business, and less self-indulgence.

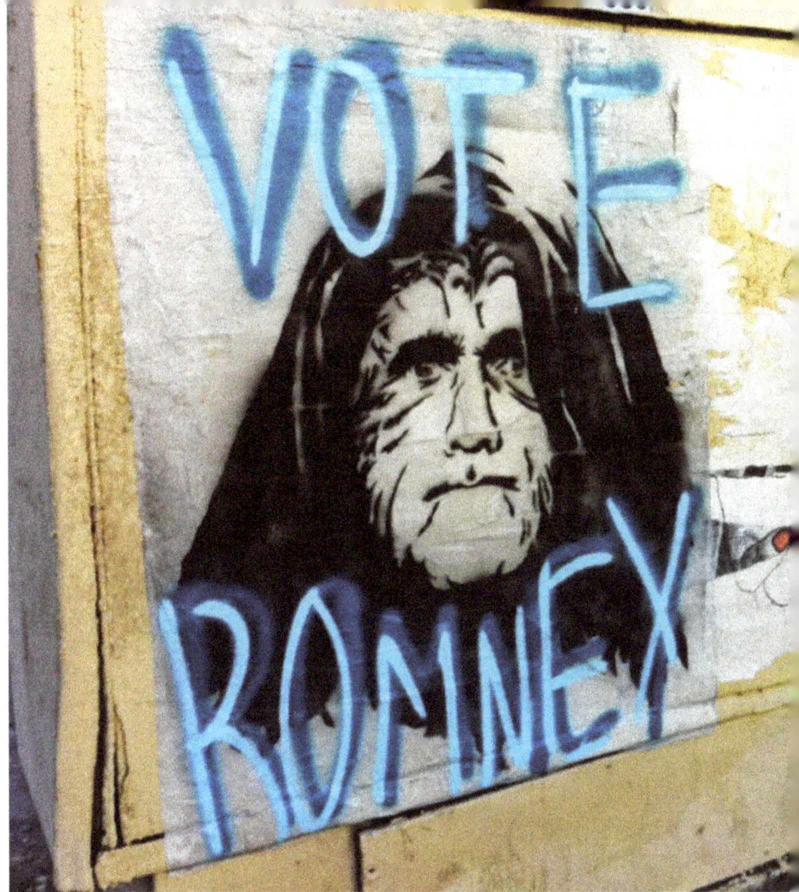

On the eve of the 2012 election, Thrashbird went large with stencils of movie villains on VOTE ROMNEY posters, as an Election Day surprise for voters to wake up to.

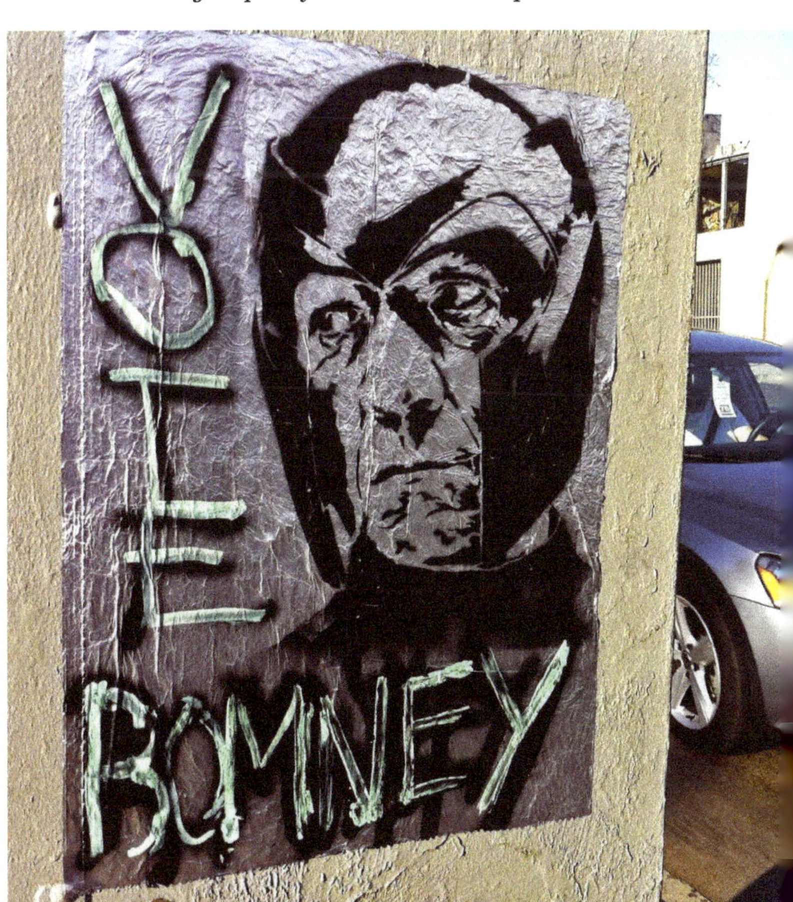

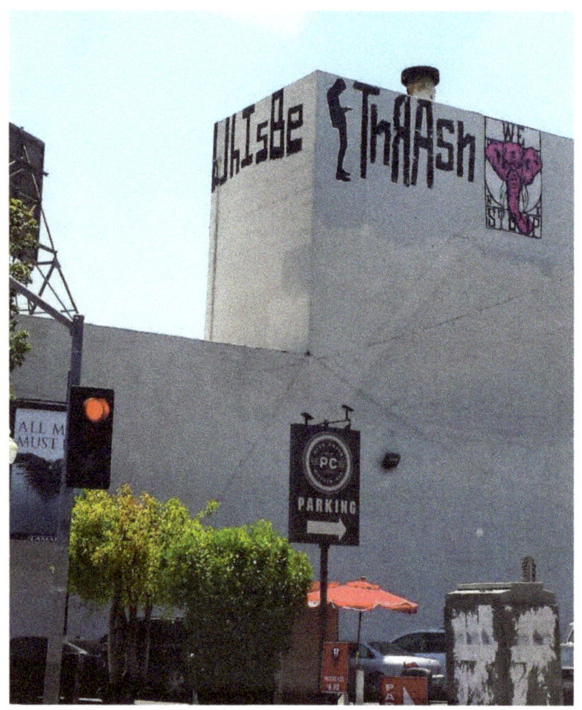

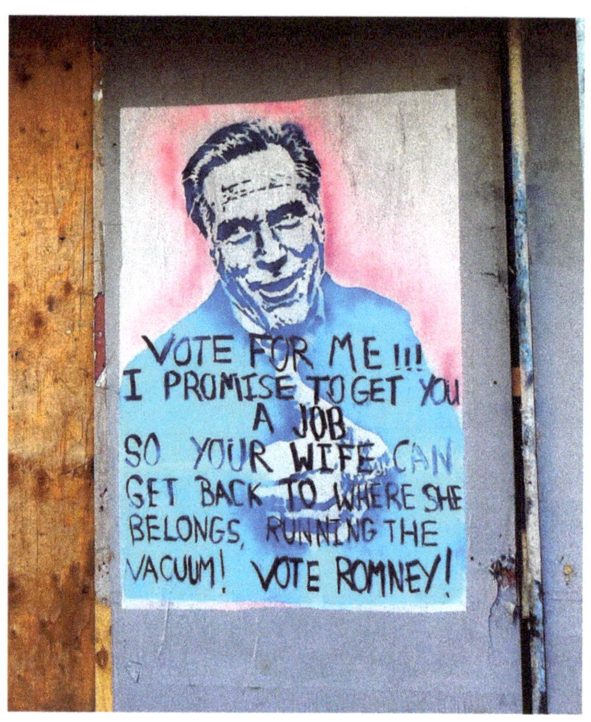

ABOVE LEFT: Thrashbird on top of a building on Fairfax. ABOVE RIGHT: Mitt Romney stencil on La Brea. BELOW: "You Need More Shit" painted over sales flyers. OPPOSITE: "U R UR BAG," multi-stenciled traffic box on Hawthorn in Hollywood.

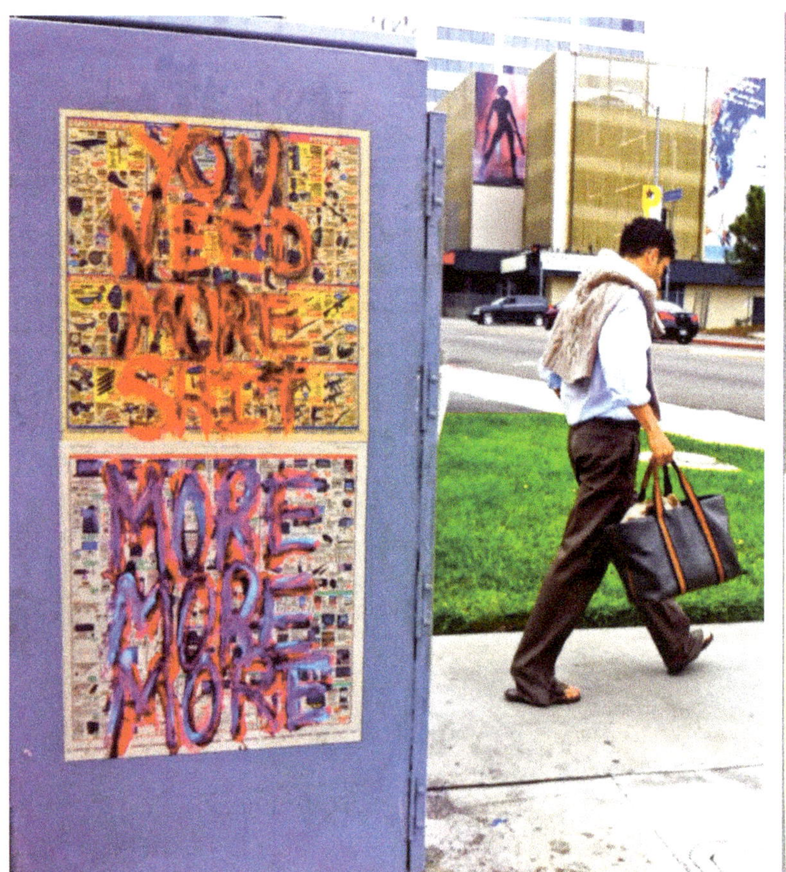

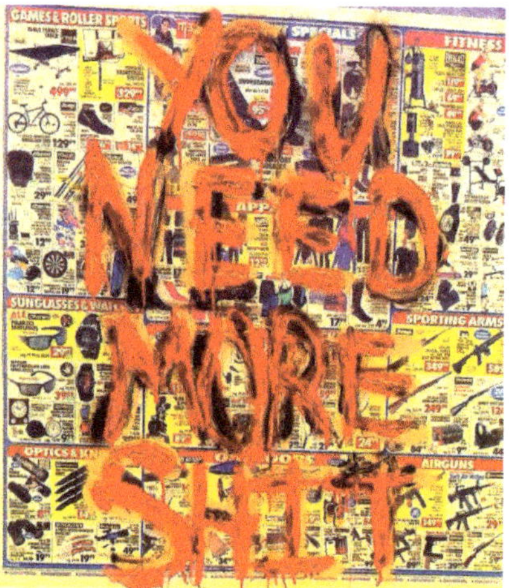

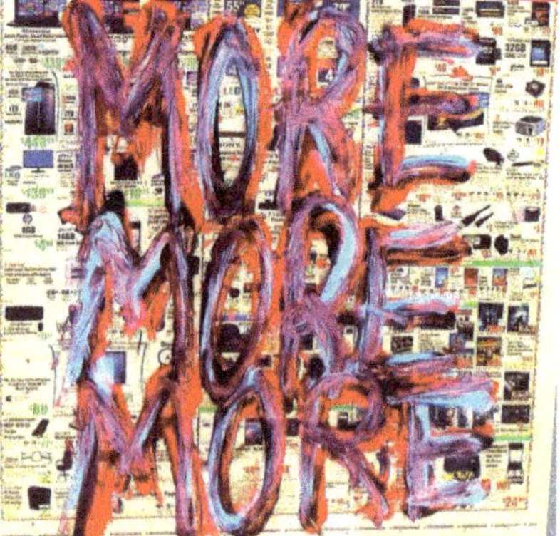

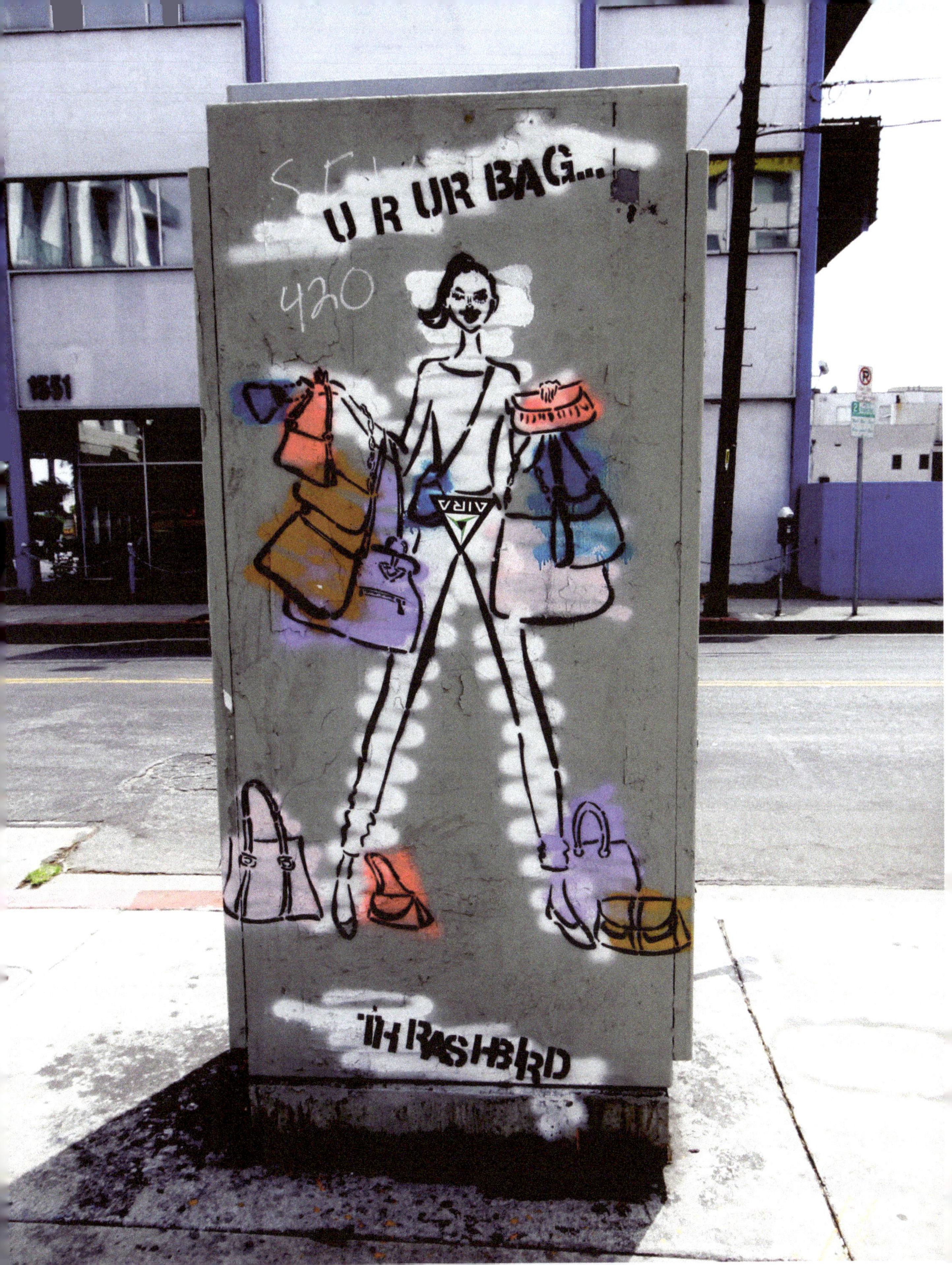
U R UR BAG...
420
1551
THRASHBIRD

SKULLPHONE

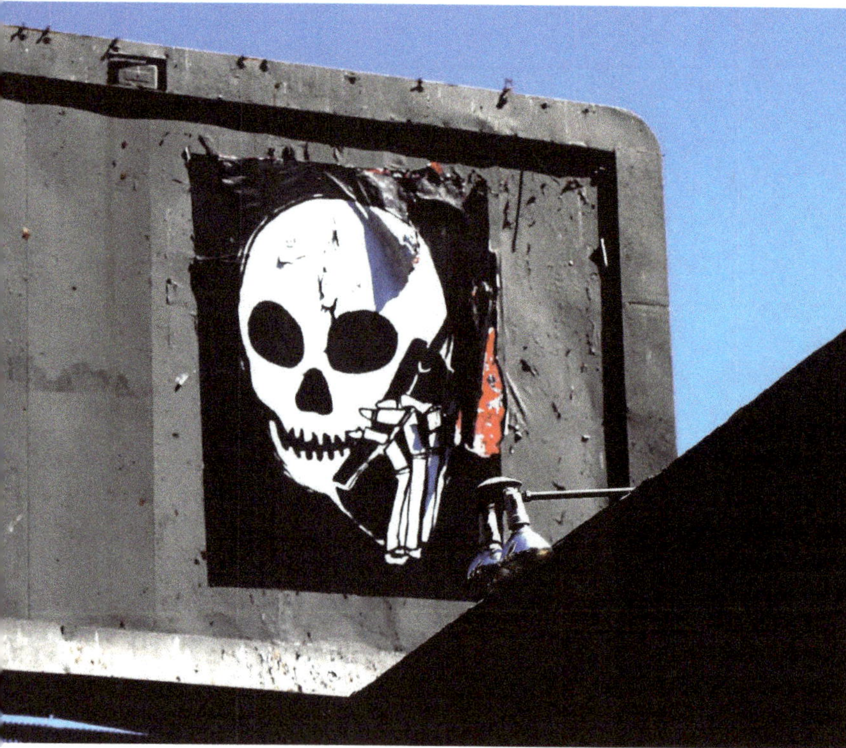

LEFT: A large Skullphone paste taking over a billboard in Hollywood on Sunset, outside Nickelodeon Studios. ABOVE: A Skullphone parody of the classic "Andre the Giant Has a Posse" sticker by Shepard Fairey, a.k.a. OBEY.

Skullphone has been a fixture on the landscape of Los Angeles since the turn of the century. The image of a skeleton talking on a cellphone seemed to be a warning about radiation from mobile devices, but like many street art images, the repetion of images placed in prominent places makes the character become an underdog or hero for getting up.

Skullphone has managed to find a life as an artist while still keeping a secretive profile. The artist's iconic image had become so recognizable that when the City of Los Angeles allowed digtal billboards, the appearance of Skullphone popping up in the rotation of digital ads caused news outlets to report that the digital billboards had been hacked by a street artist. The billboard company owner angrily insisted there had been no hack of their equipment and that their clients were secure and protected. Skullphone just happened to run an ad for the day. This was a reminder of how much people notice around the city that doesn't get mentioned. (Thankfully, digital billboards were discontinued in Los Angeles in 2013).

What prompted you to take to street art?

It wasn't what it is today. It was something else.

What does your image mean?

The image of a skull on a cellphone? It is a self portrait.

What kind of impact are you hoping to have on others?

Trompe-l'œil.

Have you had run-ins with the police?

It's not about that.

Have other people come after you for getting up so much for so long?

It's not about that, either.

How many places has Skullphone been seen?

Yes and no.

What has street art taught you?

Some walls look best unadulterated.

Why do you keep doing it after so long?

What time is it anyway?

What work are you most proud of?

My Digital Media paintings, which are most like a mirage.

Do you talk on a cellphone? How do you communicate?

Snapping Chats.

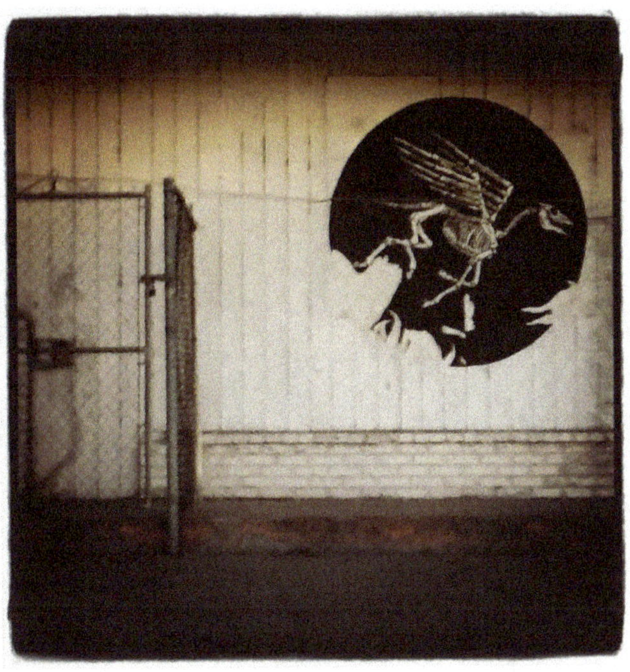

ABOVE: On a crumbling abandoned gas station off La Cienega near LAX, Skullphone added a skeletal Pegasus, resembling a decayed version of the old Mobil Oil logo. BELOW: A traffic box decorated by Skullphone which most people would probably assume to be an actual warning about being electrocuted.

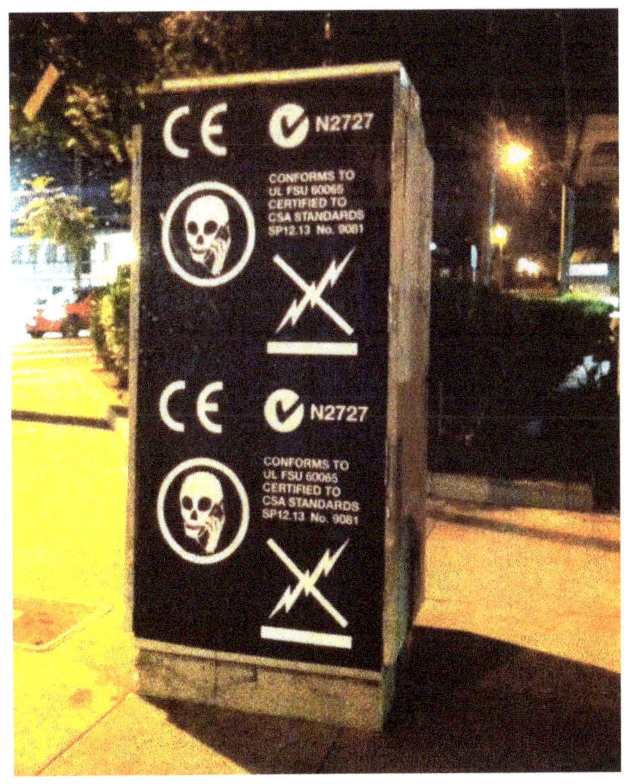

PLASTIC JESUS

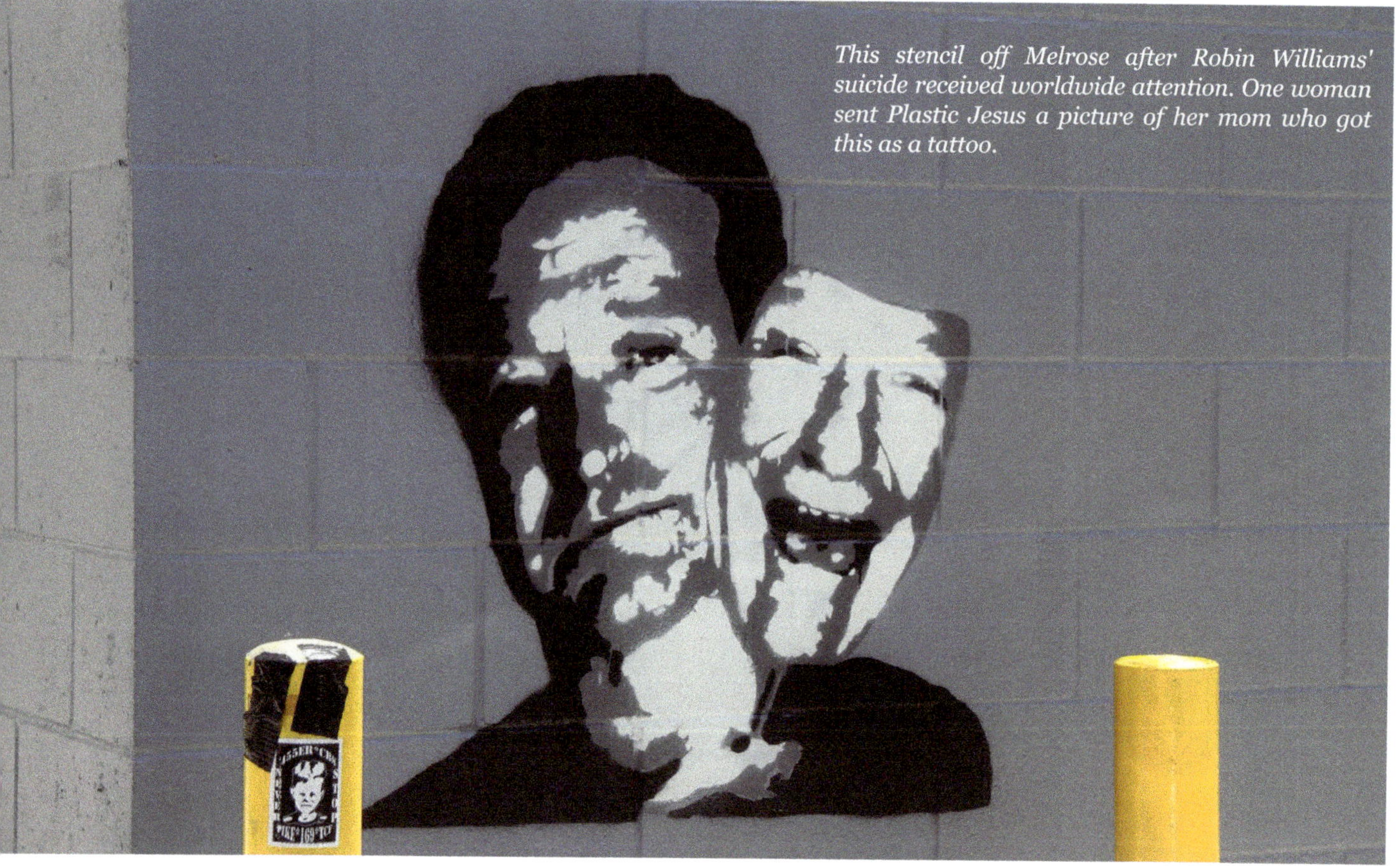

This stencil off Melrose after Robin Williams' suicide received worldwide attention. One woman sent Plastic Jesus a picture of her mom who got this as a tattoo.

What made you take to the streets?

Having spent 20 years as a photojournalist, I felt there was so much that I felt passionate about that wasn't getting addressed by the mainstream media. No one would ever read a blog with my opinions so I figured street art would be a good medium to start a dialogue on issues.

What were you hoping to accomplish?

The engagement of people with the world in which we live is truly appalling. So many people have a mindset that they have no control or influence in politics, social matters or just about anything else in their daily lives. I would like to see more people take some kind of active position on things they feel passionate about. I don't care if they don't agree with me; it's the fact that they are engaging that is important. We are not mindless clones who should sit around being fed information, rules and rights. We need to have an active role.

How did you seek to stand out?

I think street installations are very compelling to anyone who comes across them. So I try to make my work engage on a number of levels; firstly I want the piece to look good. Secondly, I want it to have an immediate engagement, whether by a photo opportunity or just a meeting point, and thirdly, I want the piece to have a deeper level of meaning, either by confronting an issue or merely highlighting it.

What is your preferred medium now for street art?

I guess installations. I love the process from inception to design to creation, on to installation and ultimate public engagement. I've always been strong on the practical side of making things. If I'm lost for inspiration, I simply spend an hour walking around Home Depot considering what can be made from the multitude of hardware components they stock.

What kind of reactions do you get?

My art initially gets a reaction of surprise and amusement.

What has surprised you most so far?

Some of my pieces are pretty controversial, but almost without exception I get positive feedback; whether the piece is about drugs, debt, or crime, the support has been right across the board. I have had great feedback from celebrities, drug addicts, cops, even state officials.

Have you had run-ins with the law?

Yes. I nearly got arrested early hours of one morning on Melrose. I managed to talk the cop out of arresting my by suggesting I paint over my nearly painted piece. I would imagine he would not have been so lenient if I were a twenty-something black guy with my pants around my knees.

What is something quintessentially American that most Americans don't realize?

Wow. good question... This is gonna be a controversial comment, but so many Americans believe the world revolves around the U.S. No, scrub that. The *universe* revolves around the U.S.

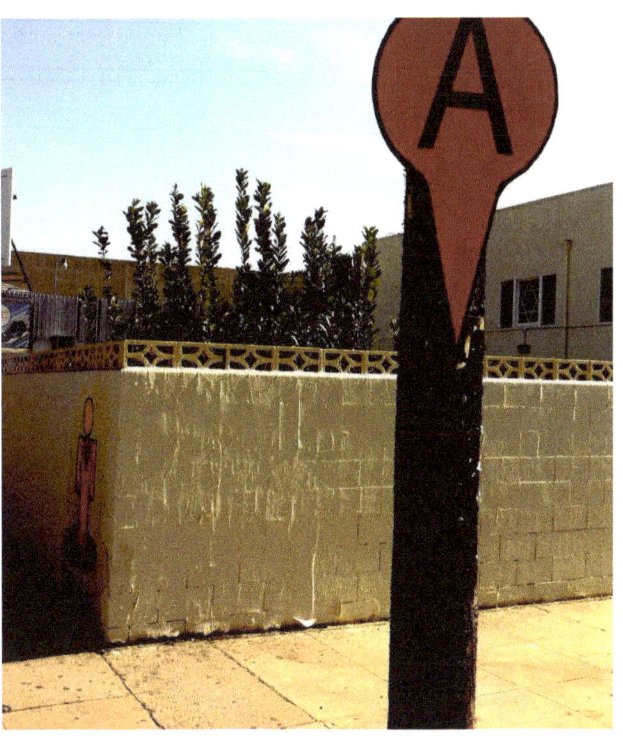

Plastic Jesus put Melrose street art on the map, literally, with oversize art works resembling the Google Maps icons that had just become ubiquitous to navigation on smart phones.

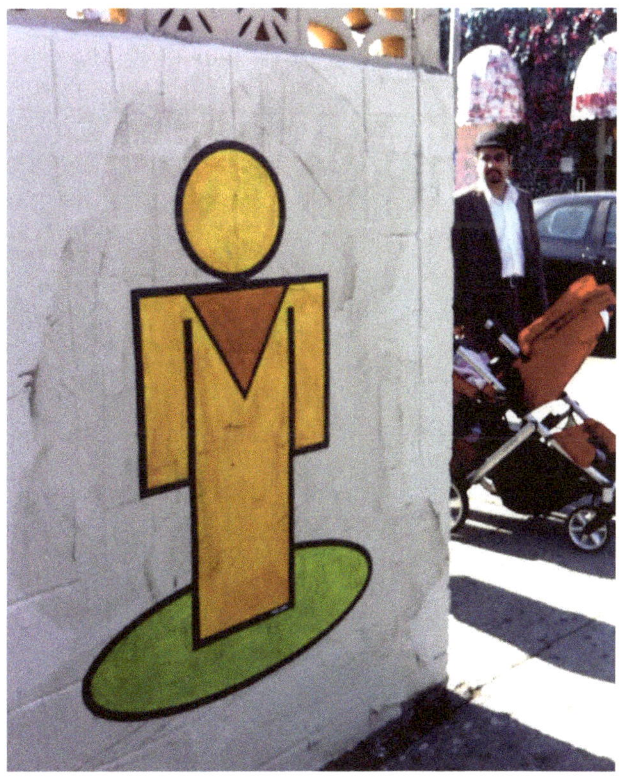

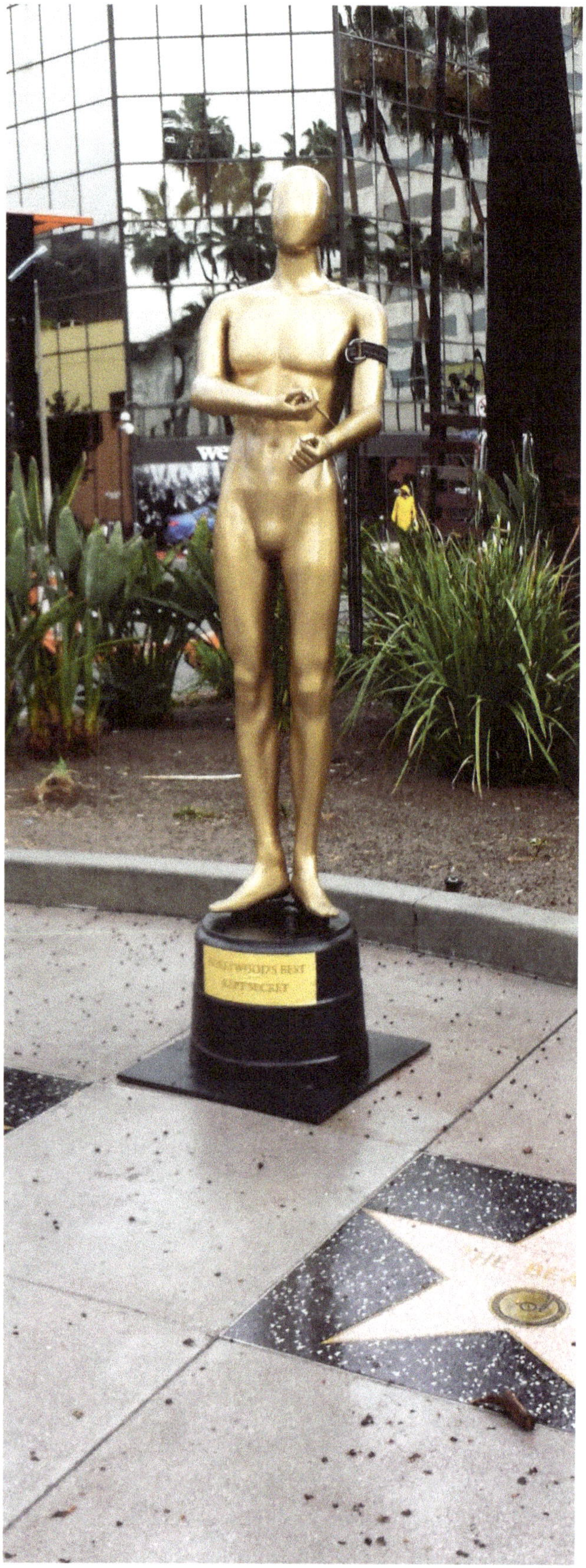

For Oscars Week in Hollywood, the fanfare and décor are so splendid, it might have taken tourists and commuters a minute to notice in 2014 that the tall shiny Oscar statue at the Gateway to the Hollywood Walk of Fame was a little off.

Closer inspection revealed that Oscar was tied off with a belt strapped around his arm, shooting a needle into his wrist.

With the award statue named "Hollywood's Best Kept Secret," Plastic Jesus made a stunning statement on the proliferation of deadly drugs in this industry town, coming just days after Philip Seymour Hoffman had been discovered dead from a heroin overdose.

The jarring piece received widespread media attention. Someone actually jumped out of their car, claiming to be from the Academy, and tried to take down the sculpture. Plastic Jesus managed to fend her off.

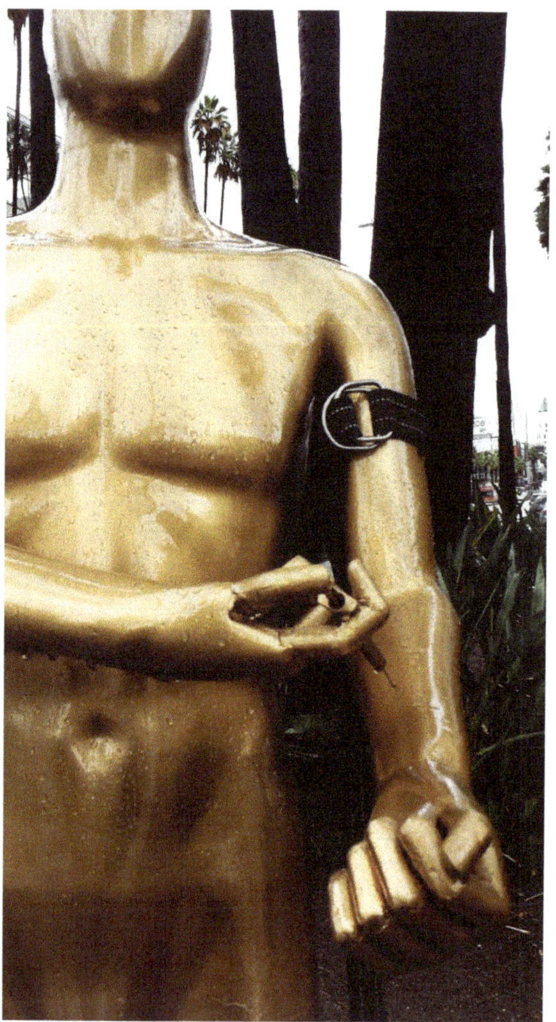

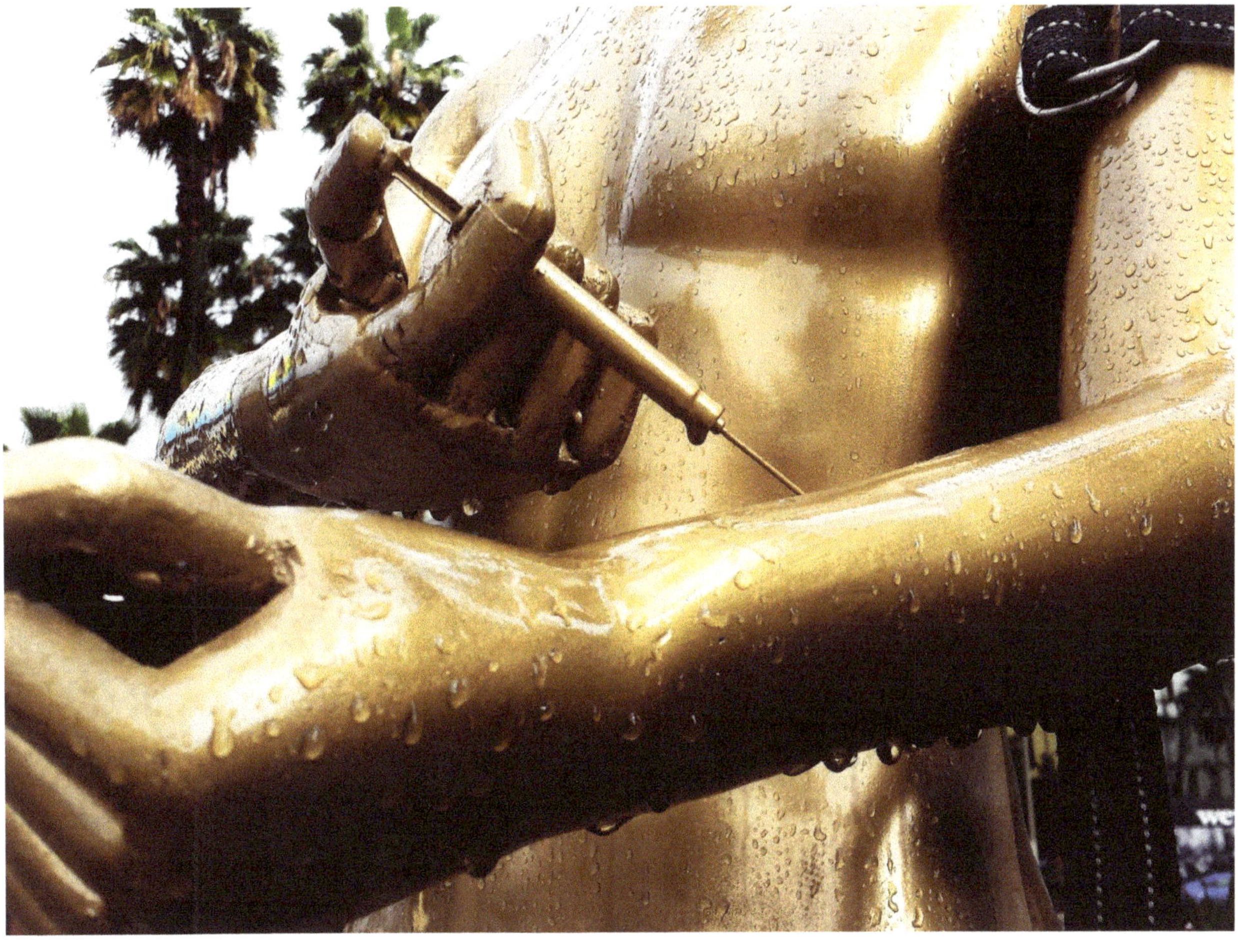

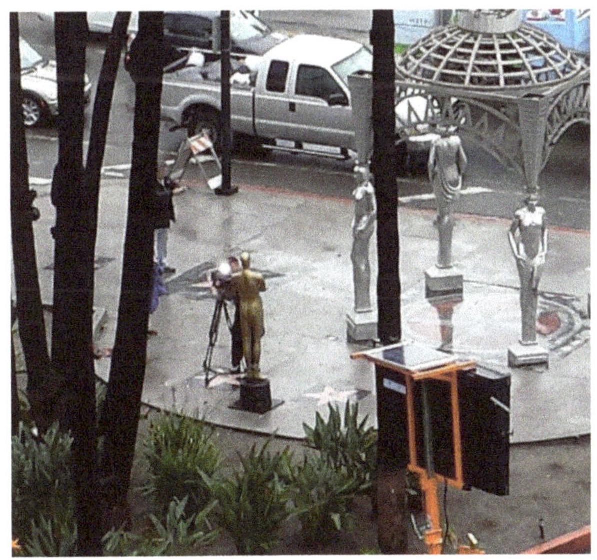

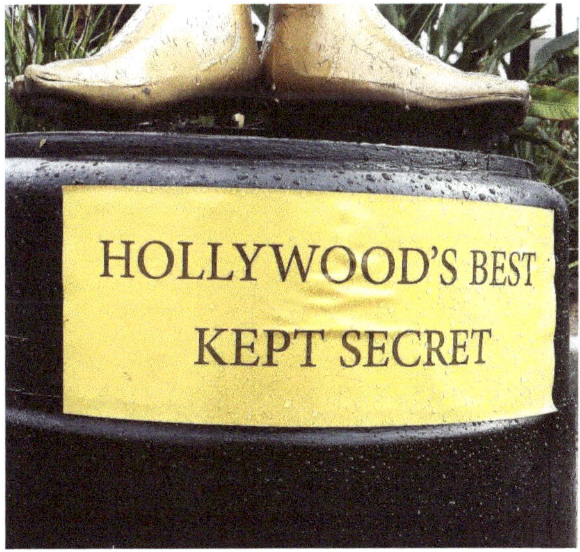
HOLLYWOOD'S BEST
KEPT SECRET

After the huge success of "Hollywood's Best Kept Secret," how could Plastic Jesus follow up for next year's Oscars? In Hollywood, a successful sequel is a rarity, but Plastic Jesus went the extra mile.

One morning, at the same gateway to Hollywood, right near the Dolby Theater, there once again appeared an oversized Oscar statue. This time, for "Hollywood's Best Party," Oscar was seen on the red carpet, but on his hands and knees. There was the cherished icon snorting up lines of cocaine, cut by a specialized Plastic Jesus American Excess Black Card.

This time, the Academy seemed to be ready for him, as someone representing the Academy immediately moved in and told Plastic Jesus's security team to shut it down. PJ and his crew held their ground for a while, until Hollywood Chamber of Commerce security threated them with arrest and confiscation.

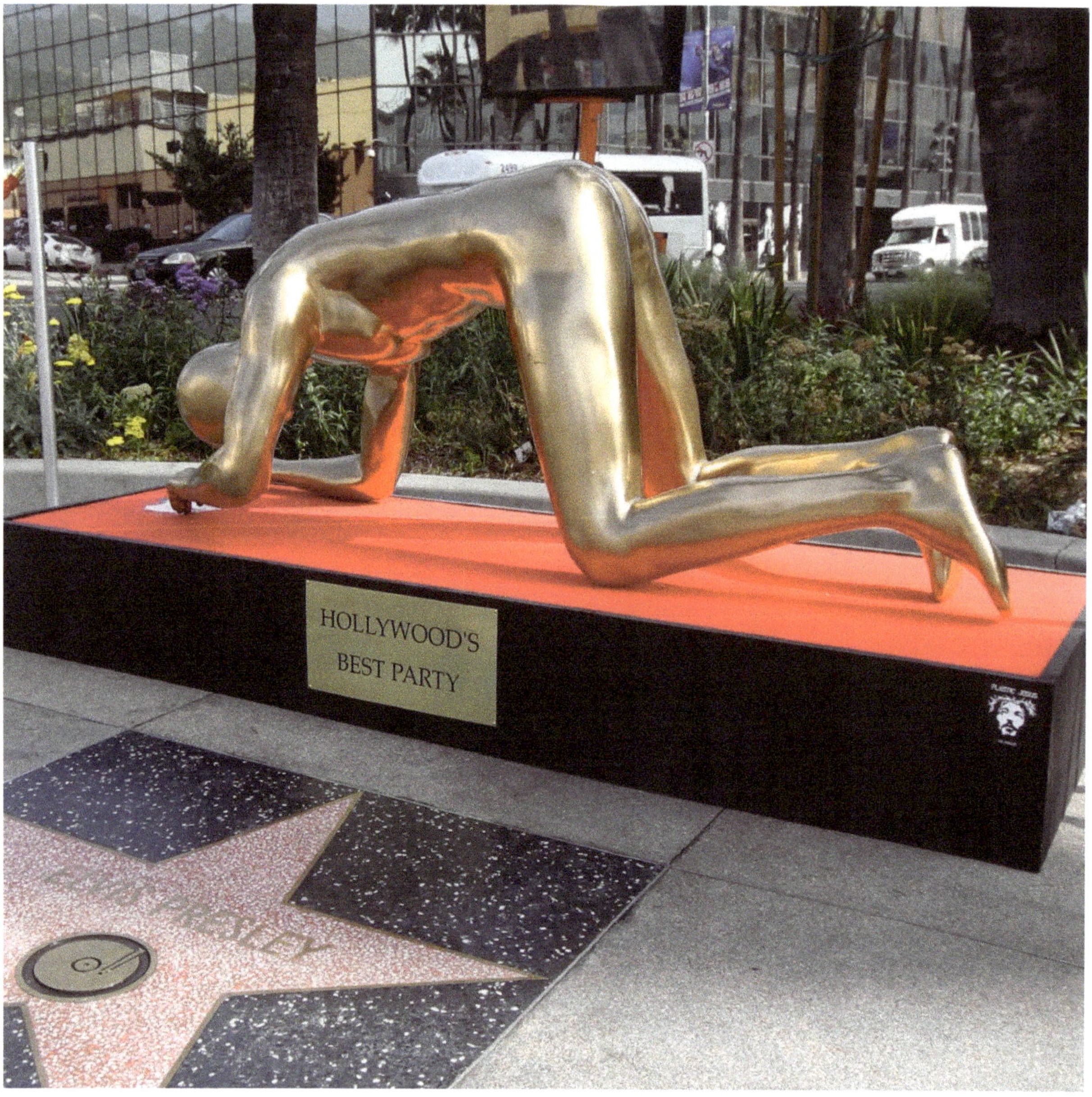

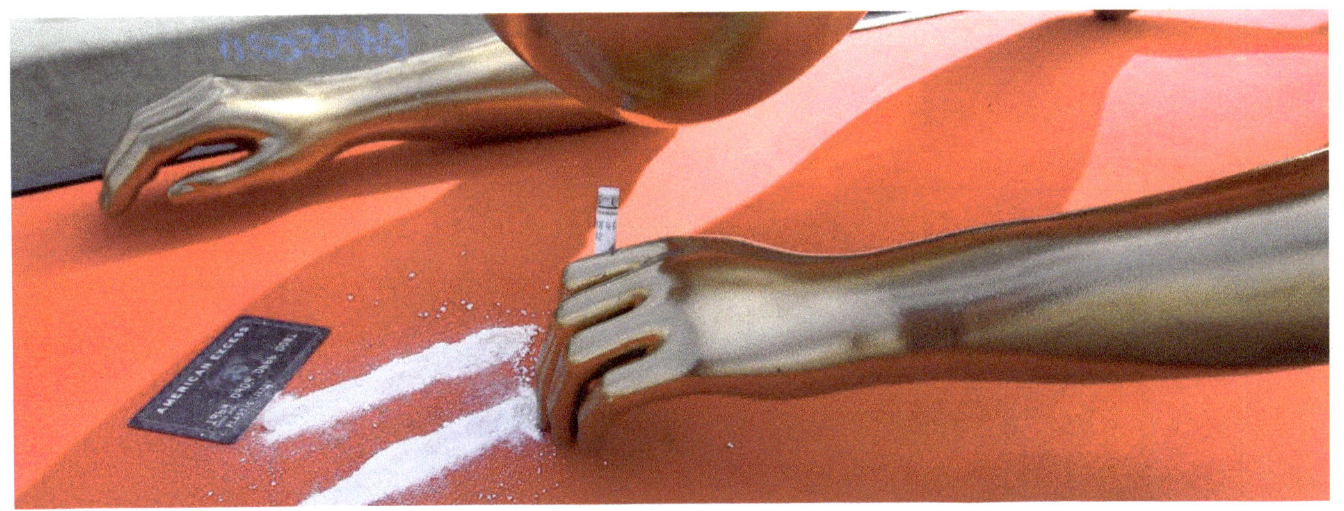

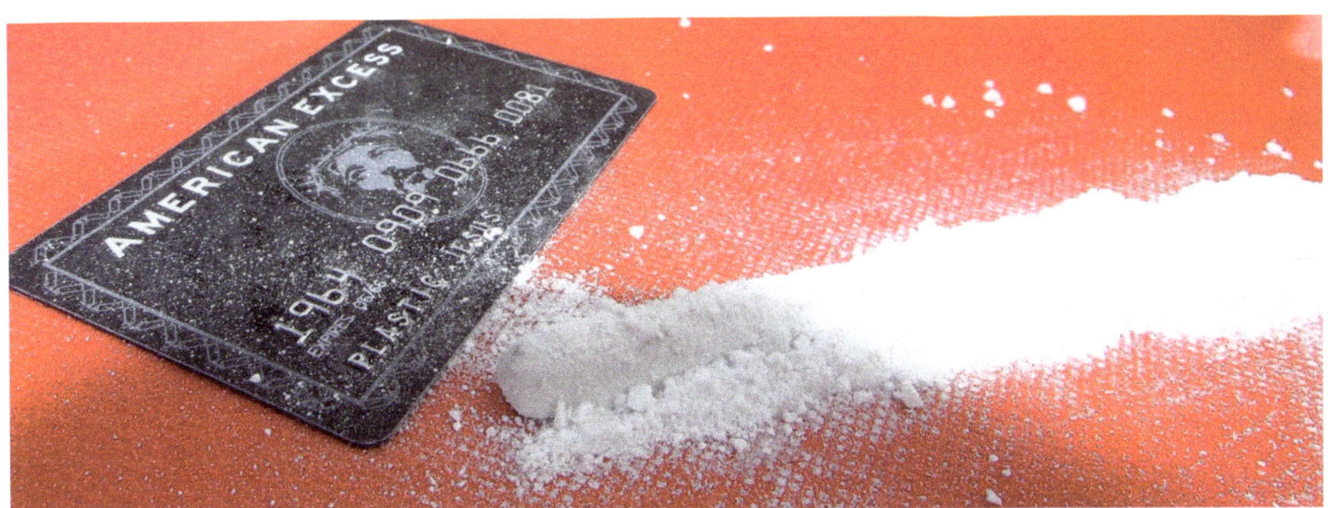
AMERICAN EXCESS
PLASTIC JESUS

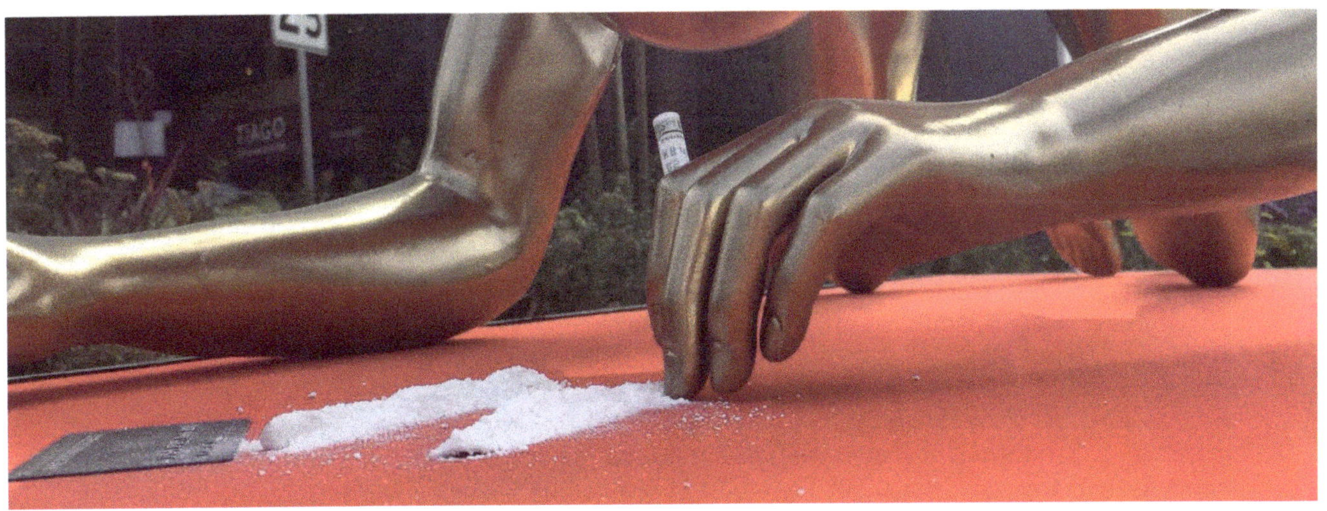
TIAGO

SABO

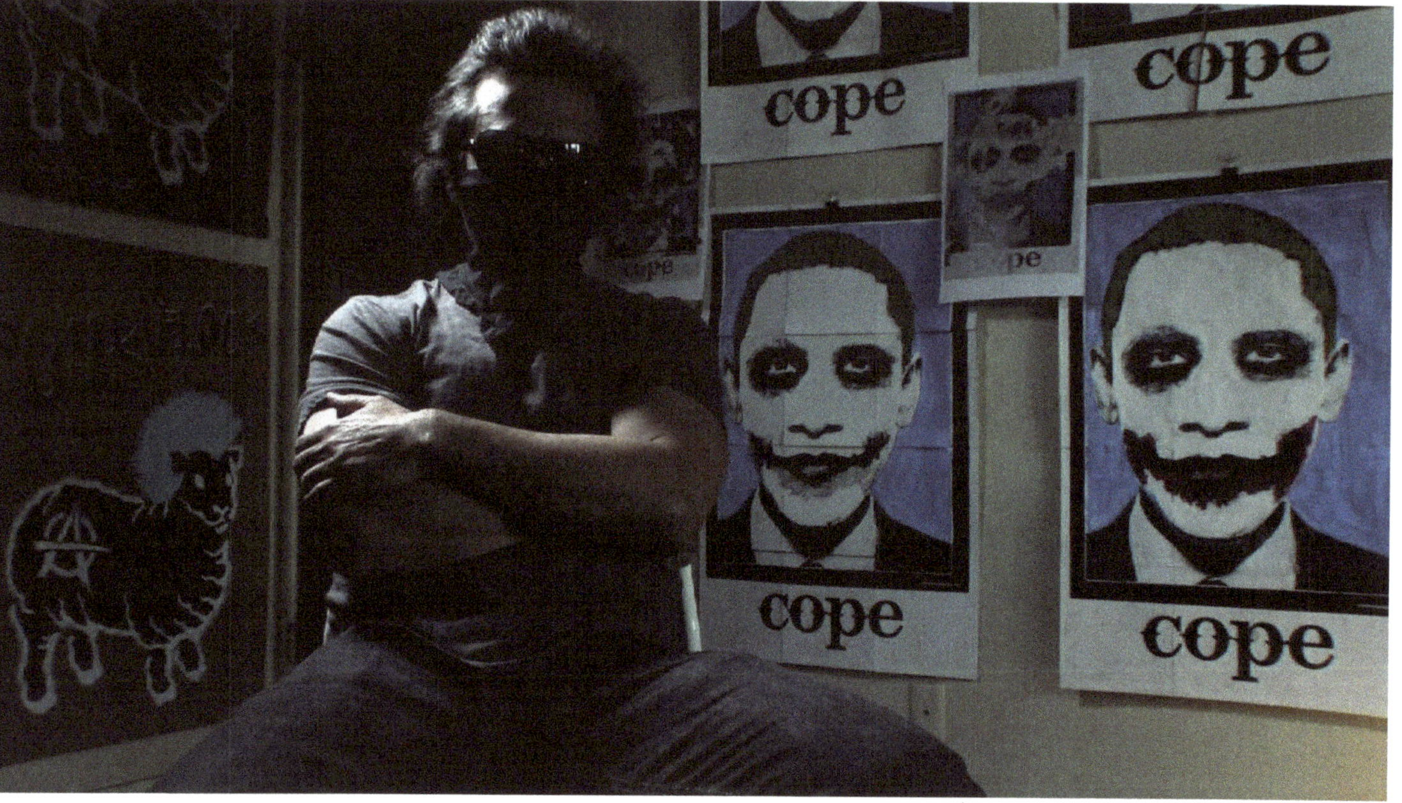

"I've always been interested in politics—I mean always. From as far as I can remember. And I remember during Clinton, when he was in office, I saw how ugly it got with him. And it was, you know...even back then I took a step back and said 'Hey give this guy a break. He's the fucking president, you know? Show him some respect.' And I even backed away from some people that wouldn't go easy on him.

"But something happened when Bush was elected. It's like, the claws came out. And I lost a lot of friends in Hollywood at that point. And what I mean by the claws came out, I almost could not go anywhere, 'cause I was barraged, no matter where you went, I'd see messages: Republicans suck. Republicans are evil. On and on, I couldn't take a girl out to dinner, or you walk into a bookstore, the books in the front are telling me my party sucks, Bush sucks, this sucks. I mean, if you're looking for a conservative book it's on the top shelf at the back, or at the bottom shelf. Or if they're lucky they may have it in the back some place. And I'm just talking about being barraged by this message, I'm not talking about walking down the street and seeing street art. And one day I went, 'You know what, I want a little bit of my voice out there.'

"So after 9/11 happened, I did these two pieces behind you, and I put them up. And I'm not going to say I'm Shepard Fairey and I'm prolific in anyway. But you know that was just my small attempt at getting my message out there. And as the years progressed, I just acquired this small body of work.

"What I'm hoping to achieve is just put a message out there for one. I mean, it's my opinion that the Republican Party, they're still living in the fifties, they've got this Beaver Cleaver mentality, like the left is going to fight fair, or we gotta fight fair. And I'm sure leftists will argue and say 'Well *they* don't fight fair.' I mean, I'm a Republican, I like to keep my ear on the ground with what's going on, and I can tell you, they don't fight nearly as dirty as the left. And they sure as hell don't jump in a car at whatever time in the morning and put up posters vandalizing neighborhoods. That's not something Republicans from Orange County do. I mean, you grab a spray paint thing, and like tag Shepard Fairey's studio, I mean, they're like, 'Wow, you know that's cool! Who the fuck did that?'

"What I want to accomplish is, if you look at the media, from the moment you sit a child down, this child is told, shaggy with a ruffled-up facial hair and sandals, he's the good guy. The evil guy is the fat guy with the cigar and a suit. The second we're sat down in front of the television. And as time progresses your teachers tell you in school who the good guys are, who the bad guys are, the evil bankers and the evil corporations, and this and that.

"And it's like, you fast forward two generations, it's just the norm. People just understand and accept who the good guys are and who the bad guys are. And the majority of the artists out there will tell you, I mean, they fall in line with it. The art speaks exactly what they've been told. I would like to introduce a new, other side. Street art in particular. How many fucking conservative rappers do you know? Not too many of them. And I'm not even a conservative, I worked at *Penthouse* for three years. I was in the porn industry for five years; I'm the furthest thing from a conservative. I'm a Republican; I'd probably be Libertarian but they'll never see office. And there's no way in hell I could be a Democrat.

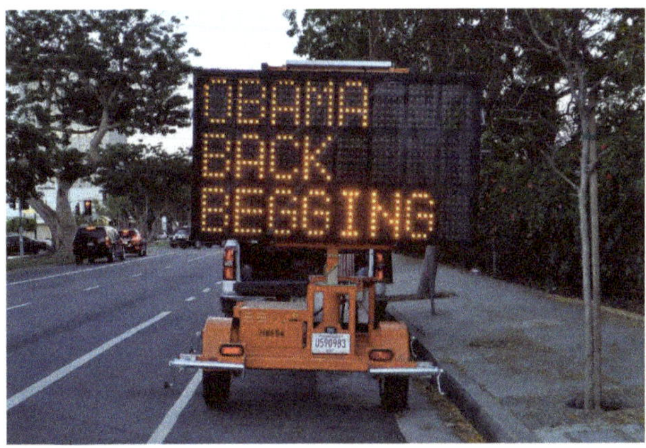

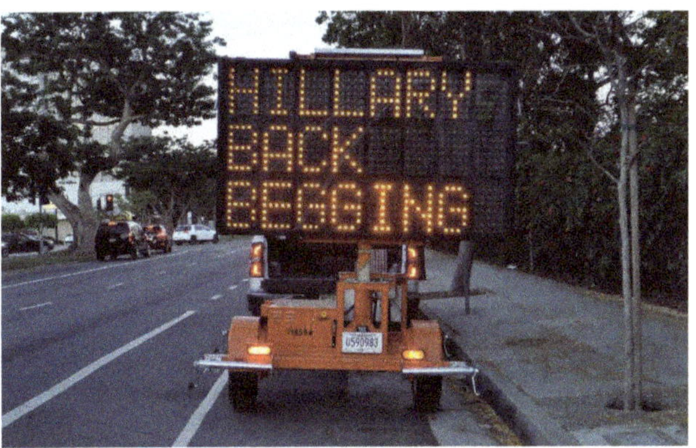

ABOVE: President Obama's frequent fundraising trips to LA create such traffic congestion, Sabo put out a traffic sign by his fundraiser. He did the same for a Hillary Clinton fundraiser. BELOW: Warped photo of Dredd Obama poster on Fairfax & Third.

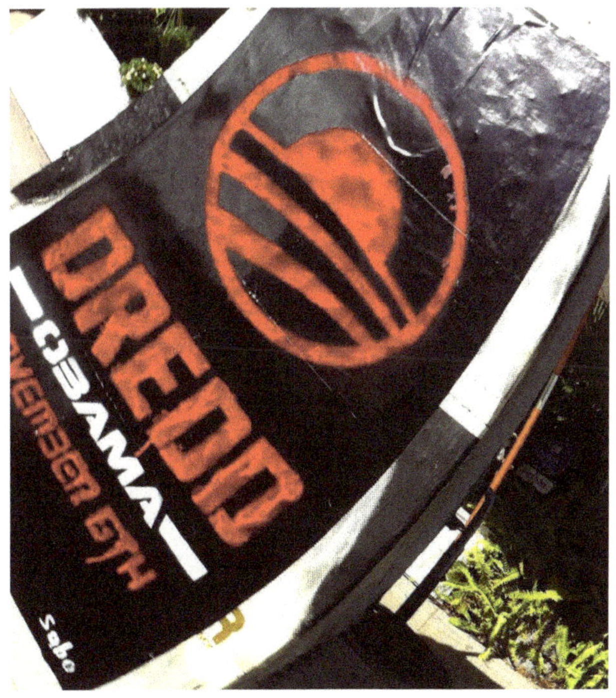

"As far as reactions go, I can tell you, when the anti-war protests started, when the Iraq War started, I had made this 'Fuck Peace' sign. That was pretty much the consensus and thought of a lot of people in America, it's like, 'Fuck this, let's go kick their ass.' What I did was, I made a couple thousand of them, 'Fuck Peace' flyers, I got 12 stories up on this building, and it was raining that day. And Jesse Jackson and all these guys are like marching down there, and I heaved them off, I heaved them off the roof. And I ran downstairs to see what the reaction was going to be. And I saw this one lady, like, lean over and pick one up? I swear to God, it was like she picked up a bolt of lightning. She like, threw it down, like, jumped back so fast. And I loved it man, because that told me something. That told me it connected. And she obviously didn't agree with the message, but it connected.

"And when I put these up at anti-war rallies, the next day they're all ripped up. A lot of my work doesn't stay up very long at all. I mean during the '08 election, if I put up something about Obama, like I was mocking Shepard Fairey with some of his posters, they didn't see the next day. I mean if I was to put up any of these Obama things they'd be lucky to be up for two days. And as far as the reaction goes, that's the reaction I get.

"The burkas is because… for decades, Hollywood is telling us the Christians are knuckle-dragging neanderthals. And, okay, whatever. I mean, you go decade after decade hearing this shit. Then you have a bunch of whack jobs take out the World Trade Center, and we're supposed to try and appreciate and understand why they did it. And I don't watch television, but I can tell you that every now and then I'll put something on, and I start seeing all kinds of pro-Muslim stuff, and I'm supposed to be open-minded, if I'm an intellectual and I've got all kinds of feelings for other cultures and such, I'm supposed to embrace it. I'm like, 'Dude, for decades you told me this religion is a bunch of dumb-asses, now I'm supposed to believe another one that's even more dumb-asses. It's like, I don't fucking think so, man. So okay Hollywood, you want me to embrace the Muslim faith? I'll put burkas on your starlets."

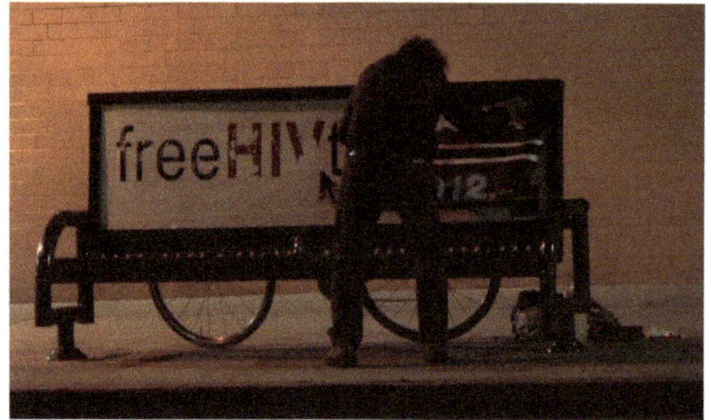

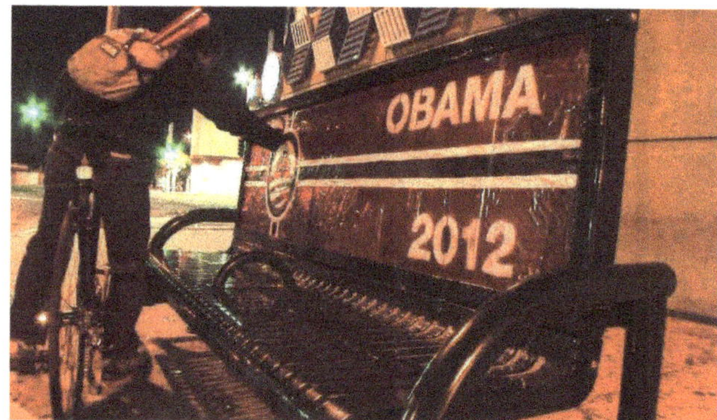

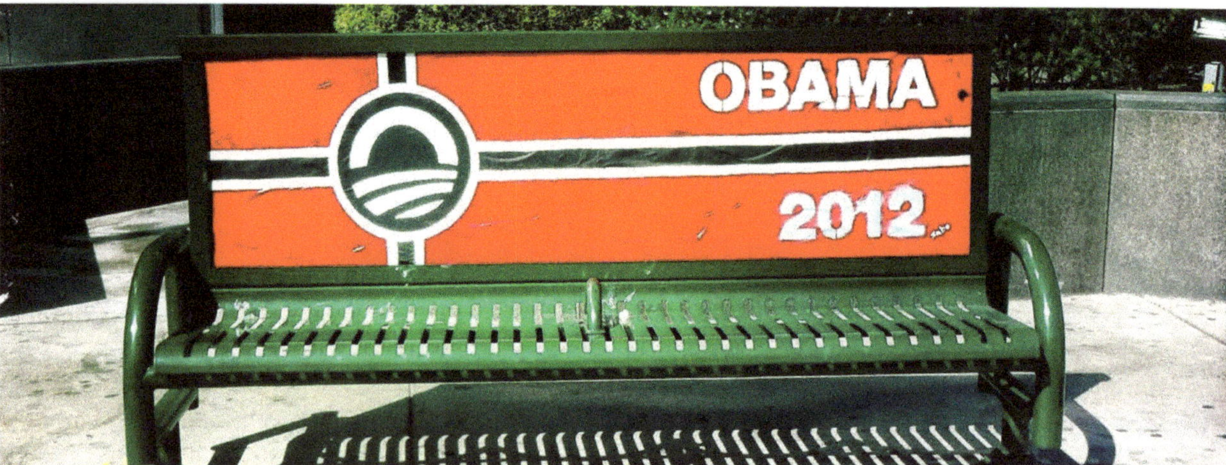

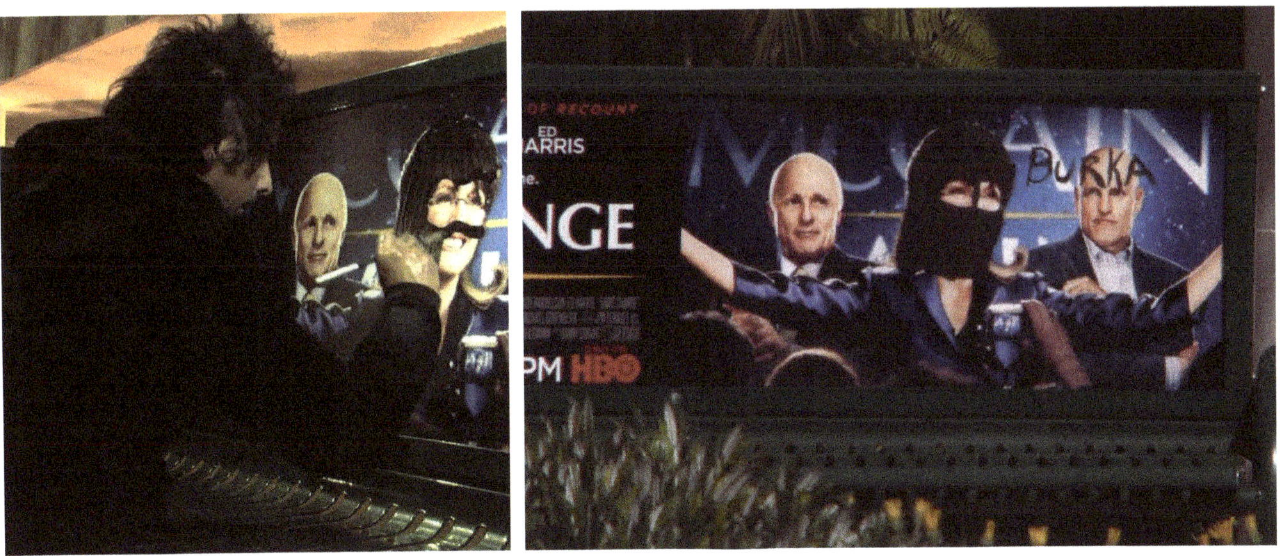

ABOVE: Sabo painting a burka on a bus bench movie ad on Wilshire. BELOW: This poster of Nancy Pelosi twerking with her tongue out like Miley Cyrus prompted top Democrats to demand an apology to Pelosi. On Windward in Venice. OPPOSITE PAGE: Sabo gets around town on bicycle. He repurposed plastic waste to make Nazi-esque Obama posters. Sabo may be one of the most eco-friendly street artists in Los Angeles.

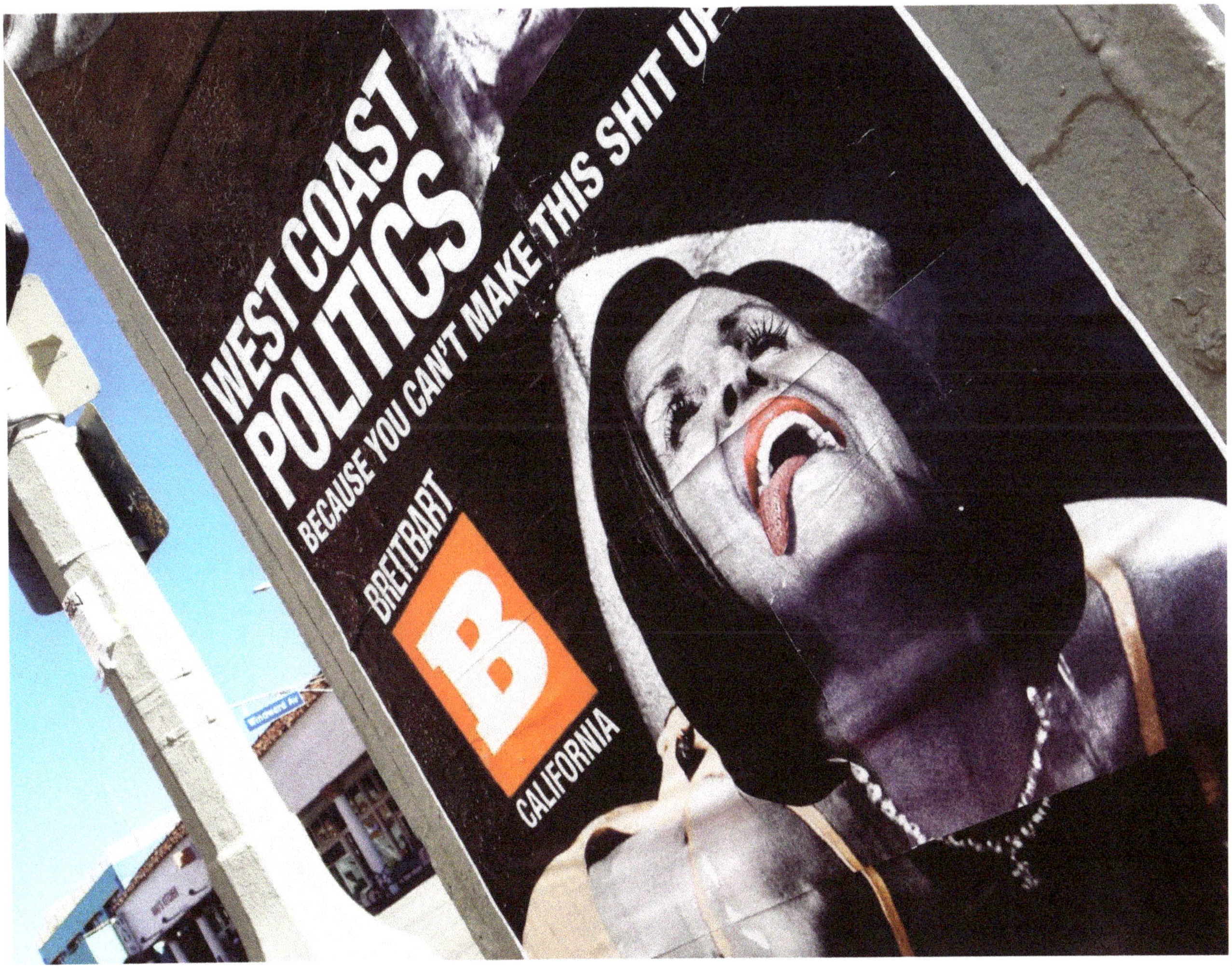

PHONE JACKS

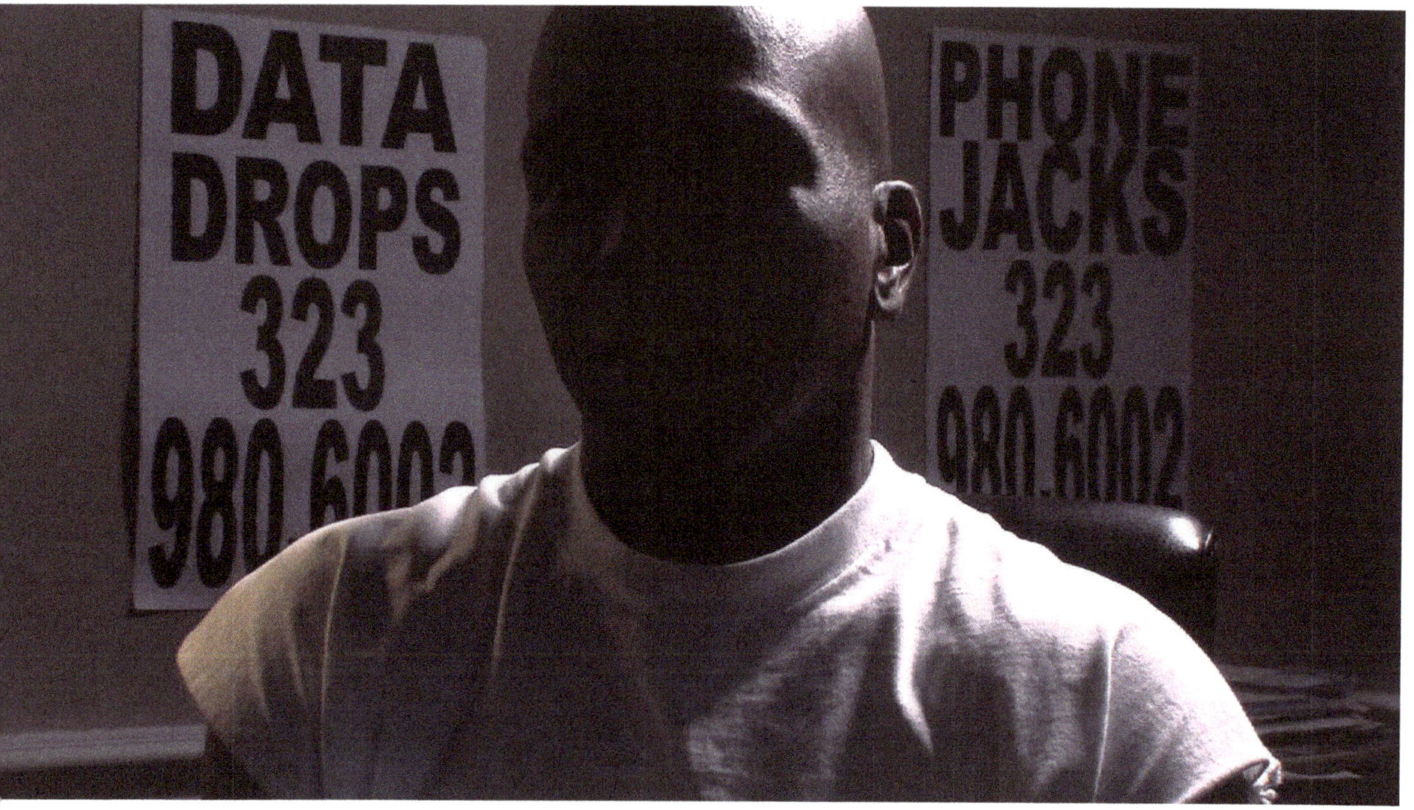

Phone Jacks is known by all street artists in Los Angeles. They all hate him. He's gotten up more than anybody, his posters are on the back of every other street sign, and he's freely capped anybody and everybody by plastering his posters over someone else's street art. A relentless grinder, he would put a poster up over a new piece of street art that had gone up earlier that night. Even artists who were out on the street every night never managed to see him. He didn't stick to one neighborhood, he was all over L.A. and the Valley. And the worst part of it? He wasn't even a street artist. He was actually some guy trying to sell phone jacks.

Melrose & Fairfax toasted Phone Jacks: "Although not an artist, arguably LA's most prolific wheat paster." The ire built to the point where other artists started making their own posters with his phone number to put up over Phone Jack's posters. I was curious, but didn't know how to track him down; so I tried the phone number he had put up all over town.

I left a message. Eventually I heard back. A man said, "First thing I gotta ask you is, do you work for the city?" Apparently he was wary of being arrested for all of his posters on city property.

PHONE JACKS: "Well, it's called low-budget advertising. When you work for yourself, you have a service you offer, you have to market yourself. And putting up posters is my marketing strategy. Throughout the years it's worked pretty well. [I service] the low-end and the high-end. I've been to places, living conditions that were so horrible, that I almost gave the work away—for free—I felt so sorry for the customer, for their living conditions. I've been to a place that was so low, I didn't think anyone should even be living in that place. And the smell was so horrible, that, when I was going back to the car, I was telling myself that I wasn't going to go back in. But, when you don't got no money... *[Laughs]* I gotta get the money.

"I've had a lot of threatening calls. I've had people claim territory. Had a lady once called me and screamed at me. 'You can't put posters in my corridor!' Your corridor? 'Yeah, my corridor!' I don't know where it was. But she kept calling me. I'd hang up and she'd call me a hundred times. 'You can't put posters in my corridor, this is my corridor!'

"I think one of the craziest things that happened was, some guy would go around, and, he made posters smaller than mine, with an adhesive back side to it, and he had them printed up, I don't know who would print this for him, it said 'N*gger Crook.' And this was when I was putting them up on poles, I'd climb a ladder and put them on poles, wooden telephone poles. He would climb up there. Obviously he'd get a ladder, he'd climb up on the pole, and he'd stick 'N*gger Crook' on my posters that said 'Phone Jacks.' And how I found out was, a lady called me and said, 'Are you the guy with the posters? Well there's somebody... there's something terrible happened. We tried to... but we couldn't reach it! We tried to take it off but you might want to come see your poster.' She told me what street it was on, but I didn't go over there.

"But I end up one day on Highland and Wilshire. That little island, there's some posters in there? And he'd come over there, too. And they were lower, right? Big sticker: N*gger Crook. Same guy, he would call me some times, late at night. Tell me I was a n*gger, and I came from gorilla slime. And I need to stay off the west side of town, blah blah blah blah. He called almost every night. He called late at night when he knew I was sleeping when the phone was off and leave his messages.

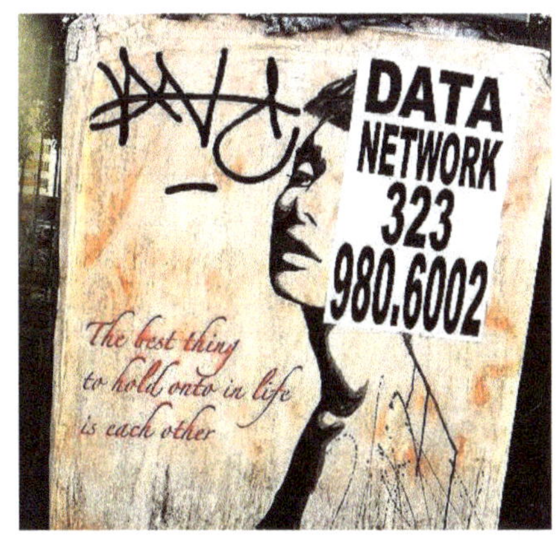

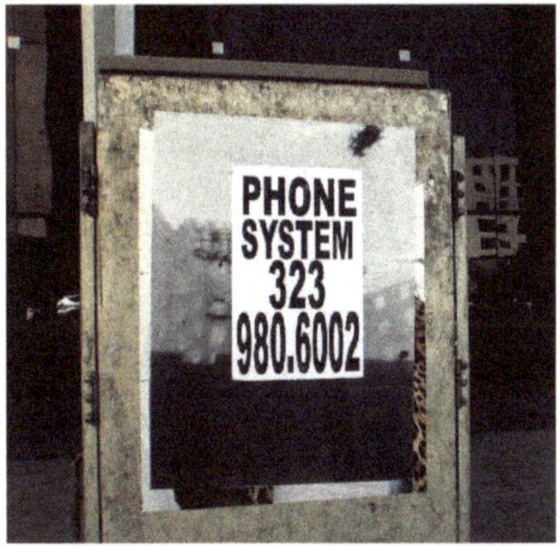

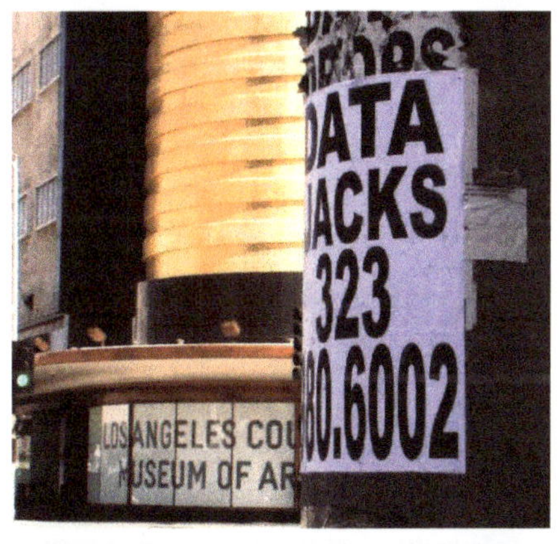

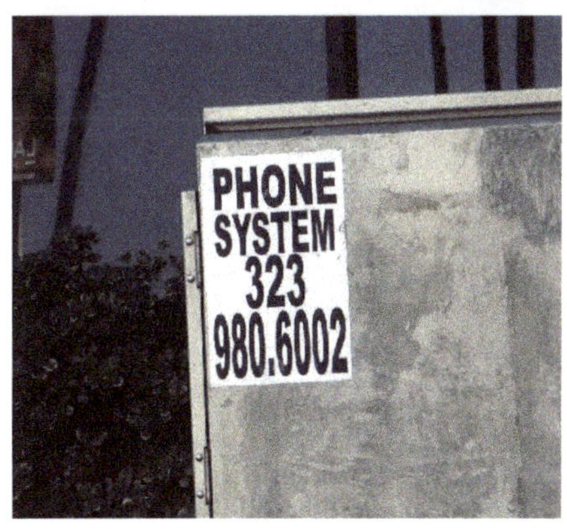

"He called so much, I saved the messages, and I took it to the police department *myself*, I said, 'This dude is crazy!' That's how much this dude called me. That's how much he called me. And then the one with 'N*gger Crook' sticker on it? I took that to the police station, I'm like, 'Can't you guys get some prints off this, find out who this guy is? This guy might be crazy!' Talked to the desk sergeant and explained to him what was happening over in the Wilshire District, and gave him the phone number and he called the guy while I was there. But the guy denied it. The guy who I suspected it was. And he denied everything, so, the desk sergeant was talking to him, and he obviously said something about being black, because the desk sergeant said 'How do you know he's black? I didn't tell you that.' He thought it was him, too, but he was like, 'There's really nothing we can do. You can't get finger prints off something that's been in public, anyone can touch it.' He stopped calling after a while. But that was, like, the worst call.

"I had guys call and scream at me, 'I'M GONNA GET YOU! I'M GONNA GET YOU!' Like those are my messages that I get. Check my messages, that's what I got. 'You put a sign up on Third Street, I'm gonna get you!' Then they hang the phone up. You know? I've had people call and ask me for drugs. Had a guy call me one night, saying he was Russian Mafia. Told me what he sold. I'm like, okay, I'm waking up in the morning and I'm checking my messages, I got a message from a guy telling me he's Russian Mafia. And he sells cocaine, and he has this, and he has that, I'm like, 'Why is he calling me telling me that off the sign?!'

"Another one of those weird calls, female calling me asked me to tattoo her private part. Okay. I said to her, I said: you *know* what my sign said. Why are you calling me asking me to put a tattoo on your vagina? And she insisted that I give her a quote, right? So I'm like okay, seventy-five bucks. I went back and forth with her a few times. But she was insistent, right? I'm like, this female is crazy. And I said okay, seventy-five. Seventy-five okay? She said okay. Hung up the phone. A day or two later she called back with her girlfriend. 'How much you gonna charge me to put a tattoo on my breast?' Now she wants tattoos on her breasts. I said, 'Yesterday or whatever it was, the other day I told you, it was *seventy-five bucks* for tattoos. I don't do tattoos, but since she, I'm just playing along with the game just to, y'know, she'd get off the phone. So that was pretty weird.

"Once a lady called, she said she saw a Phone Jacks poster, so she calls, she called from private number, blocked number. And she says, 'Hi. I was just calling because I'm here by the side of the road, and I see your posters here, nice shiny

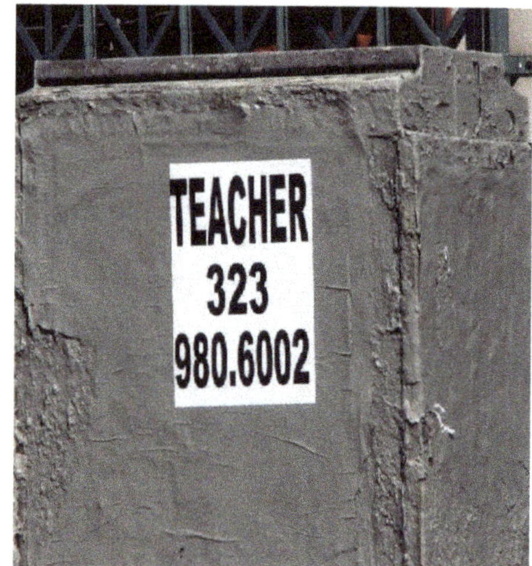

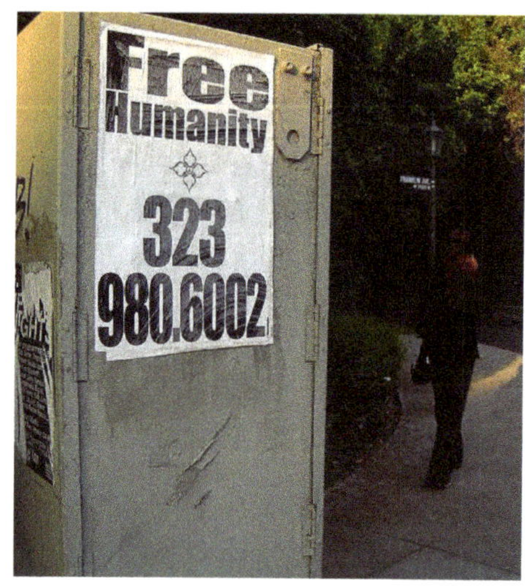

ABOVE: Teacher and Free Humanity became so irate at Phone Jacks for covering their art, they started making posters with their name and his phone number to paste over his posters.

posters, I was wondering if Jack was around. I'd like to screw him.' But she used the F word. And then she hung up. *[Laughs]*

"There's this guy, this black guy. I don't know, I don't know what his trip is. I don't know *what* he's marketing. But he started covering my posters up, oh, man, two years ago? And his posters, the ones that he started off with were him with a long jeri curl, a G-string, and some gigantic, *huge* angel wings on his back. Right? And that's it, there's no number, there's no website address, it's just him, with a red G-string on, man, and you know what I mean? And giant angel wings.

"So this dude, man, he was covering me up for a long time. I'd put up a poster, I'd look around, I'd say, 'Where's—who *is* this dude?!' No phone number, no nothing, and it was starting to... I didn't like the fact that children would see it. Why is this grown man with something up his butt, what do they call it? Shoe string? Dental floss up the crack of his butt and gigantic angel wings and a long Jerry curl, he's putting his posters up in public so children can see. So after a while he stopped. But he's back on again. Now, he's got this young lady, this white girl with him. So she's in G strings or topless or whatever. And they might pose together. Different poses. But no web address, no phone number. So I don't understand what they're marketing. I'm out here trying to *eat*, right? They're putting naked pictures out. *[Laughs]* And nobody would know whether anybody get in touch with them. I'm trying to eat. So I was figuring, like, I take precedence over that stuff because they're not trying to make money. I'm trying to make money. They can't make money if nobody can contact them, right? So I just cover 'em up when I see them or I take 'em down. Ah the dude was foul, man, that shit. *[Laughs]* Giant angel wings and a G string on. Crazy.

"One of the [LA Dept. Water & Power] guys called out, he was really upset with me, 'cause he said, you know, 'Hey man that's a brand new box! You put your poster on a brand new box!' And I just went like, 'Well, you know. Brand new box, box is a box to me!' He said, 'Naw, it's a *brand new* box, man!' And I told him, I said, 'You know what?' He said some other things, whatever he said. I can't, you know, really quote him on it. What it came down to was, I told him this, I said 'Listen. What I need is your address.' He's like, 'What?!'

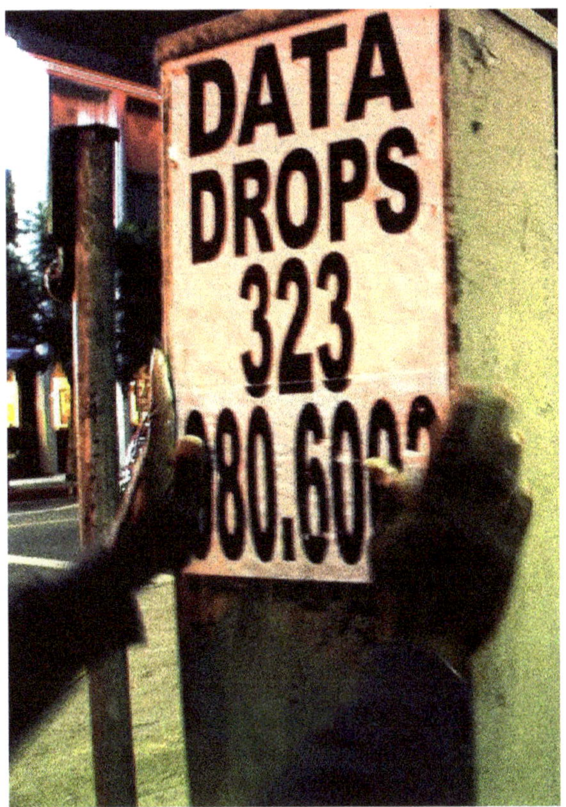

The elusive Phone Jacks getting up on Wilshire. Talk about old school: he uses Elmer's Glue.

Says like, "You tellin' me I can't market my business, so I can't eat. So I need your address, I can't take care of myself. So I need *your* address.' He says, 'I'm not giving you my address!' I said, 'Well I need to come live with you. If you don't want me to take care of me, then obviously YOU gonna take care of me.' He says, 'Well I'm not giving you my address!' I said, 'Well *give me your address!'* He says, 'How dare you call here and yell at me, how dare you!' Everything about the posters was over after that; obviously this guy had some complex about people yelling at him. All I was trying to say was: listen, man, if you don't want me to take care of myself, you gonna take care of me. So I need your address. And so, he didn't want to talk about it anymore. All his focus went on 'How dare you call here and yell at me! How dare you!' So I said, 'Man you sitting back on your fanny and you got this big old cush city job, probably work, mmm, 45% of the time? And you giving *me* a hard time?' 'HOW DARE YOU!'

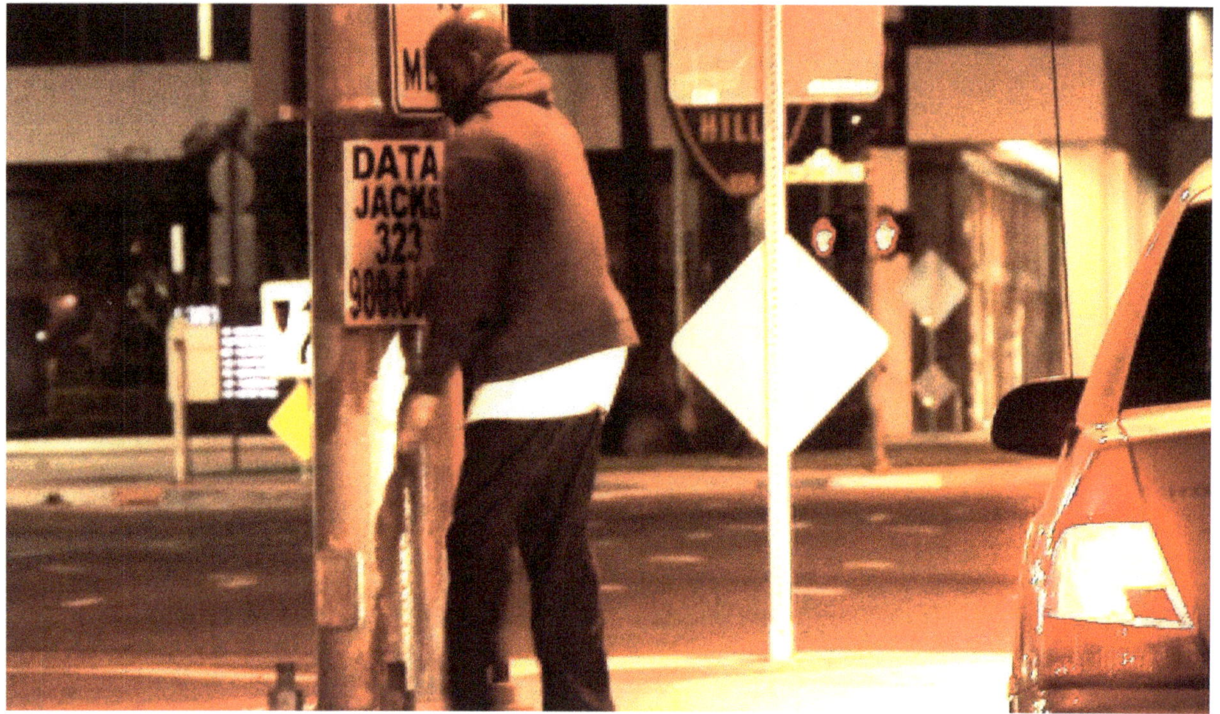

ABOVE: Phone Jacks getting up at Wilshire and San Vicente. OPPOSITE PAGE: An article about his arrest, with his business card.

"Oh yeah, you got these guys that obviously don't like me, Free Humanity, they'll put posters up with my number on there. I took a couple of 'em down. A few I took down.

"I think everybody feels like they got the right, because it's public. That's what I think. Everybody's thinking, I have just as much right to the corner as he has, so. But, I have to admit recently, somebody put up some other kind of poster, I think some kind of office building. If I'm up first they'll go below me. But they've been over me, before I think. They cover me up before. But see, with them, I don't know what they're, what they're, what kind of gain they're looking for. I'm trying to eat, this day to day to me! I'm trying to *eat*, man! You know, I don't know, if you're putting a poster up and there's no website, no e-mail address, and no telephone number on there, what are you doing? When you see me up there with a number, you *know* I'm trying to eat, man! You know, you see Phone Jacks, Data Jacks, Data Drops, Phone Systems or whatever, that brother out there trying to *eat!* And you're gonna put something up there, a building or something... Matter of fact... *[Points behind me at the wall at an Alec Monopoly picture]* Jack Nicholson! That one, right there! They'll cover my posters up with pictures of Jack Nicholson. Okay, so, what are you, his agent? *[Laughs]* You trying to get *Jack* a job? Jack got floor seats at the Lakers game, man. Every season! I don't think he's looking for work!

"Maybe it's just a hobby for them."

Eventually, the city went so far as to set up a sting operation to capture Phone Jacks. When he showed up to a job on Ventura Boulveard, he was met with "a bevy of L.A. cops," as described by the Los Angeles *Daily News*. He was charged with five counts of putting up advertising on public property, if convicted on each count he would face up to 2 1/2 years in prison and a $5000 fine. The article described the outrage of residents for years at his peristent signs. The reporter even mentioned that a local street artist named Free Humanity had begun putting up posters in retalliation for covering up his posters.

But apparently Phone Jacks was not one to be deterred. The article concludes, "Even after [Phone Jacks] was cited by Bush after showing up for the job, Cocek said, he posted two more illegal signs."

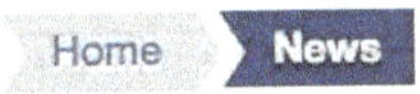

Sting helps nab suspect in ugly sign incidents

By Dana Bartholomew, Staff Writer

POSTED: 03/05/13, 12:01 AM PST

0 COMMENTS

Just before Thanksgiving, a new business prepared to open along Ventura Boulevard in Studio City.

But when businessman Rickey Reed showed up to install phone jacks in the empty storefront, he was met by more than a would-be store manager and carpet installer.

He was greeted by the chief of the Los Angeles' Building and Safety Code Enforcement Division and a bevy of L.A. cops. Reed, who had allegedly hung illegal "data drop" and "phone jacks" signs for years across L.A., was finally nabbed by a city sting.

"We'd been trying to get him for a while," said code enforcement Chief Frank Bush, who said he cited Reed after he'd begun to measure the store for a phone installation. "He caused visual blight throughout the community.

"I've seen his signs all over the place - everywhere you drive."

Reed, 52, of Los Angeles, was charged with five counts of posting advertising signs on public property, for which he faces a pre-trial hearing on Wednesday.

If convicted of each count, he faces up to 2 1/2 years in jail and a $5,000 fine.

He did not respond to a request for comment.

A potential sentence couldn't make Jules Feir happier.

For years, the Sherman Oaks resident was among the many outraged residents to complain about the placard-size phone jack and

So each Sunday, Feir would

scraper.

But no matter how much elb

he said.

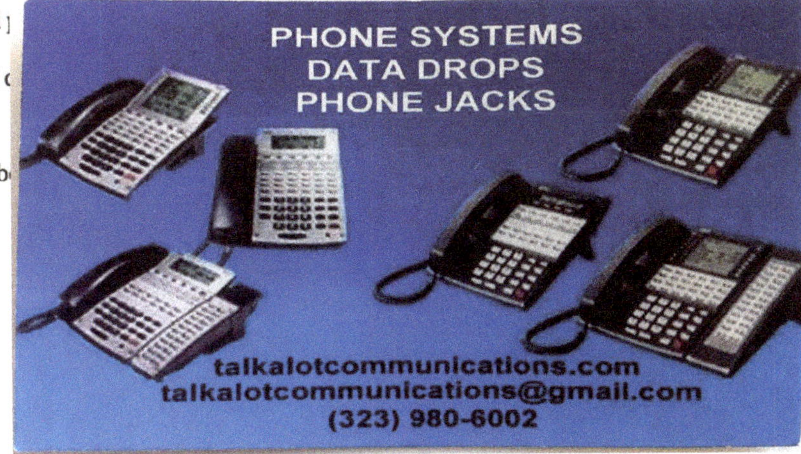

GREGORY SIFF

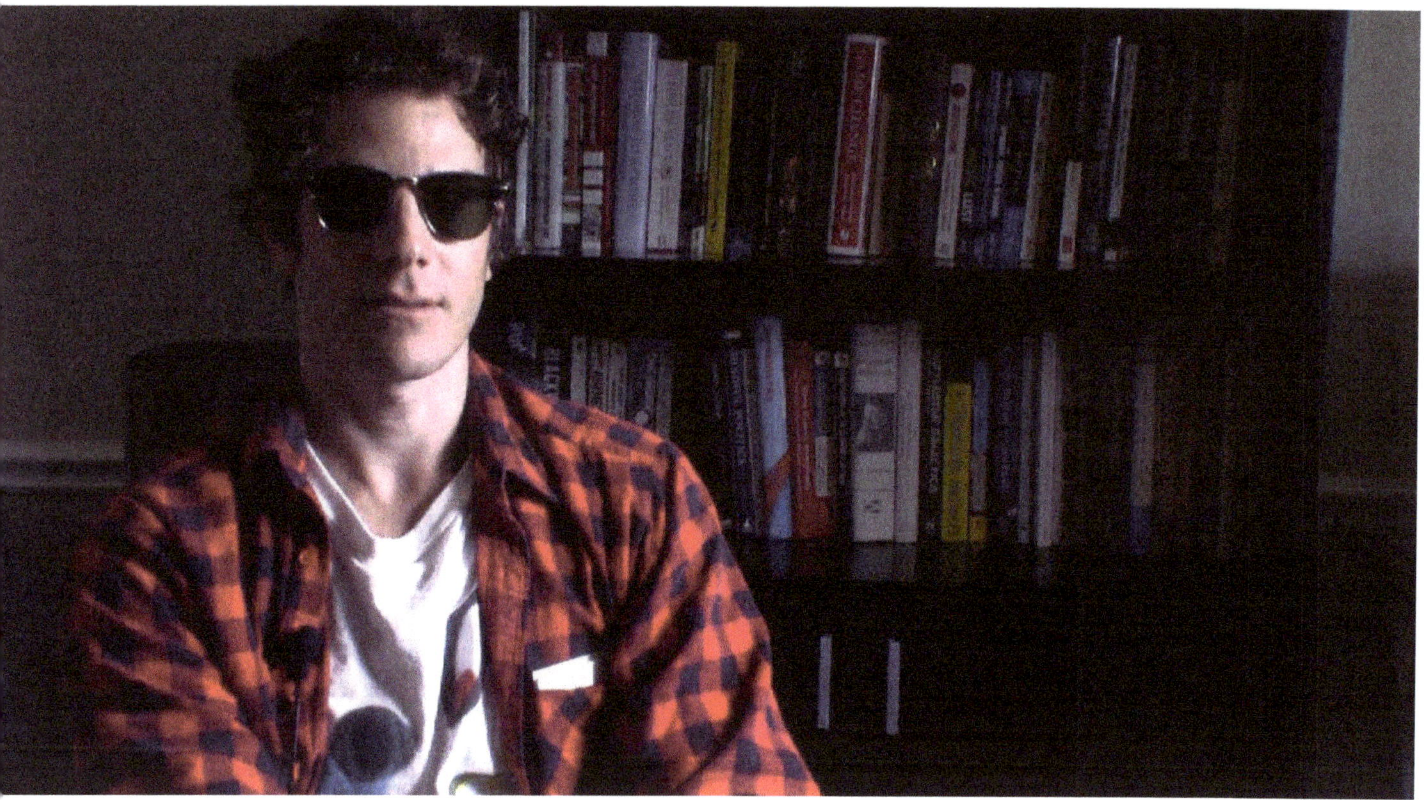

"I guess the reason that I do street art is because I'm an artist. Every day that I get up... even before I started putting work in the public eye on the street was a need for, to create—a need for creation, a need for... almost like a self-medication. It feels good to paint, to build something.

"When people see something out on the street you pay attention. What do you think people pay you, you know, like hundreds of thousands of dollars for an ad, for a billboard... is because there's a certain type of belief that comes with that, whether it's the product or the movie or whatever it is [that's] being advertised. And when you take this space yourself, you're giving people a little, like, movie into your mind, and you're getting to reach a whole larger audience... than just by painting in your house.

"It's an act of defiance, because you're able to take a space that doesn't belong to you or doesn't belong to anyone really. And it doesn't have to be on utility boxes, it could be in nature, it could be on signs, it could be hanging... it comes in various forms. And that's why it's important you choose what you're fighting for is important to you, because if it's not, it's not going to be important to anybody. If you don't have anything to say, it's going to be weak.

"[Cops] are just everywhere, because this is, like, the 'in' town to be doing this in, because of 'Art in the Streets.' And I've just heard a ton of stories, and my friends that have gotten caught, it's not a good thing. It's not fun, and you're treated like you were carrying a gun; you're treated like you're in the act of a high-crime. Their presence has always been known—especially on Melrose."

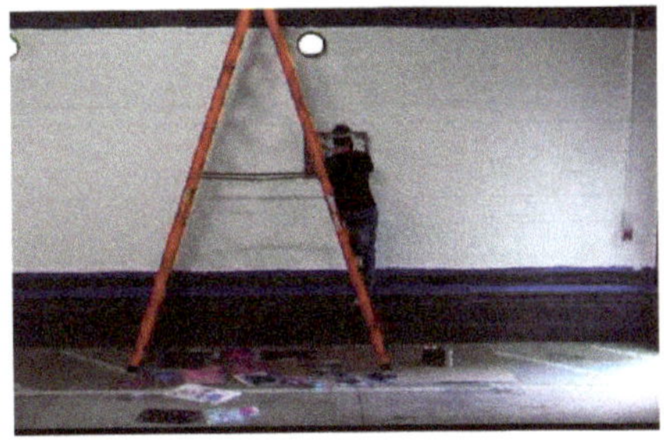

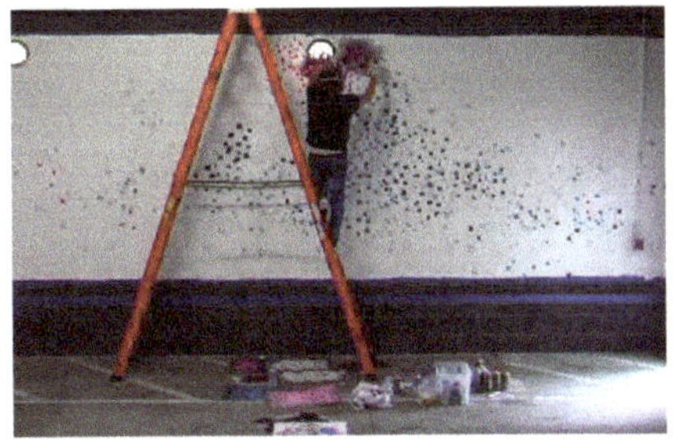

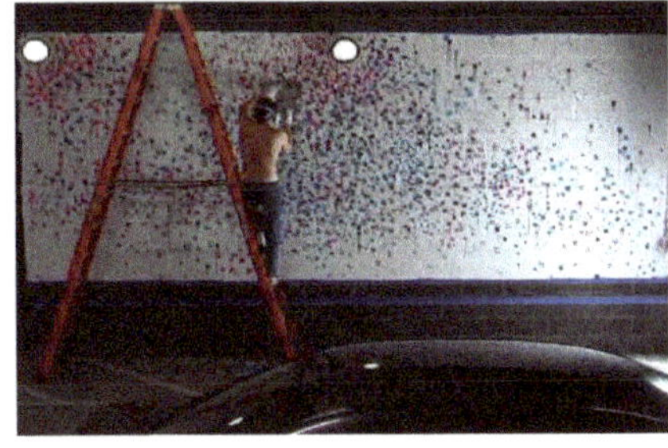

ABOVE: Gregory paints a mural at Siren Studios on Sunset in Hollywood over the course of a day. BELOW: The completed mural, created for Get Art 4, a benefit for Project Angelfood, founded by Marianne Williamson.

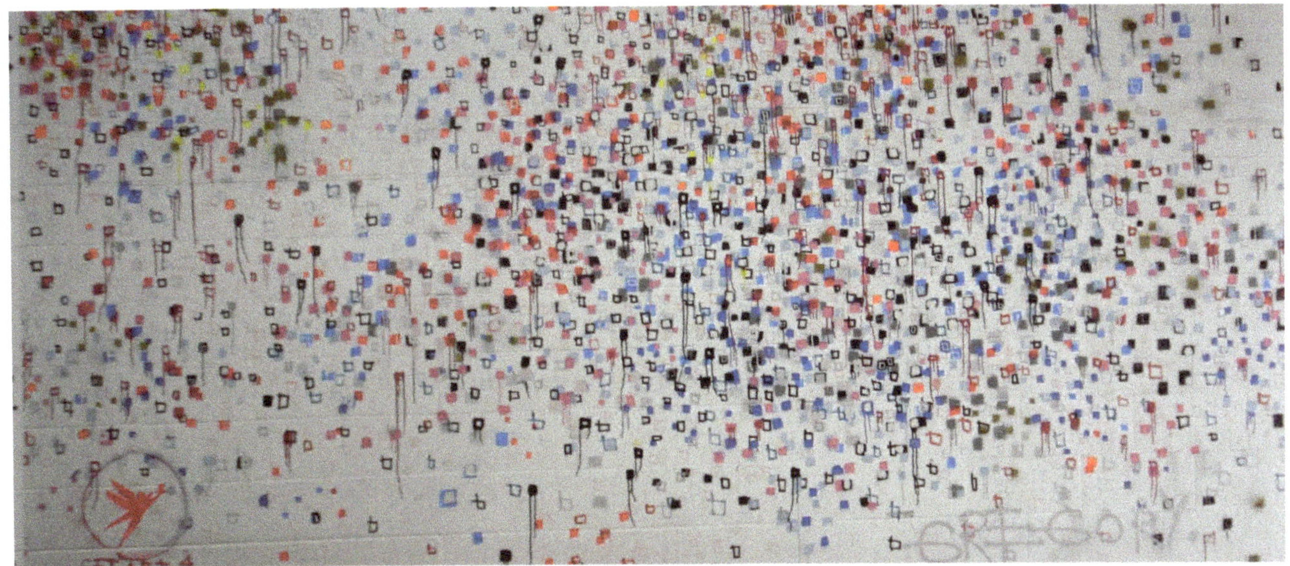

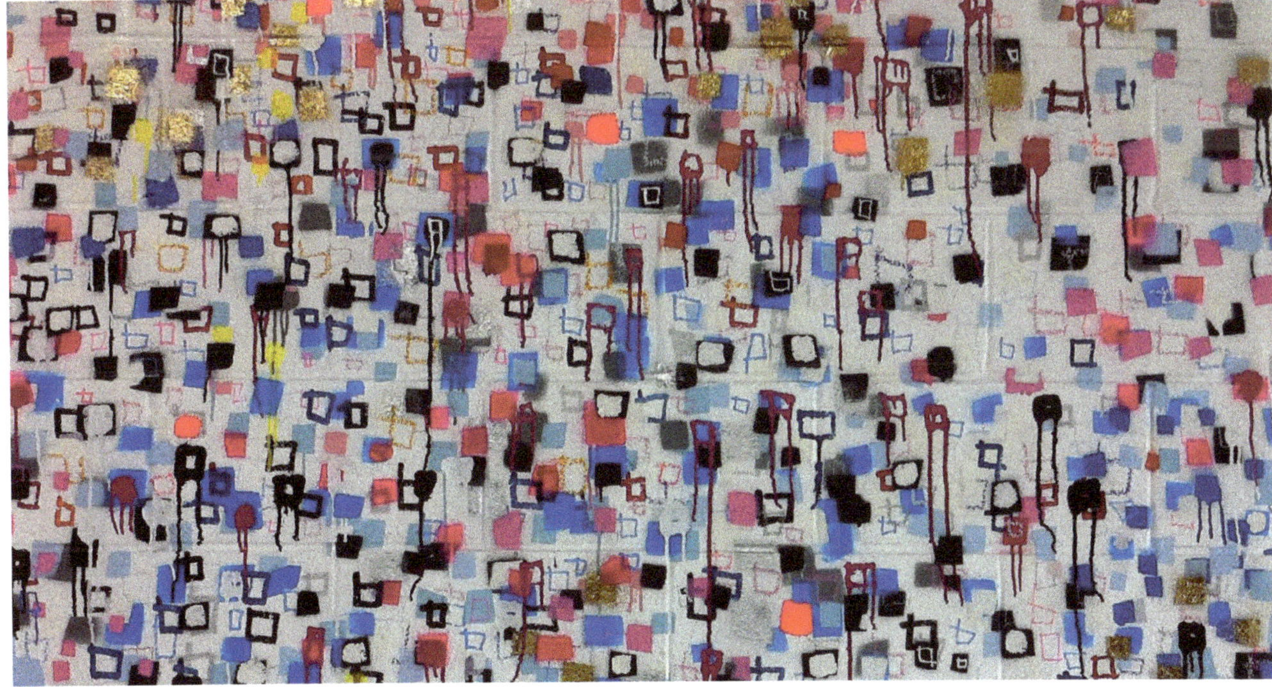

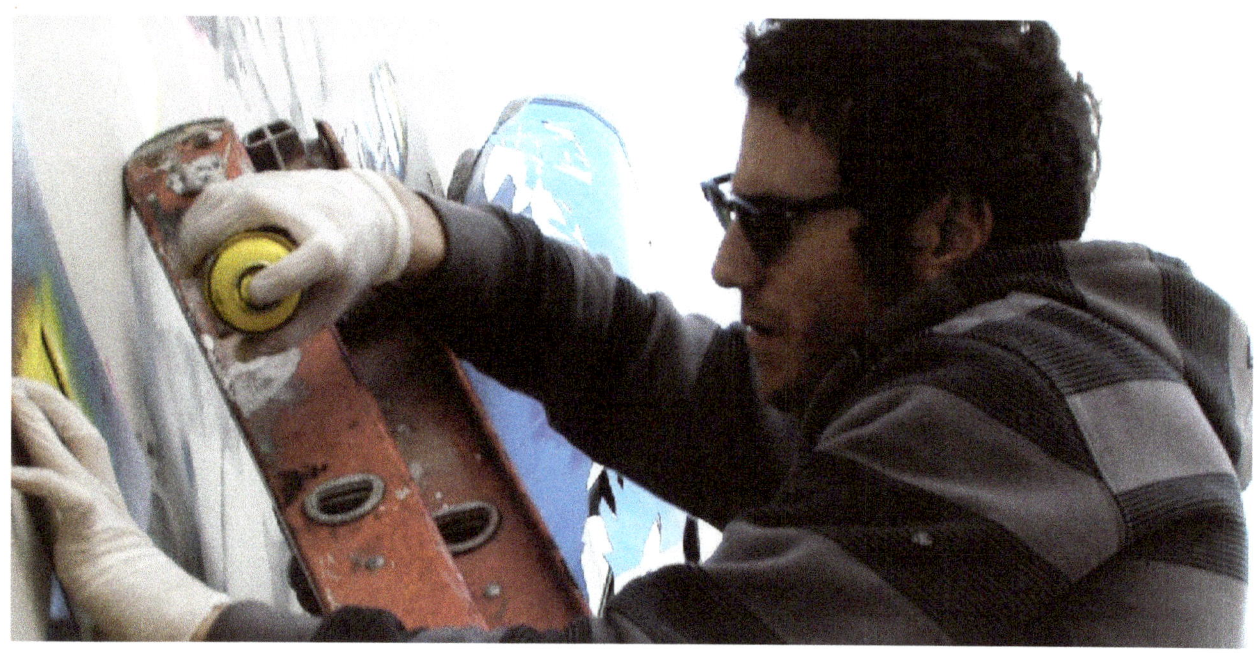

ABOVE: Gregory working on a mural on Melrose (Photo by Joe Glass). BELOW: Another mural at Siren Studios on Sunset, which has collaborated with Gregory on other projects.

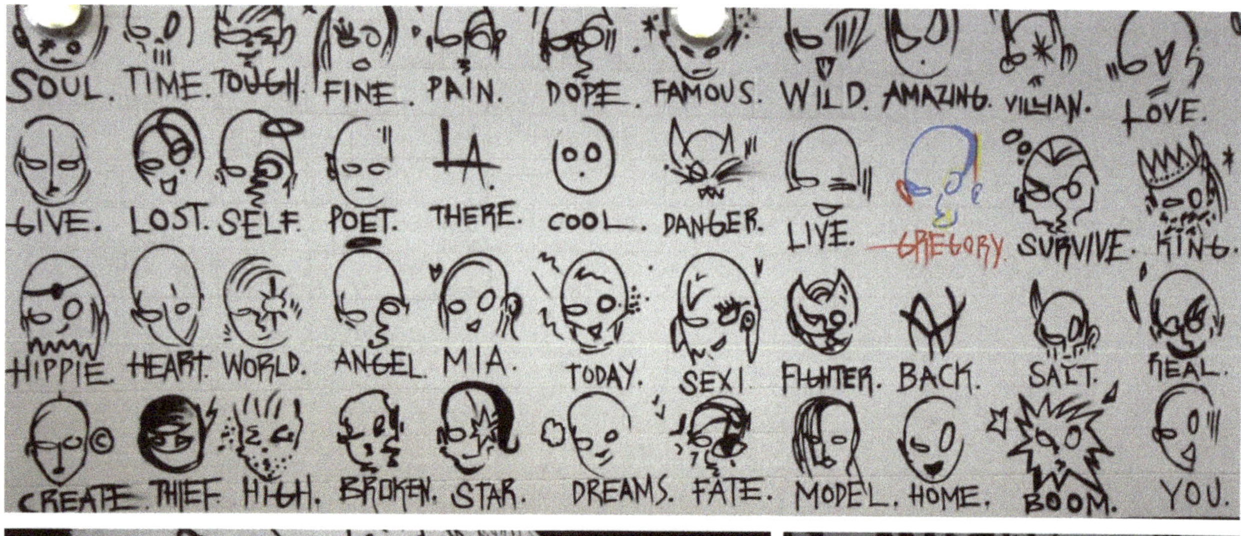

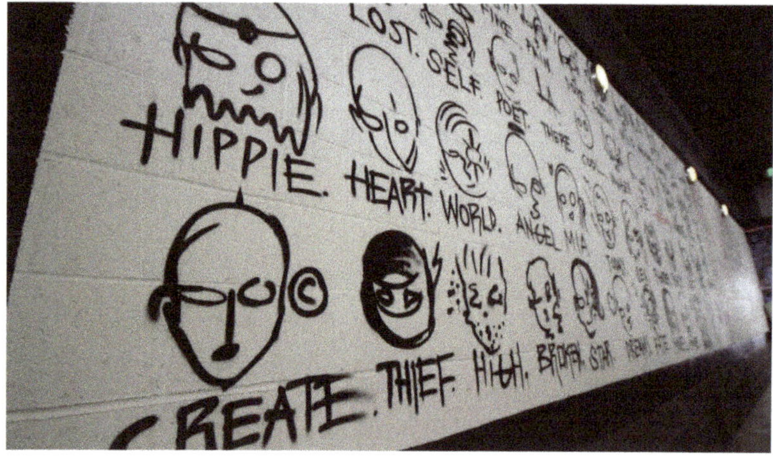

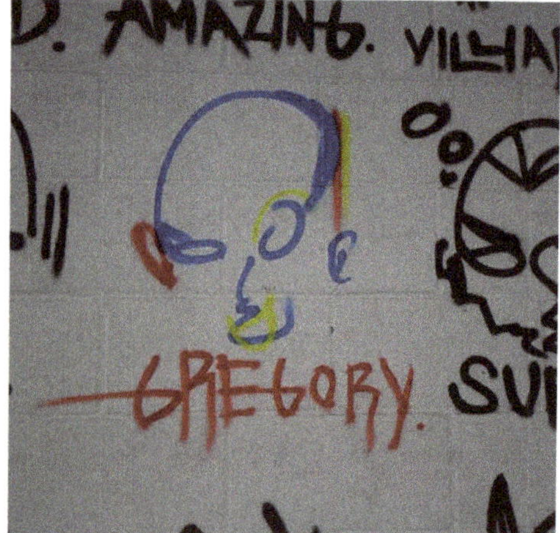

TOOLZ

"Despite all the modes of communication we have today, there is still nothing like the streets to reach people. Why else are we inundated by massive ads up and down each block in this city? If we weren't surrounded by incessant pitches for short-lived TV shows and weight loss solutions, there might not be the same need to retake the urban surfaces through personal messages or adornment. But the more corporatized and impersonal our city starts to look, the more others feel the need to make their mark in a sense of existential defiance and emotional outlet. It's still a form of community beautification.

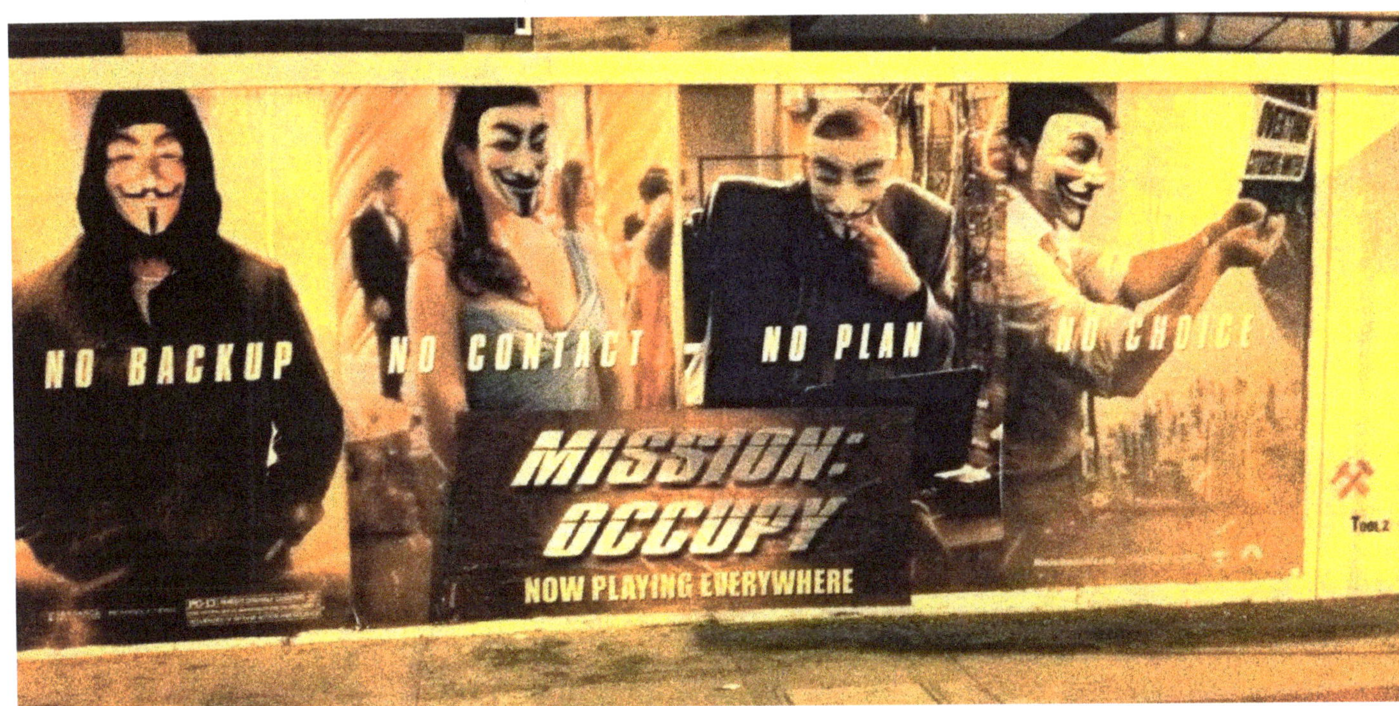

"No Backup, No Contact, No Plan, No Choice: MISSION OCCUPY" — Billboard takeover on Third Street.

"I think most street art stems from that form of alienation from your own landscape. Some people put up the alter ego they aspire to be viewed as, some wear their heart on their sleeve, some just want to be seen, like a YouTube video. I consider what I put up an 'edit' or commentary on that place and time for the viewer, whether it's talking about corruption in Washington, or the L.A. street art scene. Because street art doesn't stay up long before it's buffed or capped, the timeliness of a piece is an added opportunity for impact.

"Still, it's risky. I've been arrested, done clean-up with the Hollywood Beautification Team as community service. I heard even Brainwash has. It's part of the price you pay."

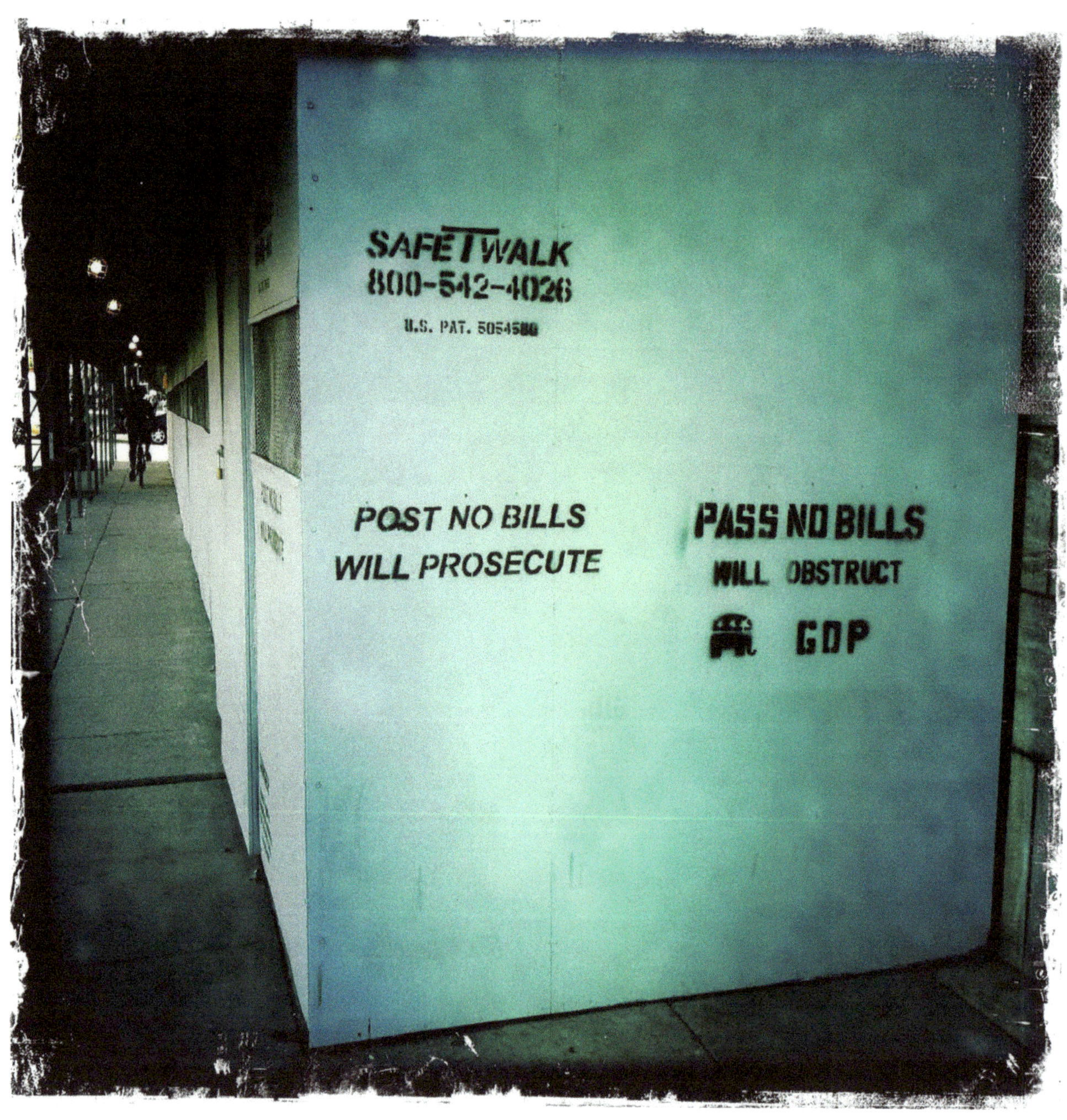

"PASS NO BILLS" – Painted on construction walls during the GOP's "Fiscal Cliff" negotiations, an acknowledgment of the Republican Party using obstructionism as their party platform.

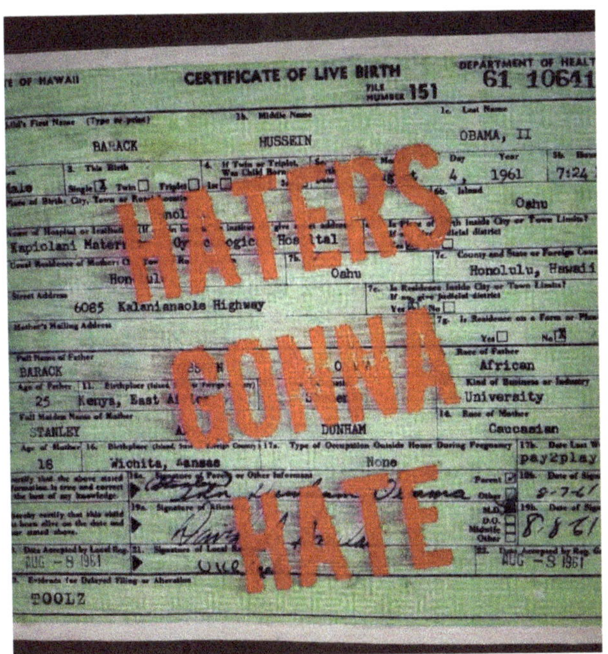

"HATERS GONNA HATE" — *The day after President Obama released his birth certificate, Toolz posted copies, with a lesson learned from birthers. (Melrose)*

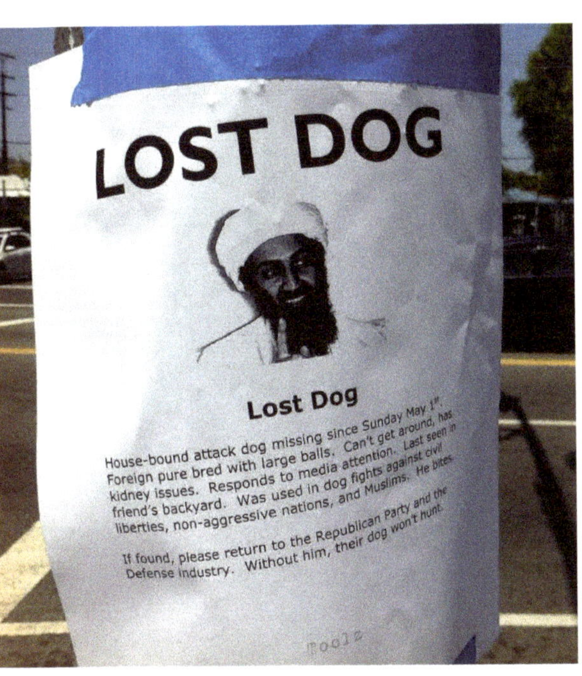

When Osama Bin Laden was killed, Toolz posted this LOST DOG poster saying the GOP's beloved fear-mongering dog could no longer hunt.

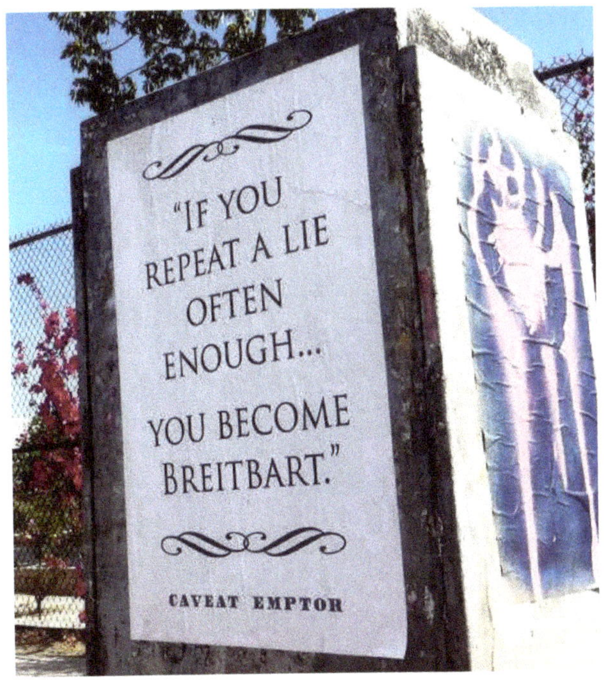

"IF YOU REPEAT A LIE OFTEN ENOUGH... YOU BECOME BREITBART." — Prior to his death, these posters mocked conservative hit man Andrew Breitbart and caused a stir online. (Beverly & Fairfax)

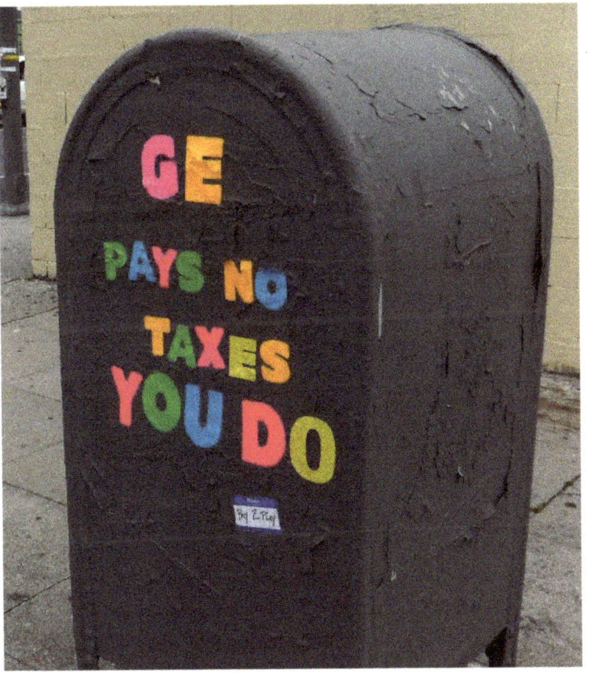

"G.E. PAYS NO TAXES, YOU DO" — Posted on Tax Day, April 15, to raise awareness about how the biggest corporations dodge taxes in the U.S. (Melrose & Spaulding)

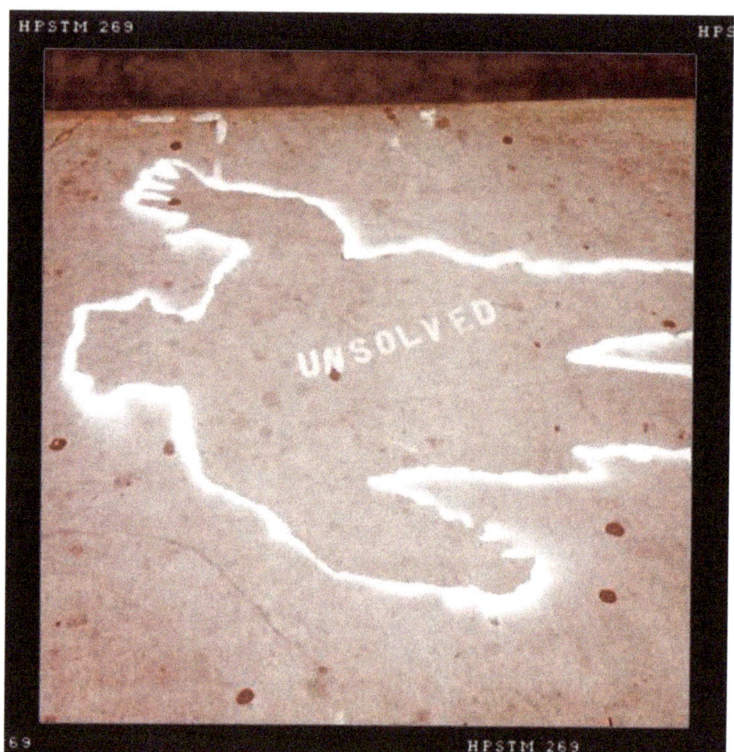

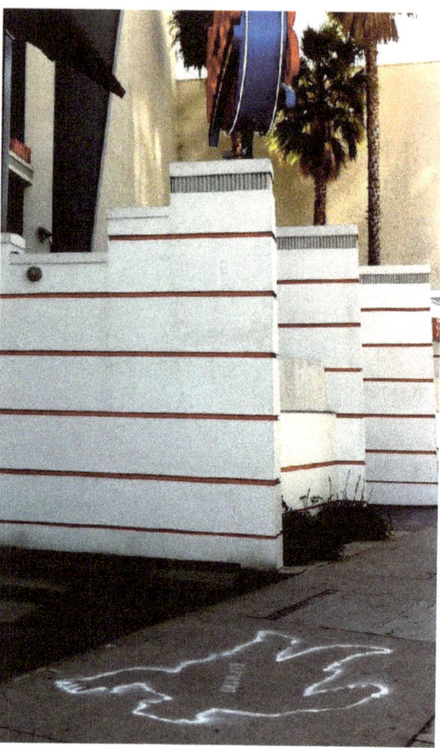

"UNSOLVED: The Murder Scene of Biggie Smalls" — On the 15th Anniversary of Notorious B.I.G.'s death, Toolz marked the spot where Biggie was shot on Fairfax and Wilshire Blvd. The LAPD has yet to solve the case, which purportedly implicates police officers within the department.

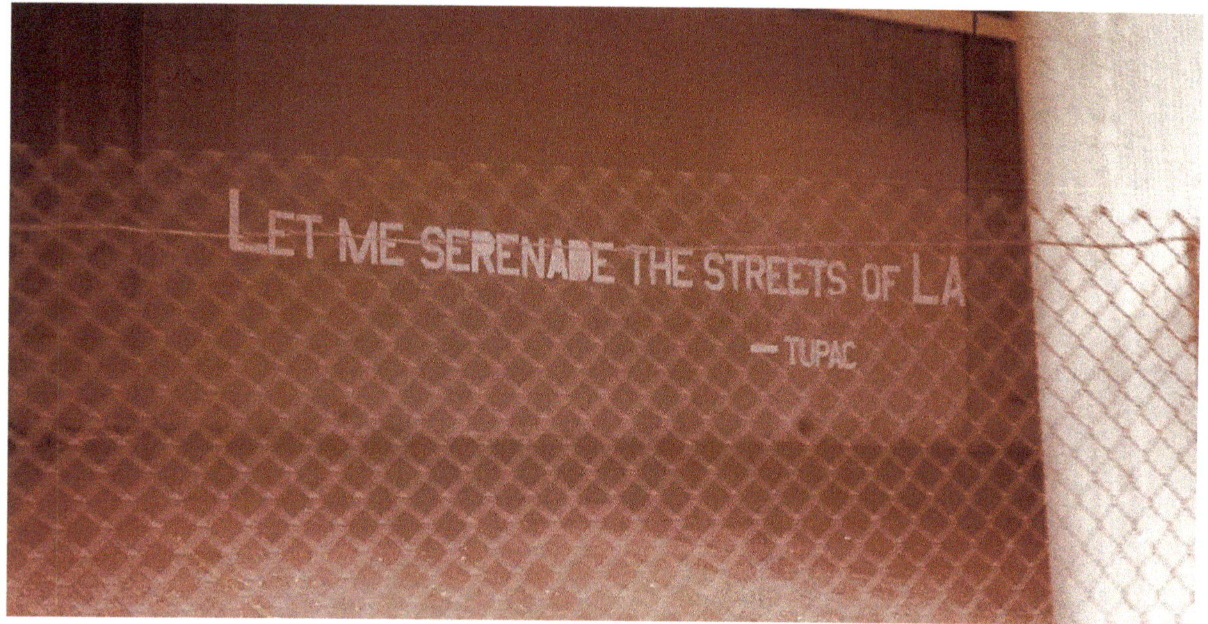

"LET ME SERENADE THE STREETS OF L.A. - Tupac" — A quote from "California Love" by Dr. Dre & Tupac Shakur, applicable to street art as well as hip hop. Under the 101 overpass on Franklin Blvd. in Hollywood.

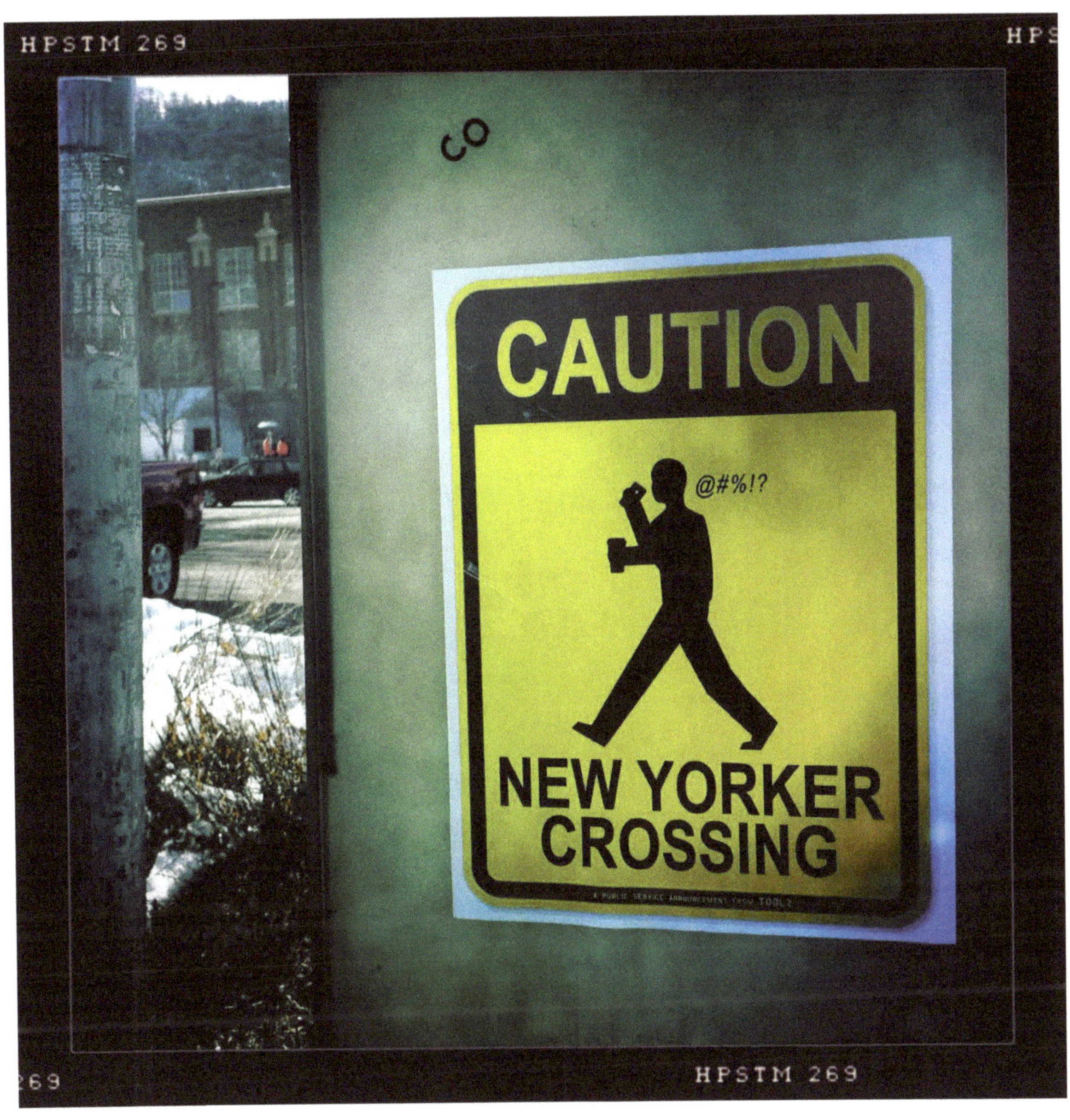

"CAUTION: NEW YORKER CROSSING" — At the Sundance Film Festival in Park City, Utah, this art served as a warning to locals about the influx of New Yorkers.

RON ENGLISH

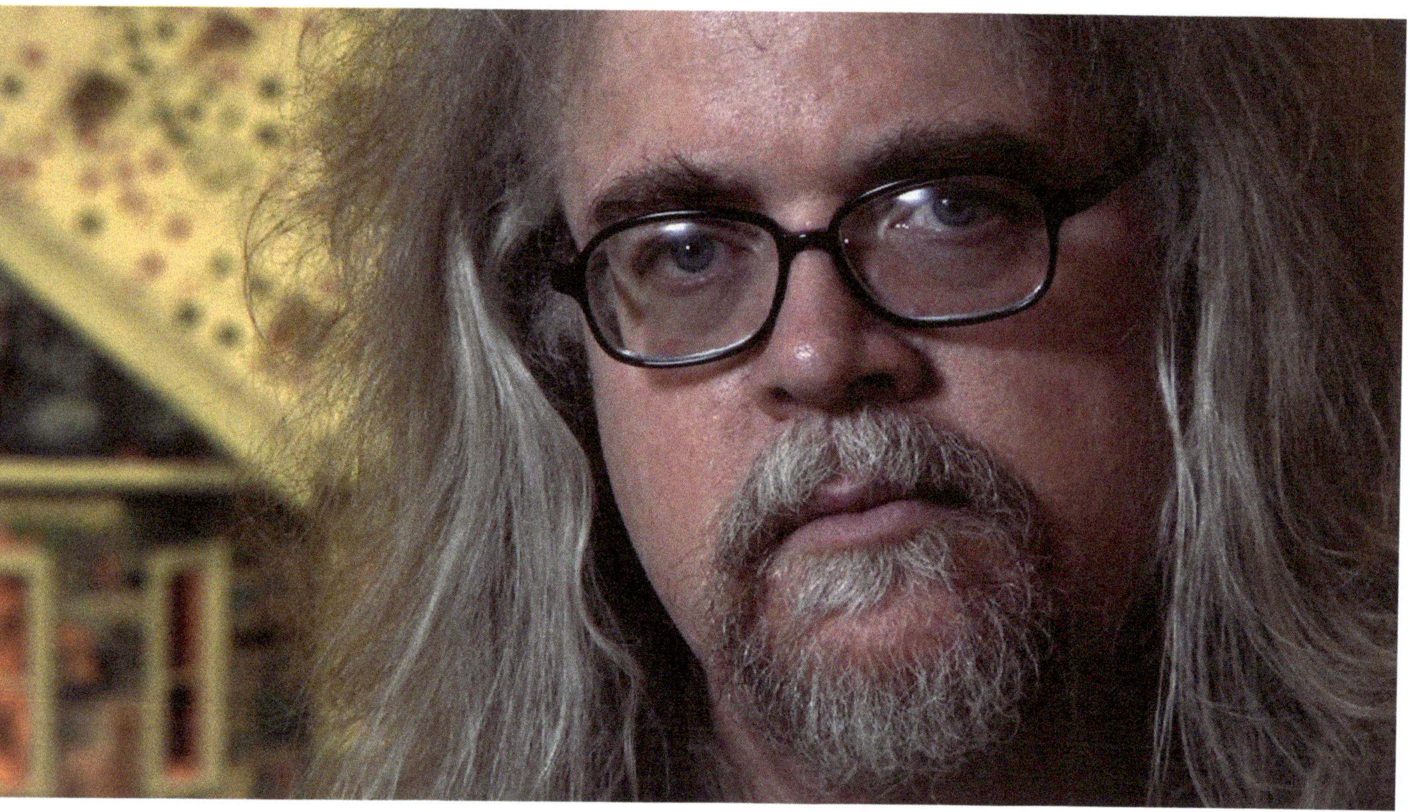

"For the last few years, I have been a part of these really big two movements. One of which is street art, which is insanely big, and pop surrealism, which actually originated out of L.A. where we are now, is the second biggest movement. And the kind of attitude that goes into pop surrealism is a lot more personal, a lot more about being the first generation of media children, and kind of our reaction to having all this media pushed at us and then how it kind of filtered through us and came out as something that was never intended to be.

"The thing that's often misunderstood about pop surrealism is, especially my work, is it seems very cynical, but it's also very embracing, too. It's like we love this stuff, and we hate it. And I think that's confusing to people, because they want you to pick one side or the other, and they don't like if you can see all sides and actually see something of value in all sides.

"One of the big characters I use is Charlie Brown, because you know growing up I was reading the Charlie Brown comic books, and I very closely identified with Charlie Brown, and I was starting to imagine eventually he ceased to be that little boy, and it was the sixties, so he probably would have gotten involved with drugs, or other things would have happened besides his quiet little suburban life as an eight-year-old boy. So I just sort of imagined a bit of that. But he's somebody I've related to my whole life that I very closely identified with. I want to make art that is about my relationship to these characters.

"With me, I became interested in pop art, and I had just moved to New York, so I needed to have some kind of job to support myself. So I was lucky to get a job for Ronnie Cutrone, Andy Warhol's main assistant, and Ronnie was a more fun-loving type of pop artist. So he made me realize that all the pop artists, like, part of what you did was you took some kind of thing from pop culture and appropriated it as your own. He had appropriated Woody Woodpecker and he just adopted that and made it his own.

"So I thought, if I'm going to adopt a character out of pop culture, I should probably adopt the biggest character, so I adopted Mickey Mouse and Marilyn, and I put them together as a mash up, and that became my most iconic image

"But it's kind of like, a thing of taking culture back. Mickey Mouse was supposed to go into public domain. And there's a reason for this stuff to exist, it should only benefit the creator, for the life of the creator, not in perpetuity. It shouldn't benefit Michael Eisner. What happened was, Michael Eisner and Trent Lott waltzed into Congress and got them to change the laws to benefit that corporation, which is a very egregious thing.

For the opening of his new pop surrealism exhibit, Ron English took over the Barracuda Wall on Melrose with a mural of his Popaganda line of satirical comic book covers.

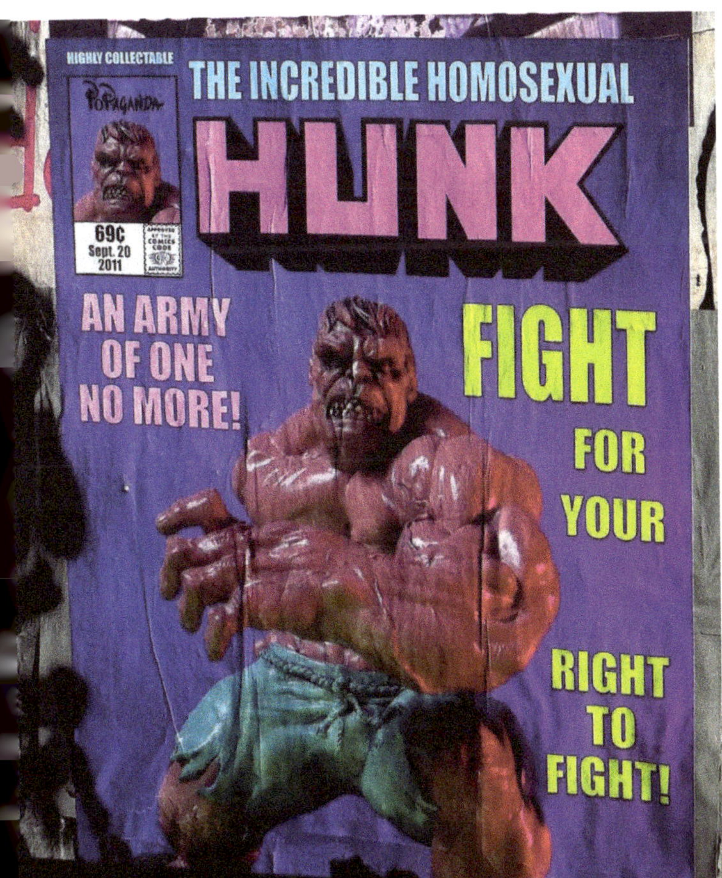

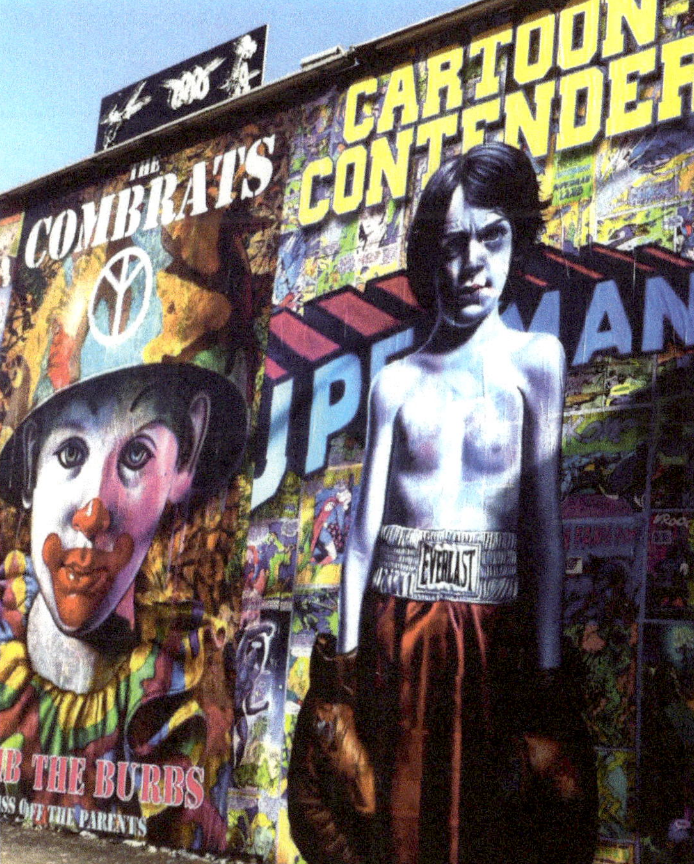

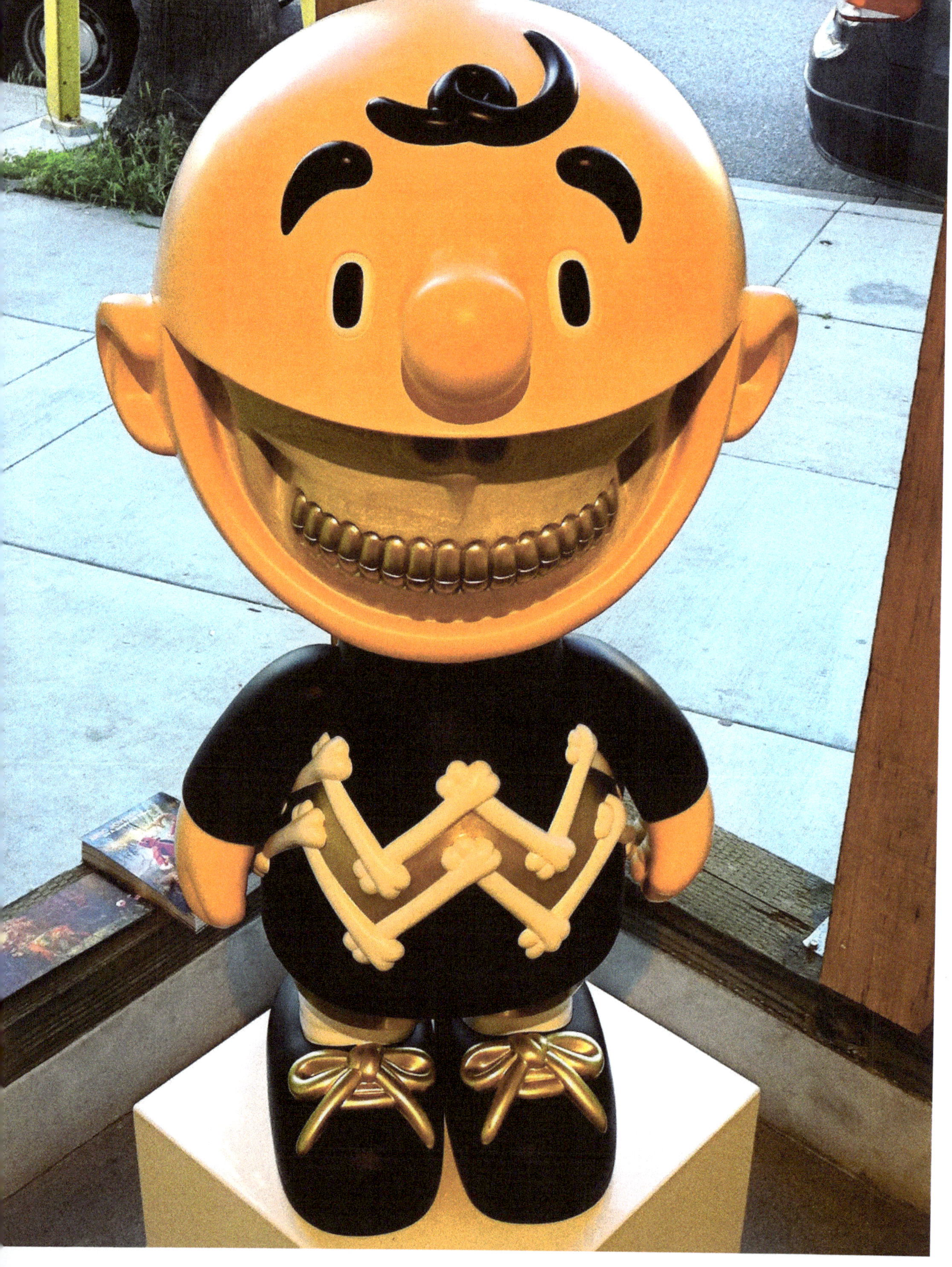

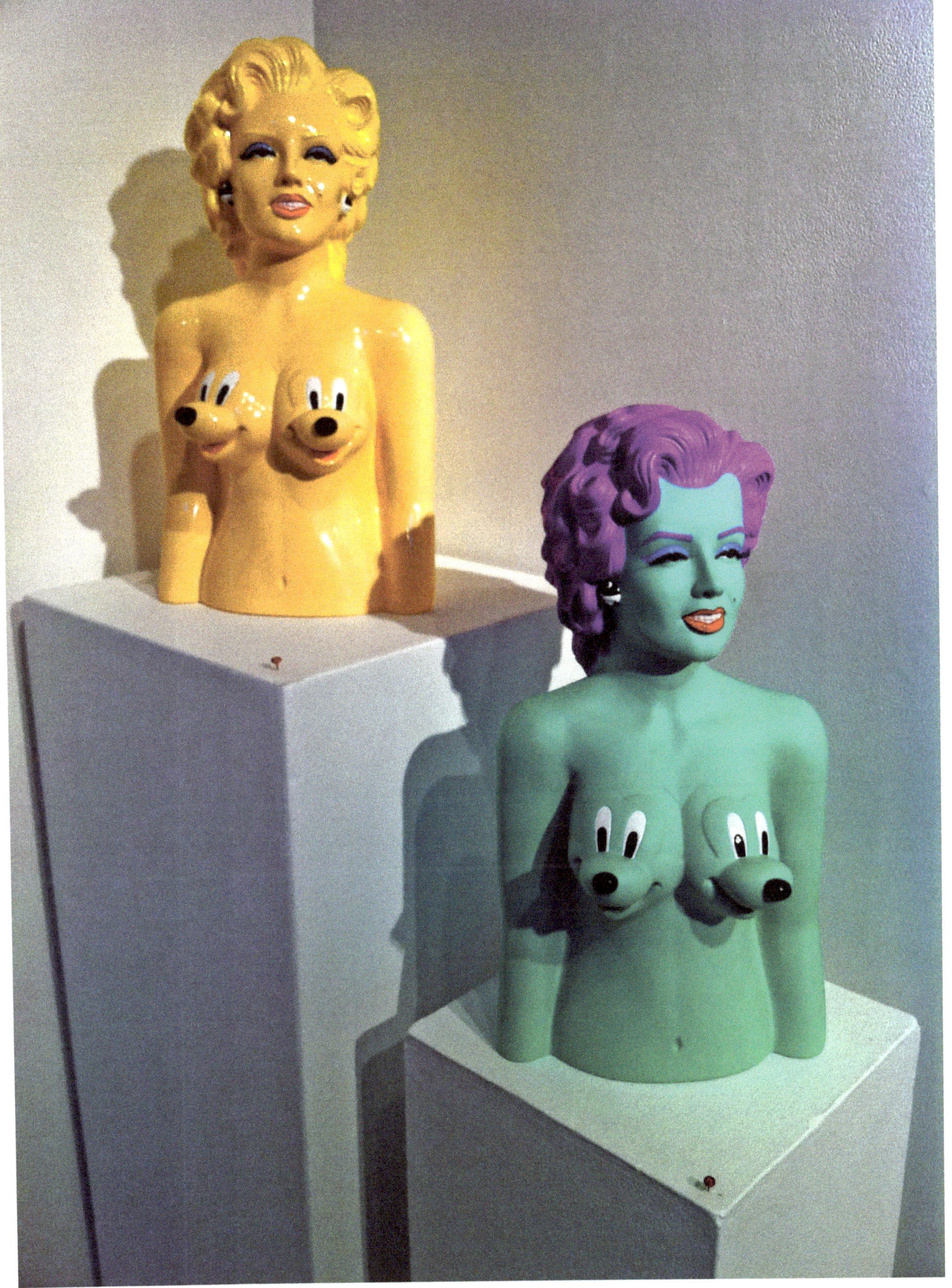

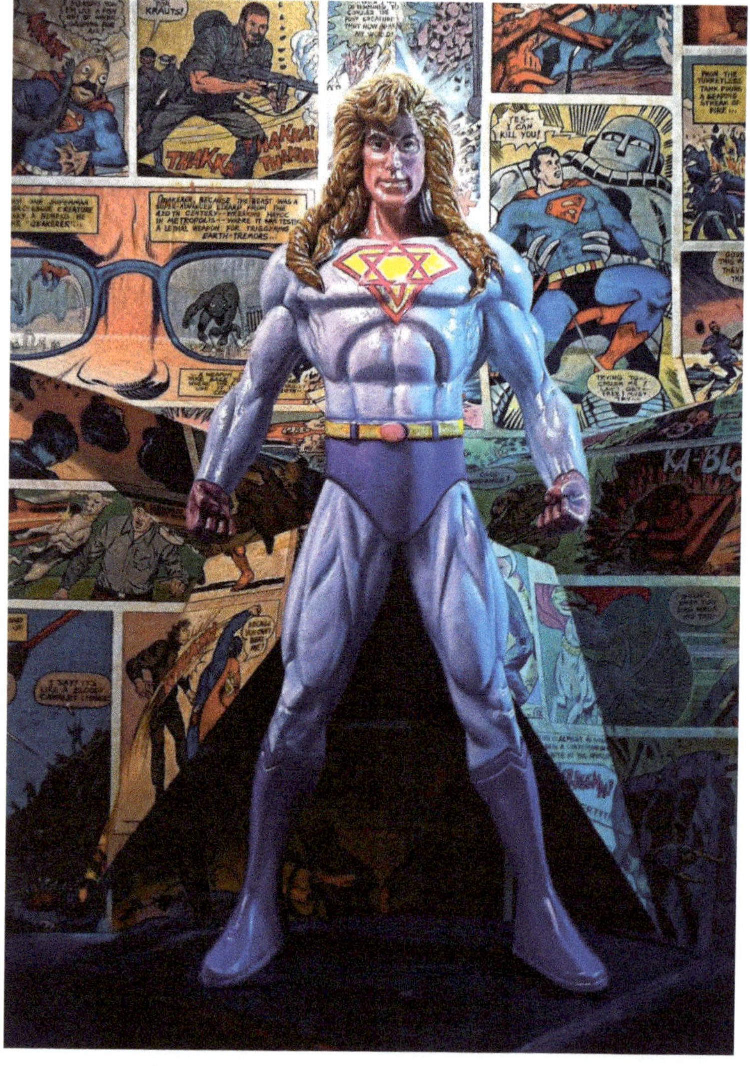

"Even before a work of art is in the public domain, it's open to parody. You can make social commentary using that. What you cannot do is, take an image like Mickey Mouse that's owned by a corporation, put it on a t-shirt because you have warehouse full of t-shirts that nobody's buying, but you know if you squeegee Mickey on there, then people are going to buy it, because they're actually buying this image that they've spent years building up and making into something.

"If I do Mickey crucified, I'm obviously making a statement, and I'm doing something that the Disney Corporation would never do to their mouse. Any reasonable person would understand that this is not something Disney put out. This is a commentary on Disney, and that's something legal. That's actually very important that that's legal. Otherwise, we would be put in a position where we wouldn't be allowed to criticize corporations or government and our society would slowly become more totalitarian."

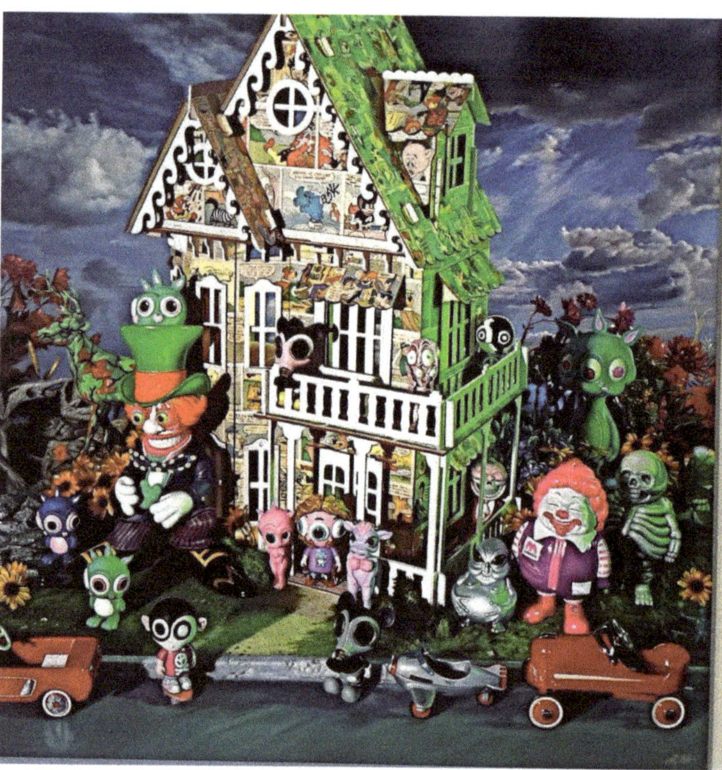

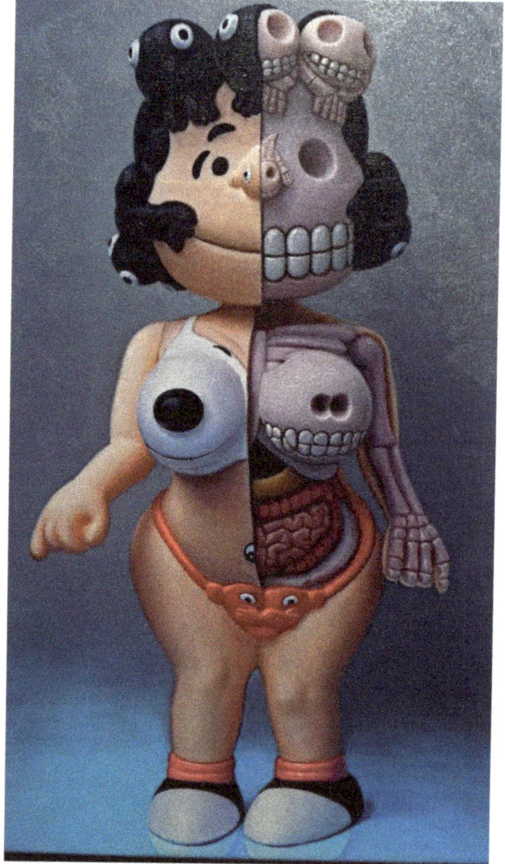

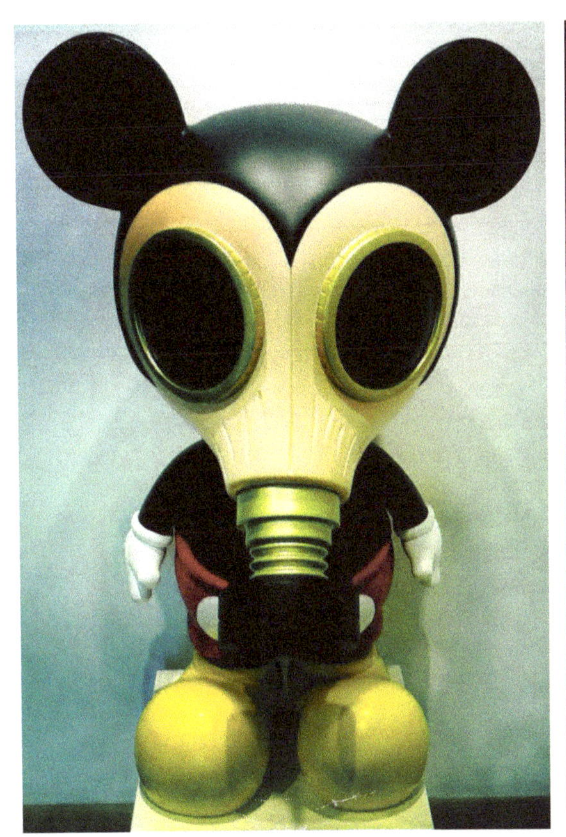

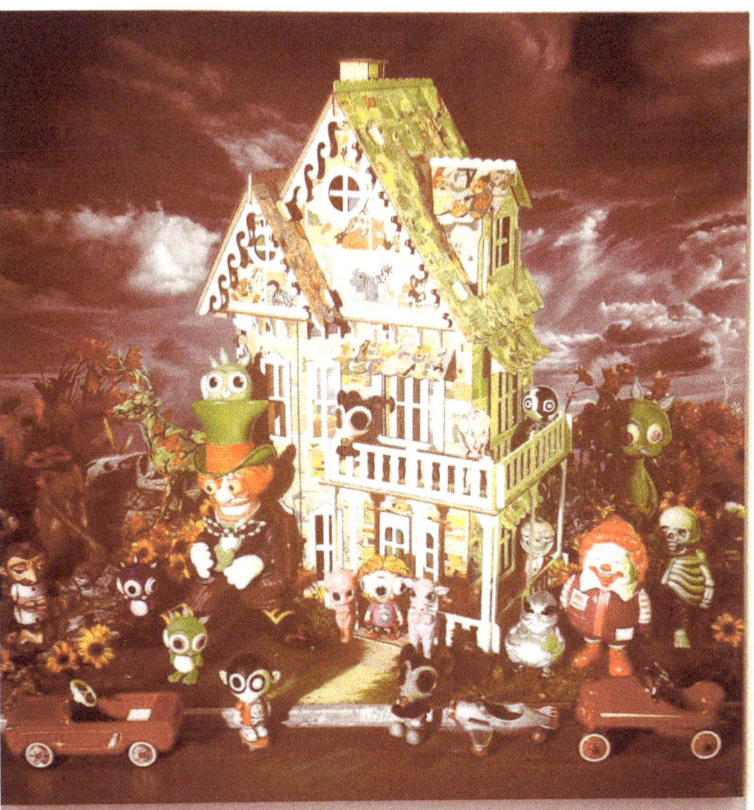

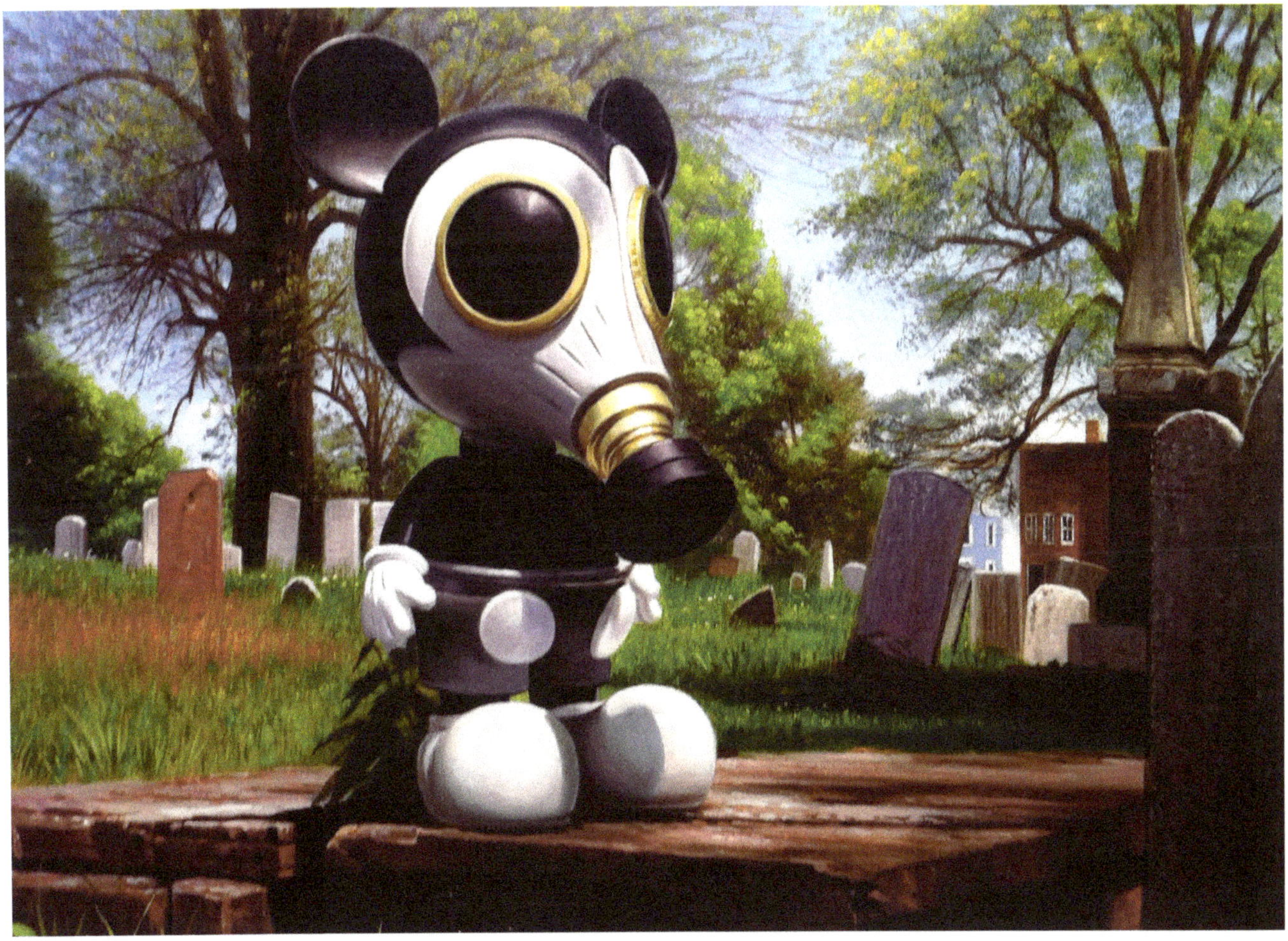

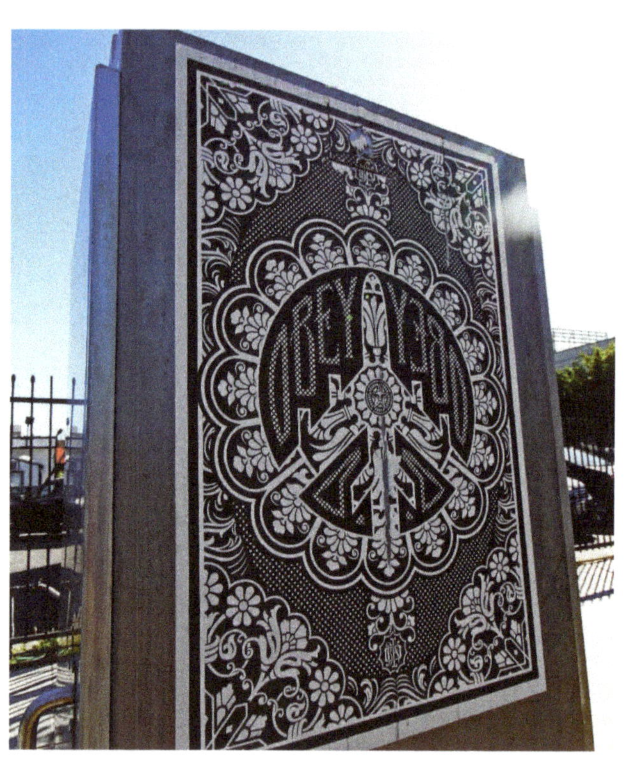

OBEY

Even though his street art stature had brought him mainstream success by this time, Shepard Fairey (a.k.a. OBEY) maintained an impressive output of street artwork making social commentary over this period.

SHEPARD: "I've made the argument for years that street art is one of the few forums for democratizing public speech. A lot of people don't understand how insidious the influence of power and money in politics is.

"The biggest problem is that the powerful rely on most of the American public being uninformed and complacent. Uninformed is actually usually misinformed, because those who control the flow of information often benefit from the info being presented a certain way. Newscasts don't want to bum out advertisers."

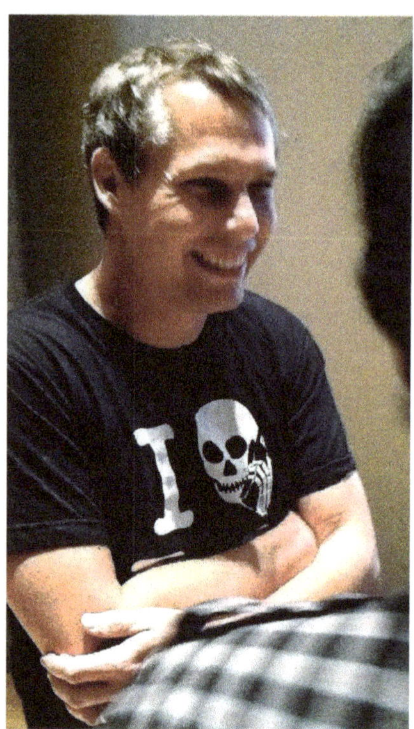

Shepard Fairey, a.k.a. OBEY: "I've been arrested sixteen times."

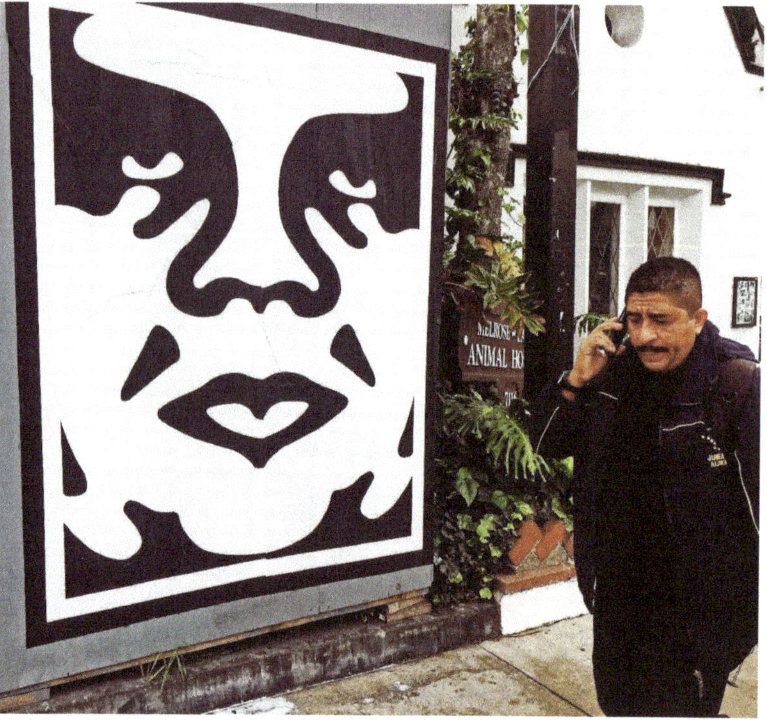

ABOVE: OBEY Peace poster; Andre staring down on Melrose. OPPOSITE: Huge poster of Ronald Reagan, "Legislative Influence For Sale," on Melrose. Seen in PAY 2 PLAY.

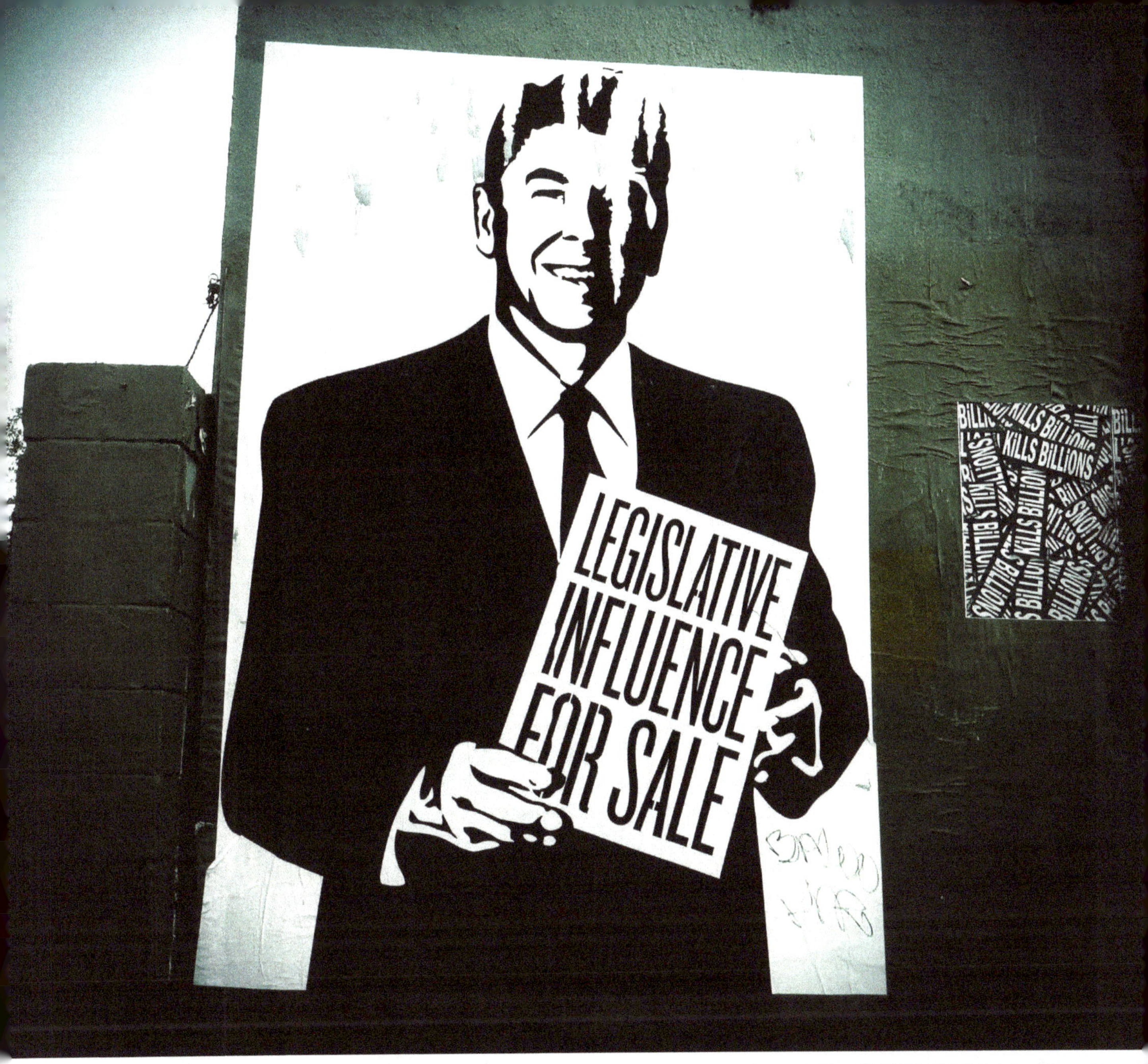

LEGISLATIVE
INFLUENCE
FOR SALE

KILLS BILLIONS

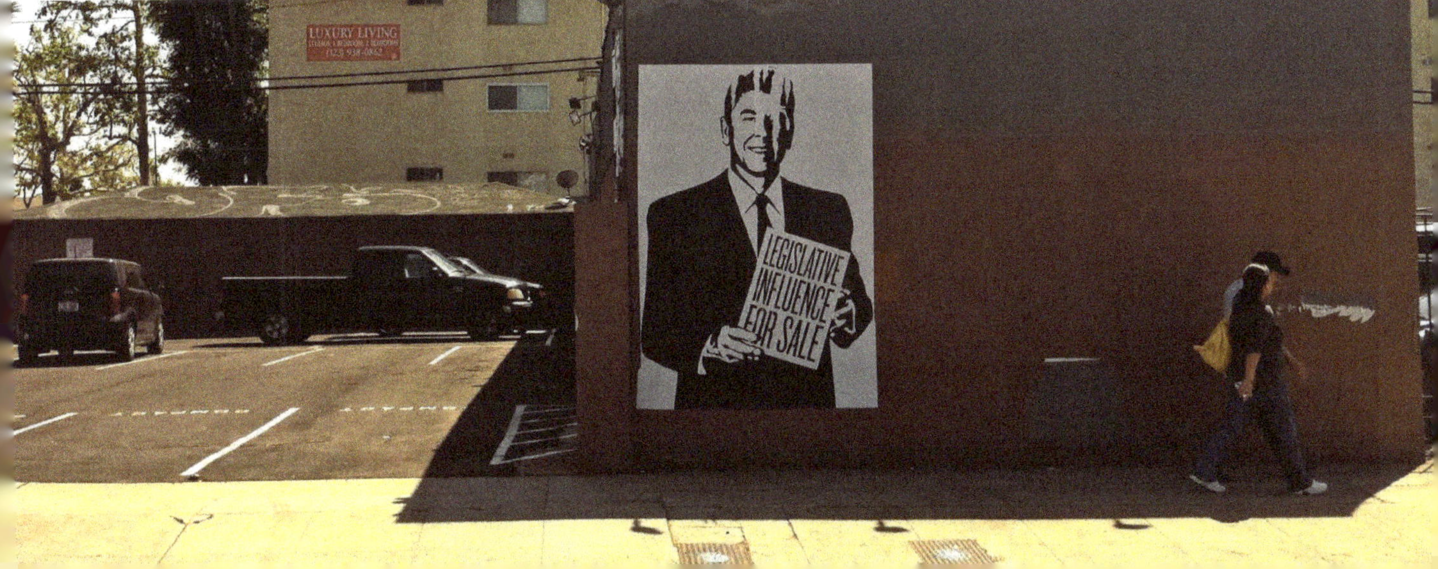

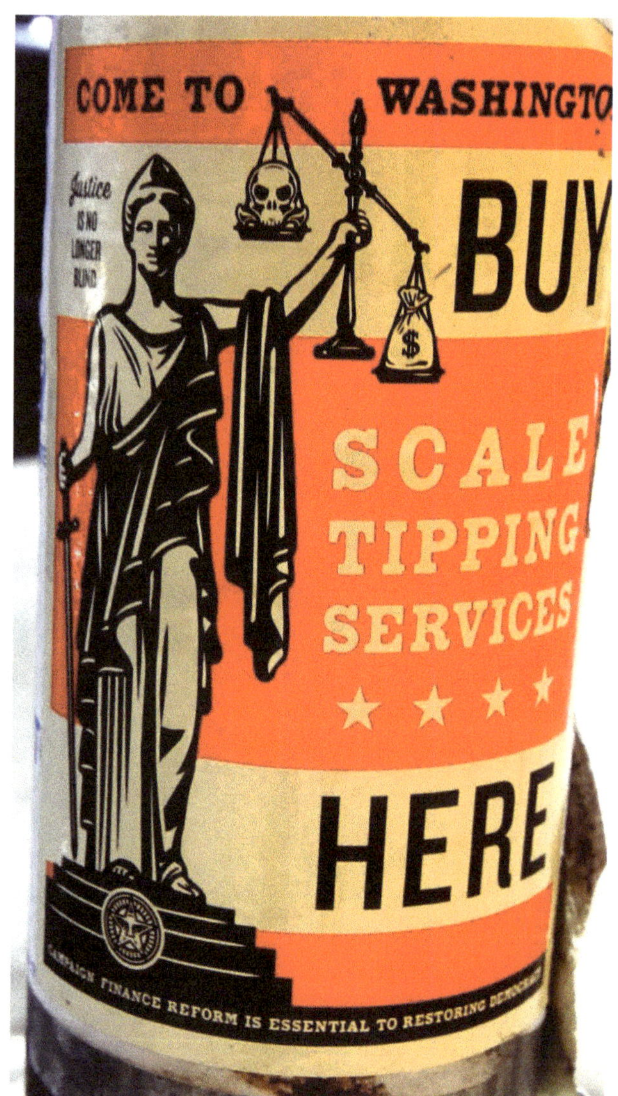

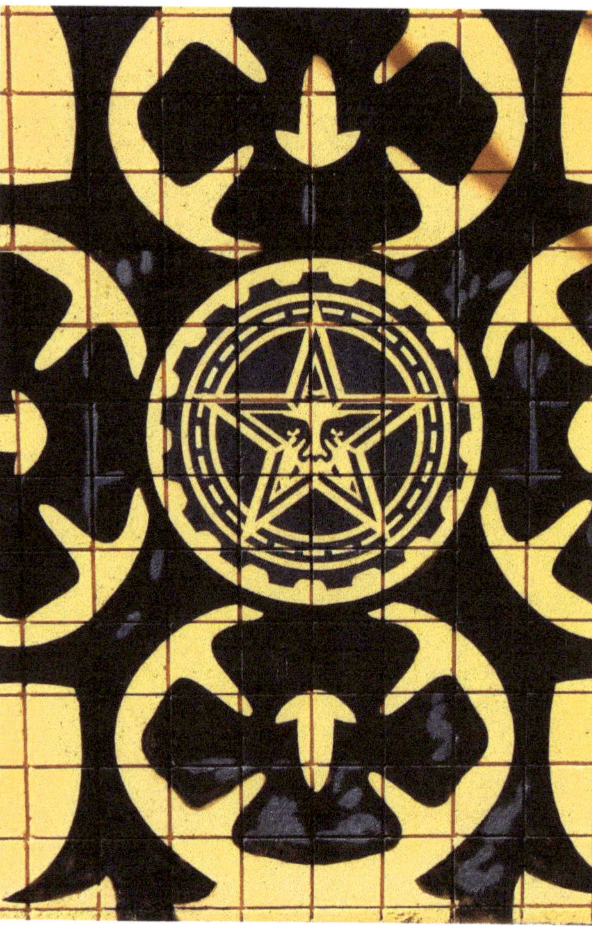

LEFT: Sticker, "Come to Washington, Buy Scale Tipping Services Here—Campaign Finance Reform is Essential to Restoring Democracy." ABOVE, OPPOSITE: OBEY mural on La Brea & 2nd St. BELOW: Andre the Giant poster looking down over Melrose, another on Fairfax.

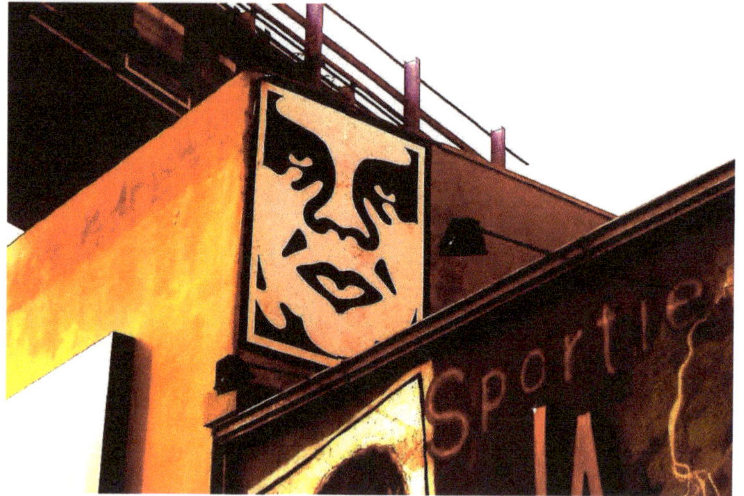

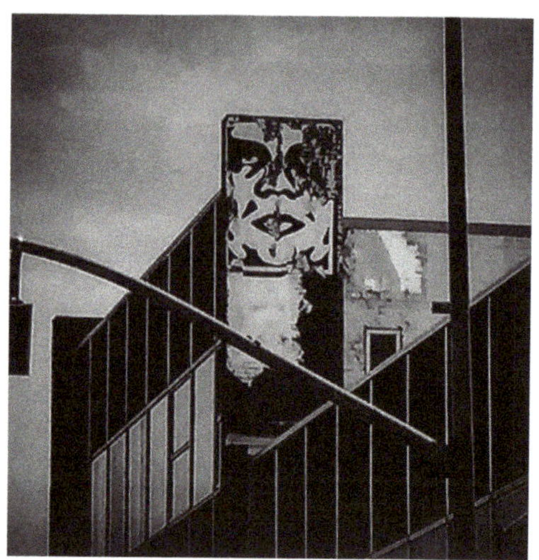

HIGH TIME
PEACE

DOUBLE ISSUE

DECEMBER 26, 2011 / JANUARY 2, 2012

PERSON OF THE YEAR

TIME

THE

PROTESTER

FROM THE ARAB SPRING TO ATHENS, FROM OCCUPY WALL STREET TO MOSCOW

www.time.com

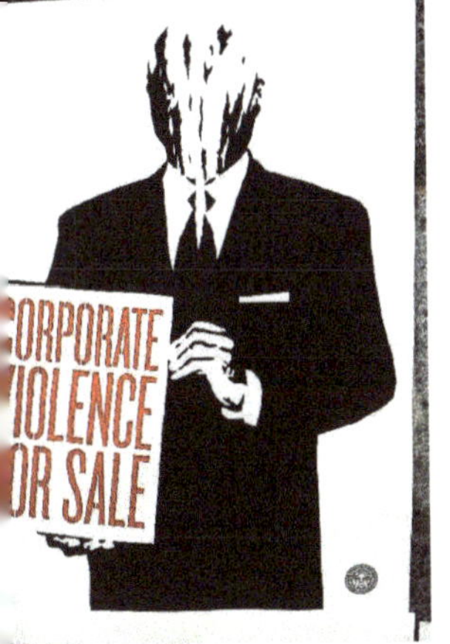

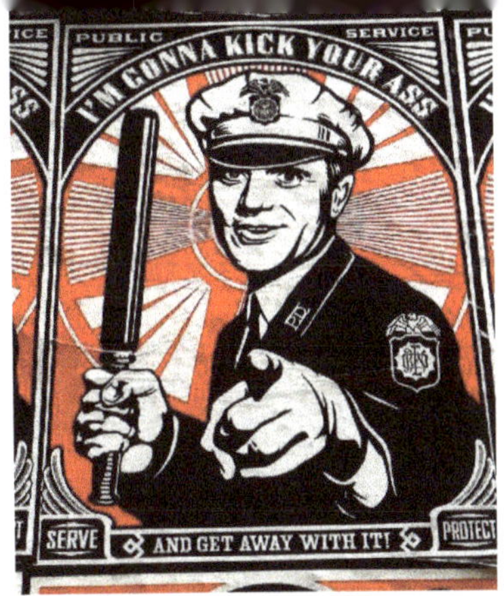

As 2011 proved to be a year of worldwide demonstrations, *TIME* magazine asked Shepard Fairey to design the cover for their annual Person of the Year edition, dedicated to "The Protester." Based on a photo of an Occupy Wall Street protester, the orginial artwork rendition was exhibited in L.A. during the 99% Spring Art Show.

In the summer of 2011, the Non-Toxic Revolution and OBEY released a series of posters and murals illustrating sources of carcinogens that we come into contact with on a daily basis. (*Left*) Commissioned OBEY murals appeared on Melrose on the Barracuda wall as well as an uncommissioned wall of posters adorning City Hall during Occupy Los Angeles *(Top Left)*.

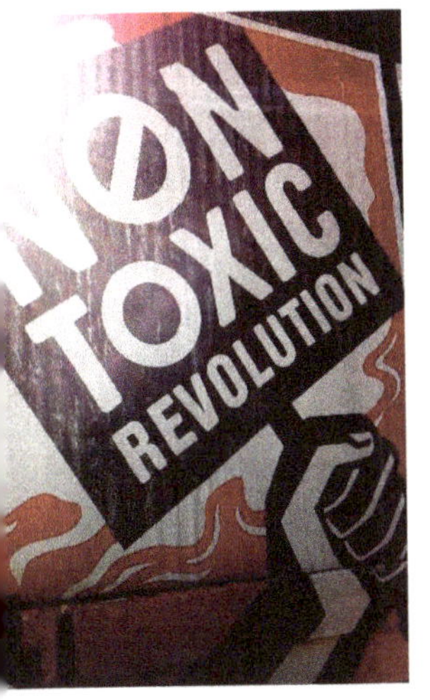

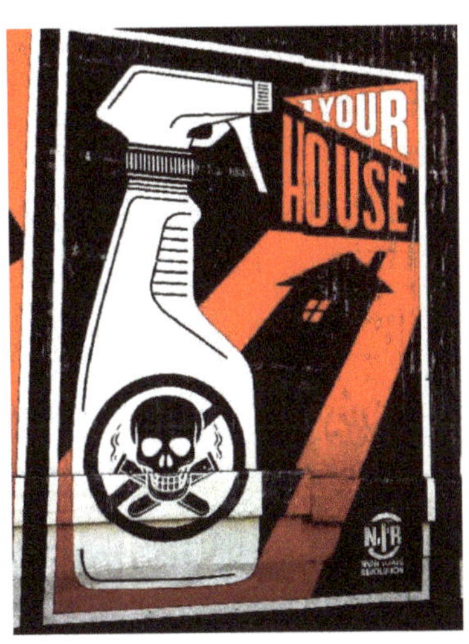

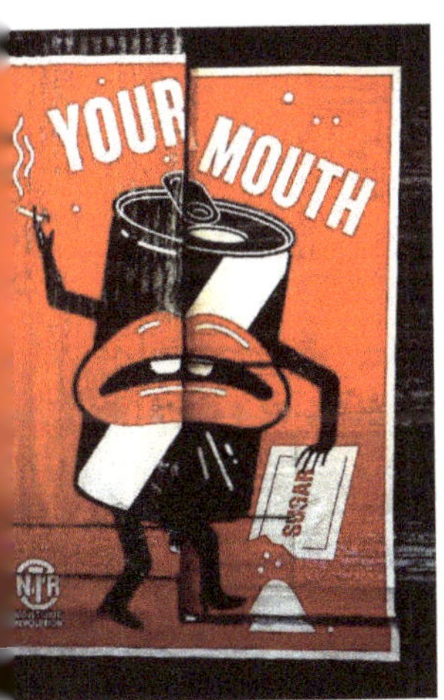

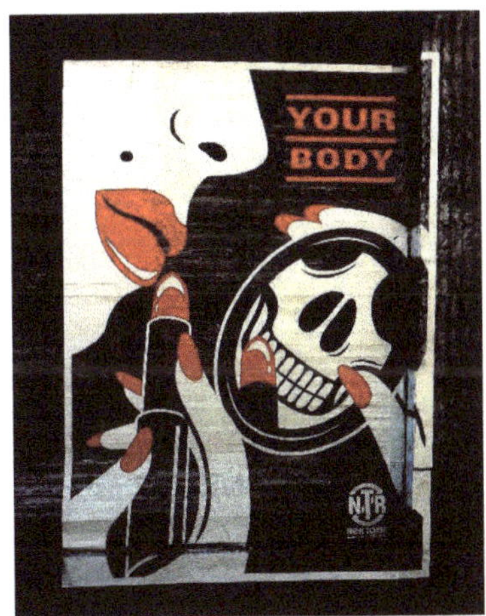

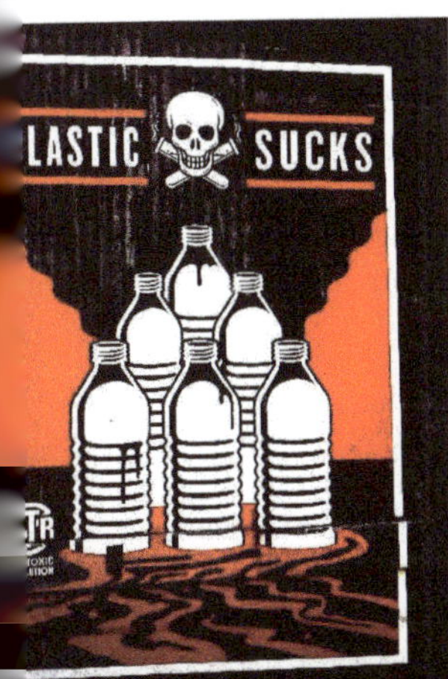

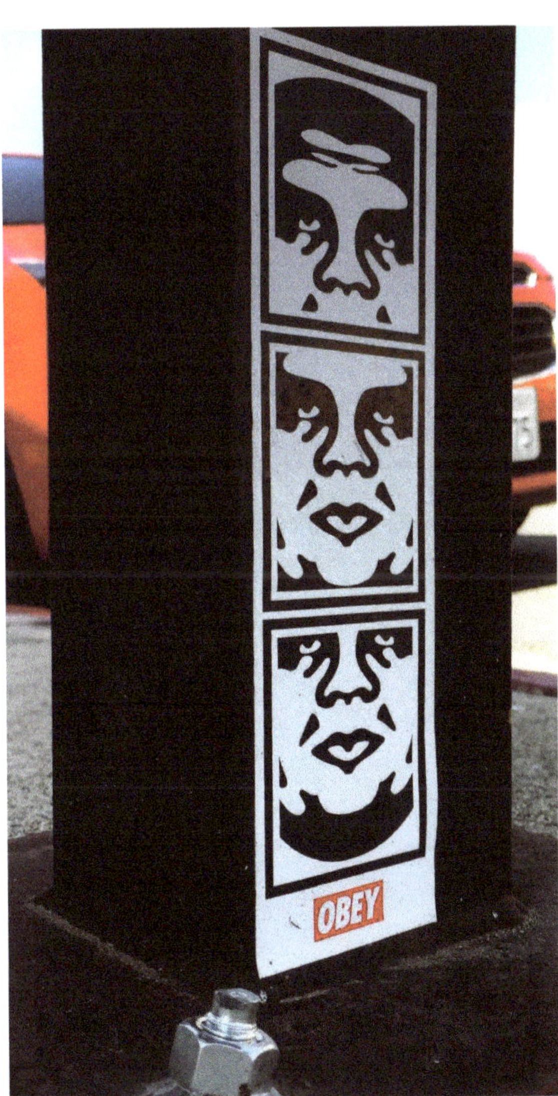

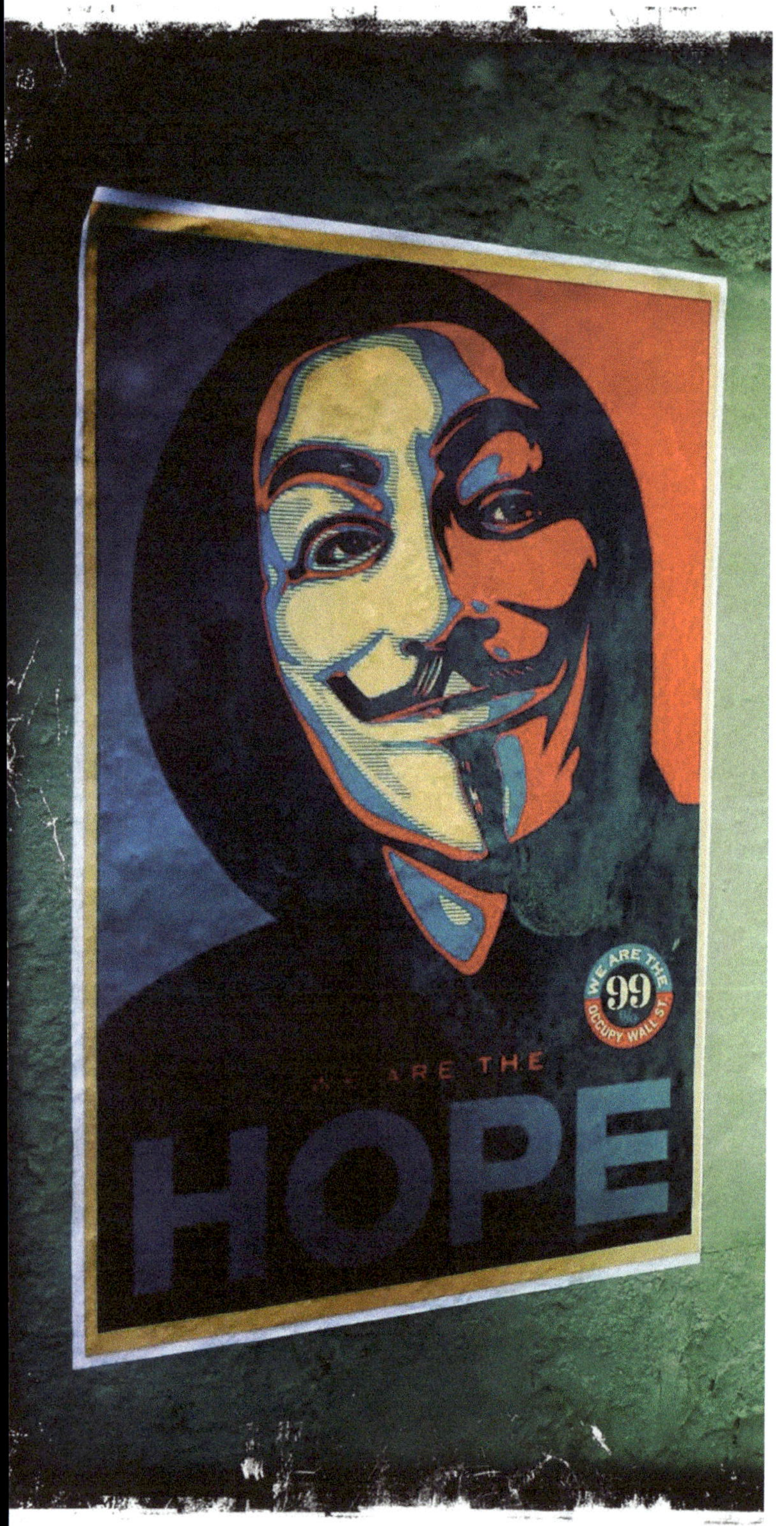

OCCUPY STREET ART

On September 17, 2011, hundreds of people convened on Wall Street to protest that there had been no arrests in the financial meltdown. They hit a nerve—in days, their numbers swelled to thousands. In weeks, there were protests in solidarity across the country and around the world.

No one saw Occupy Wall Street coming. But almost overnight, the national debate had been changed from austerity and reducing deficits to our cash-strapped youth, and the fact that the top 1% owns over 40% of the wealth in America.

At Occupy protests across the country, artwork played a major role in captivating the media and gaining public support. The Guy Fawkes mask that hactivist group Anonymous had adopted as their symbol of vigilance became the face of the movement.

Just as protesters came out from all over to rally, art sprang up across Los Angeles that joined the call for economic justice and supported the protesters, making the Occupy movement feel omnipresent.

In both dissent and art, the streets are the most vital forum.

Shepard Fairey put out this Guy Fawkes mask version of his Obama HOPE poster, reading "WE ARE THE HOPE."

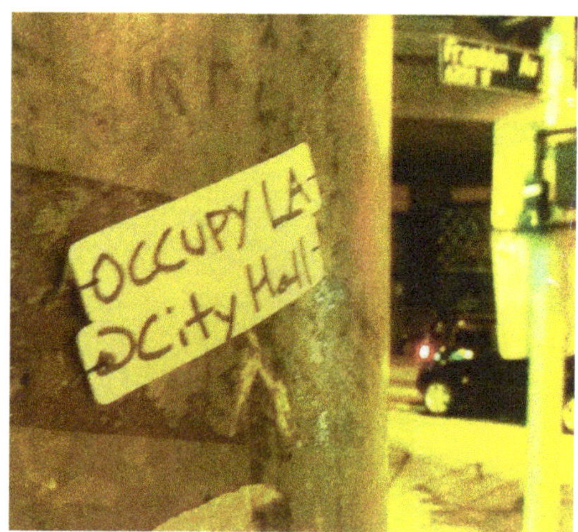

This simple mailing label at Franklin & Argyle directed people to Occupy L.A. at City Hall.

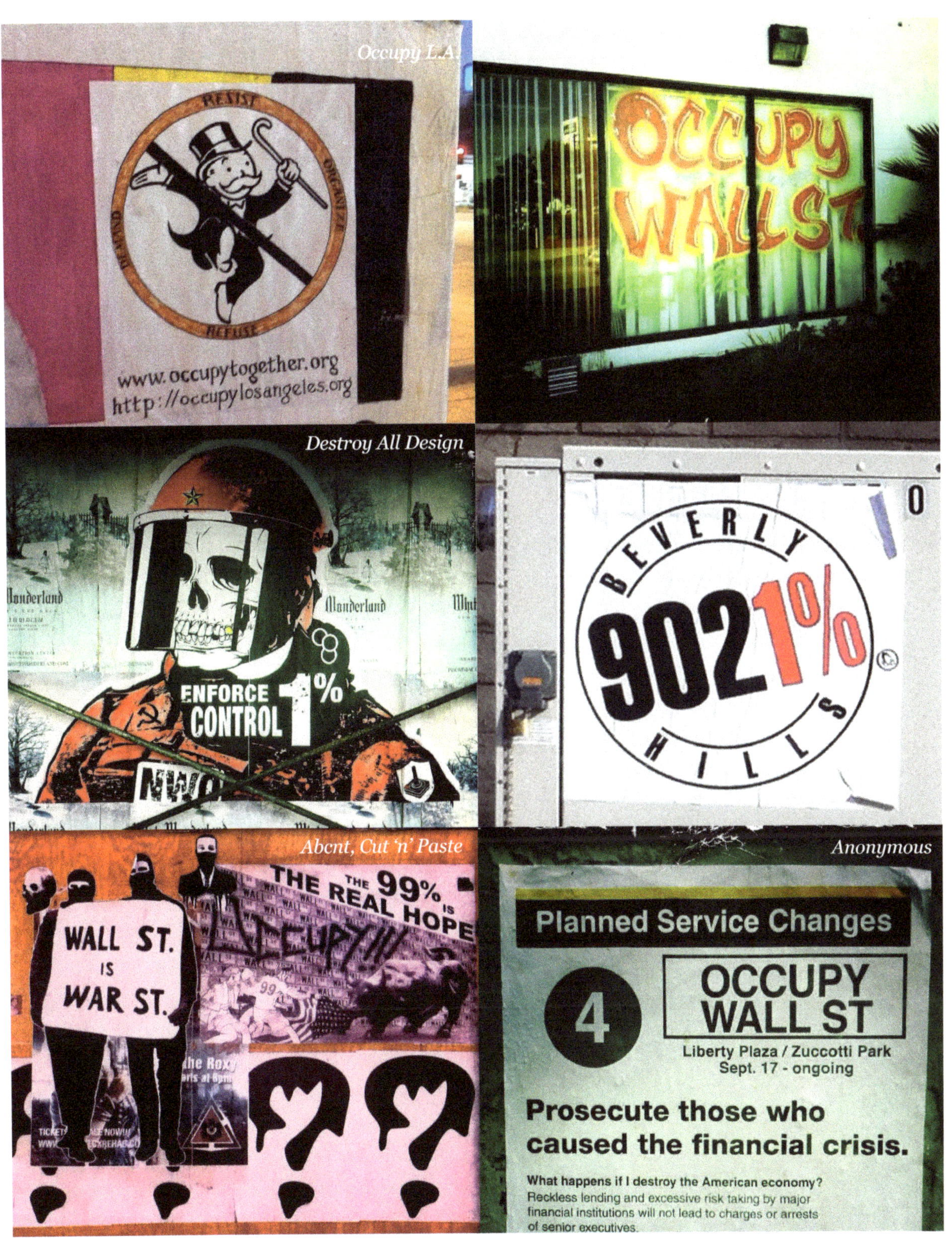

Occupy L.A.

Destroy All Design

Abcnt, Cut 'n' Paste

Anonymous

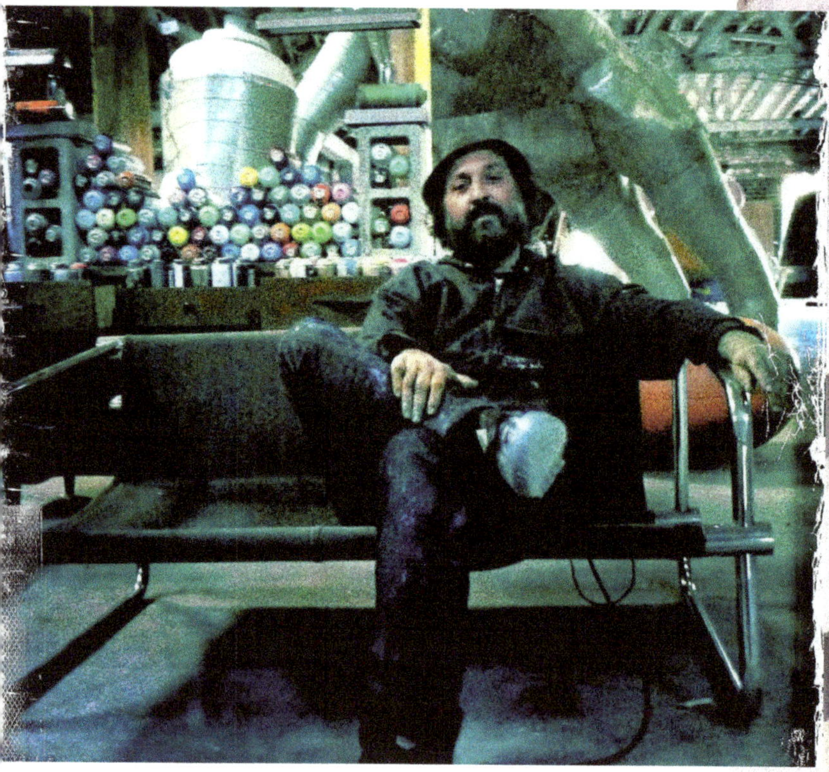

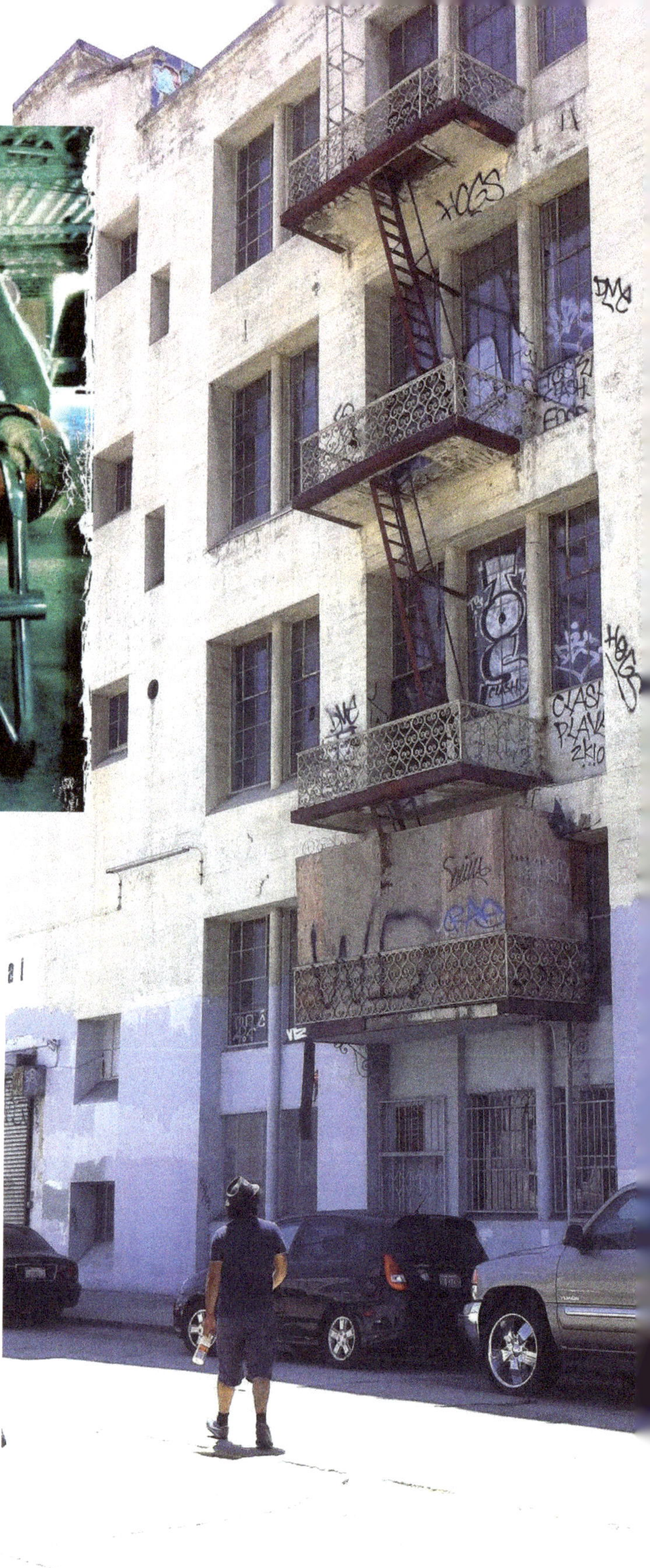

MR. BRAINWASH

"I saw this building, I saw this sign that it was available, and I look at this building, and I said, 'This... this is not even a building, it's like a Russian embassy!' You know, like, it's so big. In the middle of the city. The building, for me, it has a soul. You know, it is an art himself. The space was abandoned for many years, I guess, and when I came in I was excited and I did the deal, and I rent it for six, seven months, you know?

"I had this idea and I look at this space, and I feel like, 'It's really big,' you know? I was like, I have to share a little bit, you know? It's not about always ourself. It's about trying to do something for others. So I went to a room and I said, 'You know what? It will be cool, I invite many people to come, I donate like 20,000 square feet to all the artists who would like to be part of it.

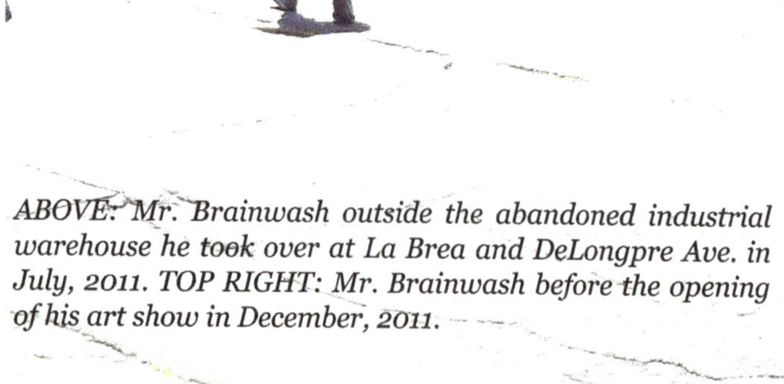

ABOVE: Mr. Brainwash outside the abandoned industrial warehouse he took over at La Brea and DeLongpre Ave. in July, 2011. TOP RIGHT: Mr. Brainwash before the opening of his art show in December, 2011.

"And that's what happened, a couple months ago, I invited people, before I started the show, to be able to come and do some stuff. I felt good about being with all these artists. What was cool about it, it was artists from everything, it was like little kid who was five years old, a grandmother I saw that was seventy years old, she did her first paste. Kind of cool to see all this energy of people having fun.

"It's all about putting everybody on the same level, in a way. It's like everyone is an artist, a good one, a bad one, there is no bad artist. Everybody is good. We are not here to judge people's art. We are here to enjoy it. That's all it is. Art is freedom.

"We are not a judge of art. We just accept it. Like I'm supporting, I'm here, you know? I'm here. I get accepted, I get don't accepted, but I'm trying to do something. I'm trying to do something. It's not like I'm trying to be on the corner and talk about people, I'm trying, I'm trying, I'm just trying.

"What it is, I'm enjoying a show in LA now and maybe you won't [see] me having a show for the next five years in LA. That's it. I might do it in Russia; I might do it in Italy; I might do it in different country. At this time I am doing it here. Because I am a support, I am with them, you know?

"And I decide to do a show here, so I change many dates, I said I'm gonna do this date, and I change, and this date, and I change. Because of what happened, I really had to work with the city to make it happen. It's like, you need a fire, they ask you a LOT, you know? And it took a very long time. Like almost six months, six to seven months. And at the end I was gonna give up."

"And I guess the city permitted me last Monday to be able to do a show. So I'm like: now what do I do? Now I have it in my hand. After a couple months I have it in my hand. What do I do?"

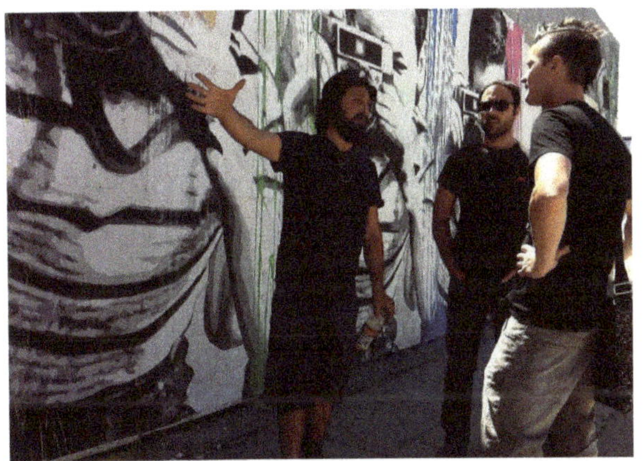

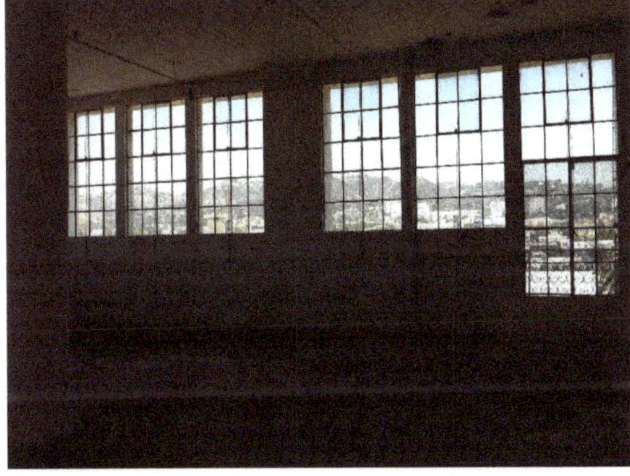

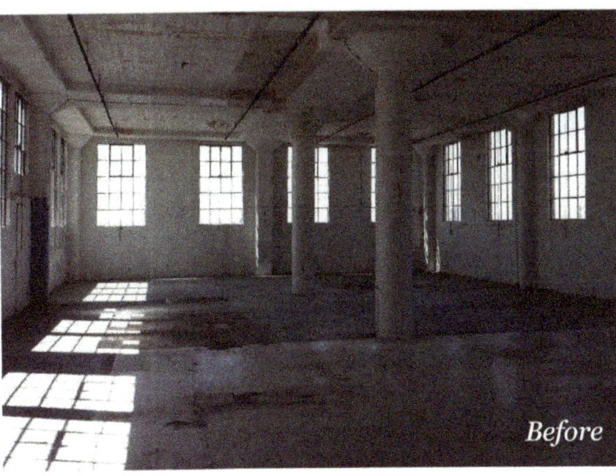

Before

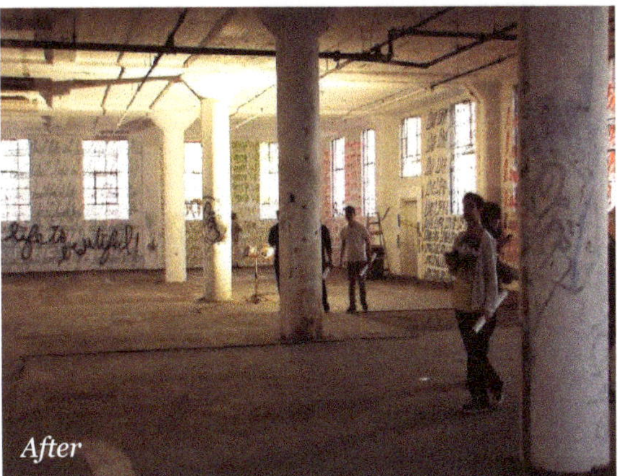

After

"And I'm trying to put the show together. I decide to do it. To see if I could make it happen. I guess it was very hard to make it happen. But when you really want something in life, you, you make it happen, and it'll happen. I believe that nothing is impossible. Everything's possible.

"I'm a person who has an open heart. Even if something does, somebody who does something bad to me, it's not like I'm going to close the door on him forever. I'm not like that. It doesn't matter. You grow up, you change, you know, there's things in life, and it's part of life.

"I believe that art is something that should be enjoyed, and if you don't like it, just let it go."

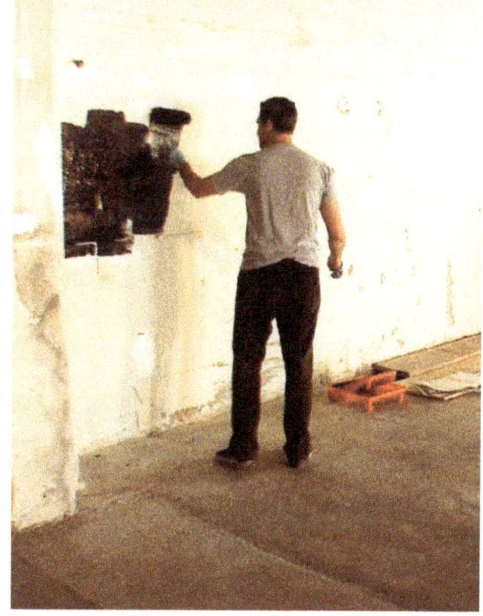

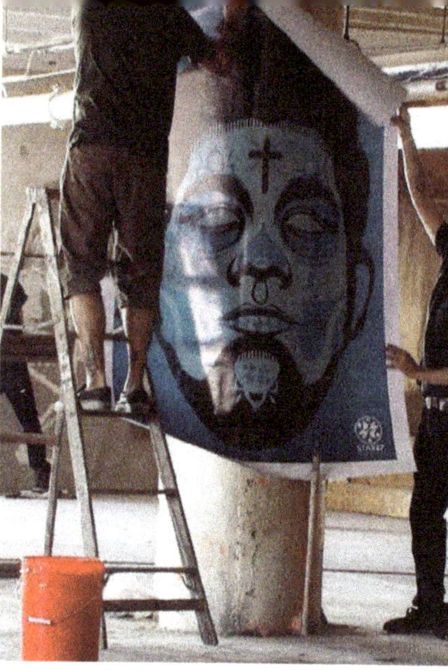

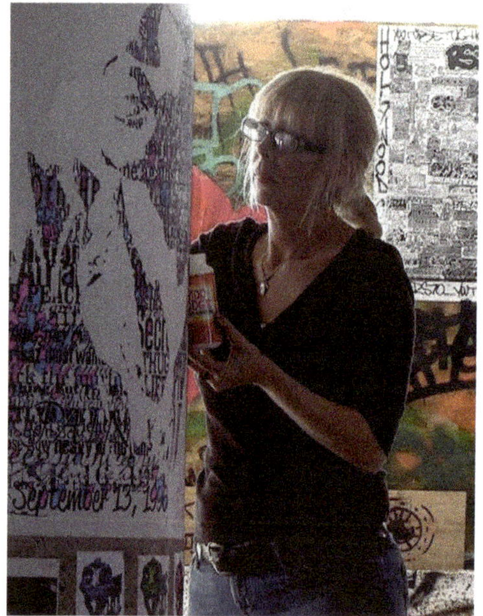

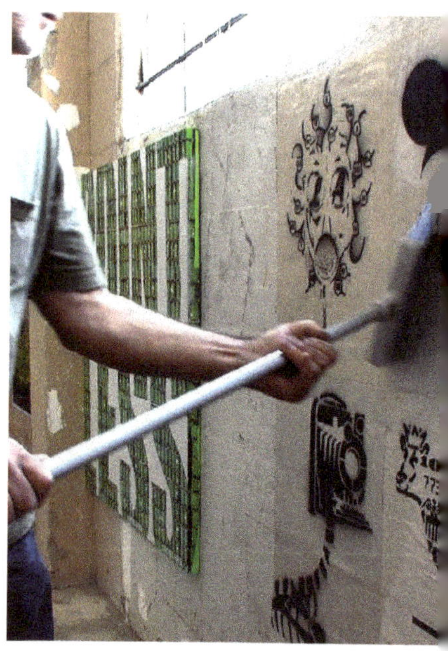

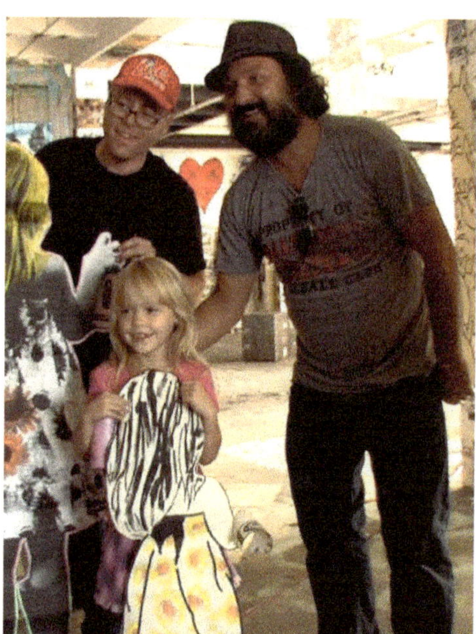

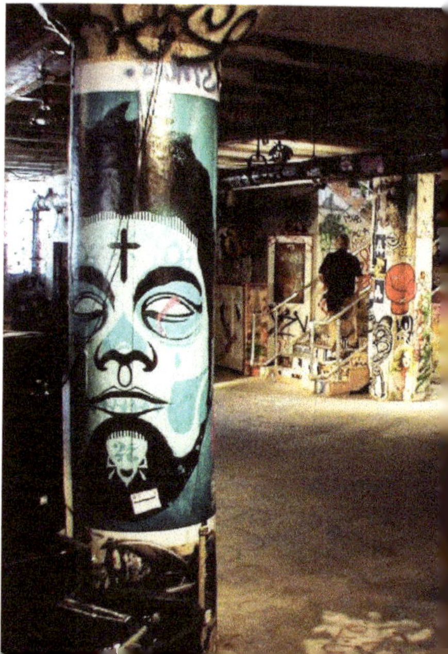

LEFT TO RIGHT, FROM TOP: Toolz preps an empty wall; Star 27 poster is hung; Random Act brush painting with acrylic; LoudLabs finishes up with the broom and paste provided; Mr. Brainwash poses with artists young and old; final exhibition space during Art Show 2011.

OPPOSITE, LEFT TO RIGHT: Mr. Brainwash's Art Show 2011 spanned outdoors and indoors, over three floors, featuring two-story tall installations and wall murals; a giant Mr. Potato Head with an MBW fedora; a stallion statue among paint buckets; a tagged-up police car; an inspirational reminder to "Never never give up."

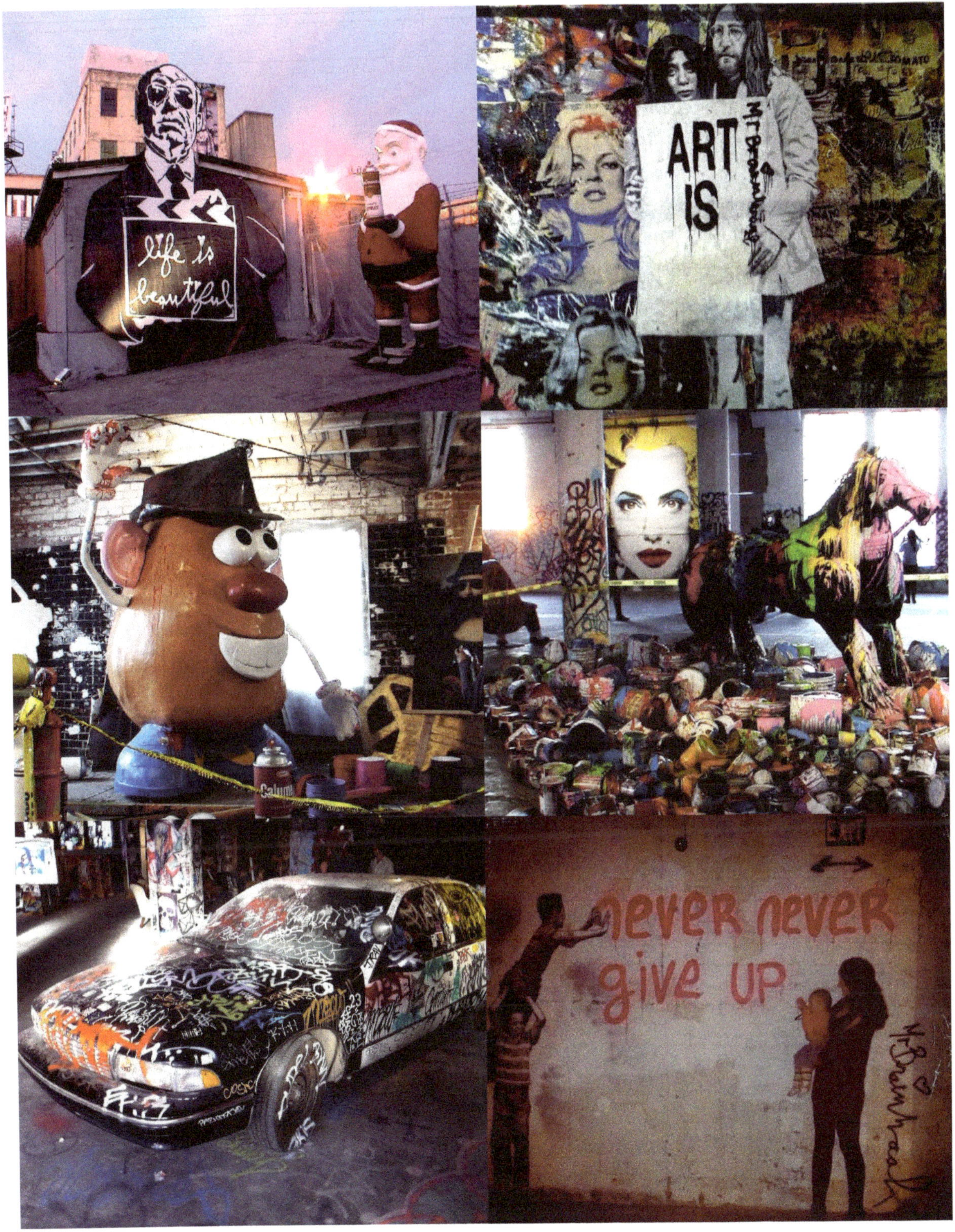
life is beautiful
ART IS
never never give up

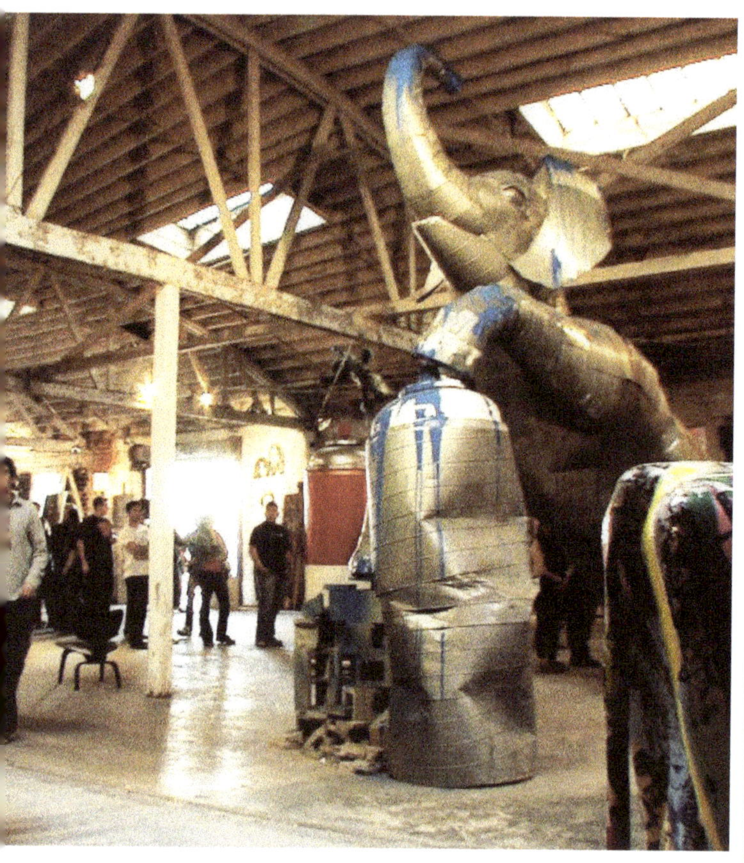

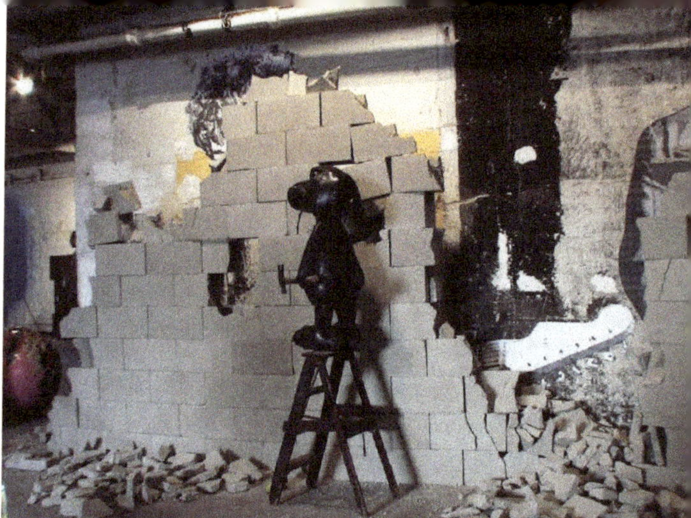

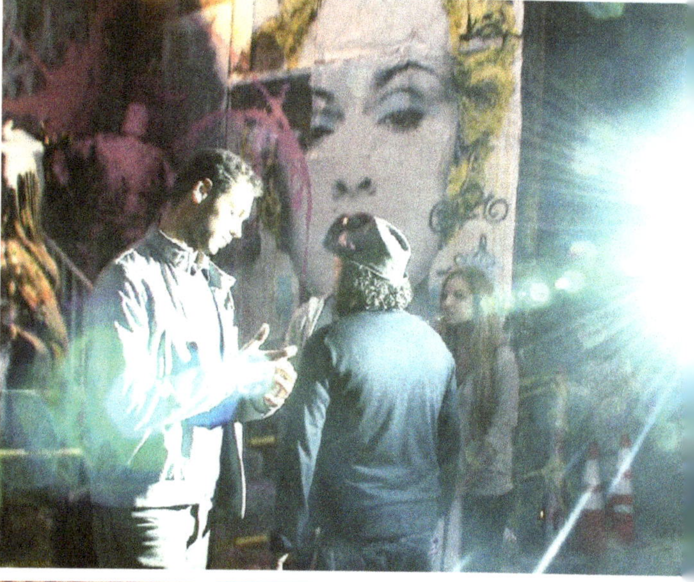

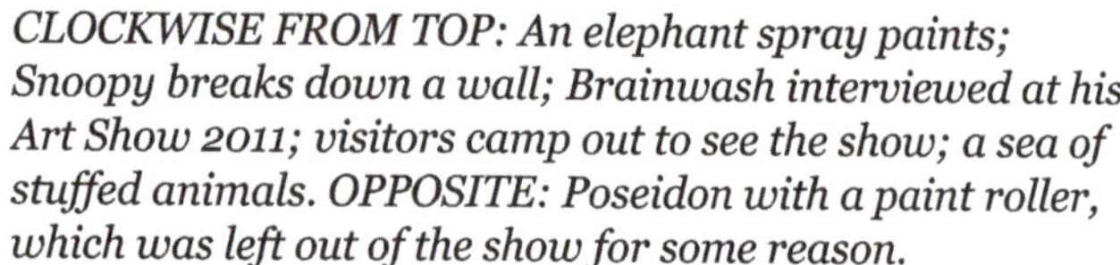

CLOCKWISE FROM TOP: An elephant spray paints; Snoopy breaks down a wall; Brainwash interviewed at his Art Show 2011; visitors camp out to see the show; a sea of stuffed animals. OPPOSITE: Poseidon with a paint roller, which was left out of the show for some reason.

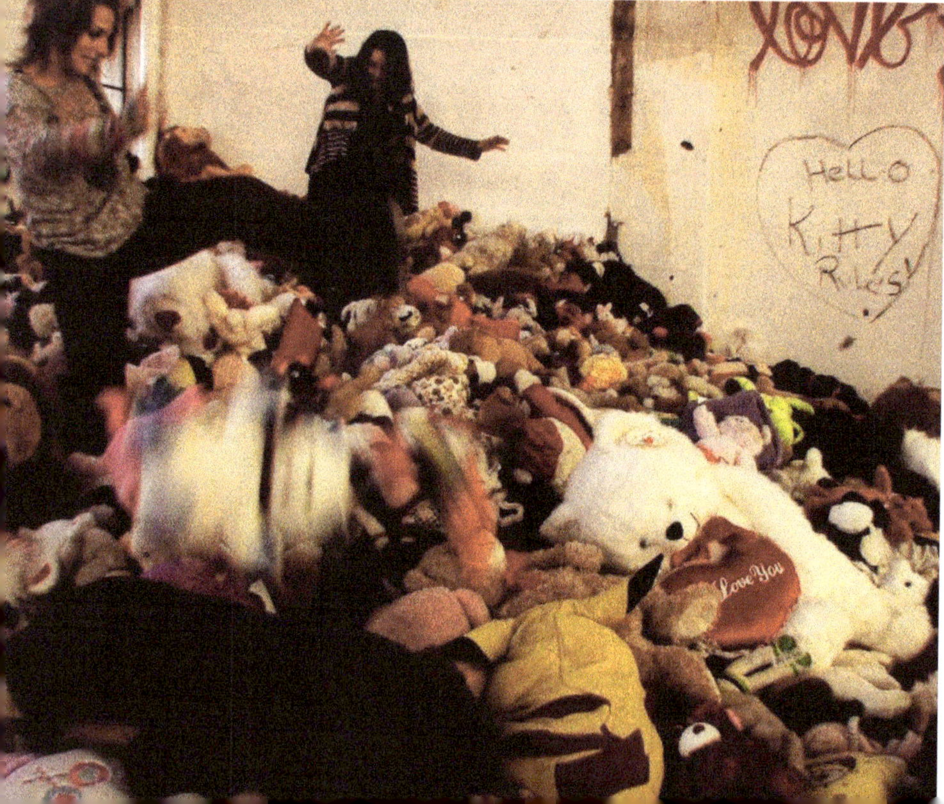

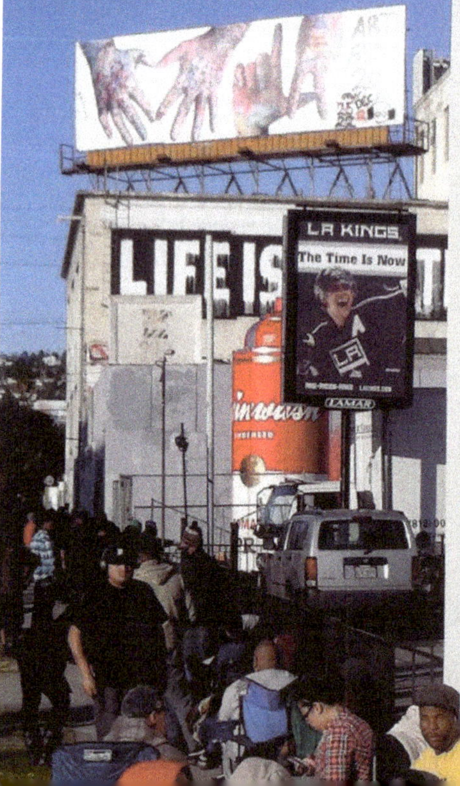

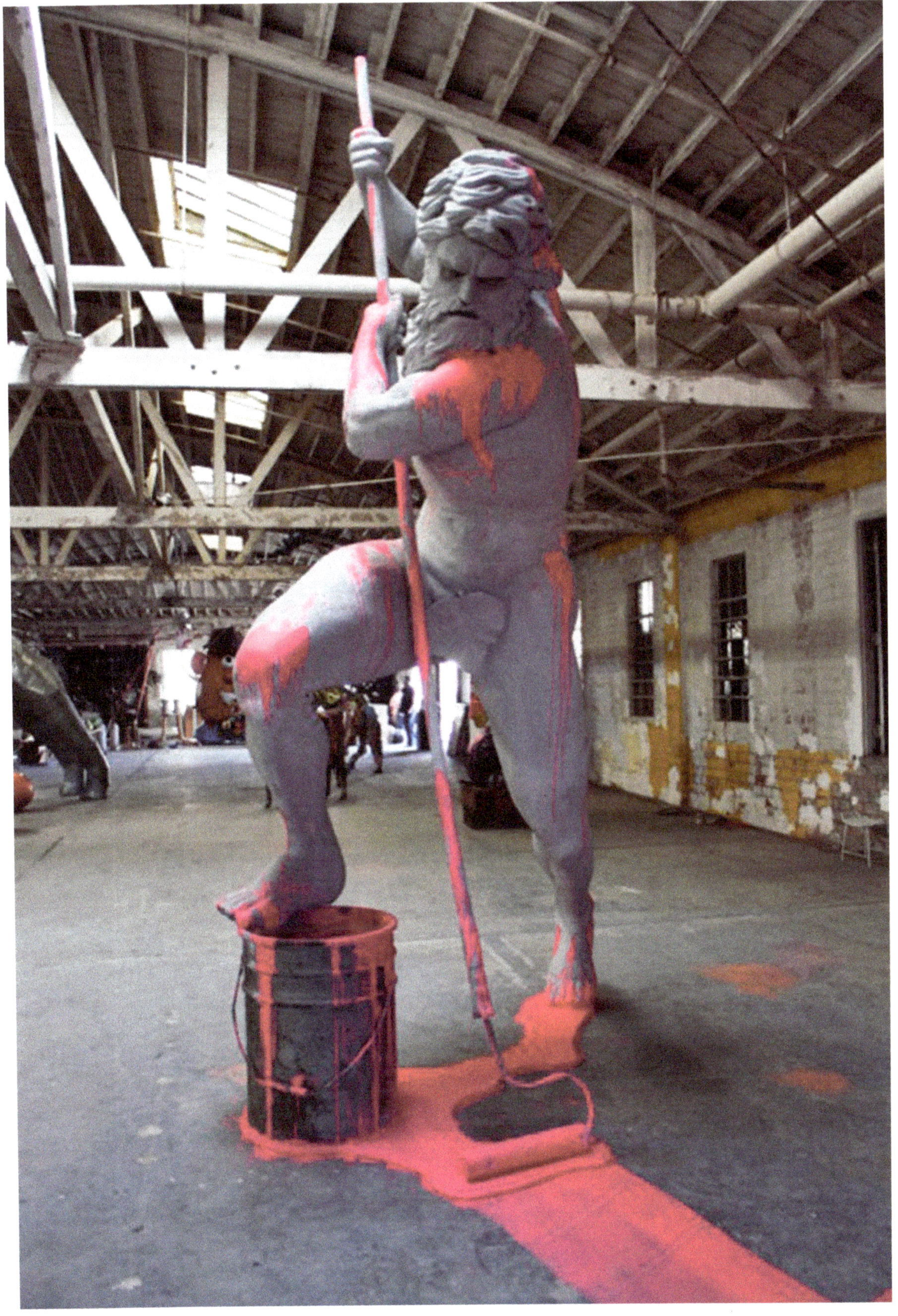

BANKSY

When Banksy came to Los Angeles to attend the Oscars for his film *Exit Through the Gift Shop*, he caused a stir by putting up street art all over L.A. for a month. Free Humanity groans, "Man, everybody and their grandma were doing street art when Banksy was in town." (Literally: a street artist named Grandma popped up who glued sarcastic messages in yarn.)

New Banksy images led the local newscasts at night, here in the media capital of the world. Opportunists tried to cut his works out of walls, frauds were sold on Ebay, security guards were posted, then plexiglass applied. Some pieces were defaced, only to be restored by supporters. All while no one knew what Banksy looked like, and could be anyone, anywhere.

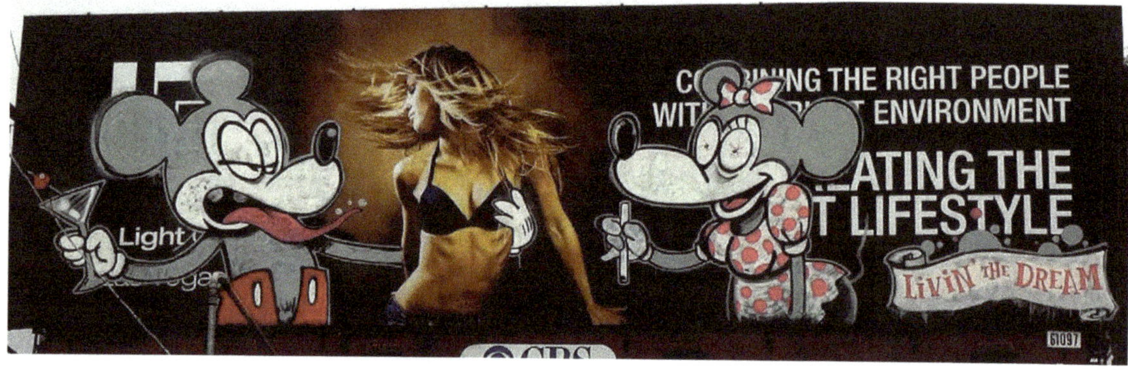

On the Sunset Strip, this billboard takeover by Banksy featured a drug-addled Mickey and Minnie. When CBS Outdoor Advertising took it down, the nightclub that had been advertised demanded it back. It now hangs over their dance floor in Vegas.

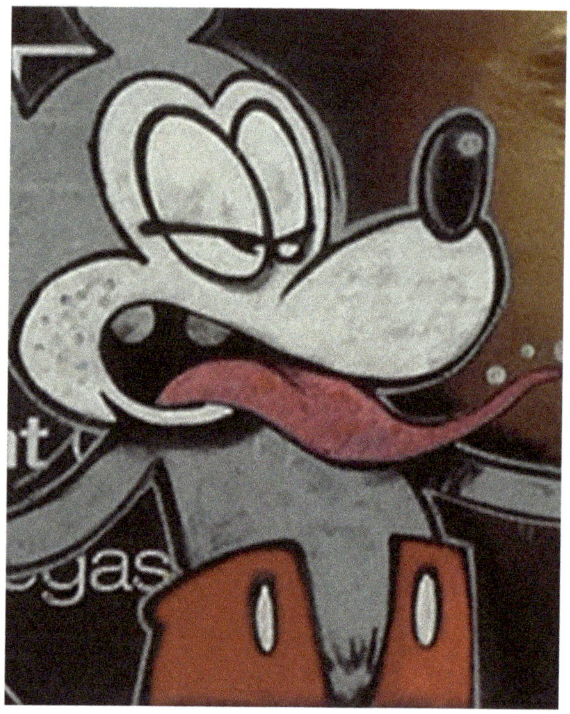

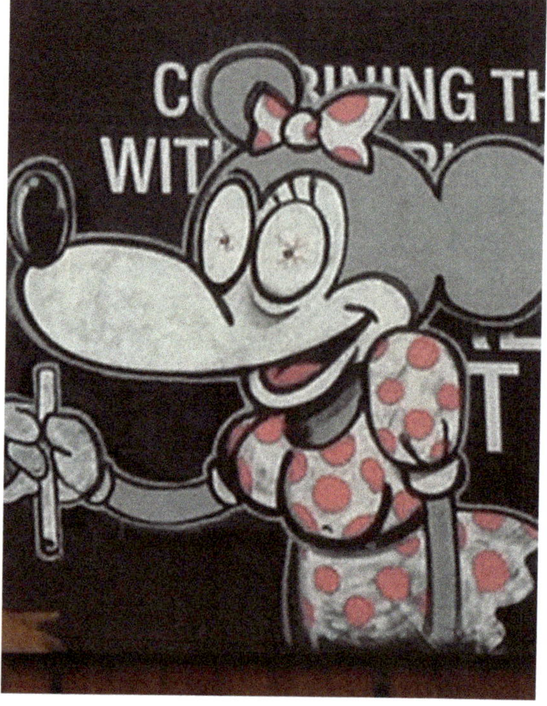

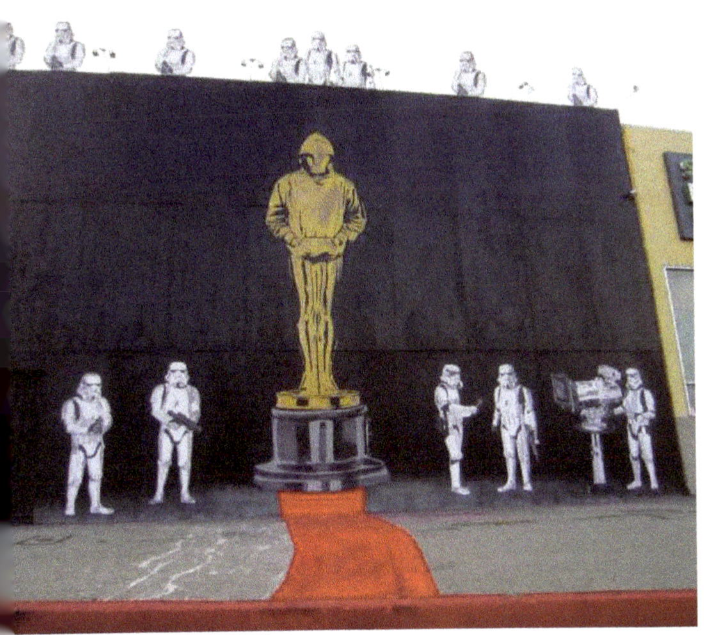

This tribute mural by Mr. Brainwash on La Brea featured a Banksy-shaped Oscar statue and Storm Troopers, with a red carpet painted on the sidewalk. (Photo by Greg Linton)

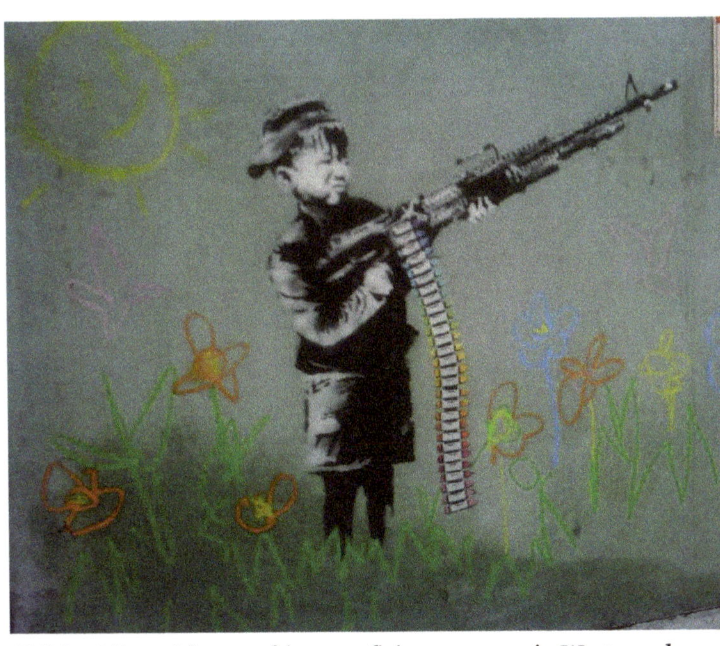

Child soldier with a machine gun firing crayons, in Westwood. (Photo by Ravi Shah)

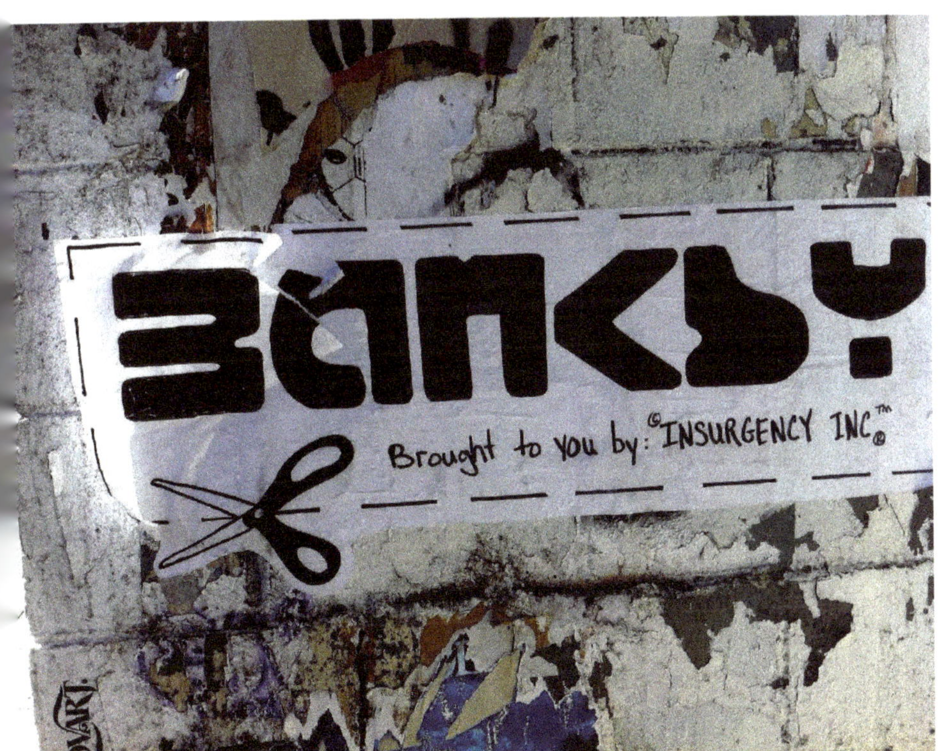

The excitement surrounding Banksy's visit was apparent, as numerous street artists put up work responding to him. Insurgency Inc. pasted up Banksy's tag for would-be collectors on Melrose.

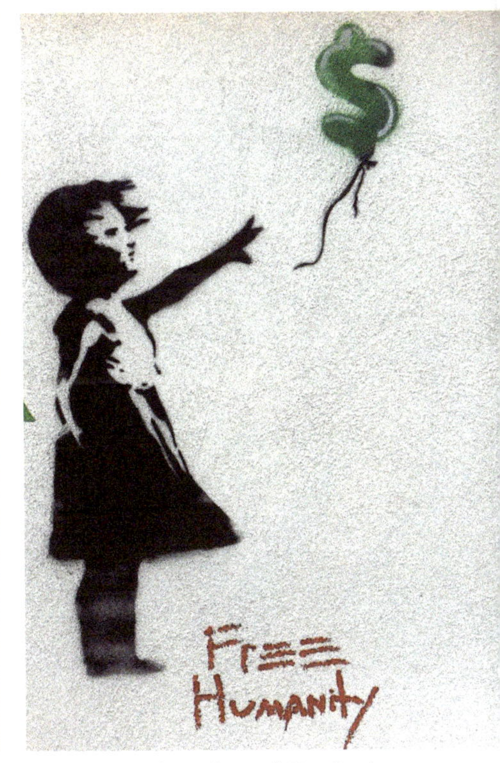

Free Humanity adapted Banksy's heart ballon into a dollar sign balloon, commenting on the inflated street art market.

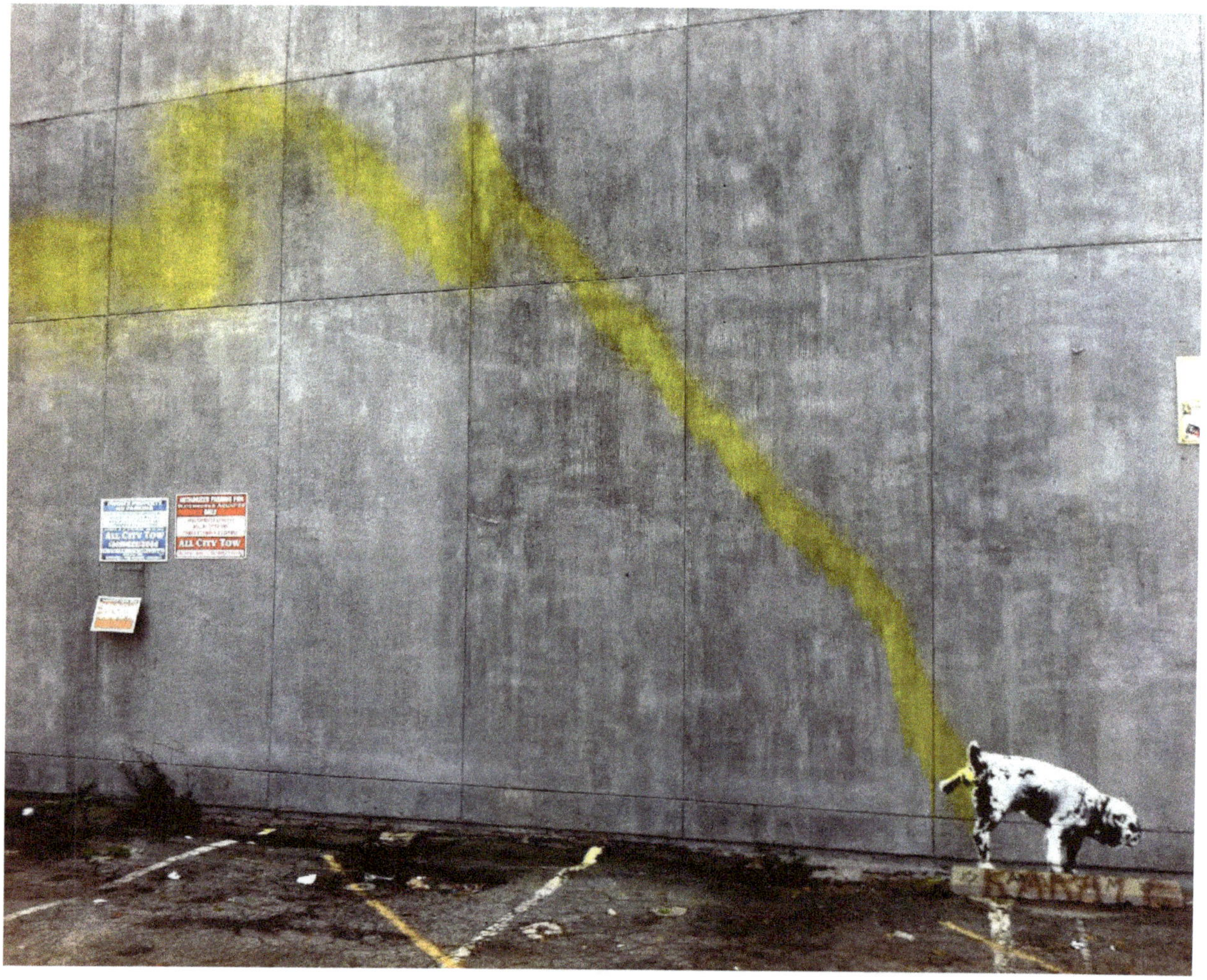

One of the longest-lasting Banksy stencils was the Peeing Bulldog, who appeared to be relieving himself on a wall, spilling onto the parking lot. Across from a rec center on Little Santa Monica in Beverly Hills, tourists would come to see this piece. But something about the attention Banksy gets really brings out the haters, and inevitably someone comes along to try to spot-jack or even cap the artwork completely. When some idiot ultimately spray painted over the bulldog and put it on YouTube, LAPD arrested him for vandalism, because the building owners called the cops—unlike when Banksy had painted on their wall.

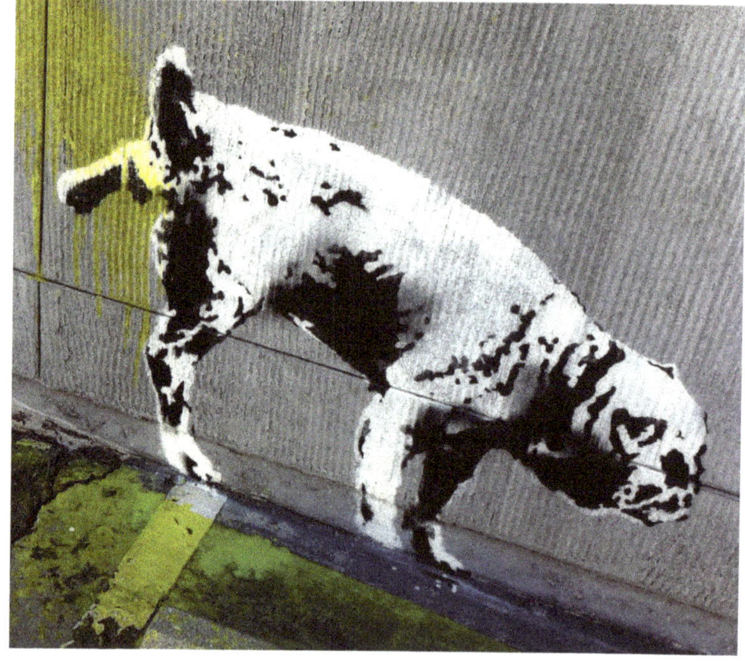

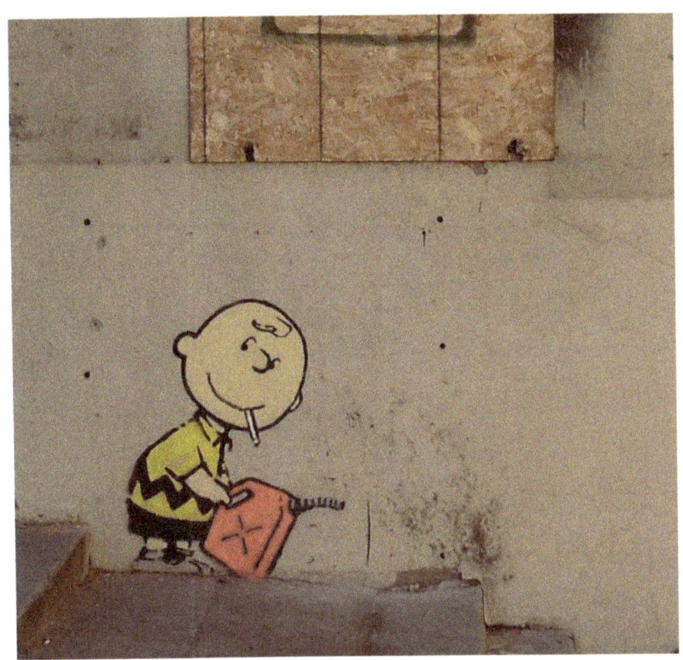

On a burned-out house along the Sunset Strip, Banksy painted Charlie Brown with a can of gasoline and a cigarette, as though he had just torched the place. At the height of the Banksy hysteria, this piece was cut out of the wall to be sold by a scavenger on E-Bay. Fake buyers then sprang up to make bogus bids to thwart the sale of Arsonist Charlie Brown.

Still intact, however, is the Banksy stencil in Park City, Utah, home of the Sundance Film Festival. The image of a cameraman uprooting the flower he is trying to film is a powerful metaphor for reckless production and a careless Hollywood. *(Photo by Tim Johnson)*

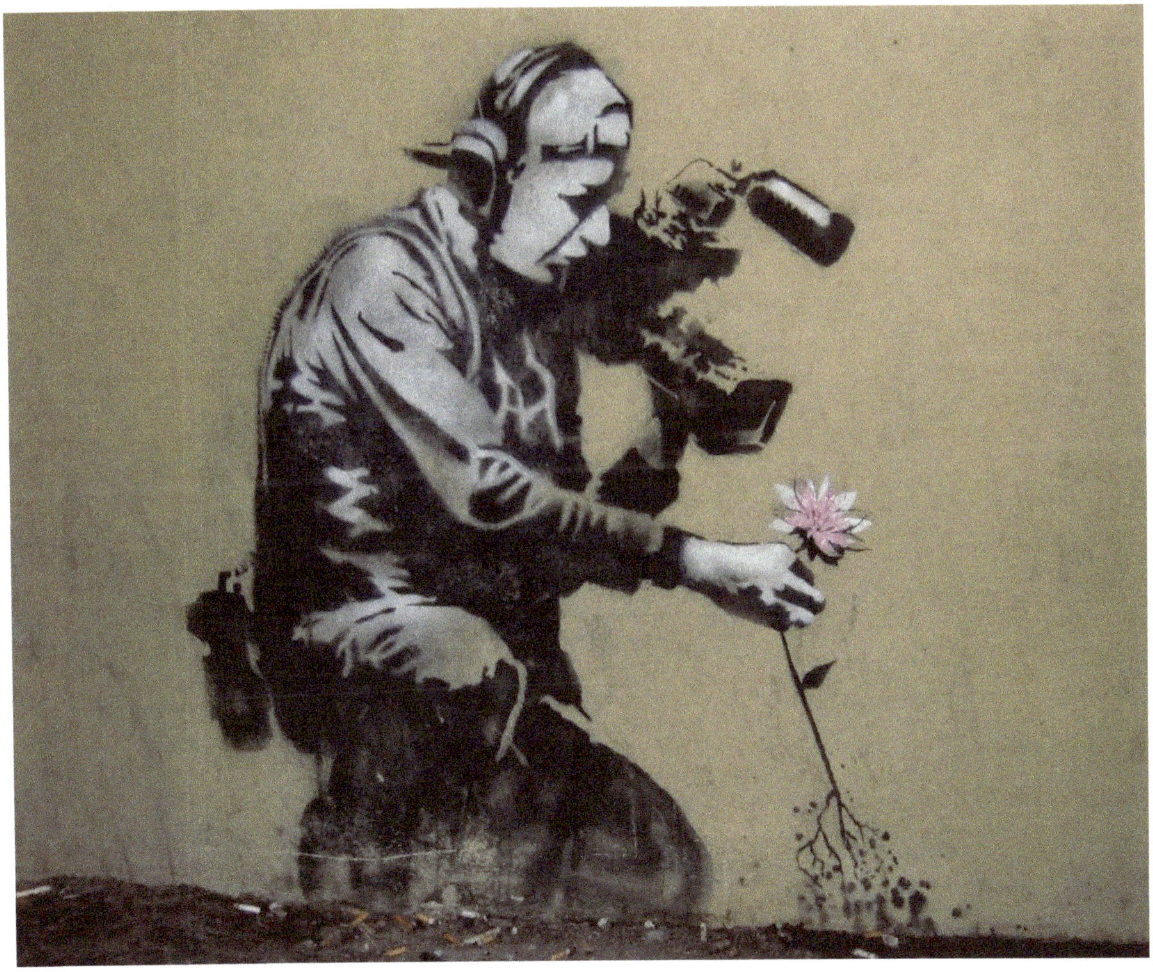

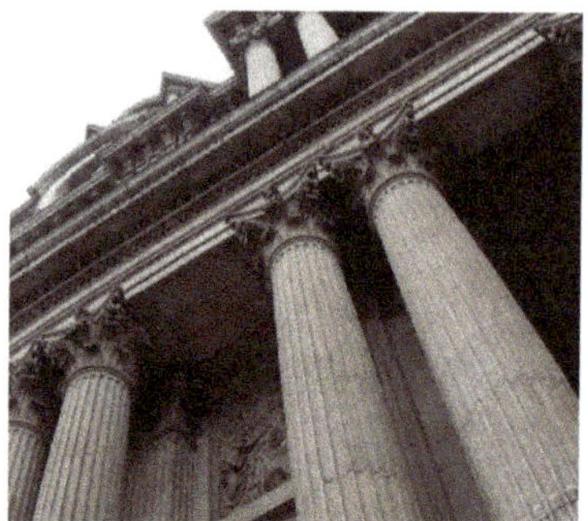

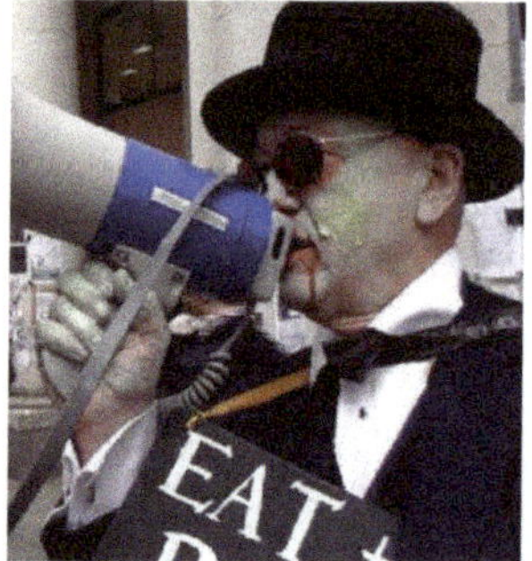

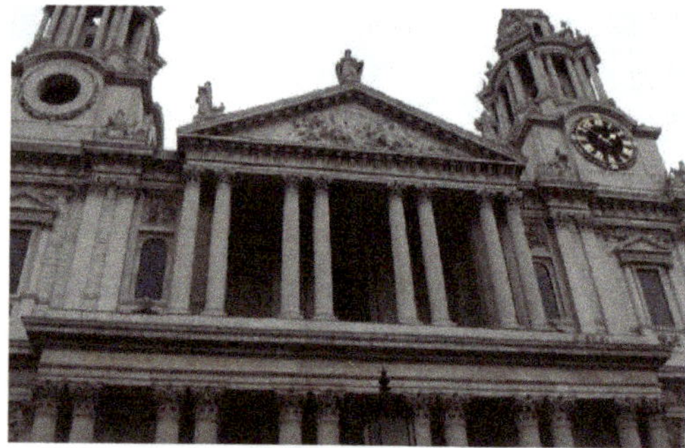

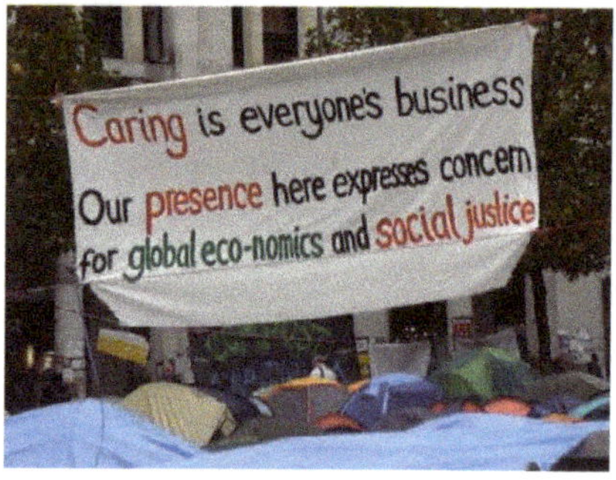

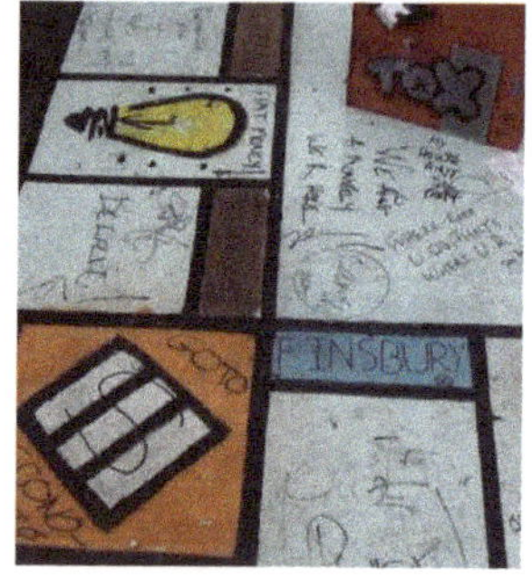

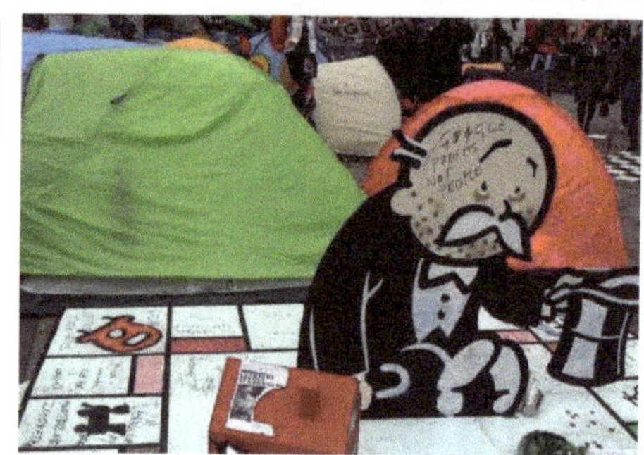

During the Occupy wave in 2011, Banksy planted a piece of street art in the center of the Occupy LSX encampents in front of the London Stock Exchange. The financial meltdown had hit everyone hard, including Mr. Monopoly, who was looking pretty run down, panhandling with his hat out. His fellow Londoners seemed happy to add to his duress by freely scribbling "Profits Not People" on his face.

Both art and protest can be a powerful way to show around the world how people are fighting their own version of a pay 2 play system.

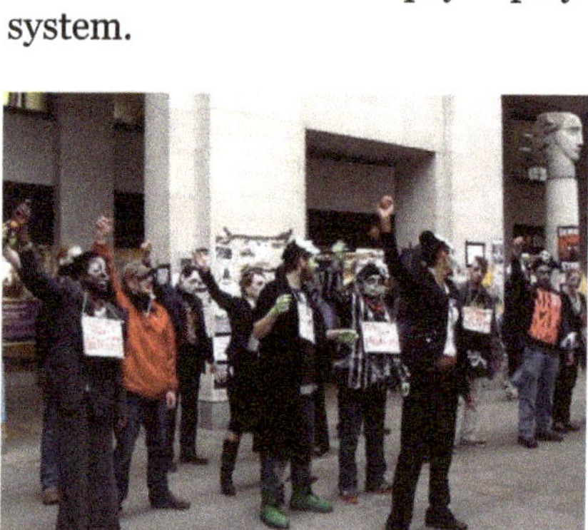

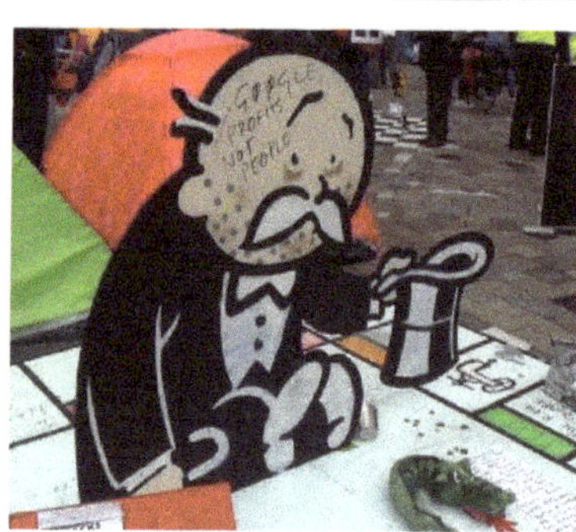

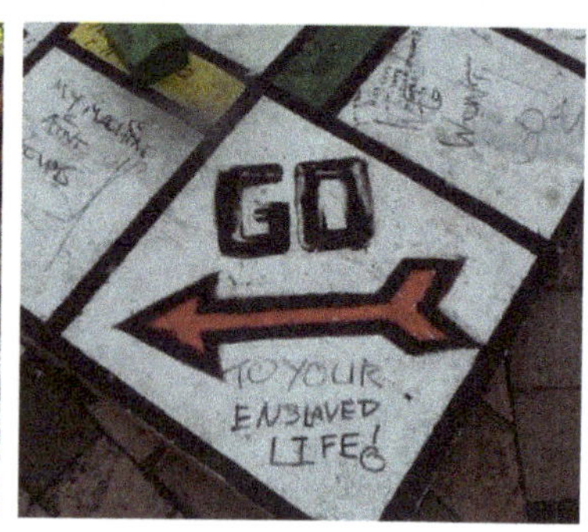

THE PSA CREW

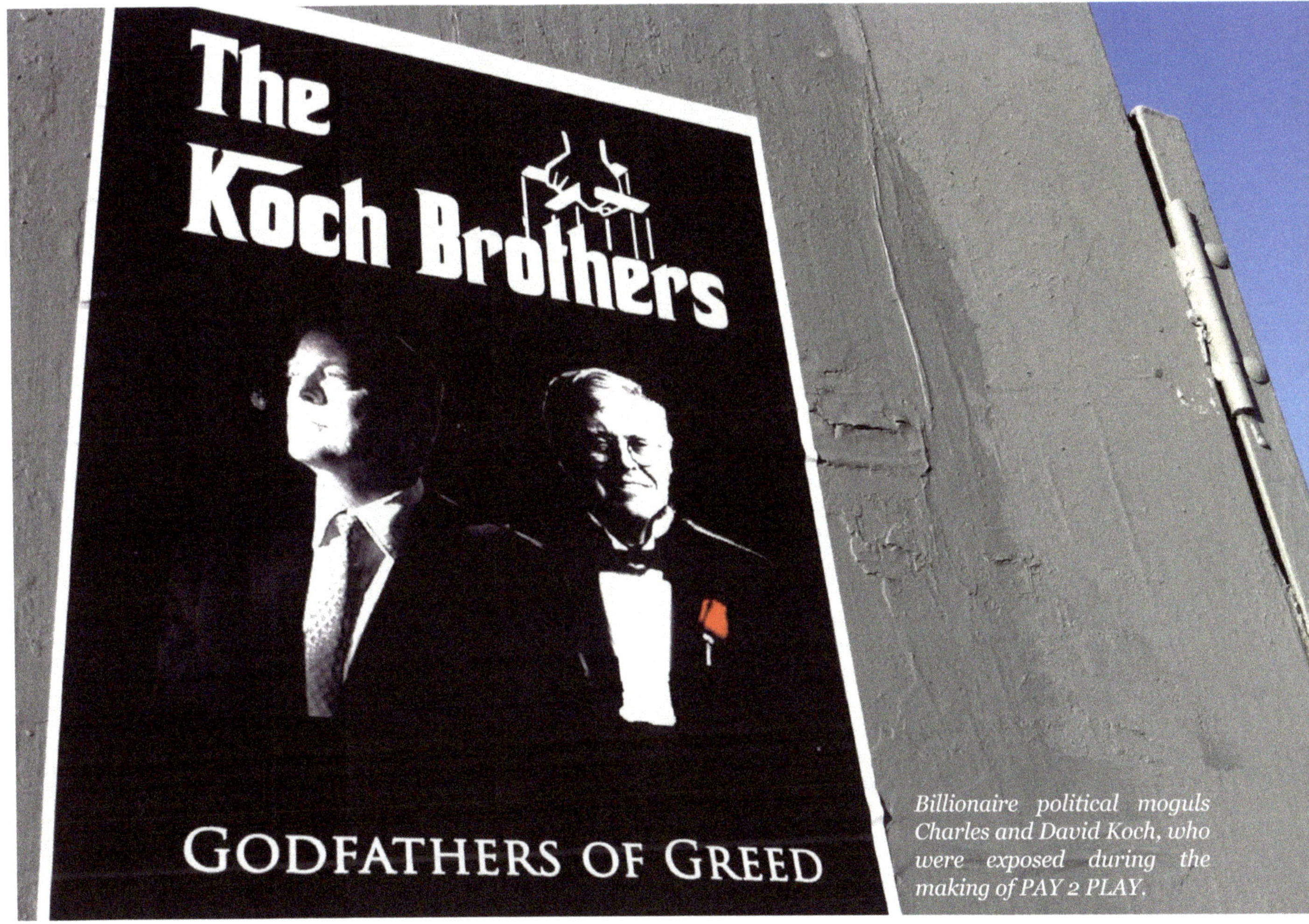

Billionaire political moguls Charles and David Koch, who were exposed during the making of PAY 2 PLAY.

Over the course of documenting street artists and chronicling corruption, something clicked. Through collaborations and creativity, a street art series was created that conveyed the issues *PAY 2 PLAY* was taking shape around. Showing others how money in politics affects them seemed like an important purpose; to me, these messages carried the urgency of old-timey public service announcements.

And so, The PSA Crew was founded to raise awareness through innovative artistic endeavors. Besides Public Service Announcement, PSA stood for Politcal Street Art. Created by L.A.'s top street artists, this crew is non-exclusive and open to others who wish to put up the message of people over profits. Even you can do it.

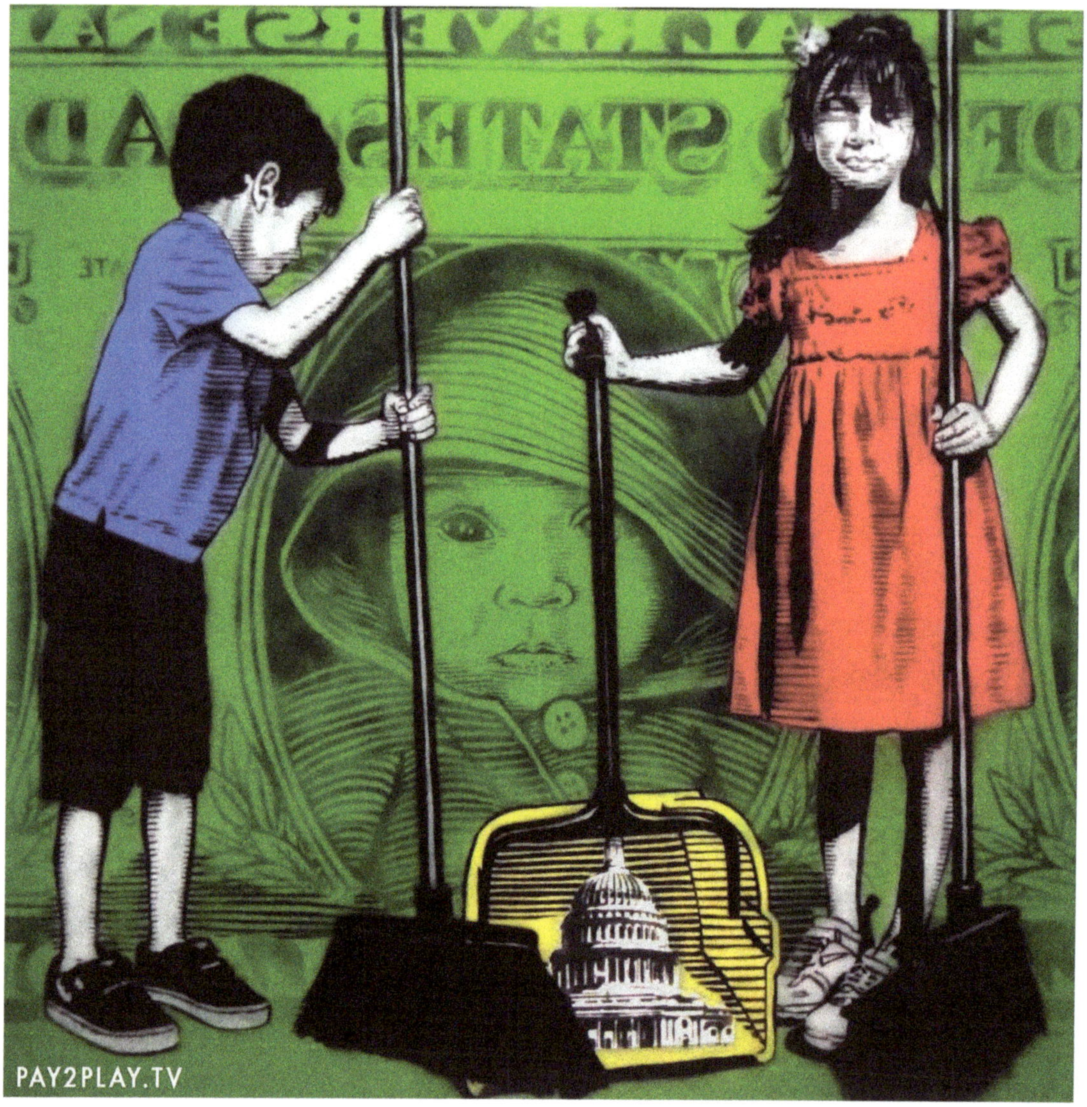

ABOVE: Teachr painted this picture of his kids cleaning up after Pay 2 Play politicians. "Sweep" was printed as stickers and posters for the 5th anniversary of Citizens United vs. FEC. *BELOW: "Wall St. Occupies US"; "Where's MY Lobbyist?" (Photo by @PhotoJenInc)*

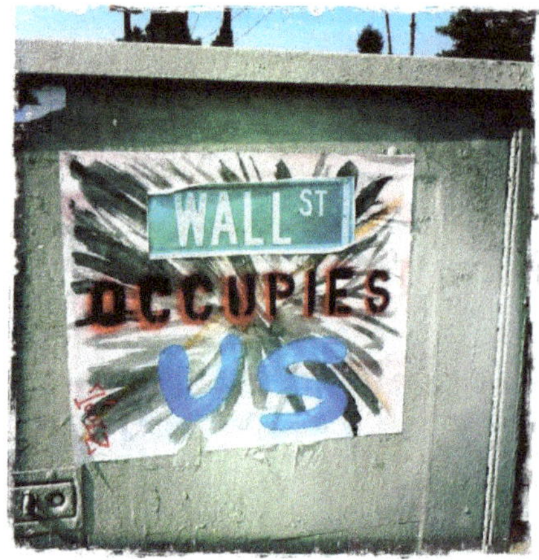

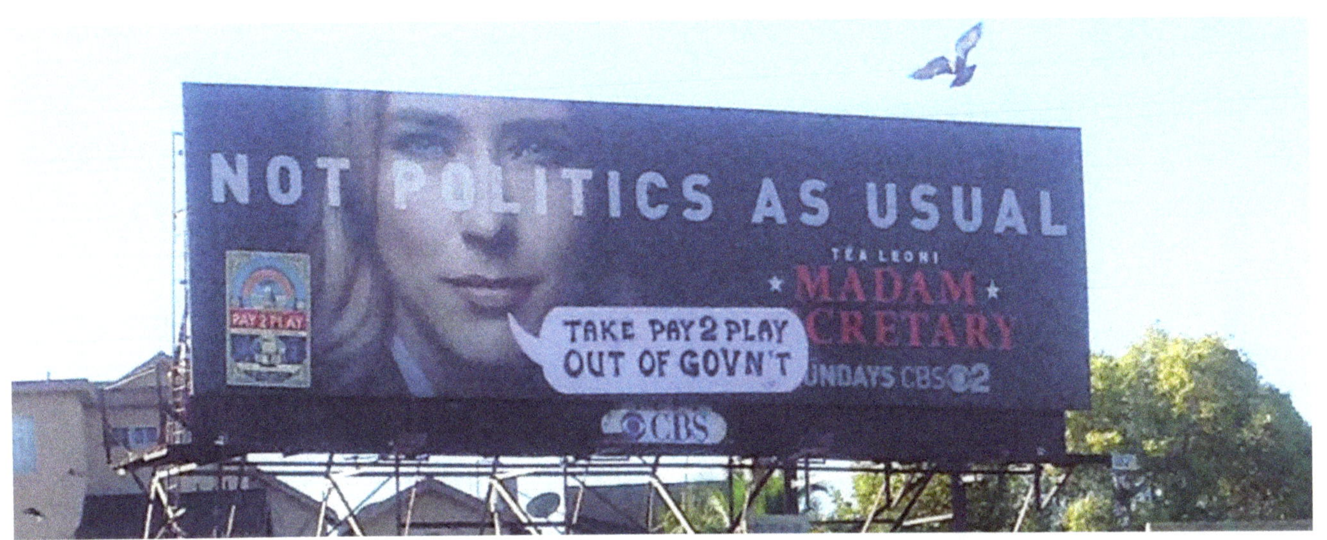

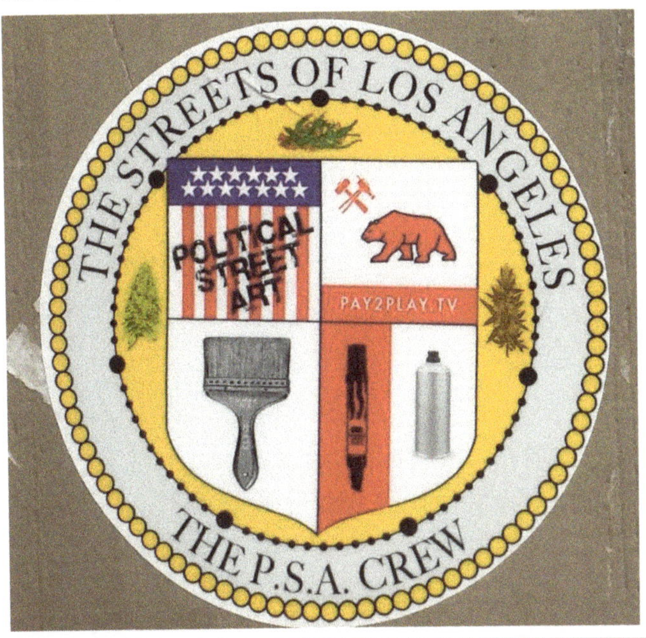

CLOCKWISE FROM TOP: A "Madam Secretary" billboard takeover by Teachr; "For The People" sticker; Wu-Tang Clan tribute sticker, "C.R.E.A.M.: Cash Rules Elections Around Me"; Teachr spray painting on Hollywood Blvd.; a sticker of the PSA Crew logo.

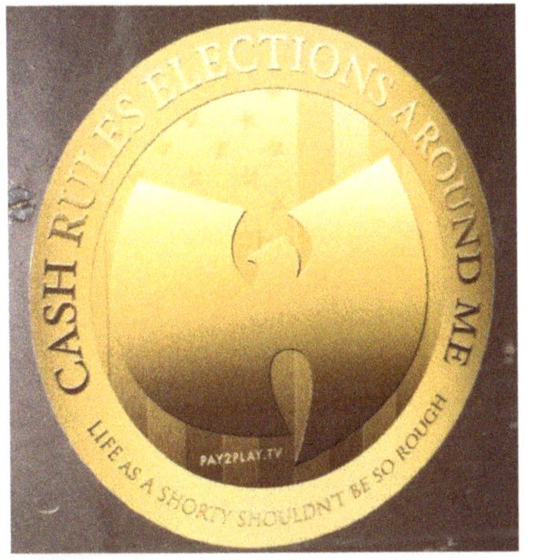

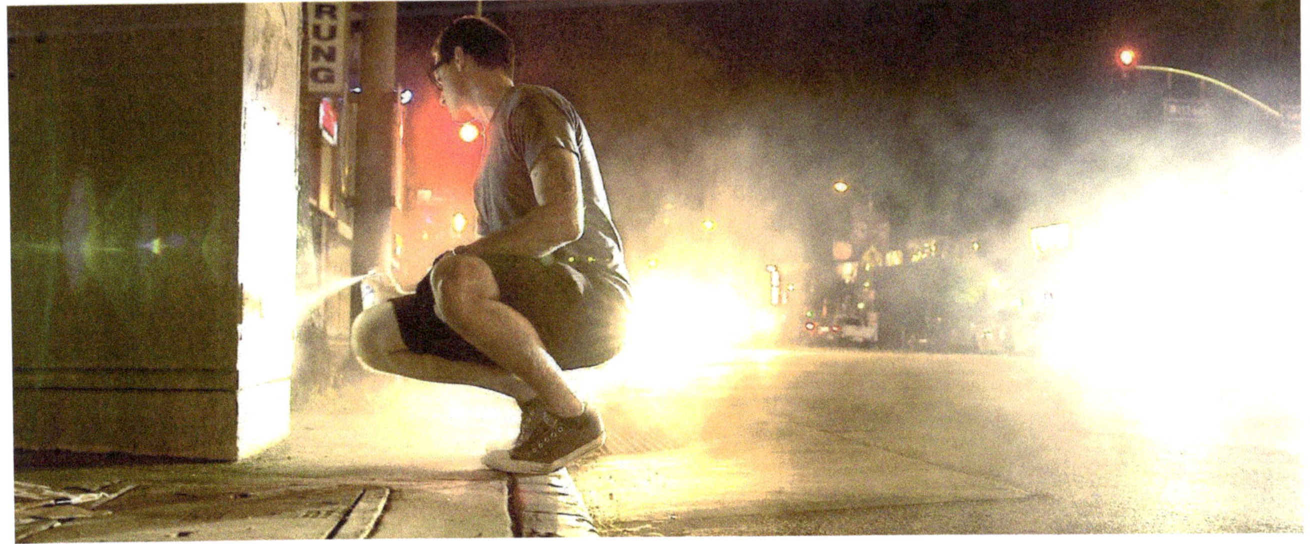

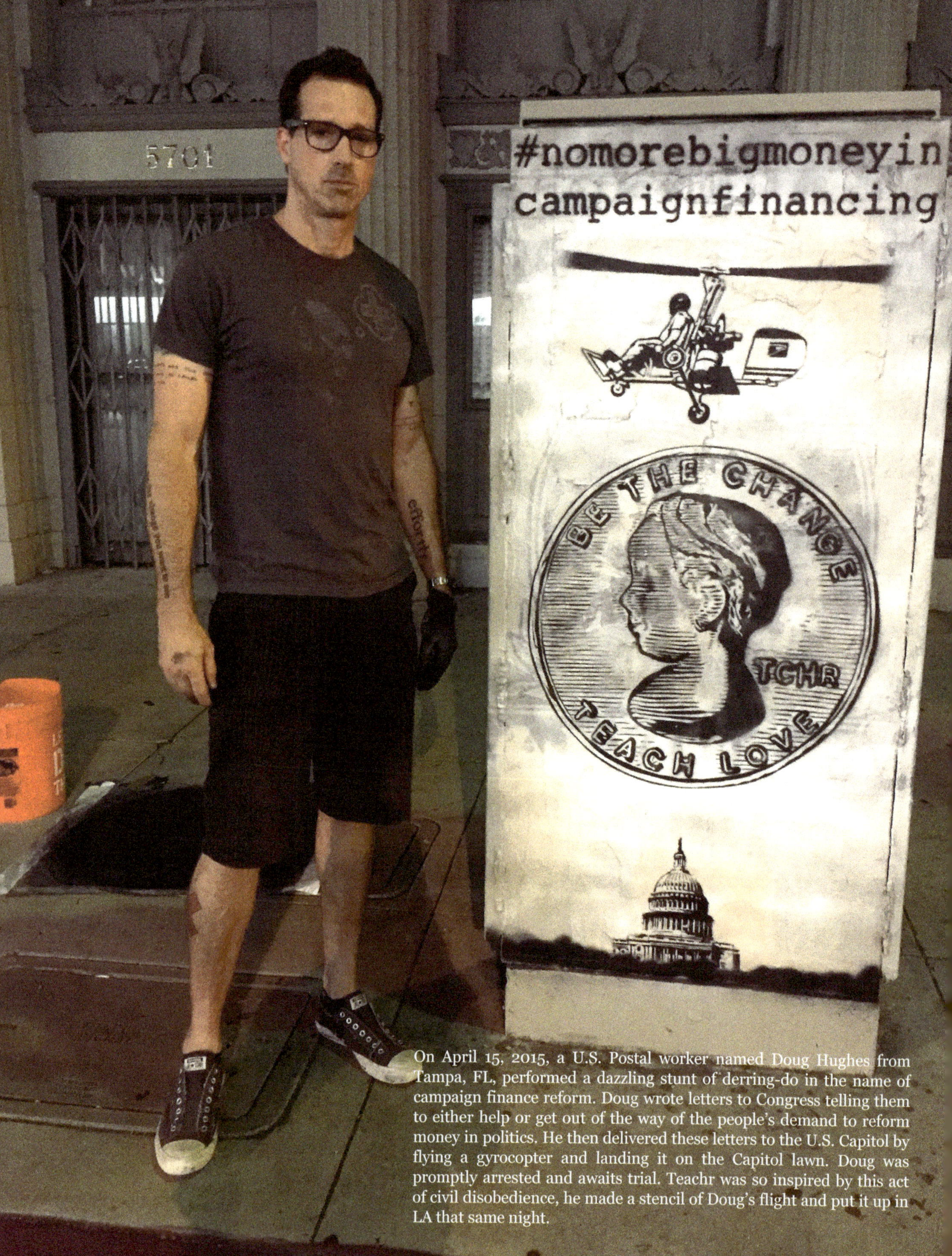

On April 15, 2015, a U.S. Postal worker named Doug Hughes from Tampa, FL, performed a dazzling stunt of derring-do in the name of campaign finance reform. Doug wrote letters to Congress telling them to either help or get out of the way of the people's demand to reform money in politics. He then delivered these letters to the U.S. Capitol by flying a gyrocopter and landing it on the Capitol lawn. Doug was promptly arrested and awaits trial. Teachr was so inspired by this act of civil disobedience, he made a stencil of Doug's flight and put it up in LA that same night.

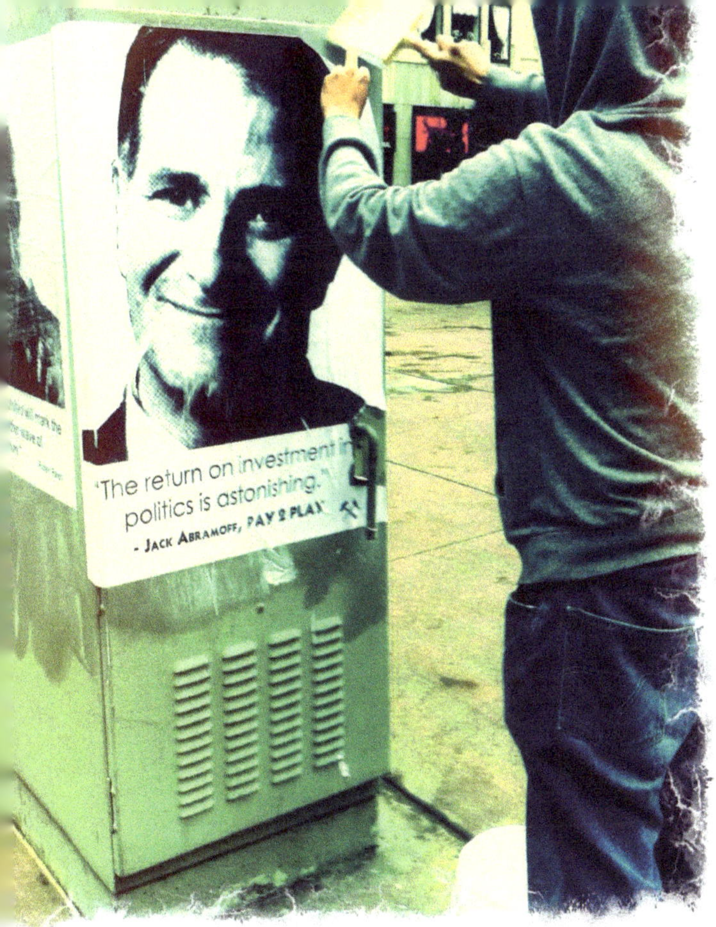

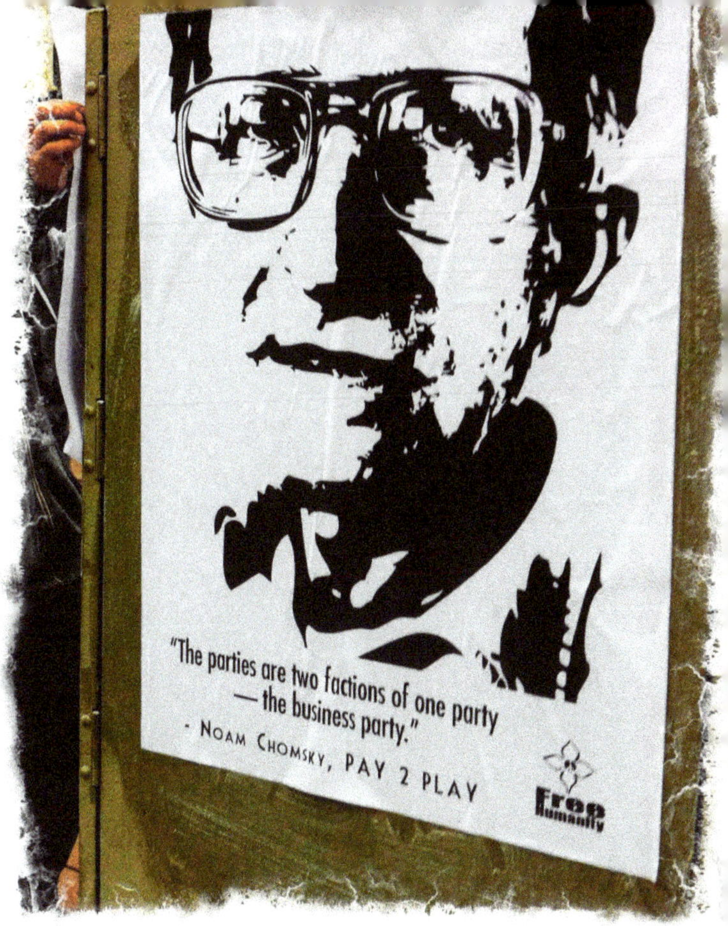

Burn One put up these posters with quotes from PAY 2 PLAY during morning rush hour in Downtown L.A. on May Day.

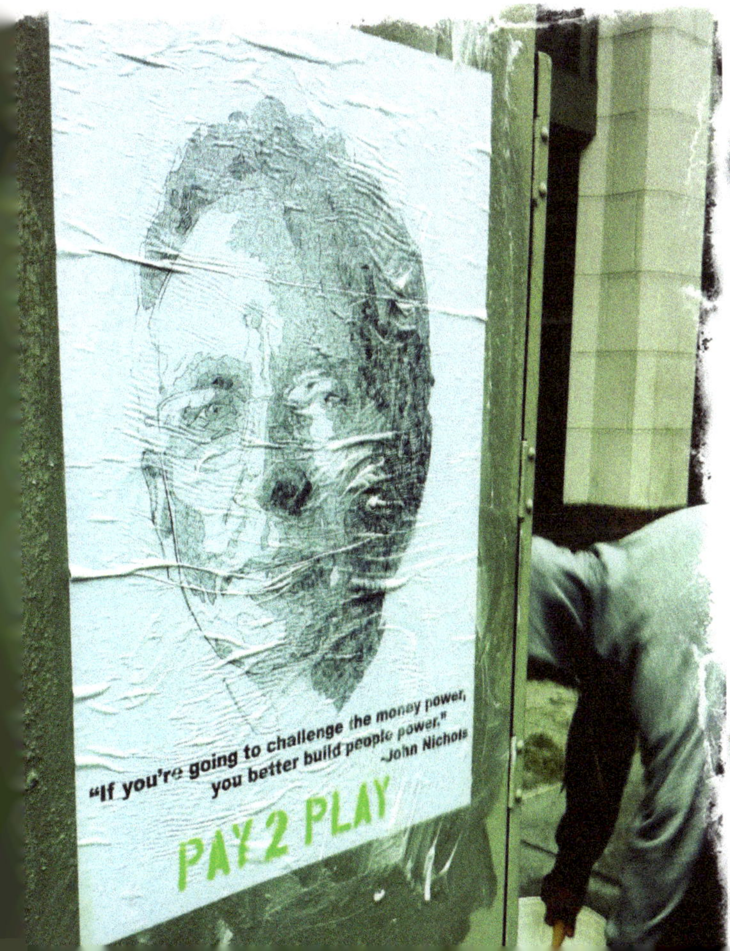

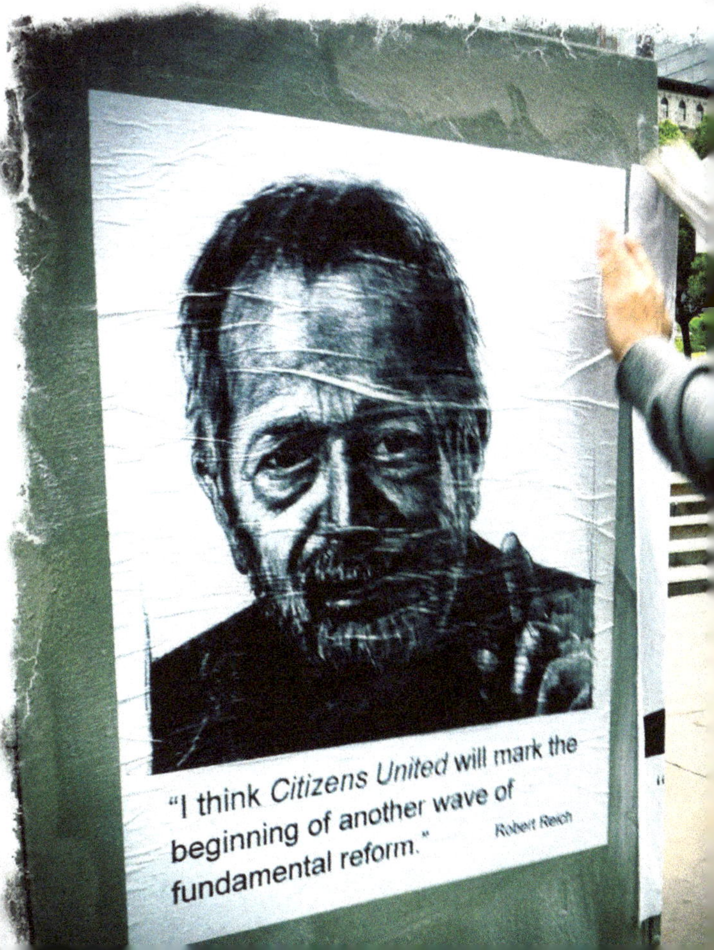

THE DISSENTER

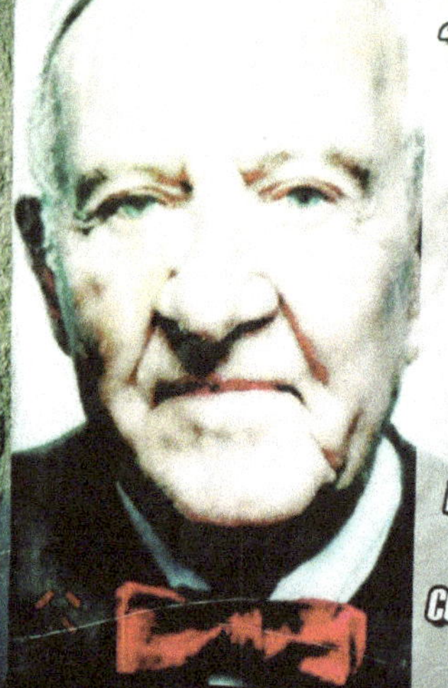

"WHILE AMERICAN DEMOCRACY IS IMPERFECT, FEW OUTSIDE THE MAJORITY OF THIS COURT WOULD HAVE THOUGHT ITS FLAWS INCLUDED A DEARTH OF CORPORATE MONEY IN POLITICS."

SUPREME COURT JUSTICE (RETIRED)

JOHN PAUL STEVENS

DISSENTING OPINION IN CITIZENS UNITED VS. F.E.C

COMPANY MAN

"The First Amendment protects more than just the individual on a soapbox and the lonely pamphleteer."
— John Roberts, *Citizens United vs FEC*

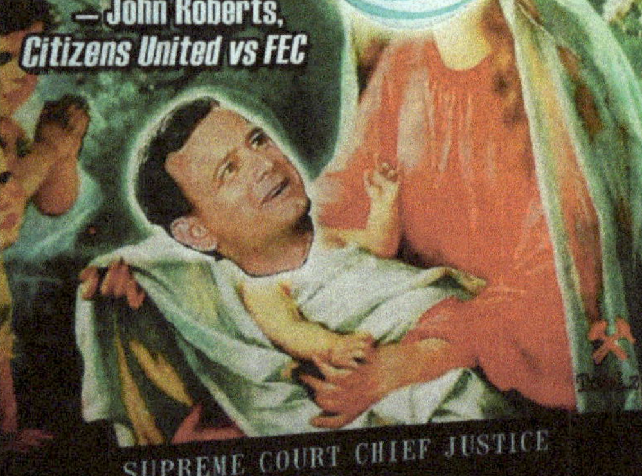

SUPREME COURT CHIEF JUSTICE

JOHN ROBERTS

MAKING THE CORPORATE INTEREST THE PUBLIC INTEREST

IMPAIRED JUDGEMENT

I'LL DECIDE MY OWN CONFLICTS OF INTEREST

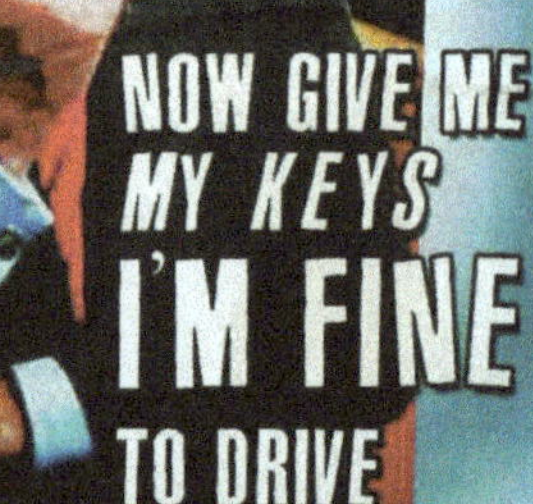

NOW GIVE ME MY KEYS I'M FINE TO DRIVE

Toolz

SUPREME COURT JUSTICE

ANTONIN SCALIA

PARTY ENTERTAINMENT FOR THE KOCH BROTHERS

"THE QUIET ONE"

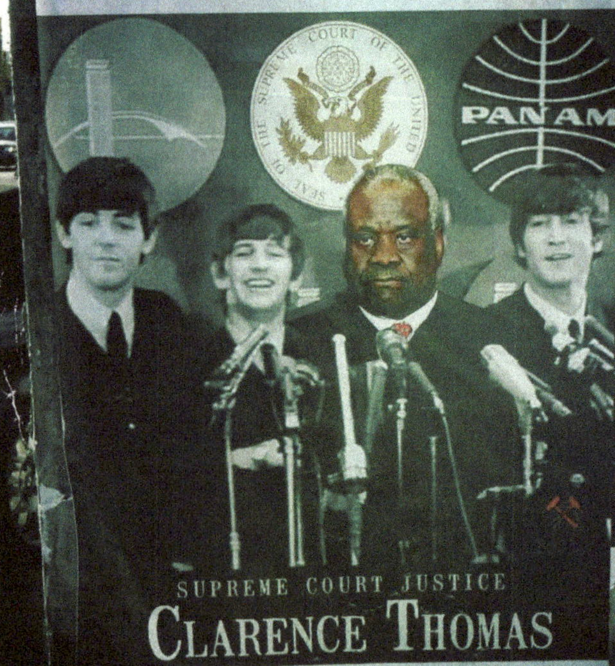

SUPREME COURT JUSTICE

CLARENCE THOMAS

SIX YEARS WITHOUT SPEAKING DURING COURT ARGUMENTS

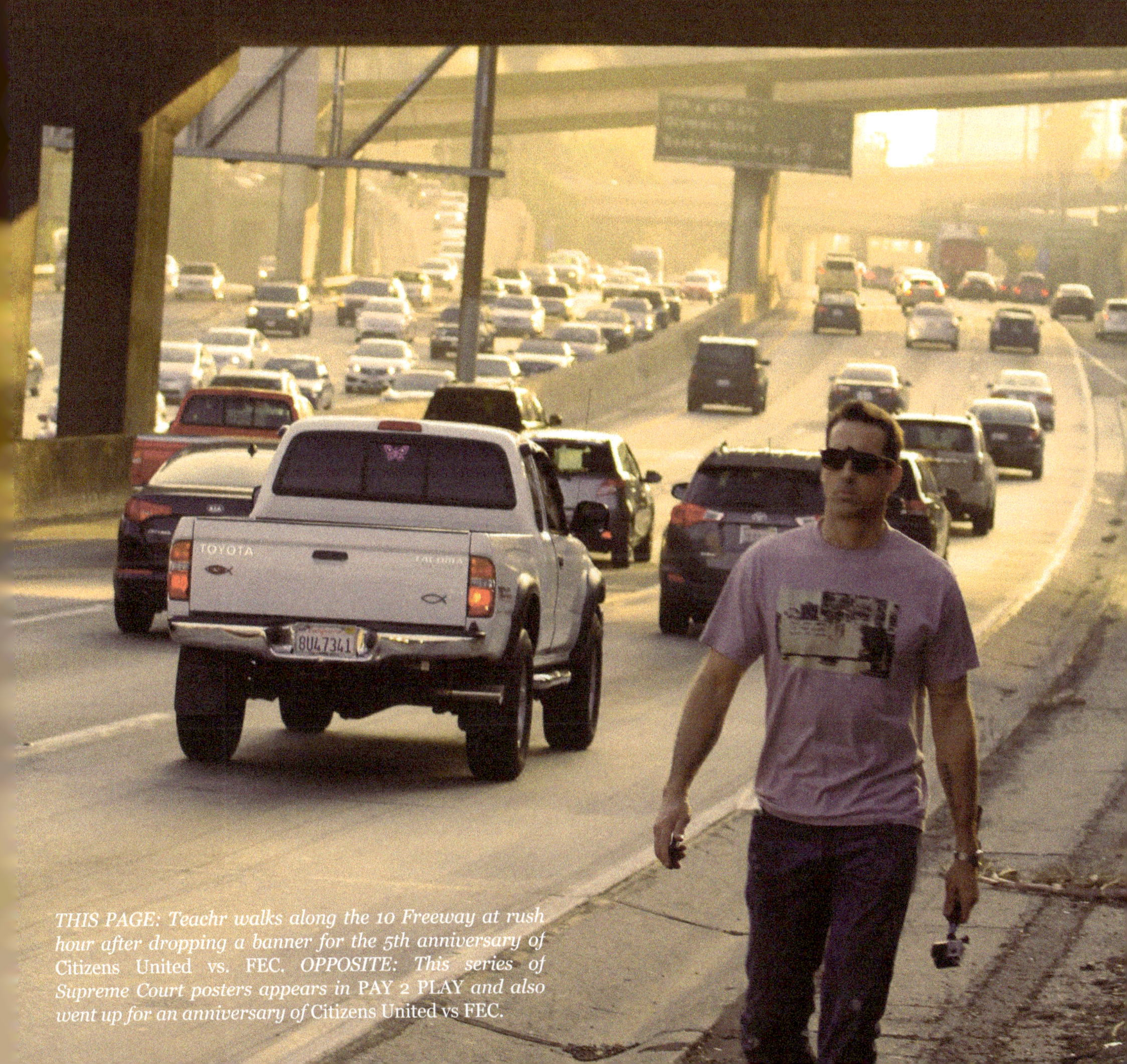

THIS PAGE: Teachr walks along the 10 Freeway at rush hour after dropping a banner for the 5th anniversary of Citizens United vs. FEC. *OPPOSITE: This series of Supreme Court posters appears in* PAY 2 PLAY *and also went up for an anniversary of* Citizens United vs FEC.

THE PAY 2 PLAY BOARD

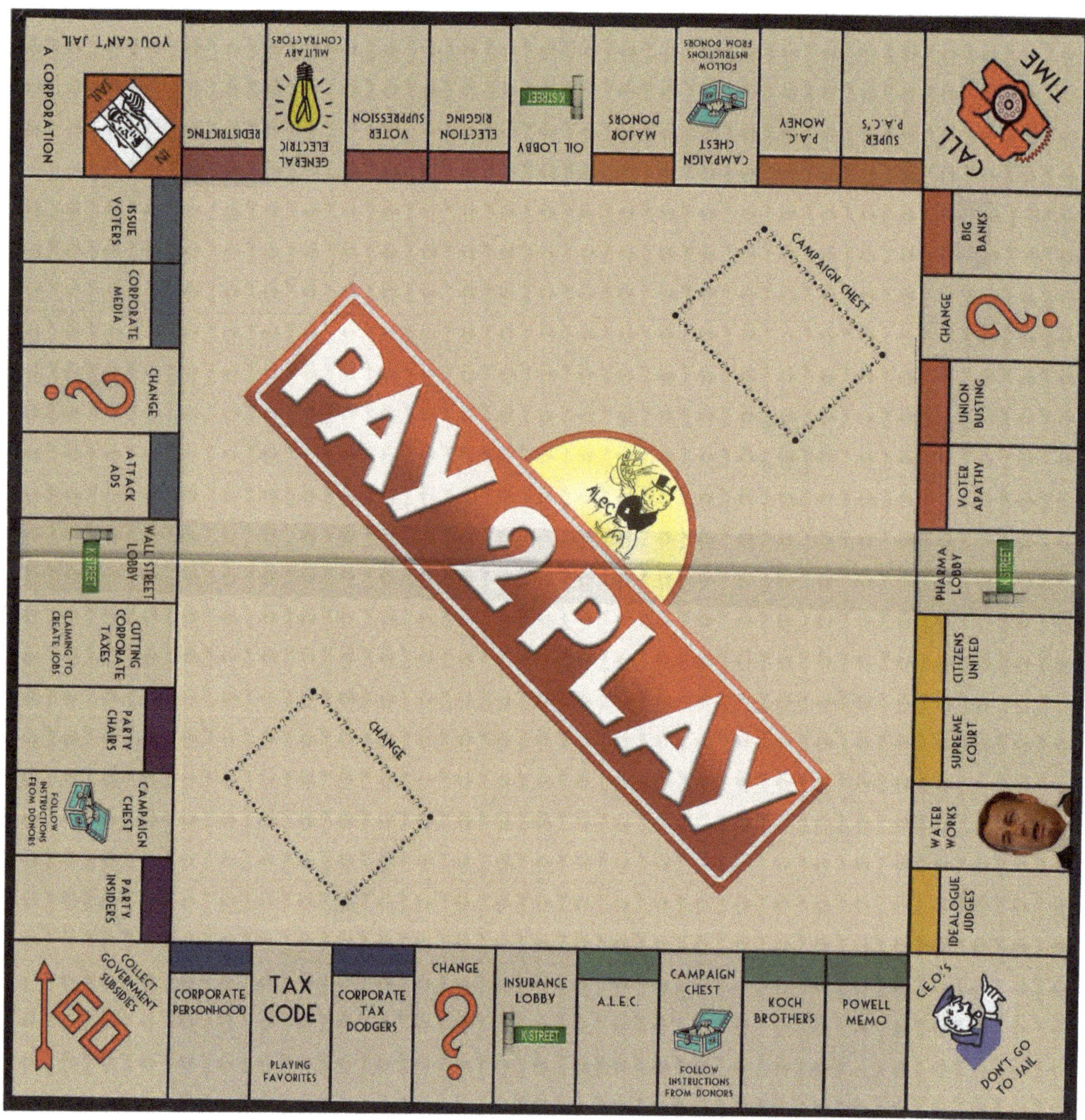

My original hope was to create a board game that showed the challenges of running for office. But this evolved a lot over the course of trying to navigate a documentary about campaign finance, corruption in Ohio, and street art. In the end result, this board reflects the Pay 2 Play System itself, which we describe in the film as a political system that shuts out ordinary people in favor of huge corporate spending in elections. But then I had a crazy idea to try to share this Pay 2 Play board with a lot of people at the 2012 May Day Parade.

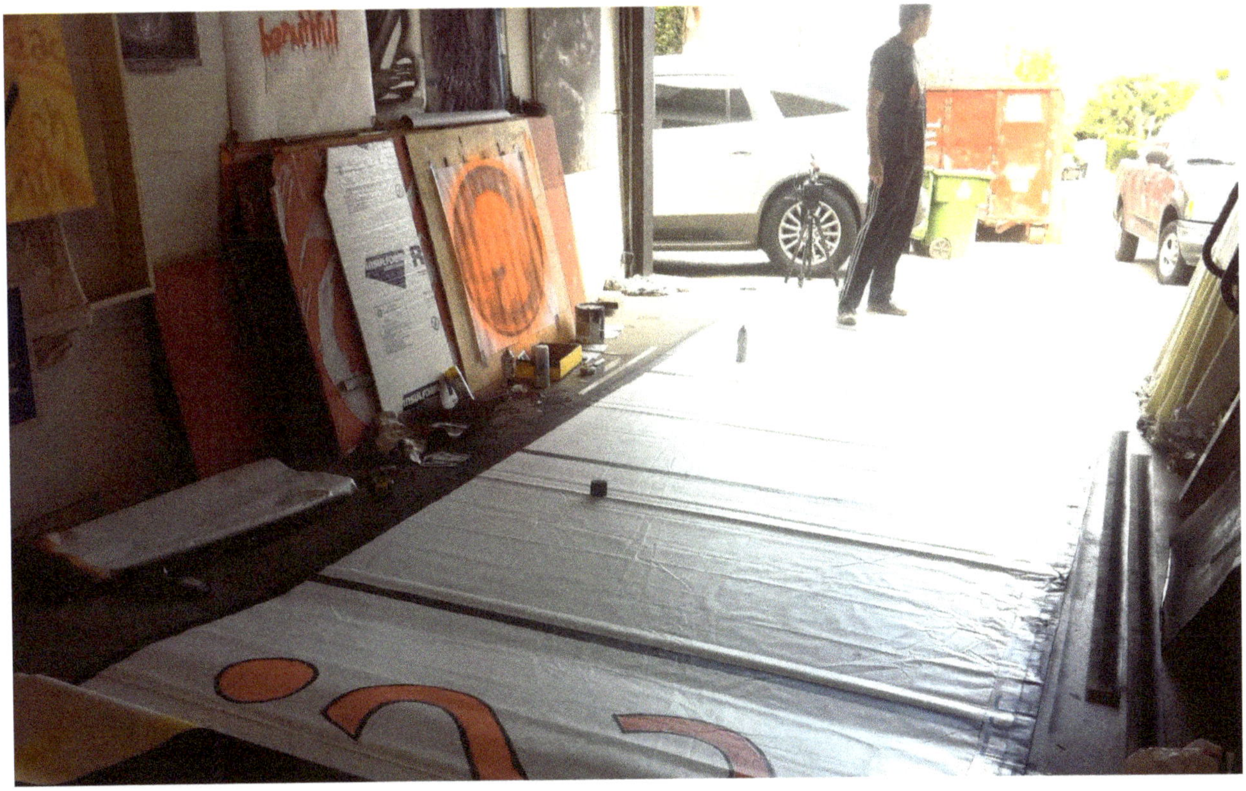

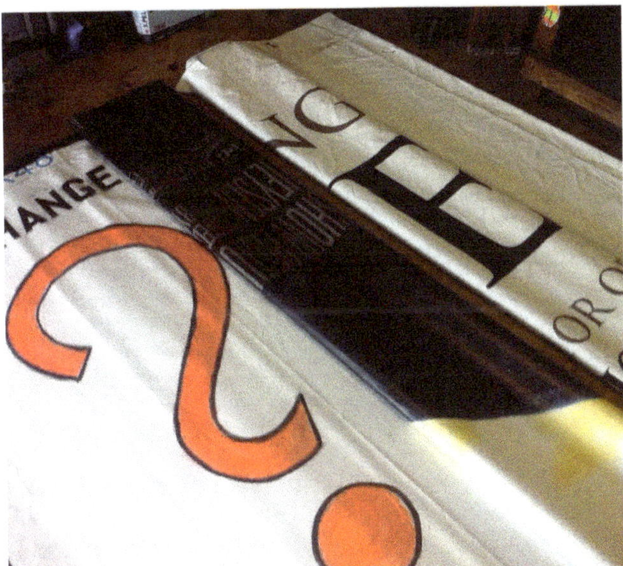

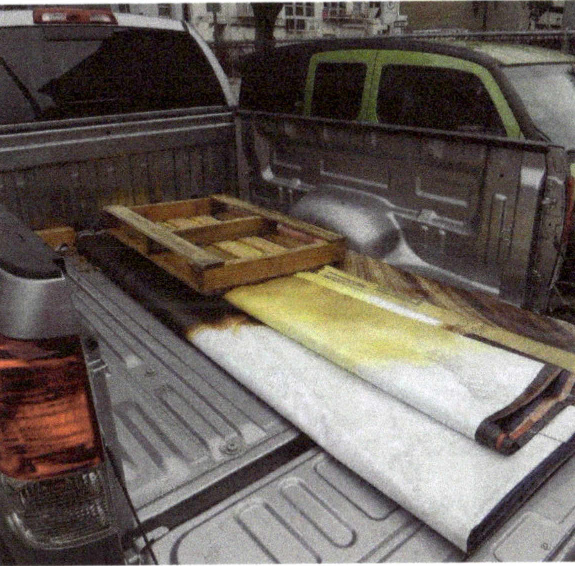

I had recently met Teachr and I knew he sometimes did large-scale street art, so I asked him for advice on how to realize this notion I had of turning an intersection into a Monopoly board for May Day. To my amazement, he said he would do it himself. He called around and managed to get two billboard vinyls donated, a miracle that provided highly durable material that could be cut, painted, rolled up, and transported. Rolled up vinyl might not look heavy, but these 45-ft. long strips are about 300 lbs.

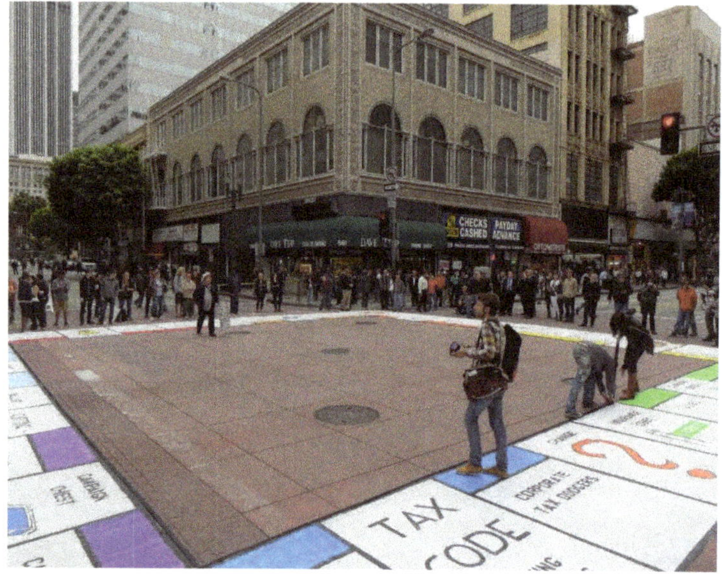

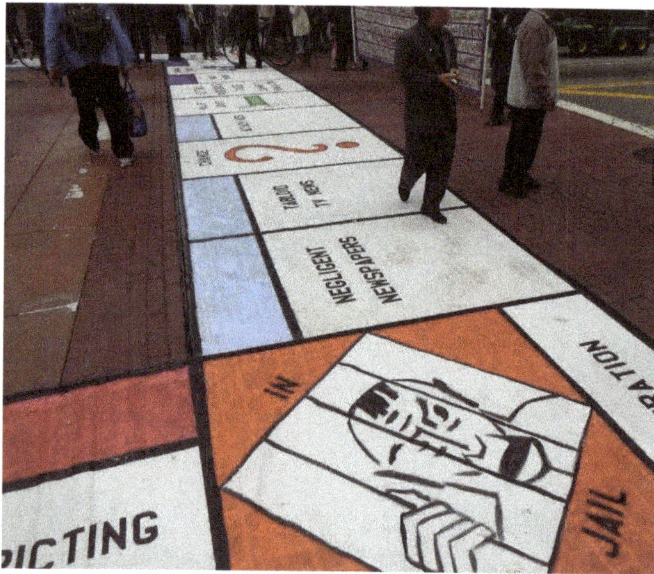

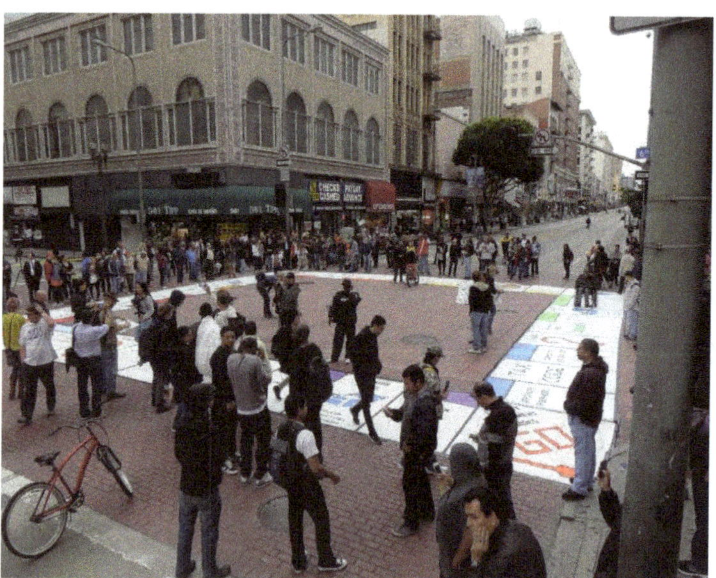

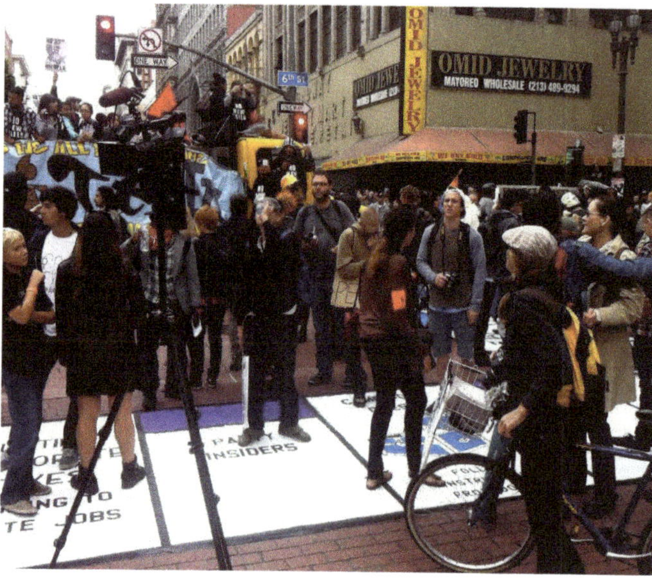

On May 1, 2012, there was a protest planned by Occupy L.A. Four separate protests were to converge on an intersection in Downtown LA, just a couple blocks from the May Day Parade. Coming from the north south, east, and west, they were dubbed the "Four Winds." We showed up that day at the intended convergance point, 6th St. and Main, where Gallery Row meets Skid Row, to find a heavy police presence. Officers posted, helicopters circling, a corner apartment had even been taken over by LAPD for surveillance by plain clothed detectives. Getting anxious, Teachr and I scoped out the May Day Parade route on Broadway and decided to go for it there. It's not like we had a permit, or forethought, into how exactly this was going to go down. But we had come this far.

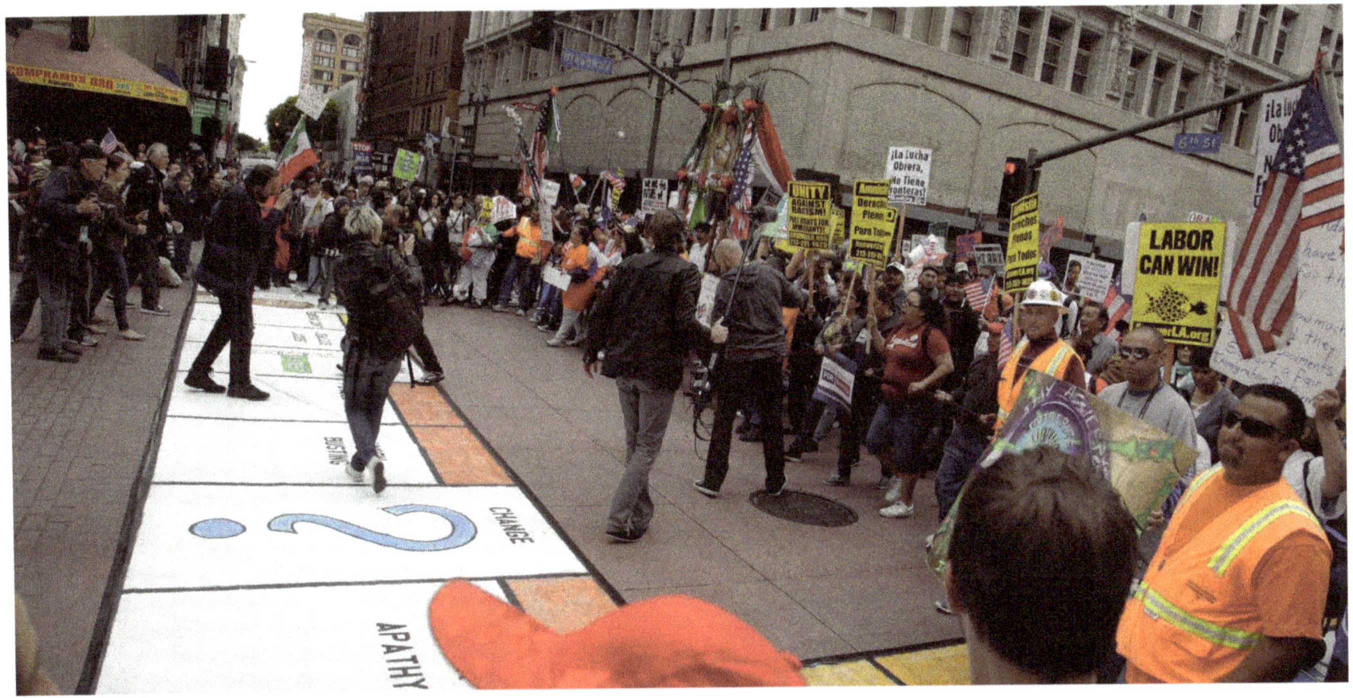

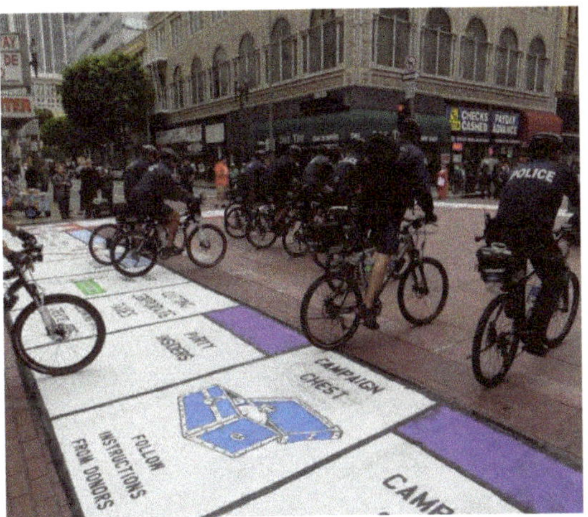

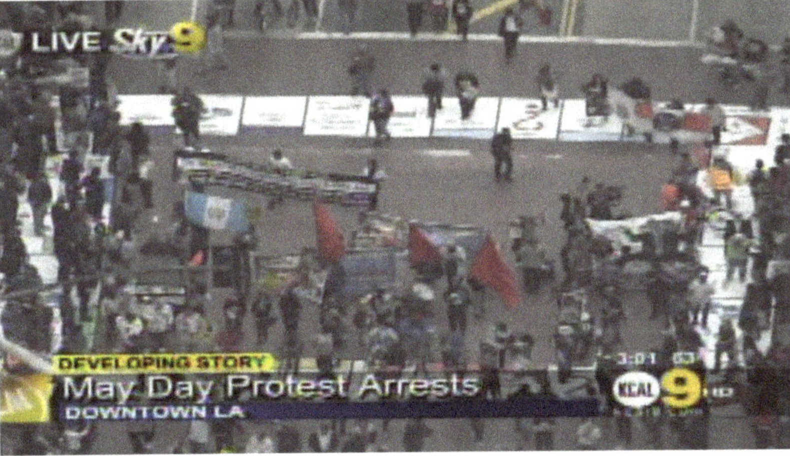

With no announcement, Teachr and the rest of the PSA Crew began to unfurl the long strips of the Pay 2 Play Board in the intersection of Broadway and 6th St. A lot of people had been standing around on the sidewalks, waiting to see what would happen when the Occupy contingents arrived, but were leery of the police posted everywhere. These people now stepped forward, gathering around the huge gameboard, looking down at it in wonder. To my surprise, the cops were not stopping us. After ten minutes, people began to gather in the center of the board/intersection, and a festive atmosphere took hold. Then each of the different Occupy marches began to arrive, excited to be greeted by the crowd. Then the May Day Parade started, and thousands of marchers traversed our board, from labor unions to immigration activists to Native American dancers.

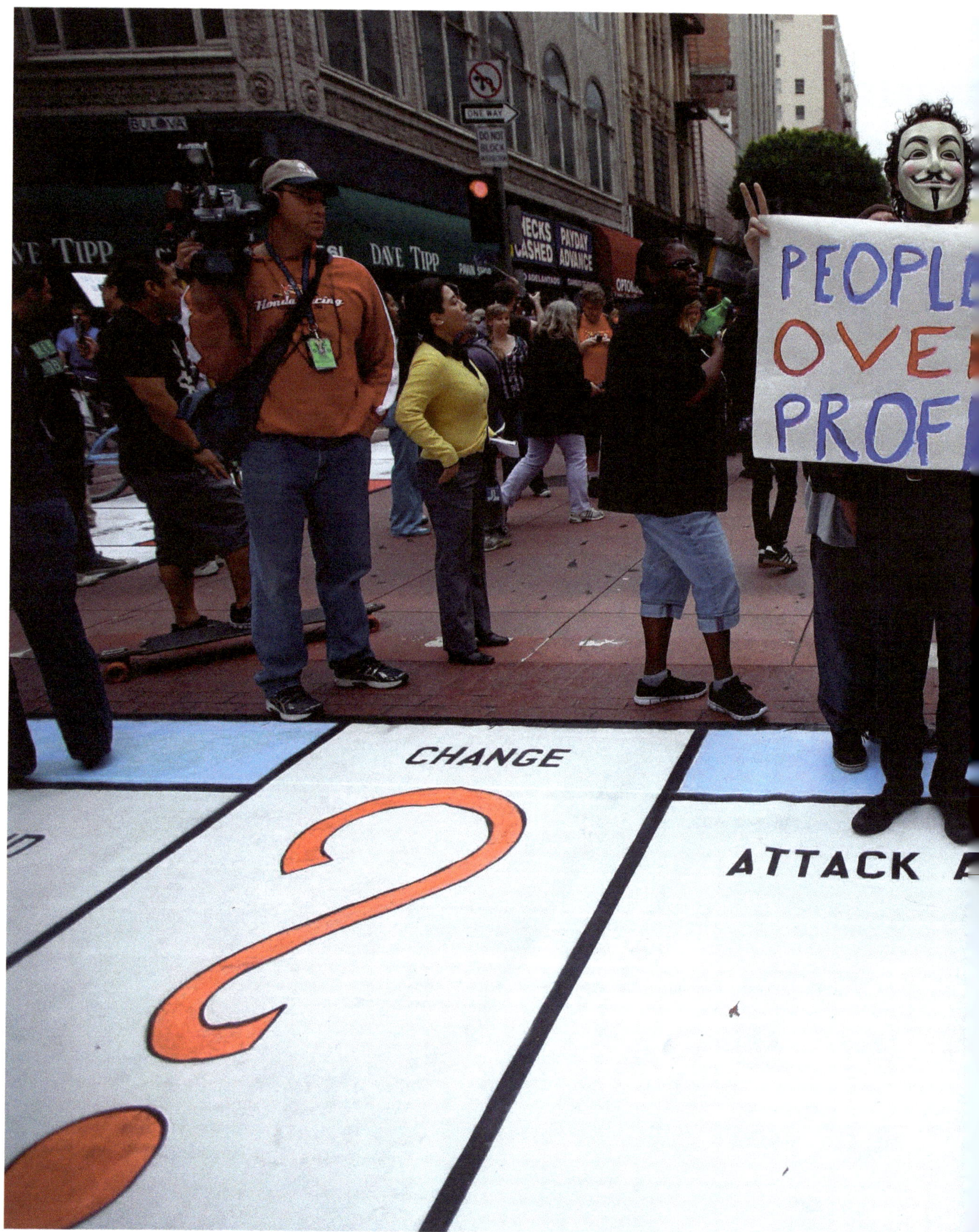
BULOVA
ONE WAY
DO NOT BLOCK
DAVE TIPP
DAVE TIPP
HECKS CASHED
PAYDAY ADVANCE
PEOPL
OVE
PROF
CHANGE
ATTACK

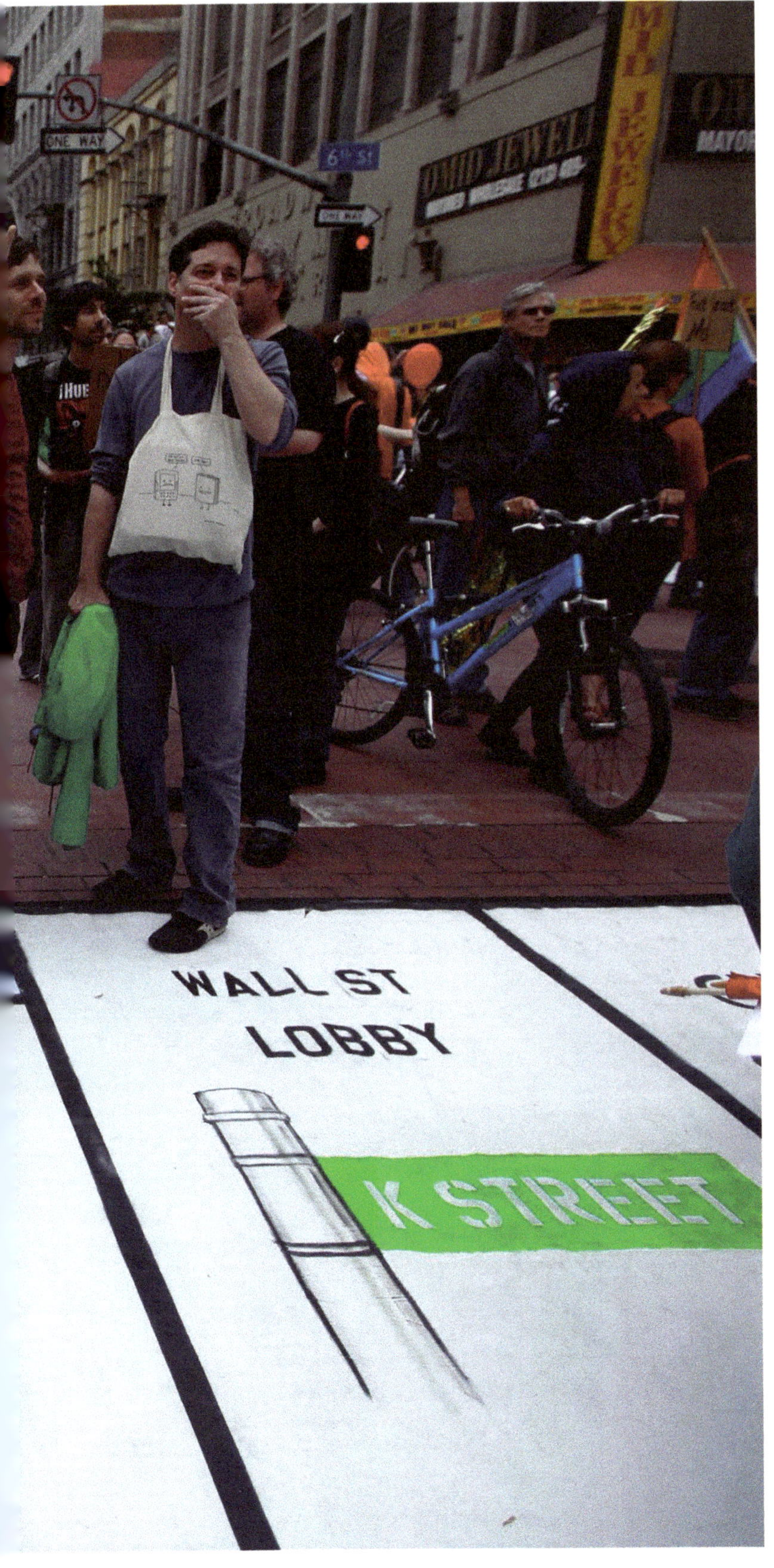

This photgraph was taken by a news photographer and ended up carried all over the world. A journalist called me and asked how I felt that a picture of our protest art was the number one photo on Reuters World News. While traveling with the movie, people have mentioned they saw it in their local newspaper as part of the May Day coverage.

I just wonder who the dude in the mask is and if he ever saw this picture. By this point, the mask he is wearing, Guy Fawkes, had gone from a symbol of Internet activist group Anonymous to become popularized by Occupy Wall Street demonstrators. To some on the right, this makes this picture a 'leftist' or liberal protest, but his sign is unmistakably nonpartisan: People Over Profits.

The essence of our movie, scawled on one sign, captured in a split second by a talented photographer who knew how to frame for perspective. This image embodies the very theme of *PAY 2 PLAY*—that when you stand up in public and use your voice, you don't know who you're going to reach. It can actually spread far and wide and inspire countless others. It seemed destined to become our movie poster.

For a fun challenge, try to find both myself and Teachr in this photograph!

Photo by Lucy Nicholson, Licensed from Reuters.

NEW YORK STOCK EXCHANGE

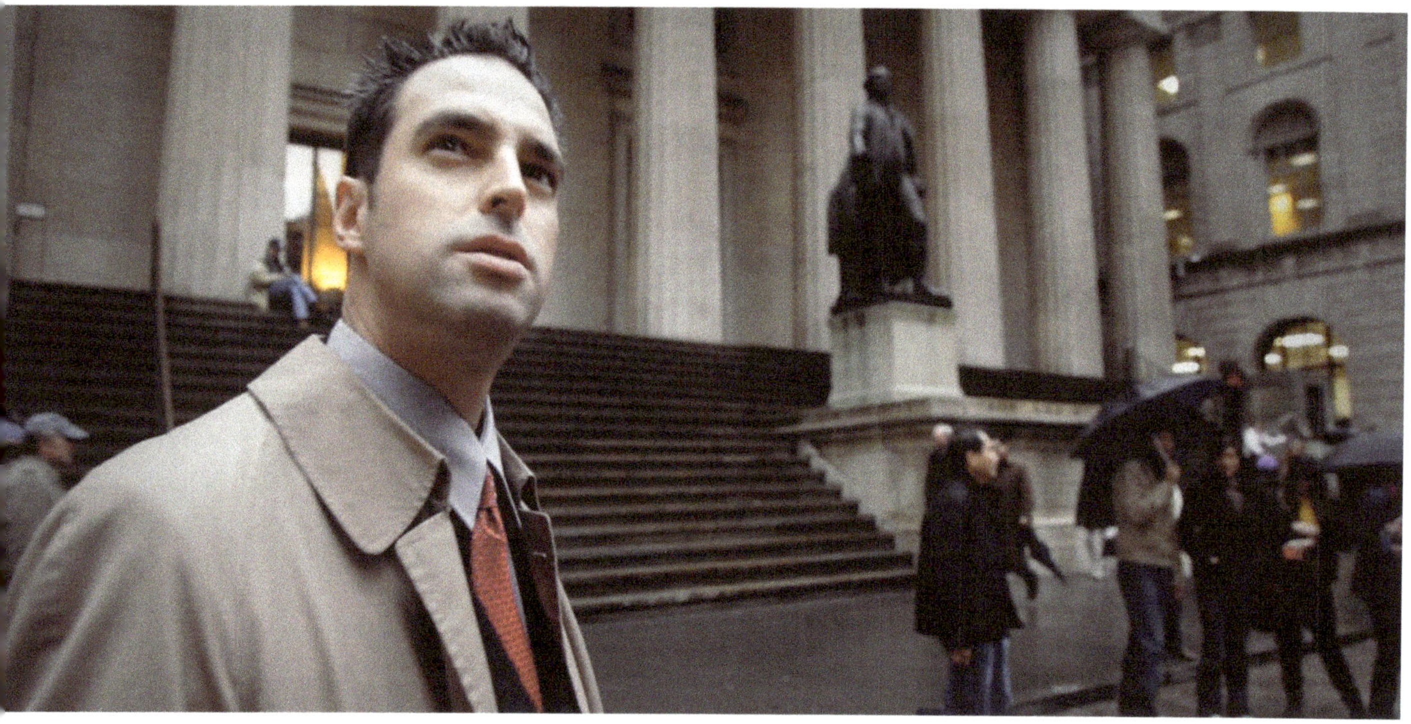

In the fall of 2010, I visited Wall Street. Right across from the New York Stock Exchange, at the Financial Museum, there was a solid gold Monopoly board on display, worth about $1 million. The gold Monopoly game comes with gold-plated cards, diamonds encrusted on the dice, and playing pieces studded with gems. If the boardgame of Monopoly had taught us that greed was the goal, this was like a trophy to the greediest.

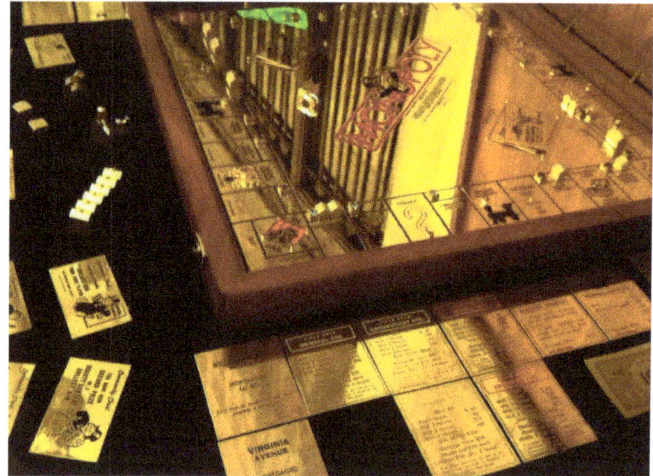

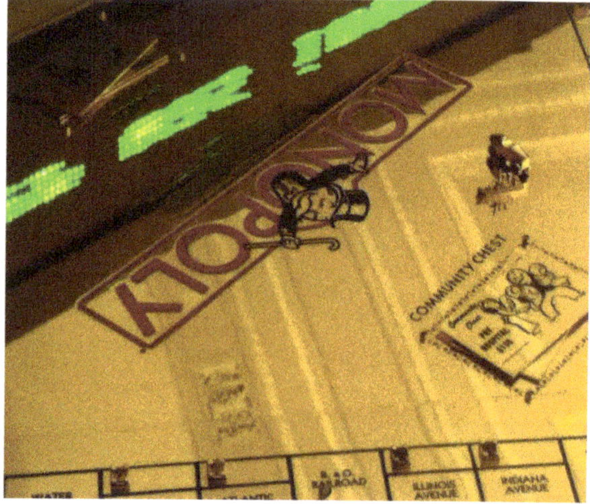

Here, Wall Street adds insult to the injury of the financial meltdown. The original board was not designed by Charles Darrow as we grew up learning, but by a progressive activist named Lizzie Magie decades before Darrow sold it to Parker Brothers as his own invention. In *PAY 2 PLAY,* we reveal Monopoly's true origins, unearthed because Parker Brothers had once maintained that they had a monopoly on the very word "monopoly." Lizzie Magie intended the game to teach others about the dangers of speculative real estate, and was the one to first write "GO TO JAIL" on the board—a step toward reform that should be seriously considered today.

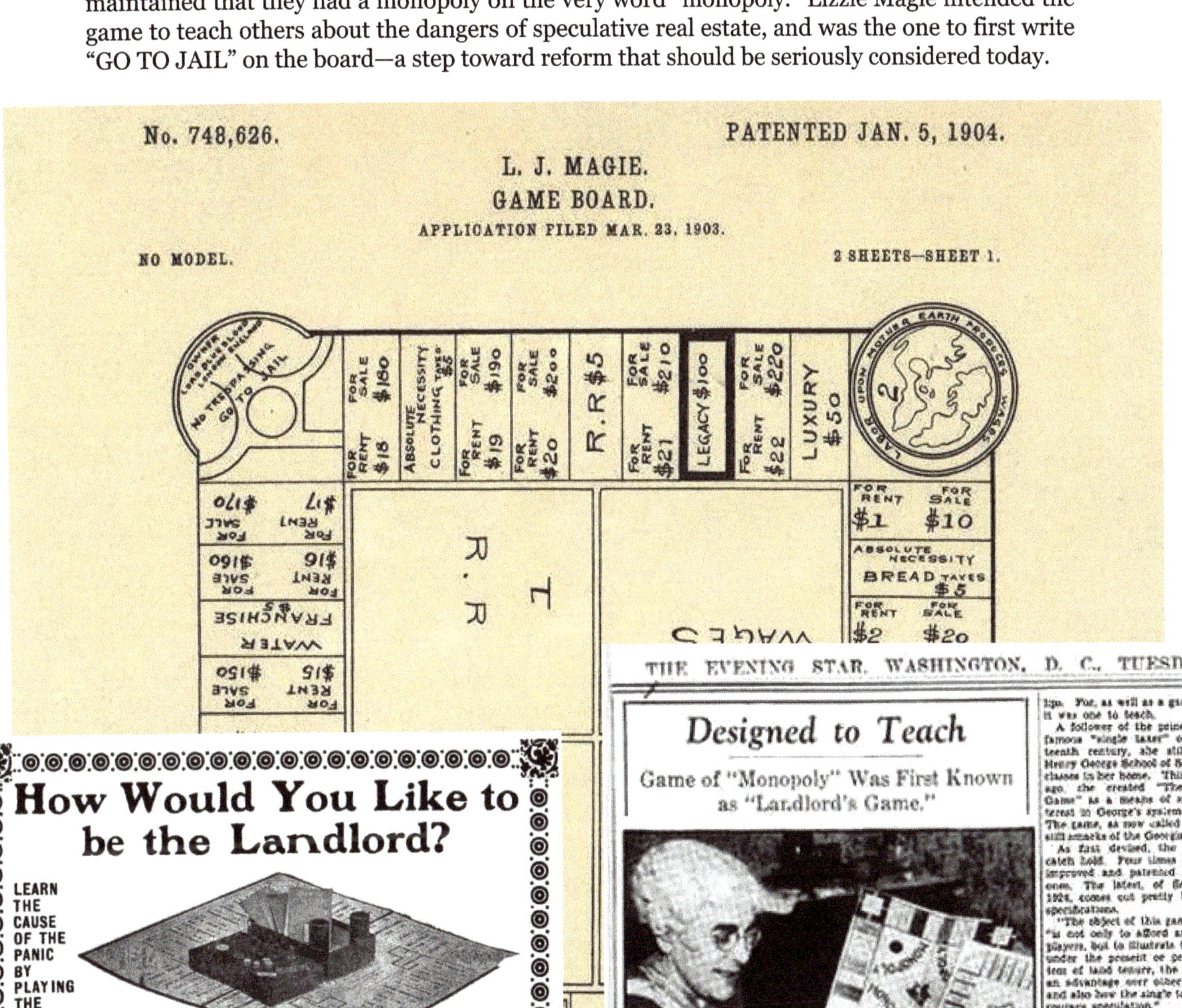

We got our chance to respond on Magie's behalf. On Jan. 21, 2015, the fifth anniversary of *Citizens United vs. FEC*, Common Cause NY organized a protest at the New York Stock Exchange and got a permit for our massive Pay 2 Play Board to be displayed. Despite freezing January temperatures, people came out to march on the cobblestones of Wall Street. To my amazement, some even made their own large-size tokens to go with the corrupt monopoly board theme--a pewter finish and everything!

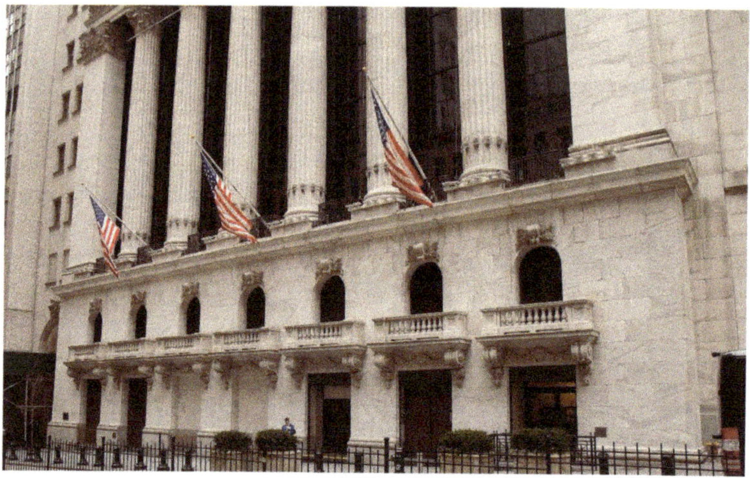

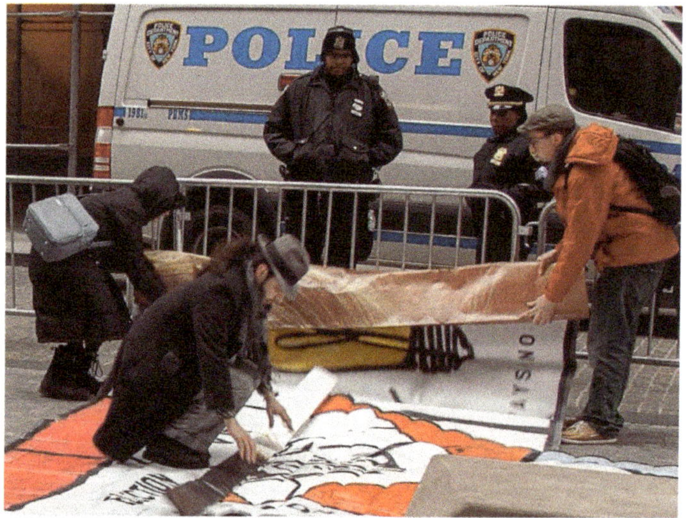

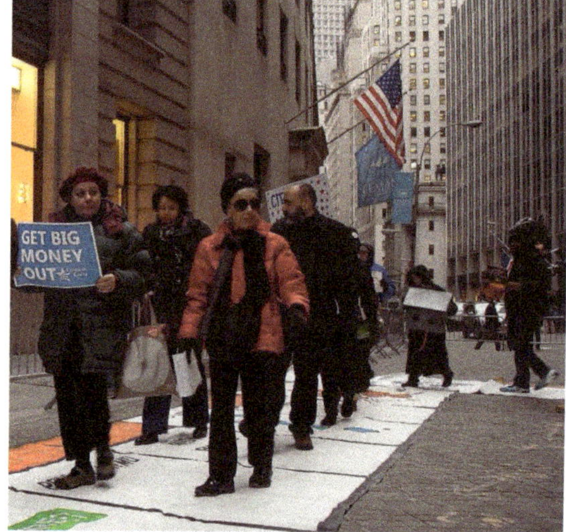

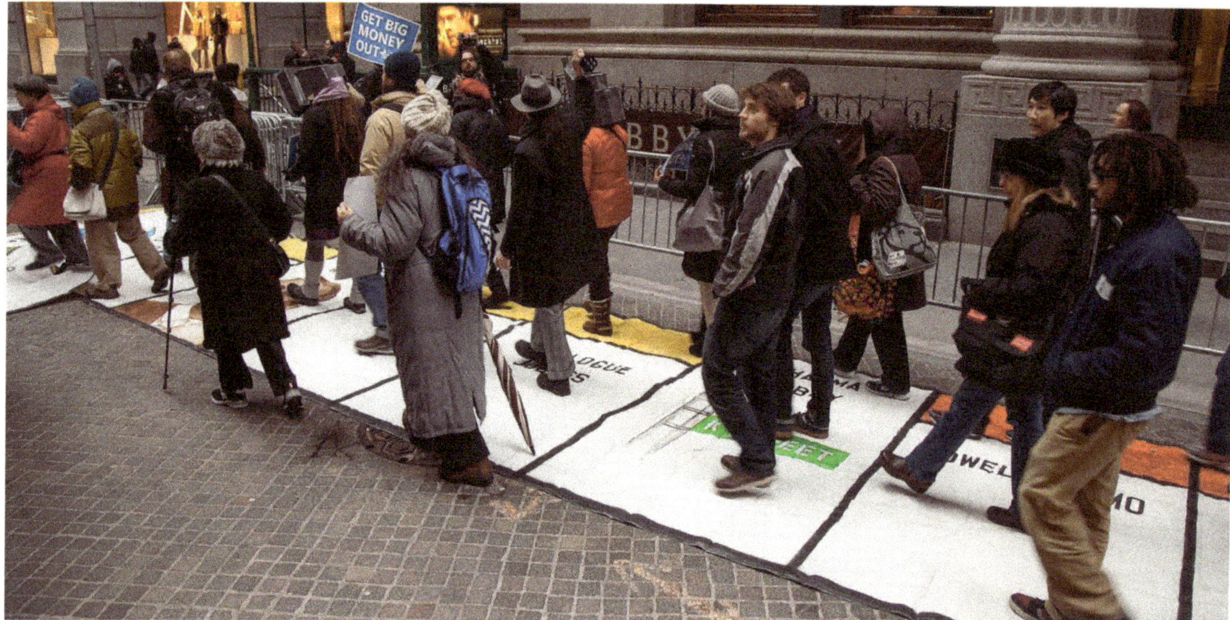

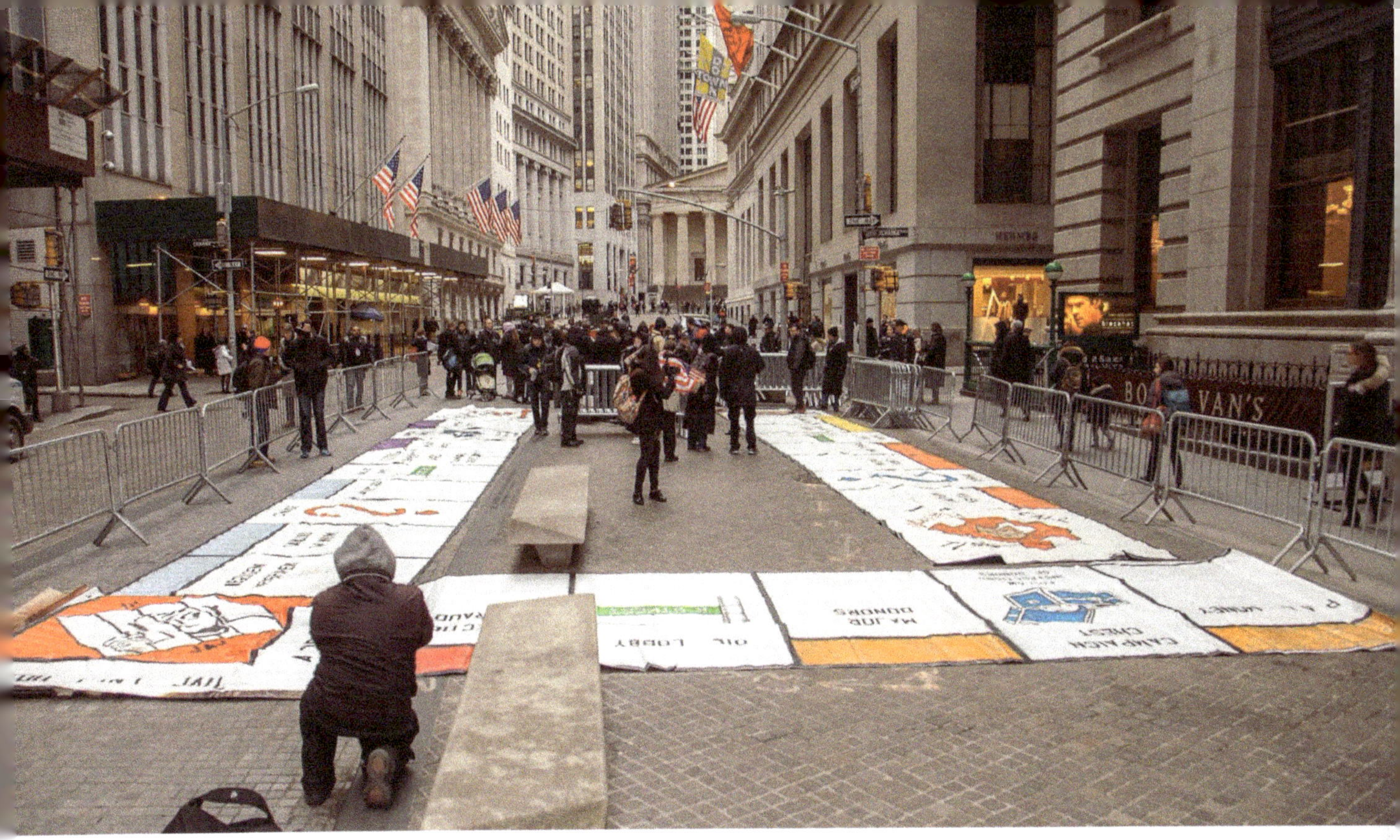

Photos by Andrew Einhorn.

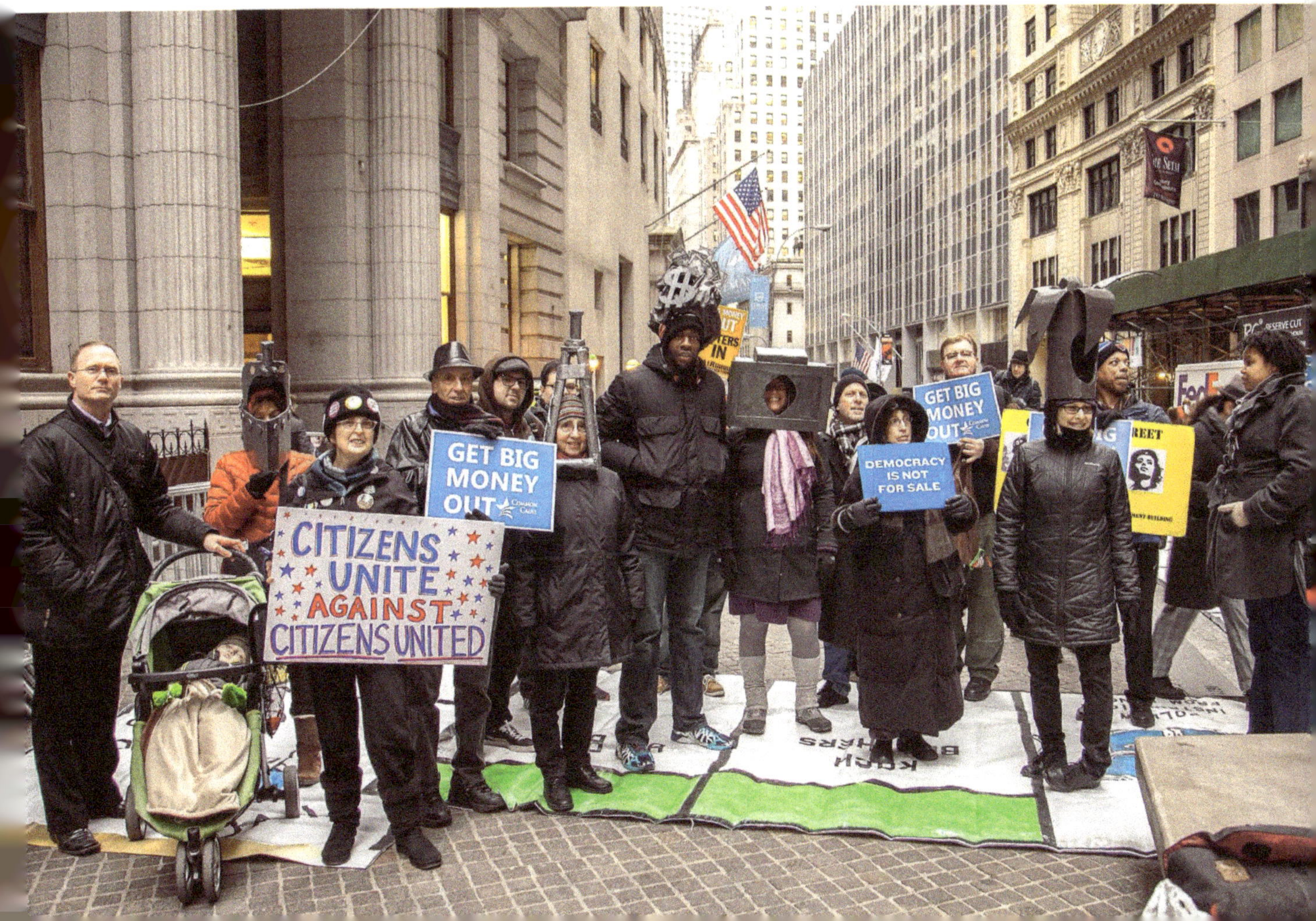

THE PAY 2 PLAY POSTER

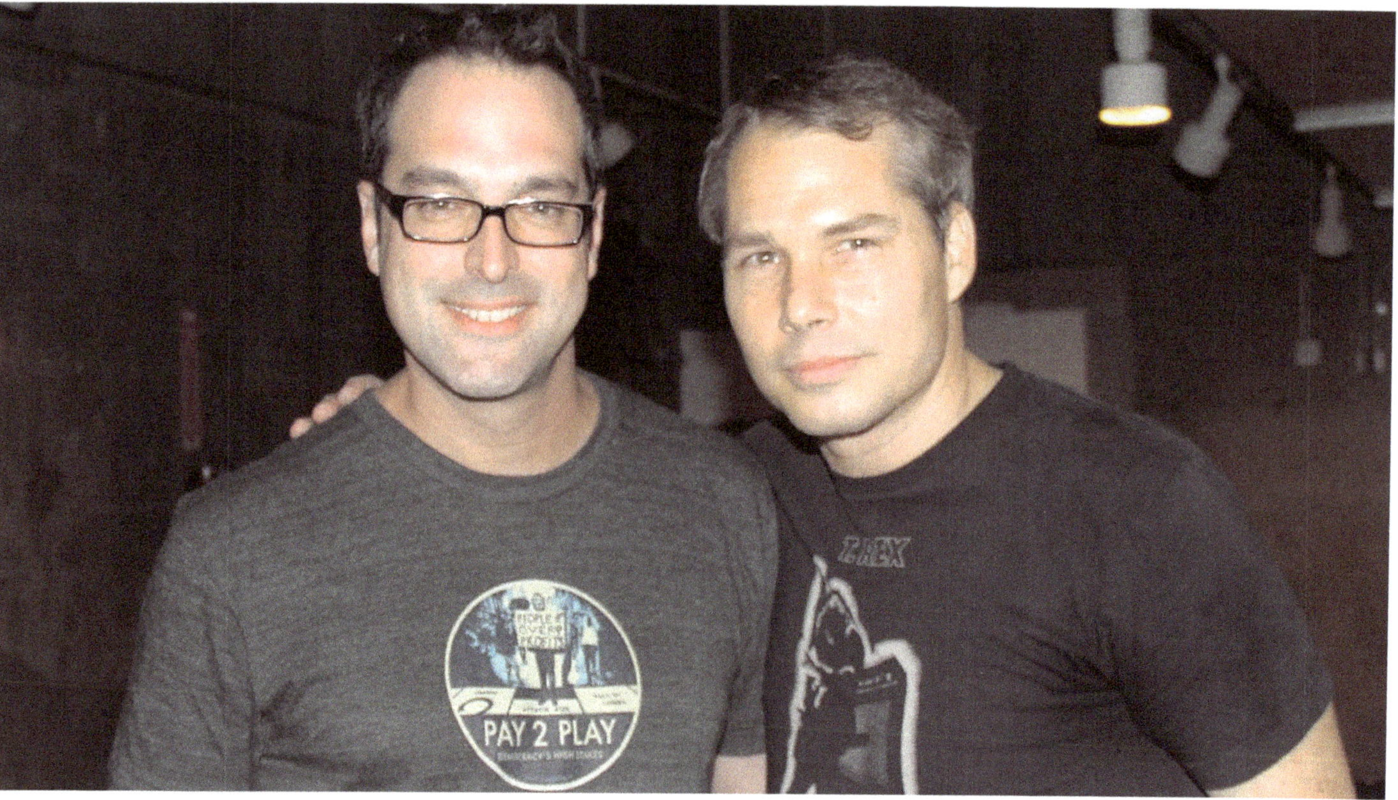

Can you imagine getting to perform with your favorite rock star? Or play a pro game with your favorite athlete? That's what it was like to get to work with Shepard Fairey on a poster. Living in New York in the '90s, I saw little stickers of Andre the Giant slowly spread around town, then start to appear with the words OBEY and GIANT. I watched OBEY GIANT rise over the ensuing years, having always loved the look of old Soviet propaganda art, an aesthetic which Shepard took to new heights. The textures in his backgrounds, the bands he worked with, the causes he supported; everything he did always seemed like what I wished I could do. I took a chance and emailed his company.

To my surprise, Shepard responded readily, saying he would be happy to help on the project. Turns out, Shepard is fiercely vocal about reforming campaign finance and getting corporate money out of elections. He also is a fan of Lawrence Lessig, who appears in our film, because Professor Lessig spoke out in Shepard's defense when Shepard was embroiled in a lawsuit with the Associated Press over using a photo of Barack Obama in his iconic 2008 HOPE poster.

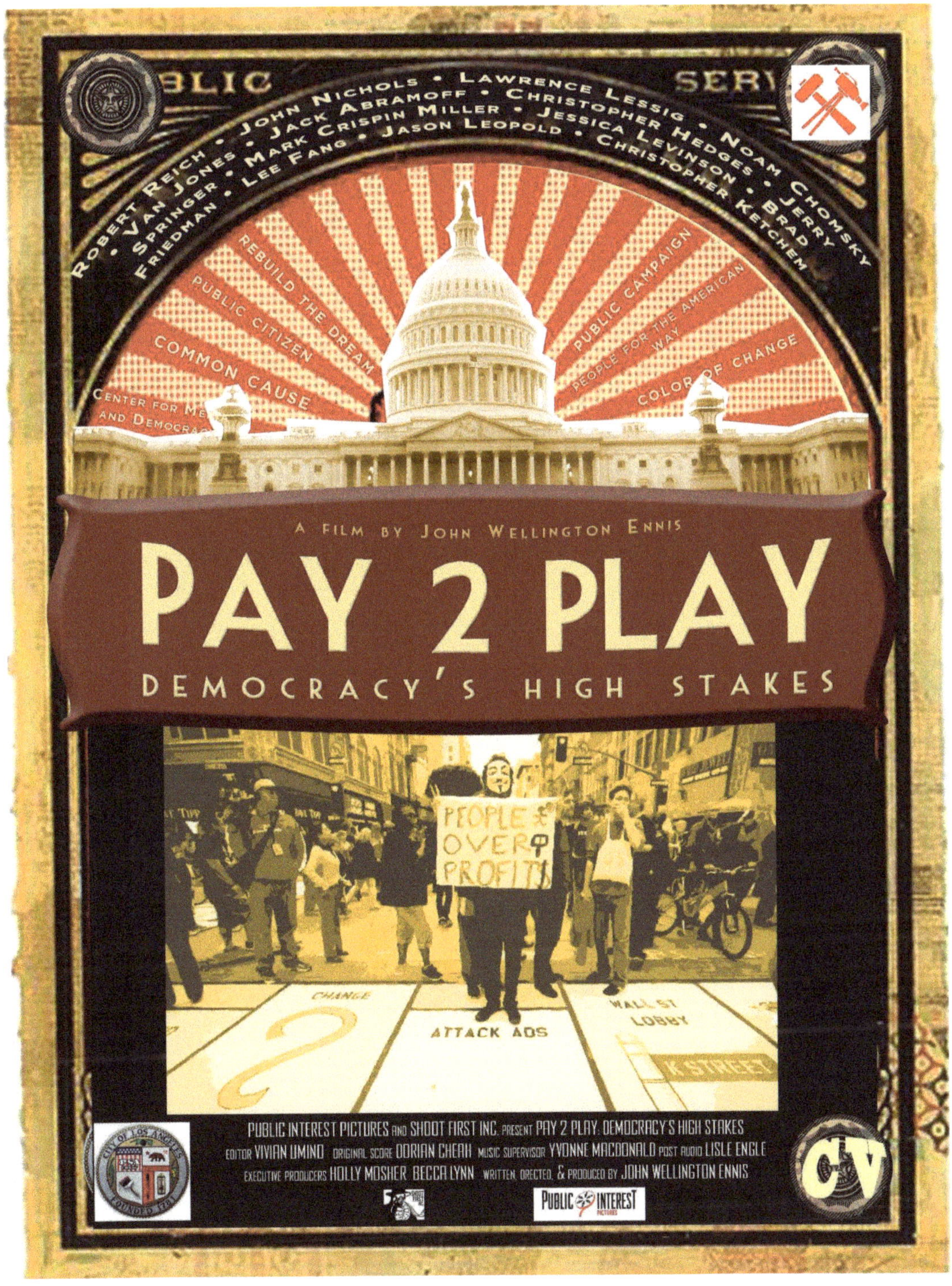

This is the mock up I shared with Shepard and his team. Like the movie itself, I didn't want it to be too grim or serious. I wanted to show that it was about politics but also people protesting in the street. I wanted it to feel like a movement. I also wanted to fit as many names of people and organizations on it as humanly possible.

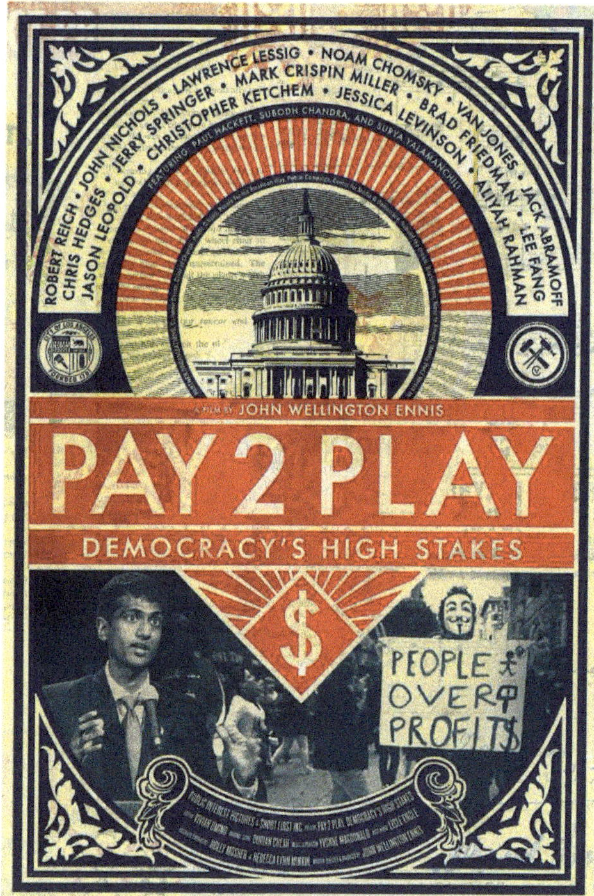
ROBERT REICH • JOHN NICHOLS • LAWRENCE LESSIG • NOAM CHOMSKY • VAN JONES • JACK ABRAMOFF
CHRIS HEDGES • JERRY SPRINGER • MARK CRISPIN MILLER • BRAD FRIEDMAN • LEE FANG
JASON LEOPOLD • CHRISTOPHER KETCHEM • JESSICA LEVINSON • ALIYAH RAHMAN
FEATURING PAUL HACKETT, SUBODH CHANDRA, AND SURYA YALAMANCHILI
A FILM BY JOHN WELLINGTON ENNIS
PAY 2 PLAY
DEMOCRACY'S HIGH STAKES
$
PEOPLE OVER PROFITS

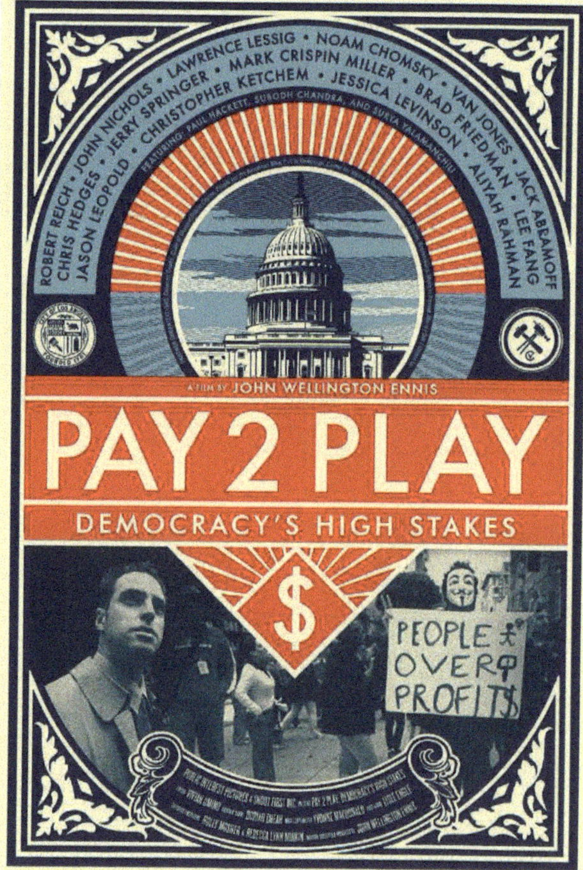
ROBERT REICH • JOHN NICHOLS • LAWRENCE LESSIG • NOAM CHOMSKY • VAN JONES • JACK ABRAMOFF
CHRIS HEDGES • JERRY SPRINGER • MARK CRISPIN MILLER • BRAD FRIEDMAN • LEE FANG
JASON LEOPOLD • CHRISTOPHER KETCHEM • JESSICA LEVINSON • ALIYAH RAHMAN
FEATURING PAUL HACKETT, SUBODH CHANDRA, AND SURYA YALAMANCHILI
A FILM BY JOHN WELLINGTON ENNIS
PAY 2 PLAY
DEMOCRACY'S HIGH STAKES
$
PEOPLE OVER PROFITS

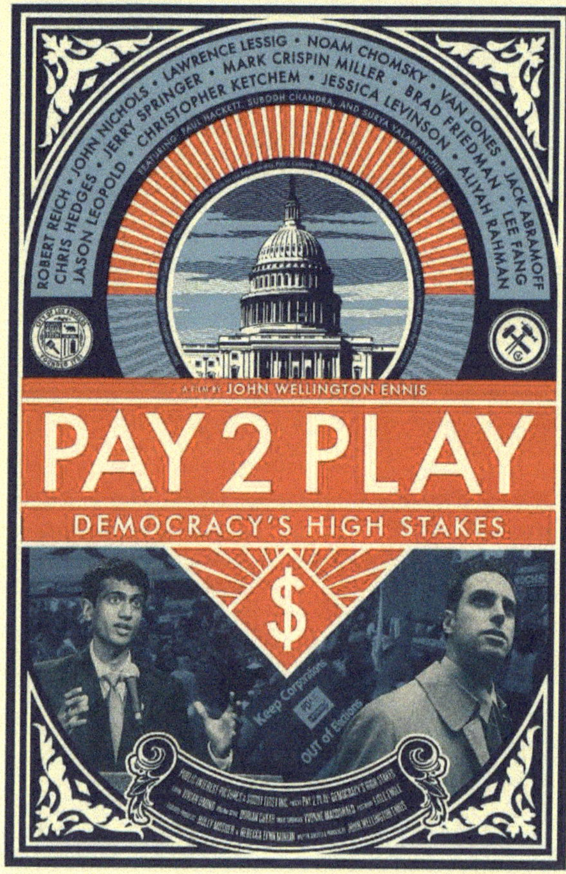
ROBERT REICH • JOHN NICHOLS • LAWRENCE LESSIG • NOAM CHOMSKY • VAN JONES • JACK ABRAMOFF
CHRIS HEDGES • JERRY SPRINGER • MARK CRISPIN MILLER • BRAD FRIEDMAN • LEE FANG
JASON LEOPOLD • CHRISTOPHER KETCHEM • JESSICA LEVINSON • ALIYAH RAHMAN
FEATURING PAUL HACKETT, SUBODH CHANDRA, AND SURYA YALAMANCHILI
A FILM BY JOHN WELLINGTON ENNIS
PAY 2 PLAY
DEMOCRACY'S HIGH STAKES
$
Keep Corporations OUT of Elections

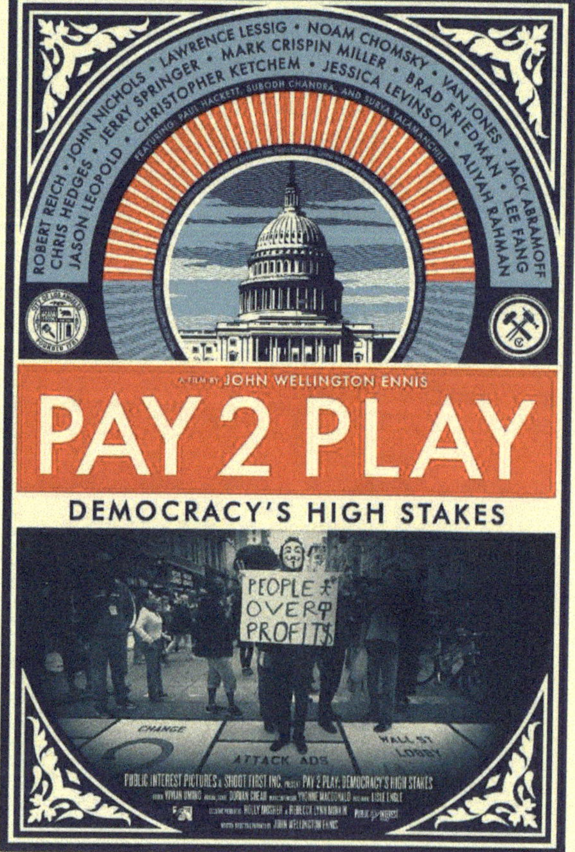
ROBERT REICH • JOHN NICHOLS • LAWRENCE LESSIG • NOAM CHOMSKY • VAN JONES • JACK ABRAMOFF
CHRIS HEDGES • JERRY SPRINGER • MARK CRISPIN MILLER • BRAD FRIEDMAN • LEE FANG
JASON LEOPOLD • CHRISTOPHER KETCHEM • JESSICA LEVINSON • ALIYAH RAHMAN
FEATURING PAUL HACKETT, SUBODH CHANDRA, AND SURYA YALAMANCHILI
A FILM BY JOHN WELLINGTON ENNIS
PAY 2 PLAY
DEMOCRACY'S HIGH STAKES
PEOPLE OVER PROFITS
CHANGE
ATTACK ADS
WALL ST LOBBY
PUBLIC INTEREST PICTURES & SHOOT FIRST INC. PRESENT PAY 2 PLAY: DEMOCRACY'S HIGH STAKES

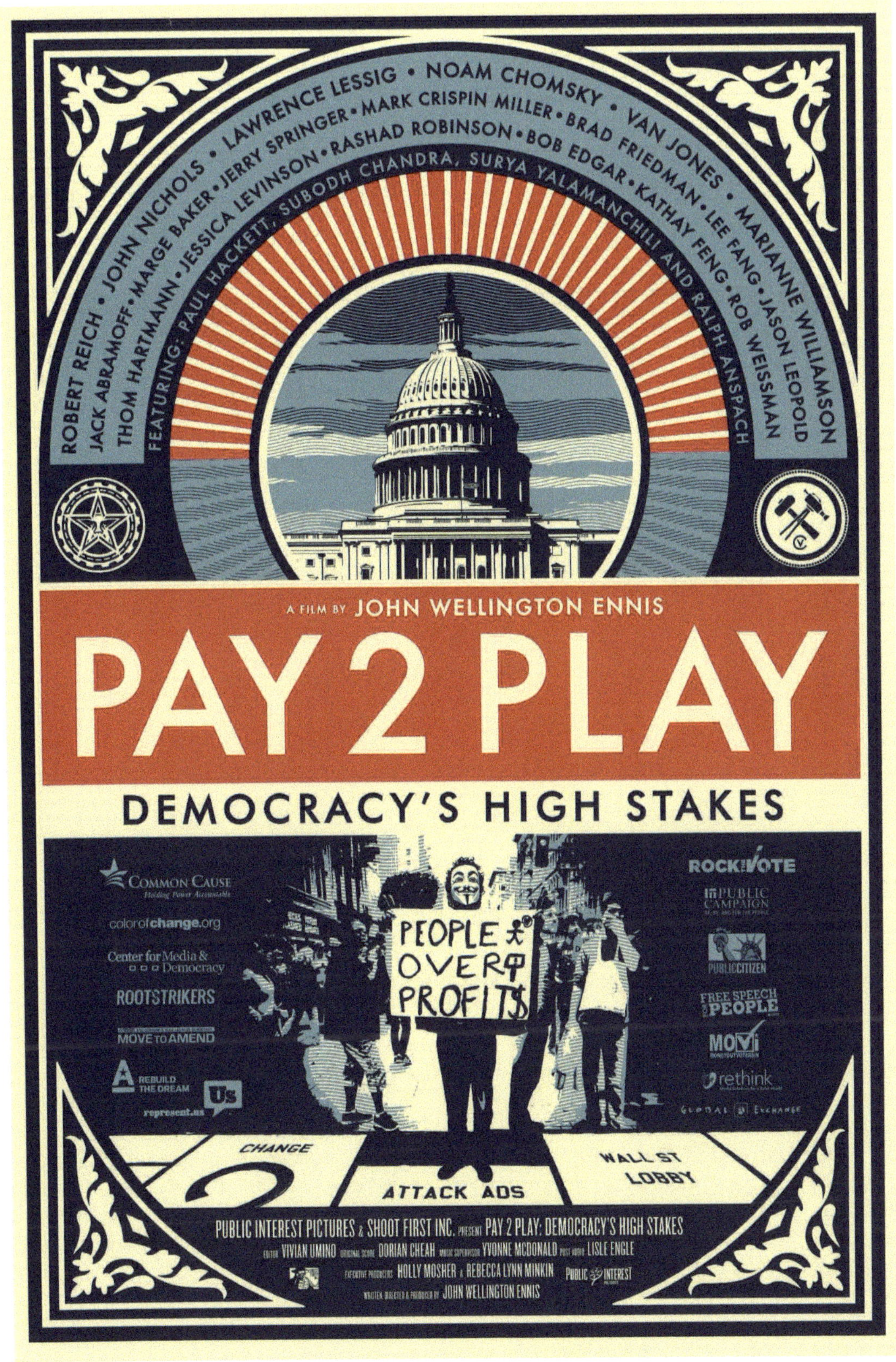

OPPOSITE: The first round of concepts submitted by Shepard's Studio One. ABOVE: The final version of the PAY 2 PLAY movie poster, by Shepard Fairey and Cleon Peterson.

WILD POSTINGS

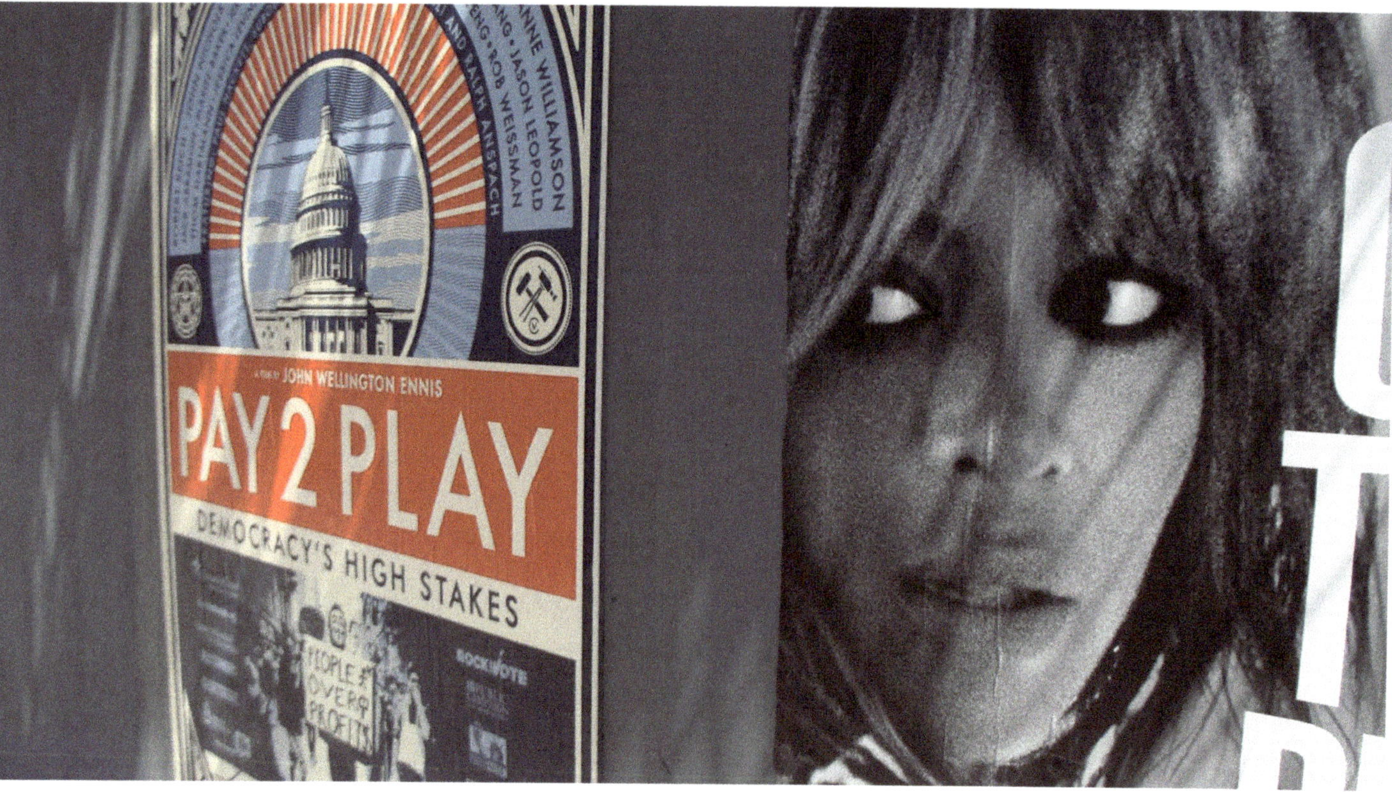

In Los Angeles around this time, there was a rise in oversize movie posters going up, known as wild postings. L.A. is already an entertainment capital, and the outdoor advertising for entertainment is like no place else. Movies and TV shows compete for billboards all over town to give their studio visibility. Wild postings became the next go-to for standing out in a city already inundated with ads. After years of ignoring posters piling up, the city started regulating walls. A permit was required for these ads, and soon construction walls and parking lots were being surrounded by plywood walls with gray paint to sell as ad space in a city already saturated with ads.

Now that we had a dream-come-true poster for our movie, I wondered: if I printed up big *posters*, maybe people will think it is a big *movie*. We soon learned that these grey walls were being regularly cleaned, and any one else's posters were painted over immediately. So the PSA Crew would have to get inventive with its placement.

As I traveled to screen the movie in different cities, outdoor advertising was not nearly as hard fought for as L.A. So I applied the lessons I learned in Hollywood. I would stop by the local Home Depot to stock up on supplies and head out at night after screenings.

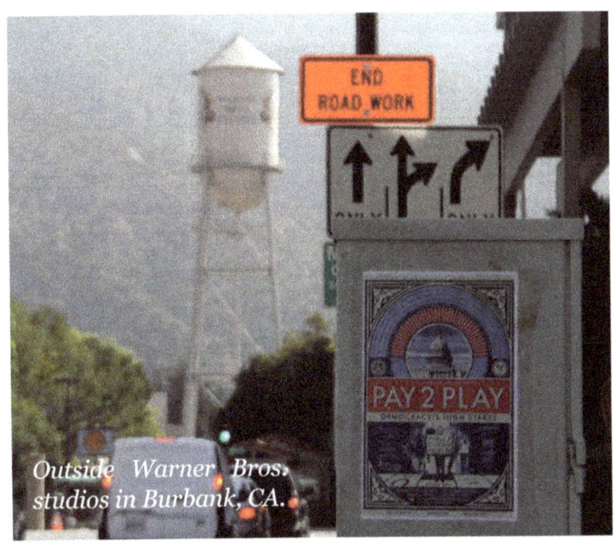

Outside Warner Bros. studios in Burbank, CA.

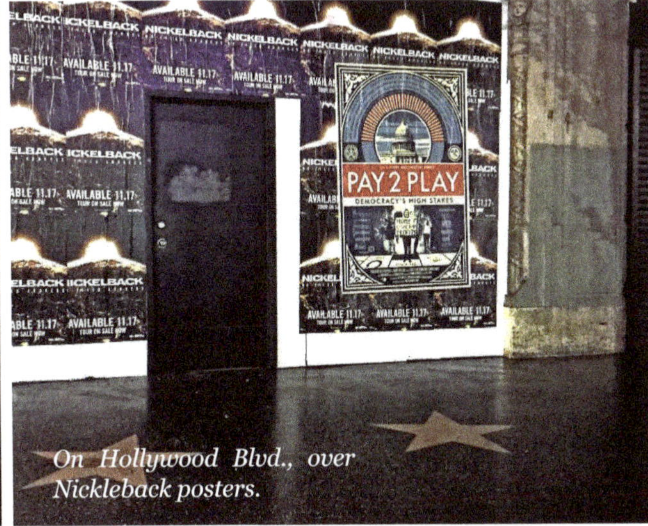

On Hollywood Blvd., over Nickleback posters.

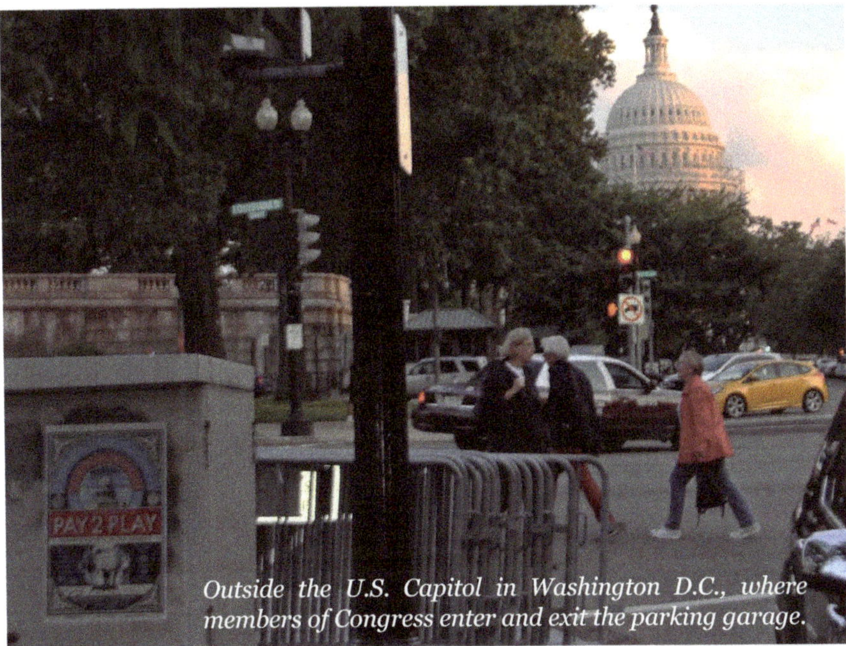

Outside the U.S. Capitol in Washington D.C., where members of Congress enter and exit the parking garage.

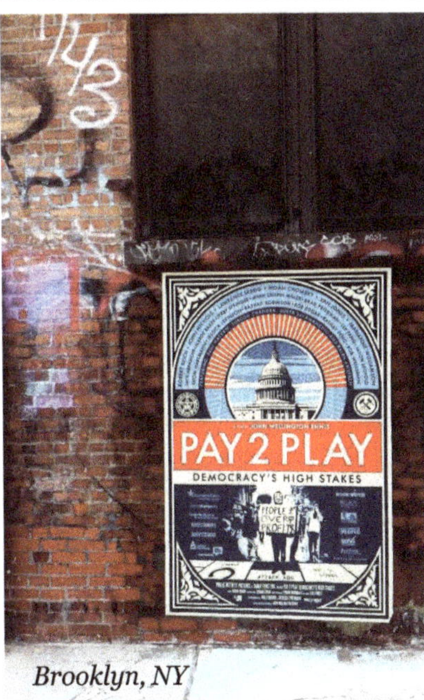

Brooklyn, NY

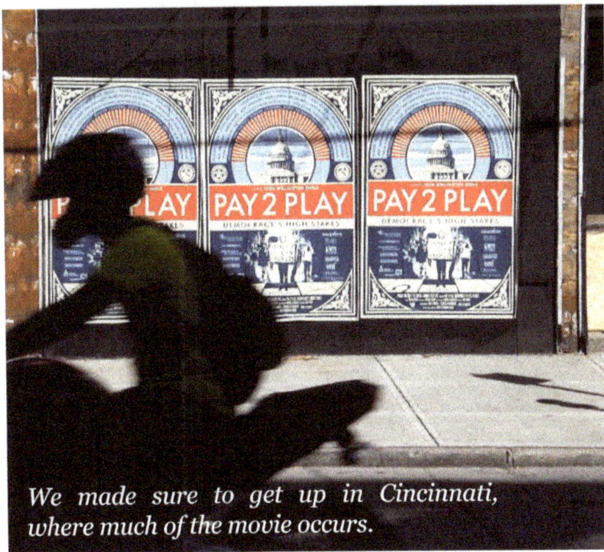

We made sure to get up in Cincinnati, where much of the movie occurs.

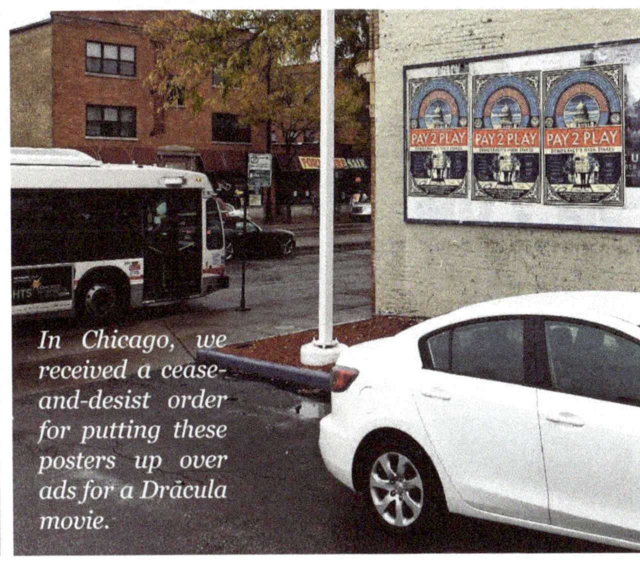

In Chicago, we received a cease-and-desist order for putting these posters up over ads for a Drăcula movie.

FOR YOUR CONSIDERATION

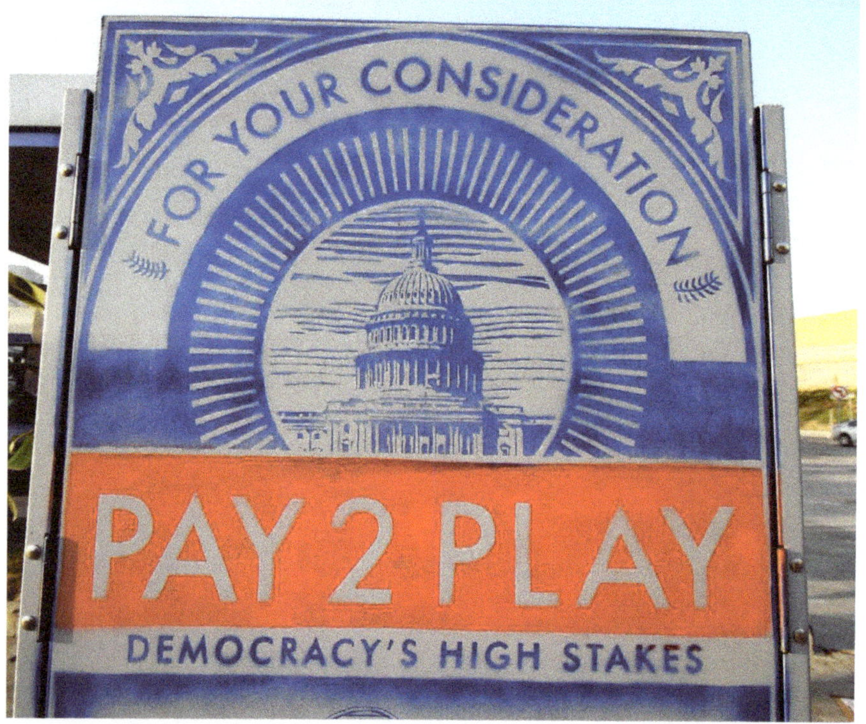

Another L.A. phenomenon is mounting a citywide ad campaign during awards season, touting movies, shows, and actors "For Your Consideration," presuming you are someone deciding awards.

The PSA Crew endeavored to make our own For Your Consideration campaign for *PAY 2 PLAY*. Teachr designed stencils based on our poster, featuring street artists from the film. We put up favorite quotes from the artists on their respective traffic box.

While the artwork looked great, we did not win any awards.

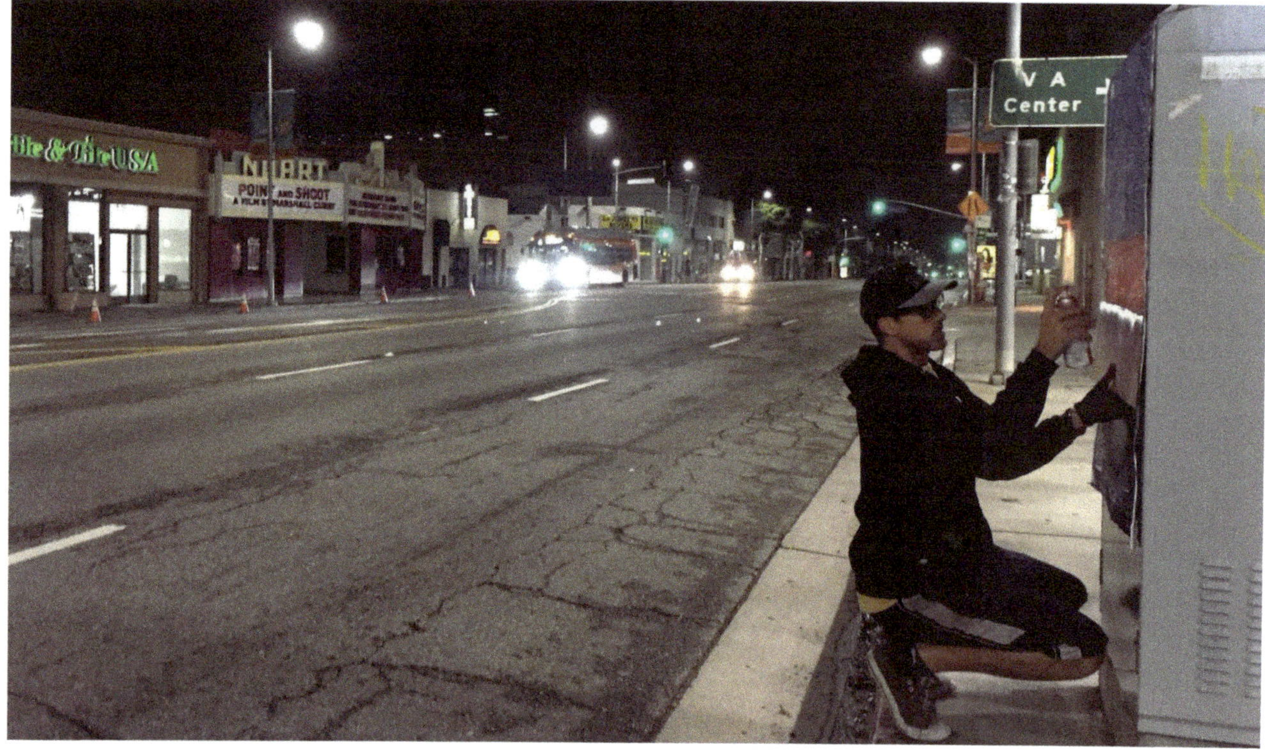

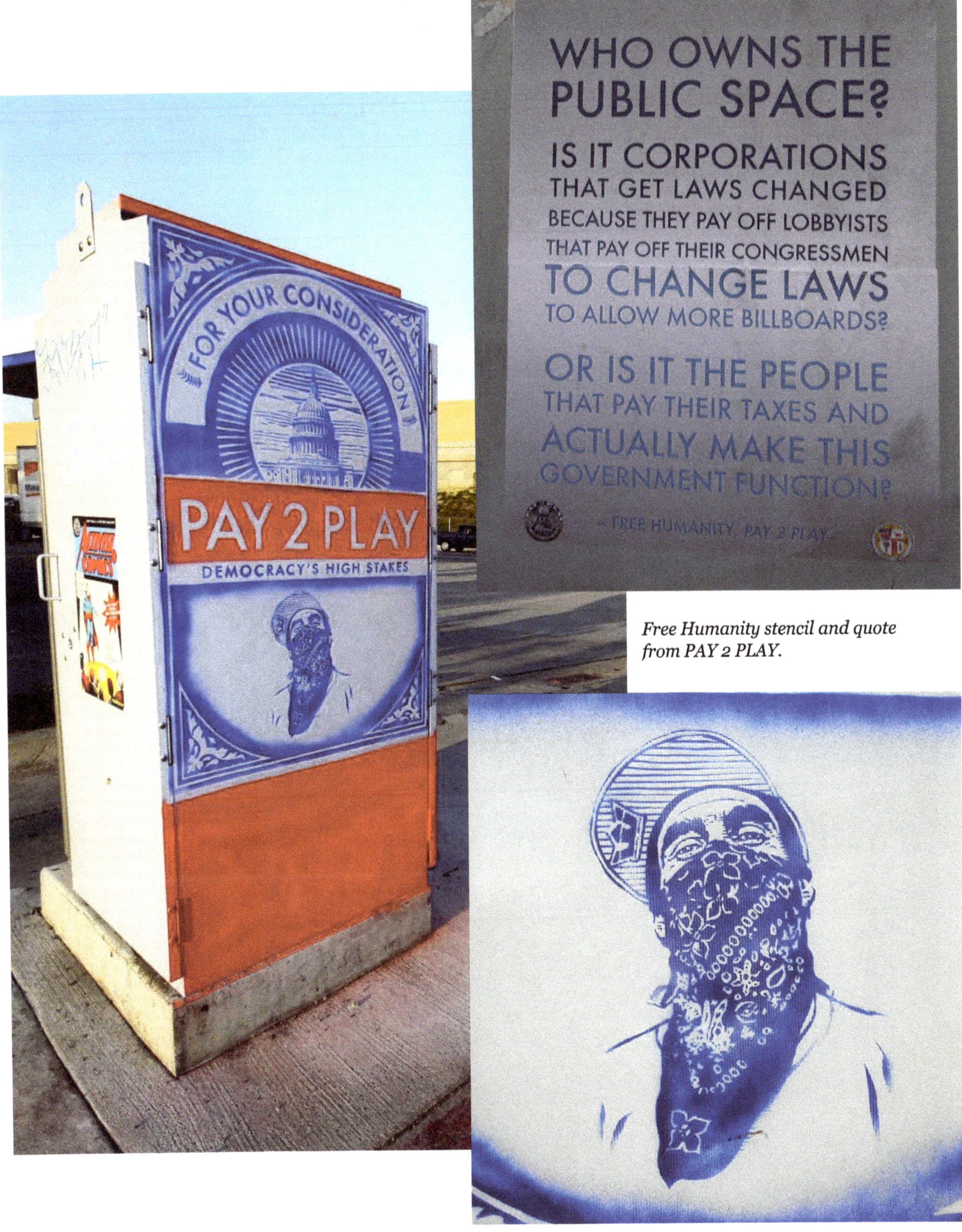

Free Humanity stencil and quote from PAY 2 PLAY.

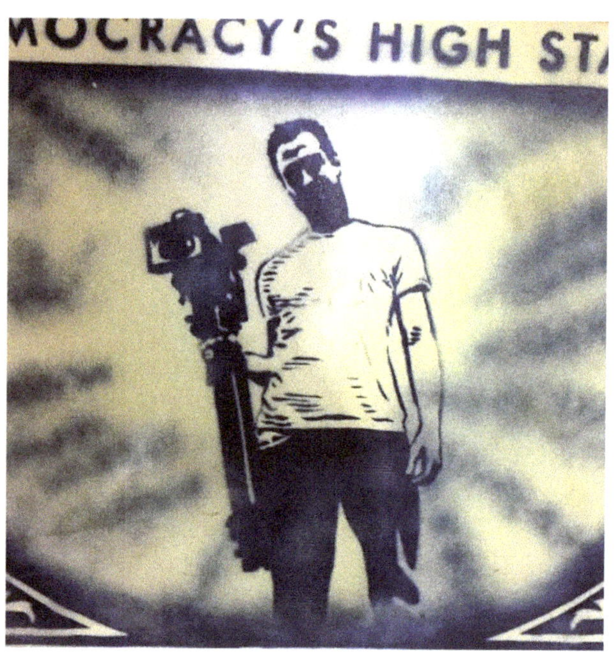

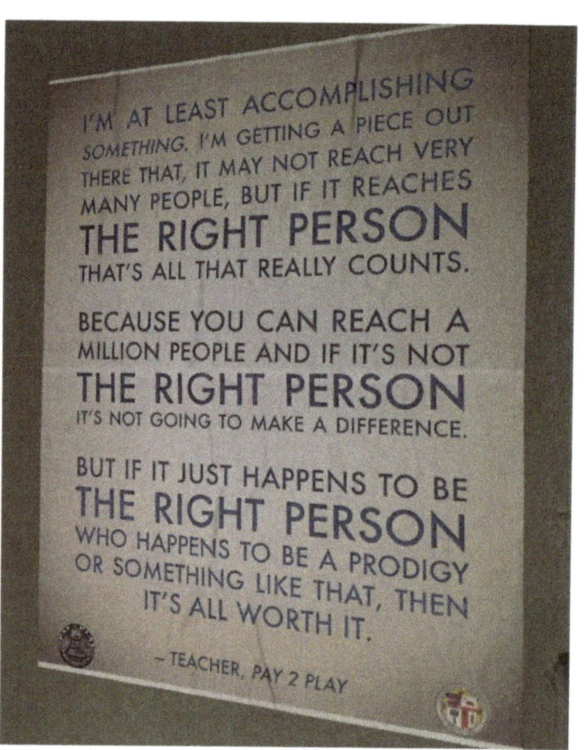

A stencil of the author, with a quote from Teachr about why he does street art.

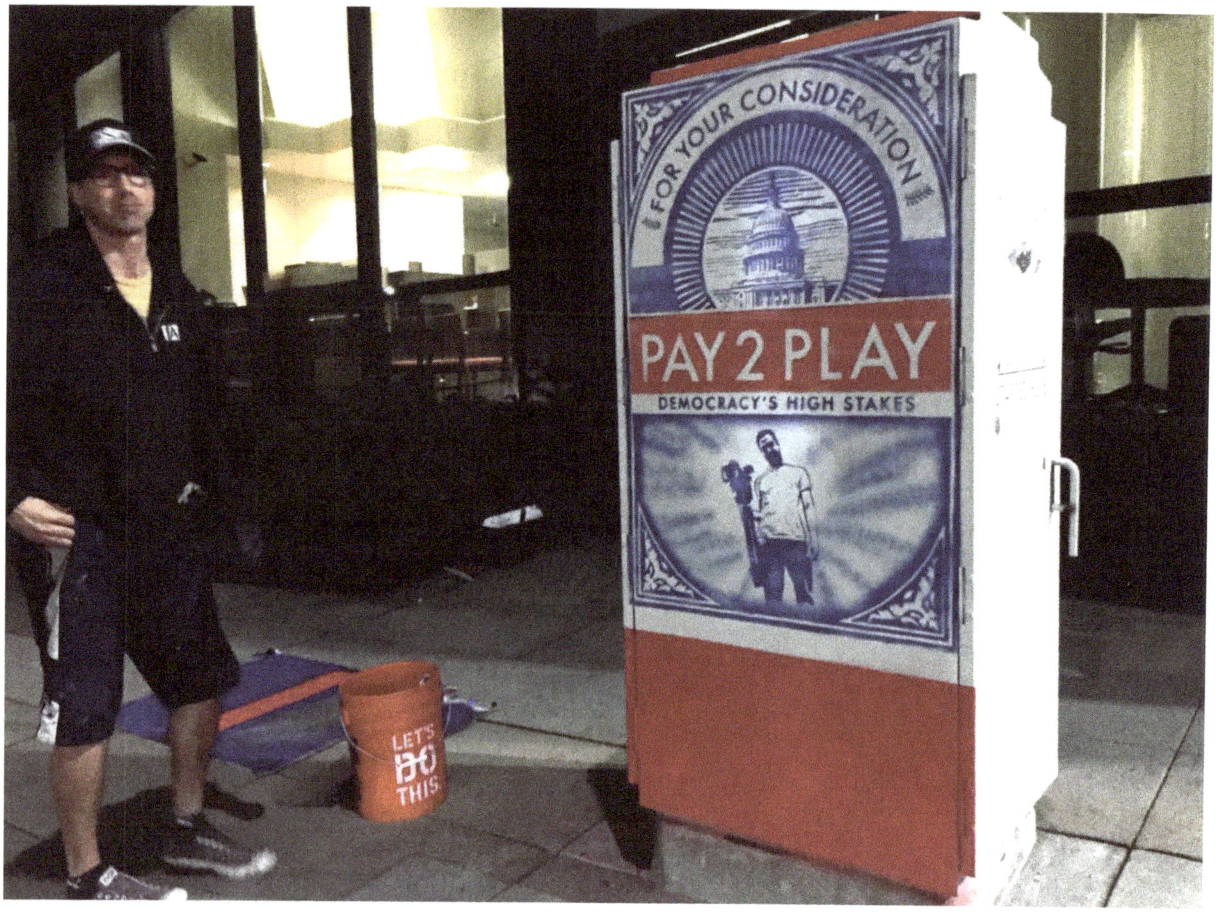

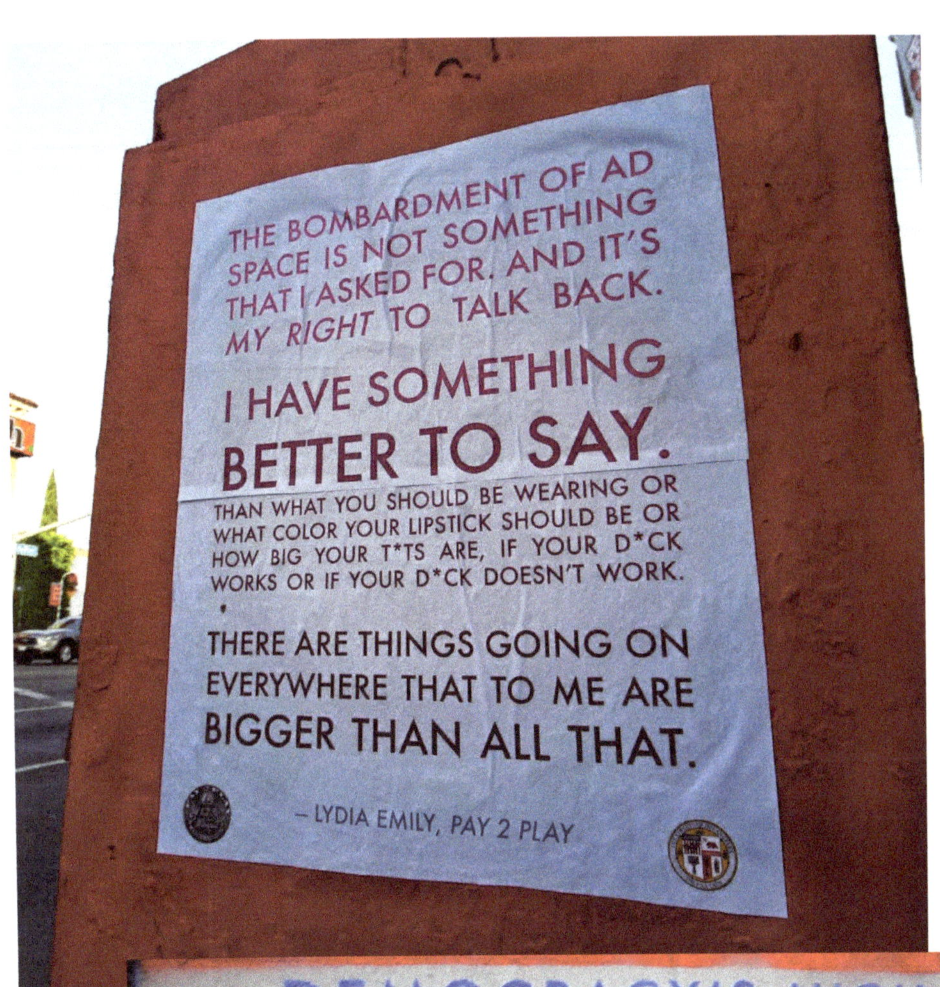

LydiaEmily stencil and quote.

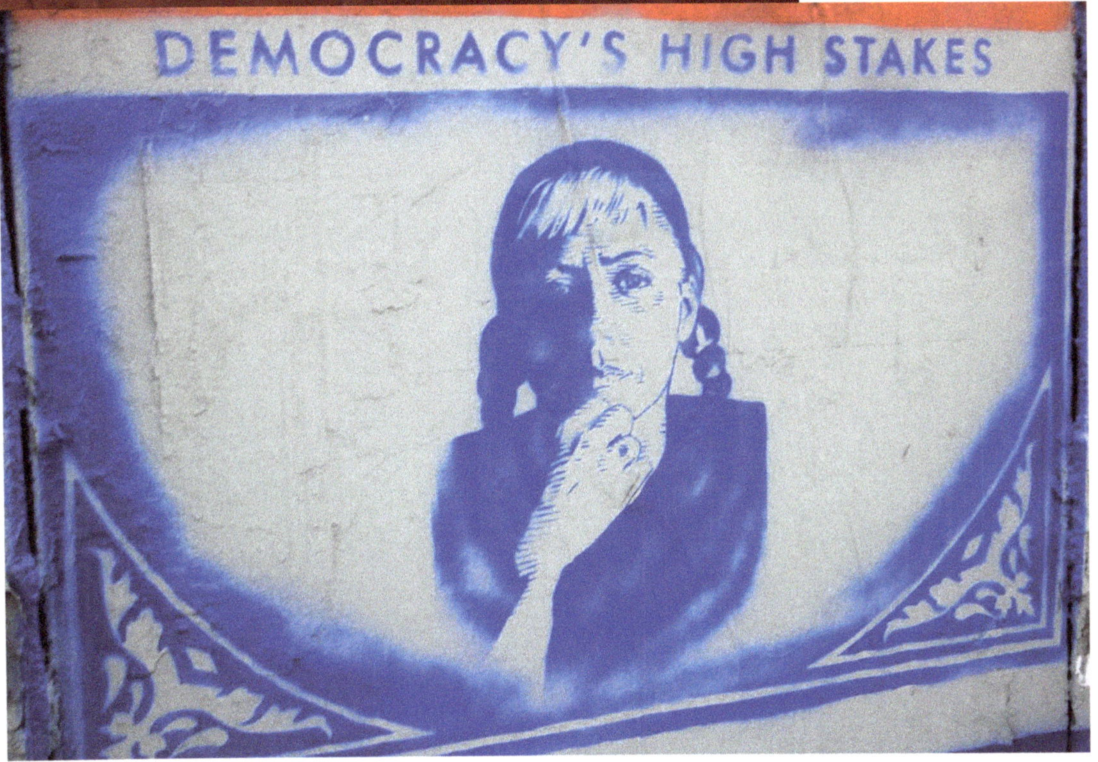

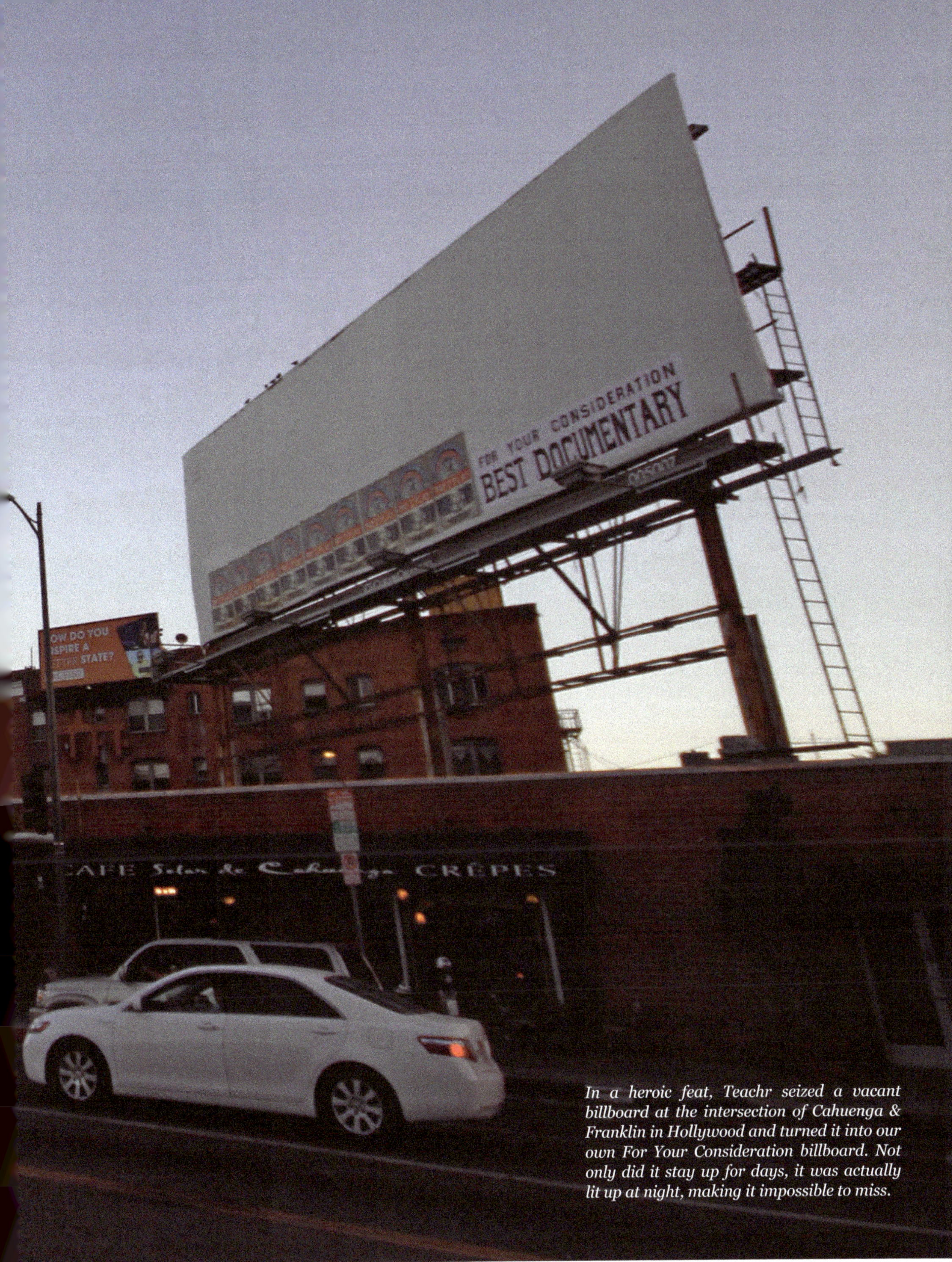

In a heroic feat, Teachr seized a vacant billboard at the intersection of Cahuenga & Franklin in Hollywood and turned it into our own For Your Consideration billboard. Not only did it stay up for days, it was actually lit up at night, making it impossible to miss.

ACTIVIST COMICS

PAY 2 PLAY concludes with solutions to the problems outlined throughout the documentary. We named them the "Fix Six" Solutions to make it more memorable. A reform explained at the end of a movie can stand out, but how to convey that idea in an image seen fleetingly while driving by?

I figured that the artwork, like the film, should feel empowering. It should look like something you would want to read. And like all decent street art, it should make you think.

The PSA Crew adapted "Action Comics" which first introduced Superman to comic book fans. Superman has always been an American symbol to many (even though he *is* an illegal immigrant) plus the viewer would relate with a childhood connection to the art. Also, I believe activism should be glamorized.

The FIX SIX solutions are:

1) Free Airtime for Candidates
2) Disclosure of Political Spending
3) End Gerrymandering
4) Compulsory Voting
5) Public Financing of Elections
6) A Constitutional Amendment Affirming That Money is Not Speech and Corporations Are Not People.

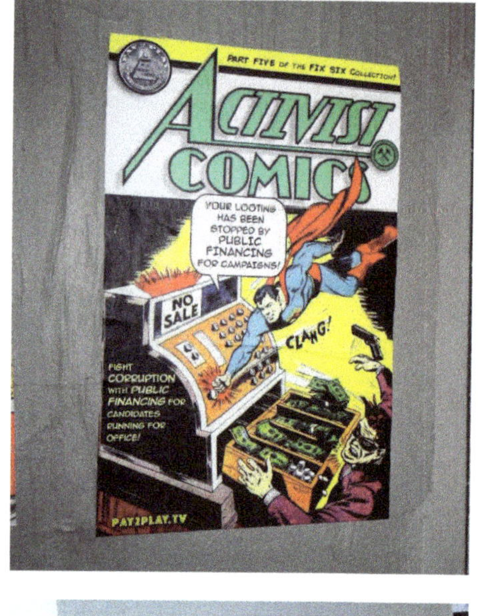

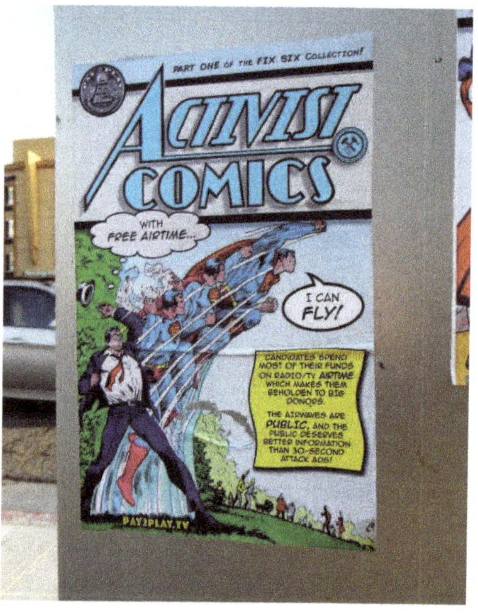

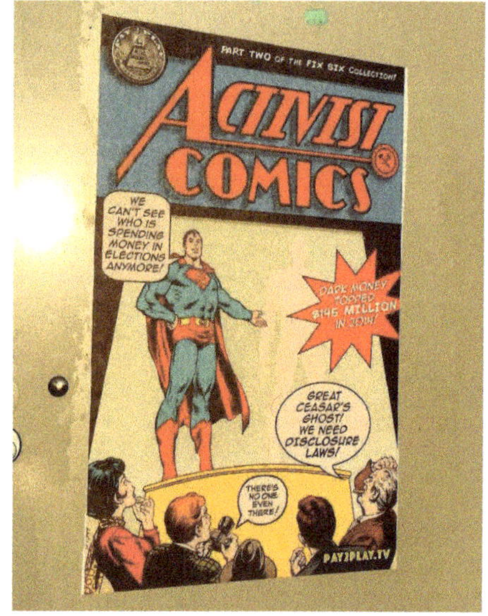

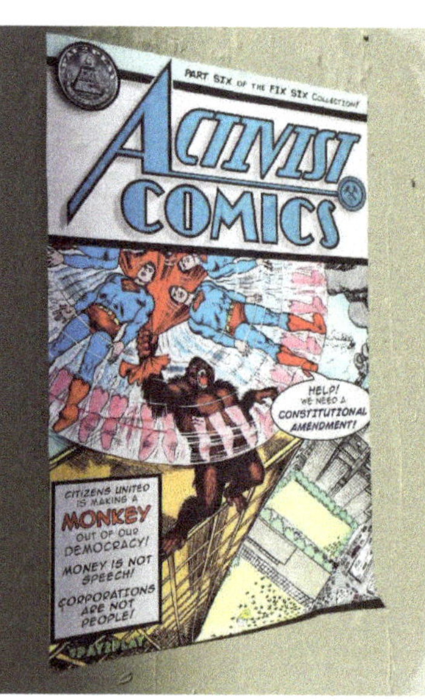

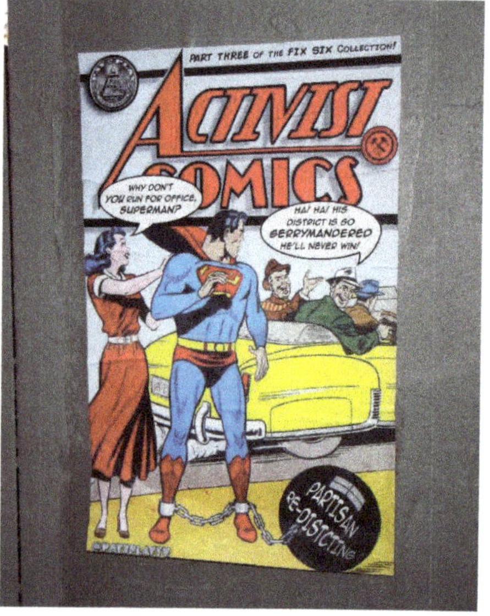

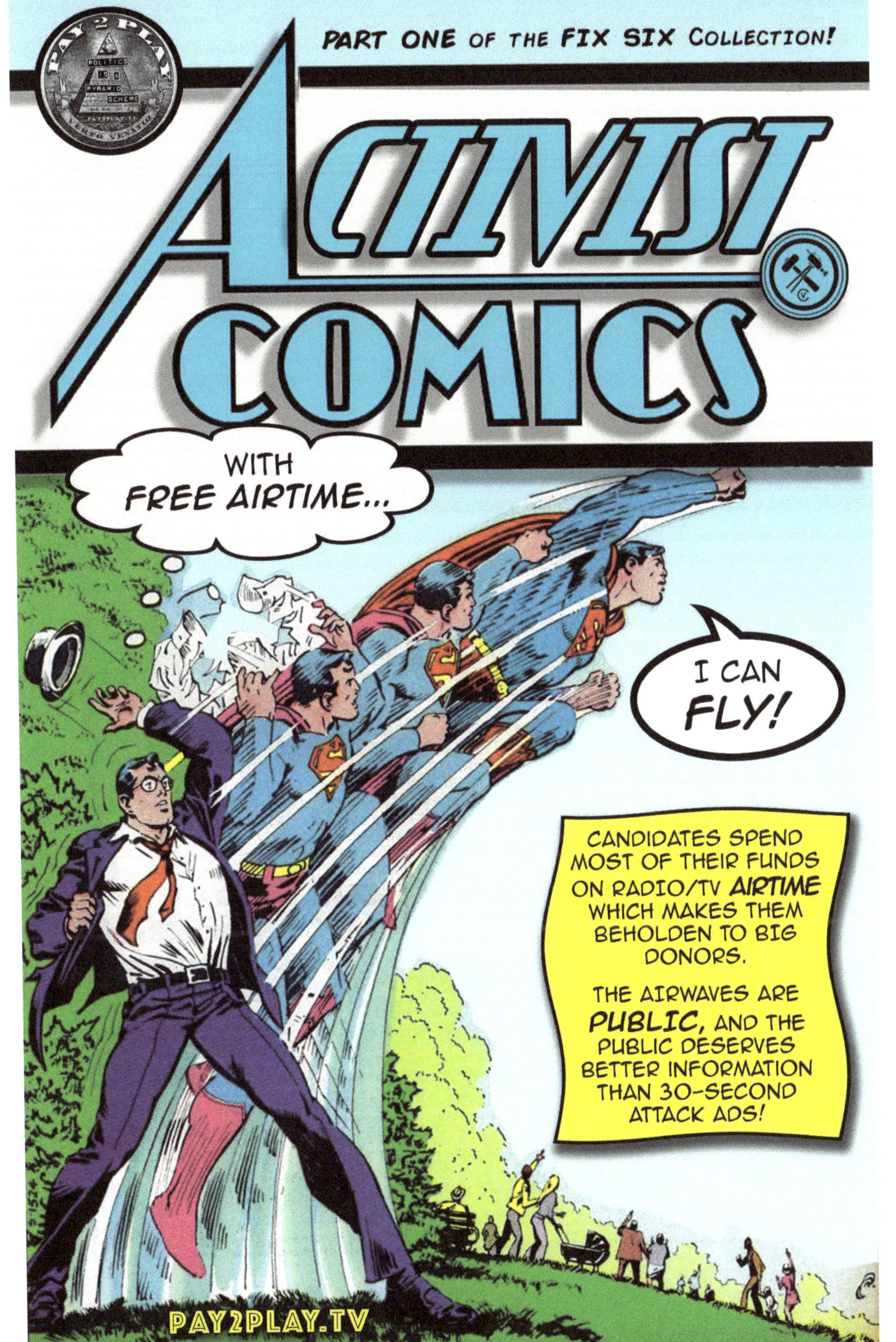
PART ONE OF THE FIX SIX COLLECTION!
ACTIVIST COMICS
WITH FREE AIRTIME...
I CAN FLY!
CANDIDATES SPEND MOST OF THEIR FUNDS ON RADIO/TV AIRTIME WHICH MAKES THEM BEHOLDEN TO BIG DONORS.
THE AIRWAVES ARE PUBLIC, AND THE PUBLIC DESERVES BETTER INFORMATION THAN 30-SECOND ATTACK ADS!
PAY2PLAY.TV

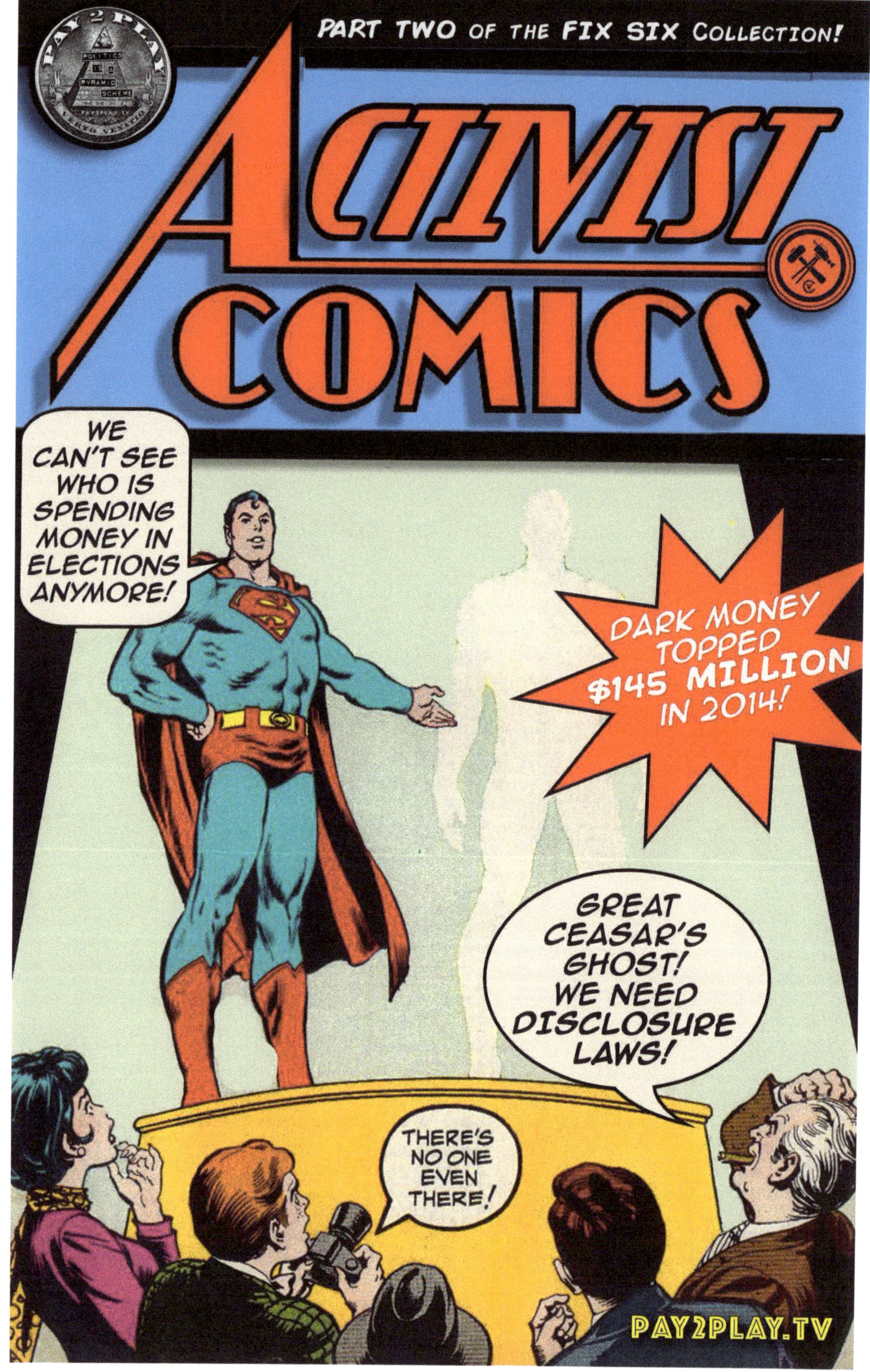
PART TWO OF THE FIX SIX COLLECTION!
ACTIVIST COMICS
WE CAN'T SEE WHO IS SPENDING MONEY IN ELECTIONS ANYMORE!
DARK MONEY TOPPED $145 MILLION IN 2014!
GREAT CEASAR'S GHOST! WE NEED DISCLOSURE LAWS!
THERE'S NO ONE EVEN THERE!
PAY2PLAY.TV

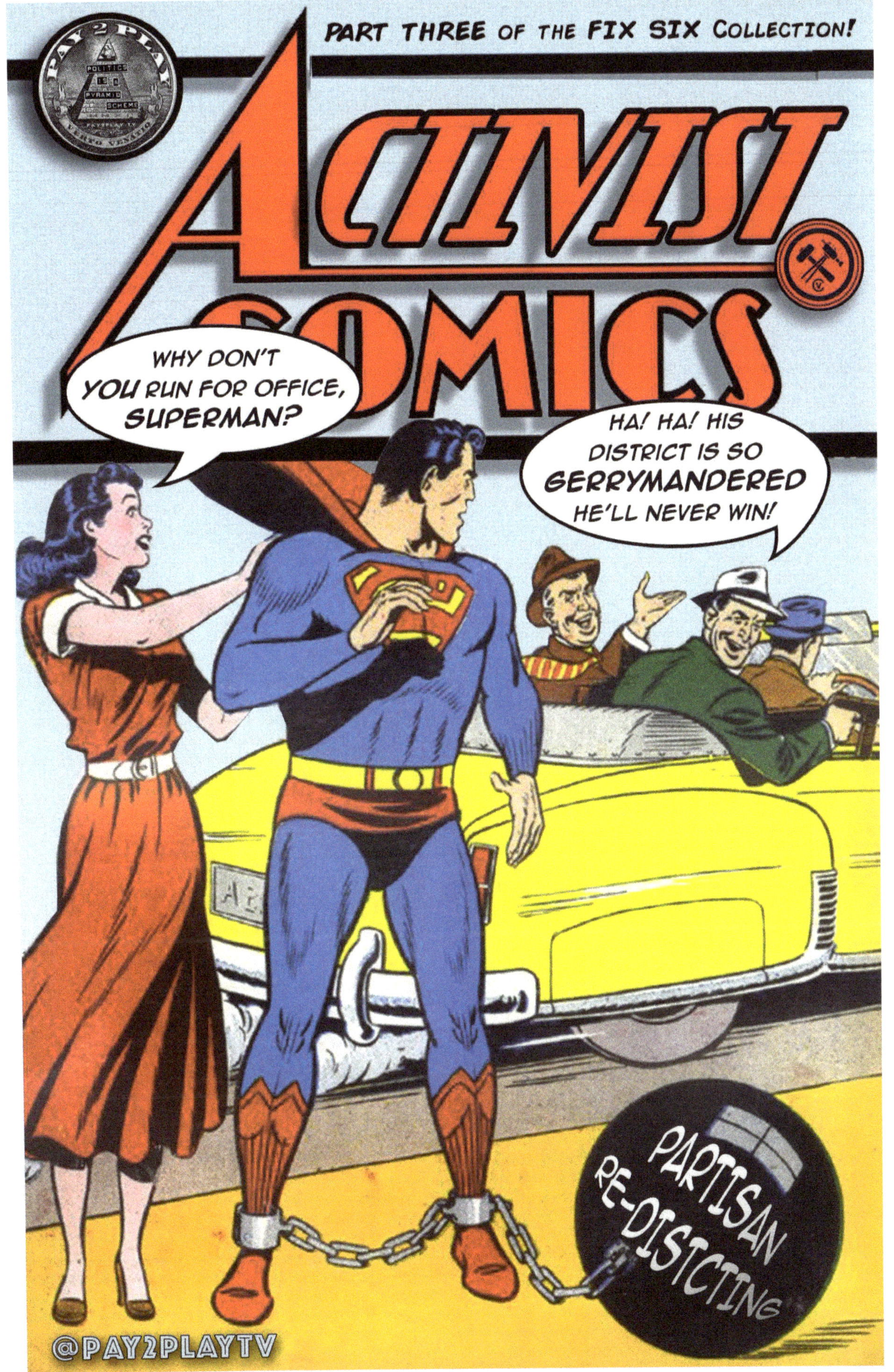
PAY 2 PLAY
PART THREE OF THE FIX SIX COLLECTION!
ACTIVIST COMICS
WHY DON'T YOU RUN FOR OFFICE, SUPERMAN?
HA! HA! HIS DISTRICT IS SO GERRYMANDERED HE'LL NEVER WIN!
PARTISAN RE-DISTICTING
@PAY2PLAYTV

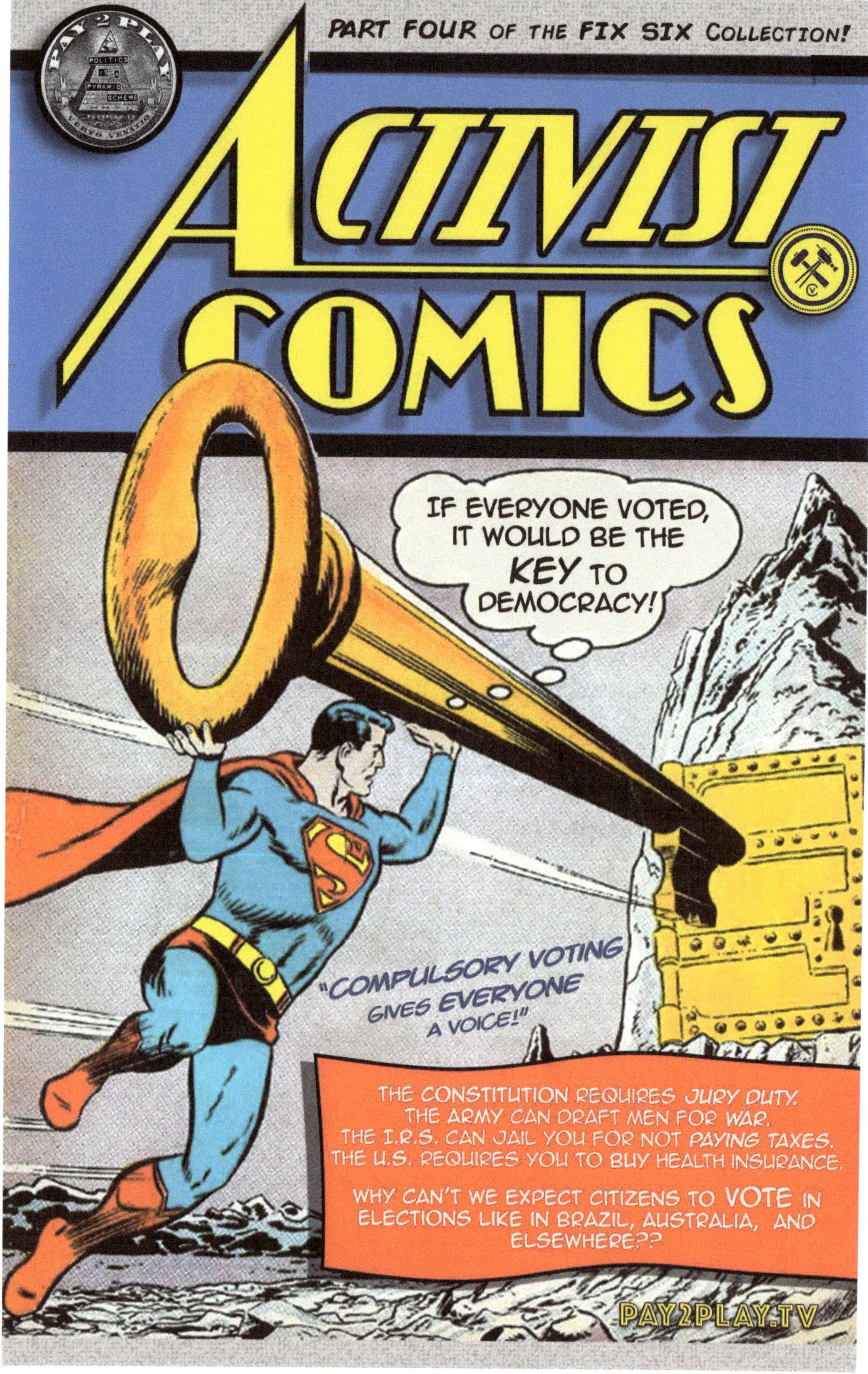
PART FOUR OF THE FIX SIX COLLECTION!
ACTIVIST COMICS
IF EVERYONE VOTED, IT WOULD BE THE KEY TO DEMOCRACY!
"COMPULSORY VOTING GIVES EVERYONE A VOICE!"
THE CONSTITUTION REQUIRES JURY DUTY. THE ARMY CAN DRAFT MEN FOR WAR. THE I.R.S. CAN JAIL YOU FOR NOT PAYING TAXES. THE U.S. REQUIRES YOU TO BUY HEALTH INSURANCE.
WHY CAN'T WE EXPECT CITIZENS TO VOTE IN ELECTIONS LIKE IN BRAZIL, AUSTRALIA, AND ELSEWHERE??
PAY2PLAY.TV

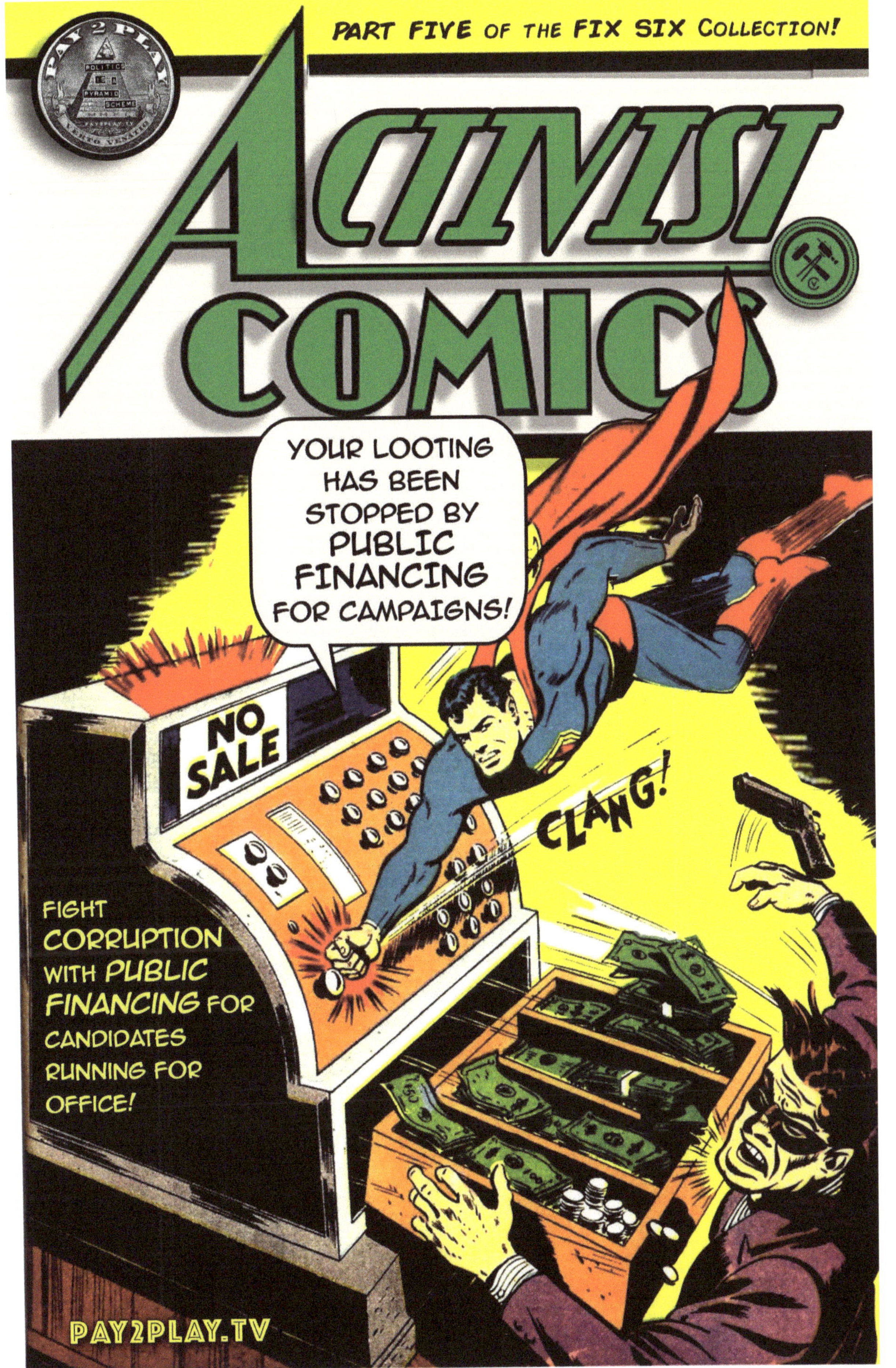
PART FIVE OF THE FIX SIX COLLECTION!
PAY 2 PLAY
POLITICS IS A PYRAMID SCHEME
ACTIVIST COMICS
YOUR LOOTING HAS BEEN STOPPED BY PUBLIC FINANCING FOR CAMPAIGNS!
NO SALE
CLANG!
FIGHT CORRUPTION WITH PUBLIC FINANCING FOR CANDIDATES RUNNING FOR OFFICE!
PAY2PLAY.TV

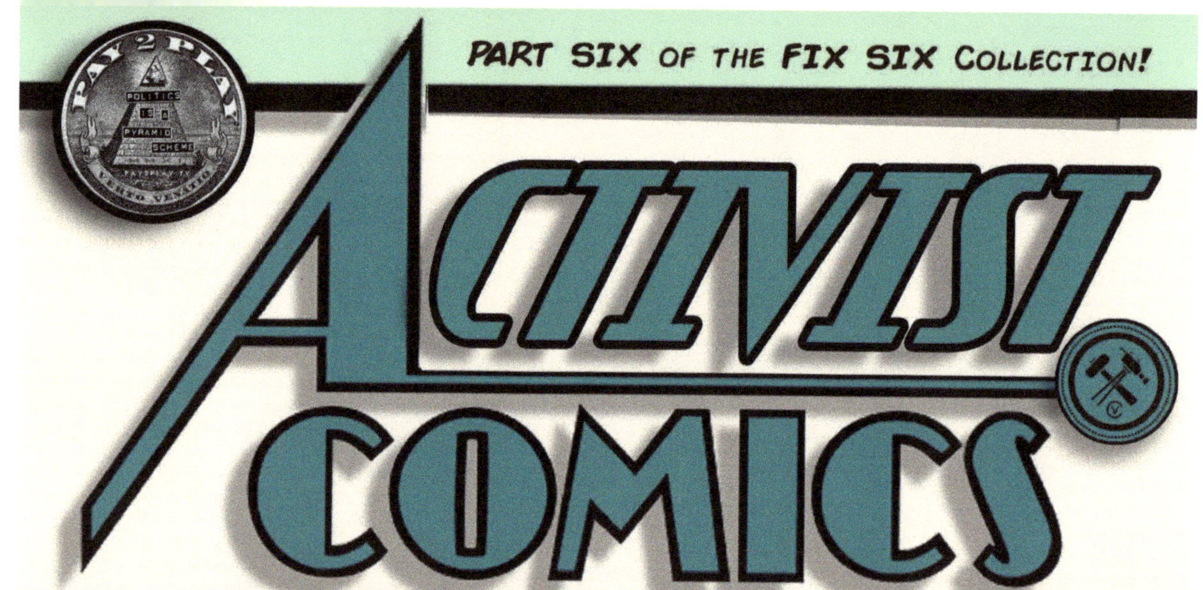

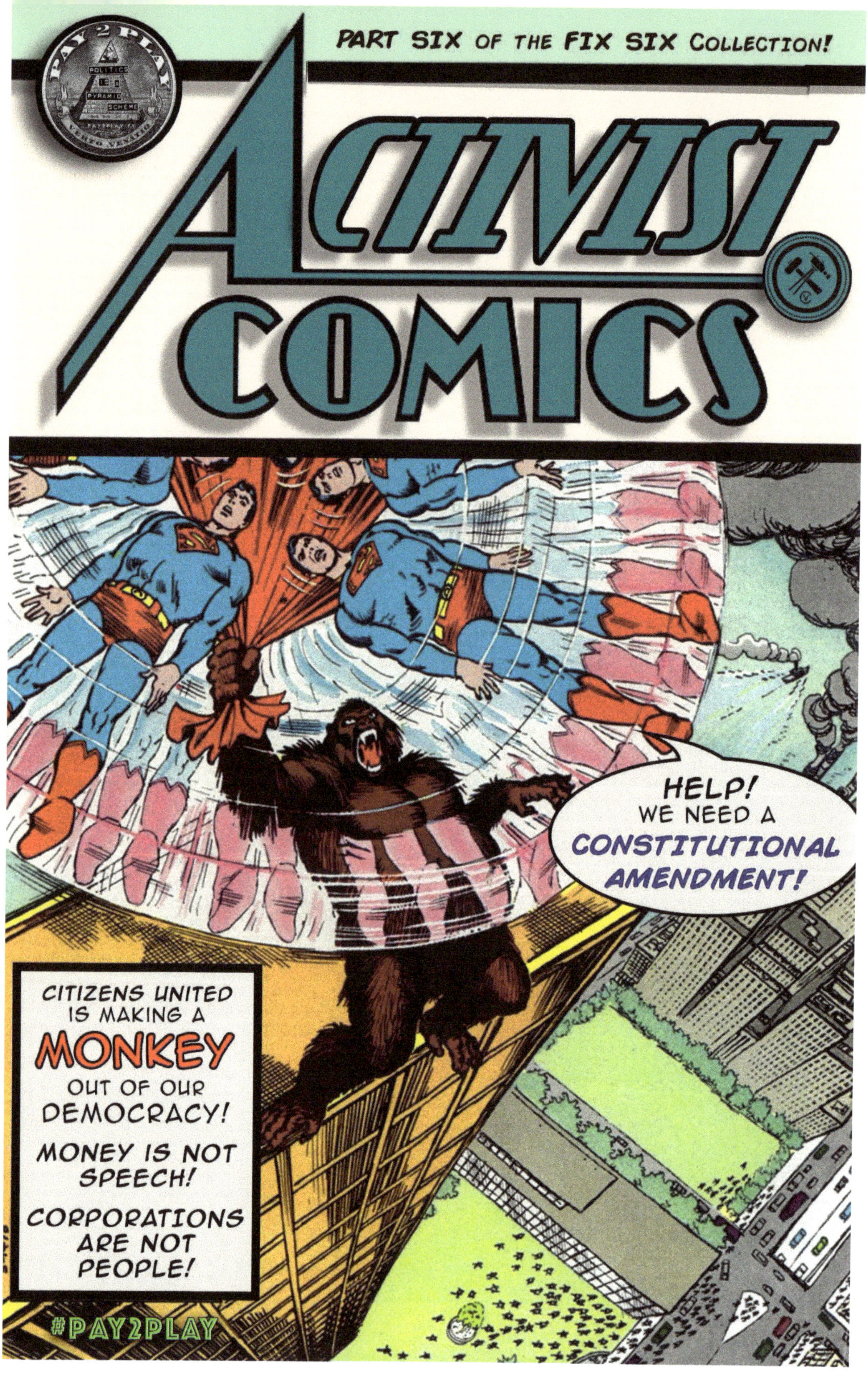

HELP!
WE NEED A
CONSTITUTIONAL
AMENDMENT!

CITIZENS UNITED
IS MAKING A
MONKEY
OUT OF OUR
DEMOCRACY!

MONEY IS NOT
SPEECH!

CORPORATIONS
ARE NOT
PEOPLE!

#PAY2PLAY

EPILOGUE

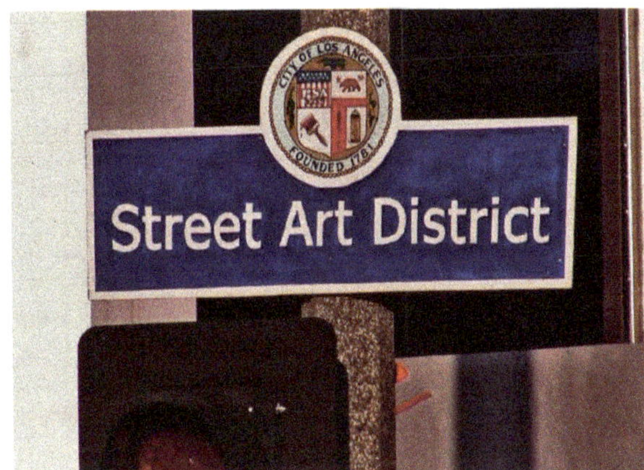

The PSA Crew mounted this street sign at Melrose & Fairfax, dubbing it the Street Art District.

By the end of 2013, *Melrose & Fairfax* had gone dark.

The remarkable streak of imaginative street artists trying to top each other had apparently run its course. Some artists had gotten big and were now in demand around the world. Still more artists were arrested in the LAPD crackdown and decided the risk was not worth the pursuit. A few of the artists in these pages are still getting up around town, though maybe not so much along Melrose these days.

Amidst this boom, of course, there were galleries suddenly interested in getting in on street art, nakedly capitalizing on artists eager for exposure, quick to screw over anyone for cash, assuming the next hot artist was bound to come along. This can quickly give hope to struggling artists, only to leave a bad taste.

Further discouraging to local street art as a whole was the emergence of ugly pastes which started appearing all over town, capping artists everywhere, all of the same drab image: a black & white picture looking up at McDonald's arches. As if the world's biggest restaurant chain did not take up enough space across the country and the airwaves, some misanthrope decided to put up even more McDonald's signage, ultimately covering more surfaces than any single paster in the city.

But more destructive than anything, the scene itself had become ferocious, as competition yielded to animosity and rivalries dimmed the collective enthusiasm. In a culture where supposedly all surfaces are fair game, street artists fiercely defend their art once it is up, and if anyone else defaces a piece of theirs, it becomes deeply personal. These grudges carry out to destroying a rival's art all over town, outing one's identity, even violence.

In its sign-off, *Melrose & Fairfax* took stock of what had been a fertile era: "It is sad, because it's hard to hold any community together when the hate is stronger than the shared bond. This situation might be similar to the way that Banksy is reviled in some graffiti circles. In the graffiti and street art worlds, currently, disdain is kind of like a badge of success. *Melrose & Fairfax* believes that the street art and graffiti community, as a whole, have some growing up to do. If there is going to be a productive community, it's got to be supportive of each other. Battle the ideas that keep people down. Battle the authorities. Battle the buffman. But don't waste time and energy battling each other. The street art community will finally come into its own when people stop bickering within the community, and come together, as a whole, to fight the good fight. Remember people, it's us against them—not us against us."

Here's looking forward to that next era.

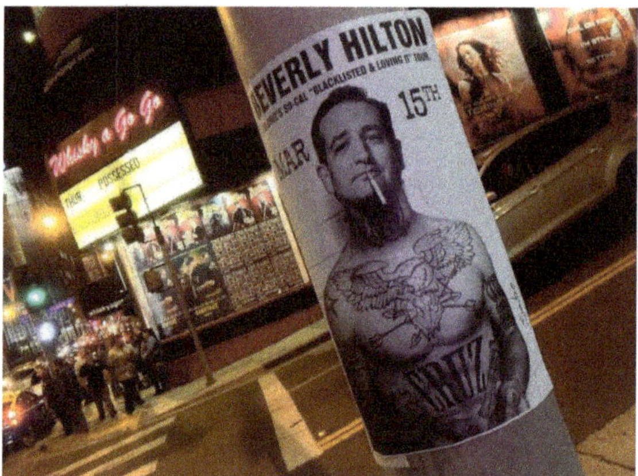

Ted Cruz now sells Sabo's street art on his website.

POST SCRIPT

I was talking to my friend Robert about having been on a rooftop filming with Alec Monopoly in the middle of the night, when someone showed up to work in the building we had climbed on top of and was blocking our access back down. Alec and I took our time before venturing down a telephone pole on the other side of the building. What I always appreciated about Robert, a black guy from Detroit, was his unhesitating honesty.

"Maaan, that is some white privilege right there," he lamented. "If it was a black guy up there they caught, they'd be like, 'You did ALL the street art!'"And of course, he's right. There are two systems of justice in this country, and the past year has shown that even saying "Black lives matter" can be controversial, something that should not even need to be said.

While making *PAY 2 PLAY*, I found I was unable to articulate the parallel I was attempting to draw between street art and protests; I had to intercut the two to even be able to start to describe it. But taking to the street to protest, and taking to the street to put up art seemed so similar to me. Both were an act of using your voice. Both went down in the streets. And both risk arrest.

In recent protests surrounding police brutality, some demonstrators exercised nonviolent tactics of civil disobedience with the possibility of being arrested. But seeing as how unequal treatment by law enforcement is at the core of this crisis, it is understandable that some black protesters would say to their white ally activists: for black folks, arrest holds uncertain dangers, but as white people, you can use your privilege to make an important point and raise awareness.

I feel the same is true with street art. As you can tell by this dossier, once you look behind the pseudonym, most of these street artists turn out to be white. The one black guy getting up was putting up ads, trying to eat. Thus, if you are someone who does not fear an arrest on your record to prevent you from getting a job, or if you are not afraid that police will lay hands on you, then use that opportunity to speak for others who cannot speak for themselves. There's already too much self-promotion on the streets.

While finishing this book, I checked in on Phone Jacks to see how he was since his arrest a few years back. He wrote back that he was in federal court. But now he was the plaintiff, as well as his own attorney. He had taken someone to court for stealing a TV show idea he'd emailed them. Not just anyone: The NFL, the $9 billion/year non-profit for domestic abusers. He had sent them an idea for the NFL's version of "American Idol," and when the NFL came out with a show called "The Draft" a few months later, Phone Jacks contacted all of the NFL's advertisers until the advertisers asked the NFL what was going on. Once he got them in court, a federal judge denied the NFL's request for dismissal based on the evidence presented, and now they had to settle. Phone Jacks said it would be for "a lot." This in L.A., where people steal show ideas with impunity, daily.

Let the lesson of this book be the same one from *PAY 2 PLAY*—that one person really can make a difference, even against some of the biggest corporations in the world.

GLOSSARY

A helpful guide to some of the terminology used in this book. Not like it's all that exotic, there just aren't normal terms for the practice. Hence, people came up with euphemisms that make sense.

All-City Means your art is seen all over town. Derives from graffiti culture in NYC in the 1970s/80s, when the aim was to spray paint on subway cars that would travel through all five boroooughs.

Bombing Adorning many surfaces in an area with your art.

Buffing Painting over or removing street art, usually by the city or people working community service (although there has been at least one old guy in the Fairfax District who went around painting over street art by himself).

Capping Covering up another's street art with your own. Usually taken as a hostile act.

Getting Up To spread street art around town however you do it: posters, stickers, paint, etc.

Going Large To put up a lot of street art around town in one night, so it can't not be noticed.

Pastes A poster that has been mounted outside with adhesive glue or wheat paste, which is just flour mixed with water into a smooth, sticky fluid.

Piece Any piece of street art: poster, stencil, decorative, hand drawn, etc.

Riding A piece of street art staying up, before it is painted over or taken down, e.g., "That Teachr piece has been riding on La Brea since July."

Slap A sticker. Also can specify a sticker with a tag written on it, like a mailing label from the Post Office or a name tag.

Smashed A spot or wall that is covered with lots of stickers or street art.

Spot-jacking Placing your street art next to a prominently displayed piece, thereby hijacking the attention the previous artist was attracting.

Tagging Scrawling of intitials or a street art psuedonym, usually with marker or paint pen. Unlike street art, it's not meant for the general public to understand, it's more to jockey for visibility among other taggers.

Toy A "toy" is a new street artist who thinks they are the shit but don't know what they are doing, e.g., "The author of this book was a toy trying to get up." Can also be used as an adjective to describe inferior street art.

Up If you are "up," it means your art is widely seen on the streets at any given time.

"The Street is My Gallery," by Septerhed on La Brea & Third St.

ACKNOWLEDGEMENTS

Thank you to my amazing *PAY 2 PLAY* partner, Holly Mosher, who first inspired the film and then inspired so many more people with the film. Thank you to every single person who contributed to the film in its long journey, everyone who hosted a screening, everyone who shared the film with a friend. Much gratitude to Shepard, Cleon, Victoria, everyone at Studio One, Ric and Primary Color. Thanks to Christine, Rob, and Richie for making this book a reality.

Thank you to the artists included in this book. I hope to share your inspiration with others. Just as much, thank you to the street artists that made the scene, if not this book: Bankrupt Slut, Leba, AMK, Snyder, Jose Fever, Kill Yrslf, Random Act, Bod Bod, Muse, Cali Love, LA_Blue, Serf, Pike, TCF, the 169, Sprout, K-47, Wil, Jaber, Johnny Digital, Desire Obtain Cherish, Bran One TRB, Sand One, Louie XV, Ramiro Gomez Jr., 47, Destroy All Design, Smear, Thefl, Lush, Common Cents, Felix, Cali Killa, Granny, Cut 'n' Paste, Army of One (RIP), Trigz (RIP), LoudLabs, Homo Riot, Smog City, Herbert the Hippo, J.R., Blu, Annabelle, Revok, Skyler Grey, Septerhed, the 86'ed Crew, The Status Faction, Insurgency Inc., Madman, Phobik, The Seventh Letter, Saber, Lister, Kills Billions, Wheat Peace, Dogbyte, Lord Jim, Inseyet, Xvala, Swift, D*Face, Neckface, Street Art Sanctuary, Cha$e, Bandit, Kenny Scharf, Retna, Casio, Shark Toof, AJL, SicKid, Valak One, Eyesore, and more I missed. Special thanks to the Hollywood Beautification Team for keeping the streets a clean canvas.

Extra special thanks to Gregory Linton of *Melrose & Fairfax* for creating a scene for artists to meet and collaborate. Get up, stay up!

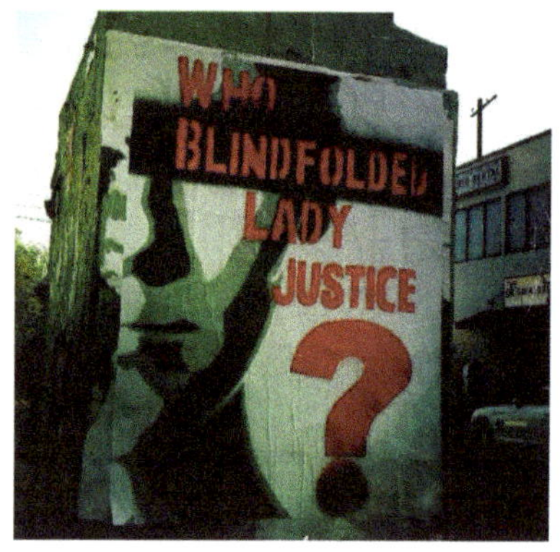

Profound thanks to everyone involved in making and releasing *PAY 2 PLAY*: Adam Winkler, Aliya Rhaman, Brad Friedman, Brad Nye, Brianna Bodine, Brodie Alexander, Cheryl Dickinson, Ciara Torres-Spelliscy, Clark Davis, Cynda Collins Arsenault, Cynthia Beard, Dan Kattman, David Dayen, David Walker, Derek Cressman, Dorian Cheah, Dorit & Green Lifestyle Network, Doug Hughes, Earl Katz, Ed Erikson, Fortunato Procopio, Gary Bush, George & Julie Mosher, Grant Abert, Greg Palast, Heather Burgett, James Honaker, Jason Leopold, Jessica Brackman, Jessica Levinson, Joanne & David Goldblum, Joe Glass, John Ford, Jonathan Schell, Judy Branfman, Karen Wilkinson, Kent Moorehead, Kristin Tieche, Laura Paglin, Lawrence Lessig, Lee Fang, Libby McInerny, Lisle Engle, Marc Ostrick, Marge Baker, Marge Tabankin, Marianne Williamson, Marjorie Roswell, Mark Crispin Miller, Mark Stuckey, Mary Jack, Michael Wuten, Michelle Fawcett, Mike Chamness, Mike McCabe, Mike Way, Miles Curtiss, Mitchell Reichler, Nick Nyhart, Nicole Berns, Noam Chomsky, Paul Hackett, Pluma, Ravi Shah, Rebecca Lynn Minkin, Rep. John Sarbanes, Rep. Ted Lieu, Rich Bridge, Rick Perez, Rob Mosher, Rob Weissman, Rocker Meadows, Russ Rayburn, Sally & Richard Ennis, Sean Patrick, Sharmila Ourdesray, Shawn Taylor, Stephanie Bleyer, Stephen Chace Bass, Subodh Chandra, Surya Yalamanchili, Tamra Raven, Thom Hartmann, Tim Munson, Timothy Johnson, Van Jones, Vivian Umino, Yvonne McDonald, Zach D. Roberts. Thanks to Steve Fagan at Sky Island Films, Gary Baddeley, Dan Gurlitz, and Marcie Gainer at Disinfo, Caroline Briggs and Antoinette Juneat at Free Speech TV, Matt Radecki at Different By Design Post.

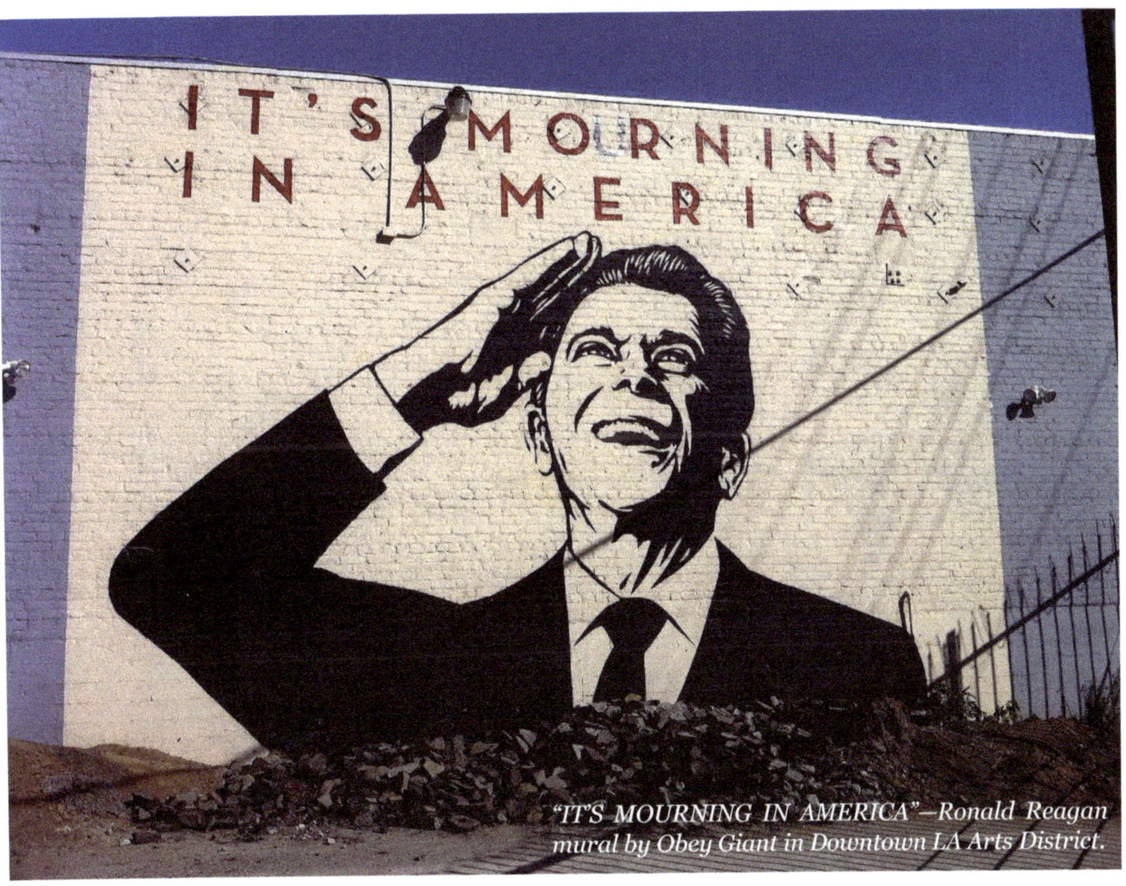

"IT'S MOURNING IN AMERICA"—Ronald Reagan mural by Obey Giant in Downtown LA Arts District.

A heartfelt thanks to the partners and advocates for others that helped spread this message as part of the Democracy Movement: John Wachenheimer and Matthew Snyder, 28 Amenders; Corinne Bourdeau, Nicole Haggard, Susan Haymer, 360 Degree Communications; Curt Ries, Kai Newkirk, Mathias Quackenbush, 99RISE; Gwendolyn Bradley, AAUP; David Delk, Alliance For Democracy; Lauren Windsor, Mike Lux, American Family Voices; Arnie Alpert, American Friends Service Committee; Eric Zulaski, American Friends Service Committee; Alison Hartson, Americans Taking Action; Sam Wercinski, AZ Advocacy Network, Andy Barker, Jay King, Ben & Jerry's; Mark Karlin, Buzzflash; Trent Lange, California Clean Money Campaign; Hinnaneh Qazi, Kathay Feng, Leila Pedersen, Sylvia Moore, Helen Grieco, California Common Cause; Zach Weinstein, CalPIRG; Bill Snape, Center For Biological Diversity; Abigail Seiler, Heather Whitehead, Center for Food Safety; Brendan Fischer, Lisa Graves, Mary Bottari, Center For Media & Democracy; Jodie Evans, Michelle Pineiro, Codepink; Arisha Hatch, Rashad Robinson, Color of Change; Allegra Chapman, Bob Edgar, Karen Hobert Flynn, Miles Rapoport, Scott Swenson, Susan Lerner, Common Cause; Eddie Kuritz, Laura Leavitt, Tim Molina, Courage Campaign; Josh Nelson, Murshed Zaheed, CREDO; Stephen Santulli, CREW; Zavé Martohardjono, Cut50; Charles Chamberlin, Jay Henderson, Ruby Reid, Eden James, Democracy For America; Marissa Brown, Sean Trambley, Democracy Initiative; Anita Lorraine Kinney, Democracy Matters; Donte Donald, Joseph Hines, Demos; Adam Smith, Francoise Stovall, Every Voice; Brenna Norton, Darcey Rakestraw, Kate Fried, Food & Water Watch; Jason Miller, Franciscan Action Network; Bri Holmes, Jeff Clements, John Bonifaz, Lindsay Van Dyke, Sarah Stranahan, Free Speech For People; Jon Fox, Semhal Tekeste, Friends of the Earth; Layla Zaidane, Generation Progress; Ashley Cline, Carleen Pickard, Derek Poppert, Global Exchange/Elect Democracy; Diana Reeves, GMO Free USA; Lawrence Gaughan, Gov360; Adam Mason, Iowa Citizens for Community Improvement; Mike Peabody, Issue One; Betsy McKinney, It's Time; Stephen Michaels, Main St. Alliance; Szelena Grey, Benj Singer, MayDayUS; Aaron Black, Chip Travis, Kathy DaSilva, Mary Beth Fielder, Michele Sutter, Money Out Voters In; Daniel Lee, David Cobb, Edgar Franks, Jessica Munger, Kaitlin Sopoci-Belknap, Keyan Bliss, Move To Amend; Jess Buckley, NASPA; Bill Gallagher, National Nurses United; Liz Ryan Murray, National People's Action; David Turnbull, Matt Maiorana, Oil Change International; The Pen, PEN; Calvin Sloan, Layne Amerikaner, Rio Tazewell, Scott Foval, People For the Amercian Way; Dustin Calliari, Physicians for a National Health Program; Conor Boyle, Janis Kay, Progressive Democrats of America; Jan Liss, Project Pericles; Aquene Freechild, Jonah Minkoff-Zern, Margrete Strand Rangnes, Public Citizen; Dahlia Graham, React To Film; Jen Kim, Nisha Anand, Van Jones, Rebuild The Dream; Lee Camp, Redacted Tonight; Graham Lynn, Isabelle Goodman, Jeff Bomberger, Mansur Gidfar, Matt Vaughan, Tzipora Lederman, Represent US; Dorry Levine, Tyler Creighton, ReThink Media; Heather Smith, Maura LaMendola, Rock The Vote; Aman Banerji, Roosevelt Institute Campus Network; Kurt Walters, Lee Woodsmall, Rootstrikers; Jeff Haggin, Say No To Big Money; Ben Cohen, Stamp Stampede; Student Debt Crisis; Beth Hwang, Student Labor Action Project; John Nichols, The Nation; Kalin Jordan, Unkoch My Campus; Emma Einhorn, USAction; Michael Eisenscher, USLAW; Blair Bowie, Dan Smith, Emma Boorboor, USPIRG; Cyndy Fowler, Yes We Can; David Duhelde, Democratic Socialists of America; Betsy Avila, Young Democratic Socialists.

Finally, a deep thanks to you, for supporting outlaw art culture, independent media, and the Democracy Movement.

ABOUT THE AUTHOR

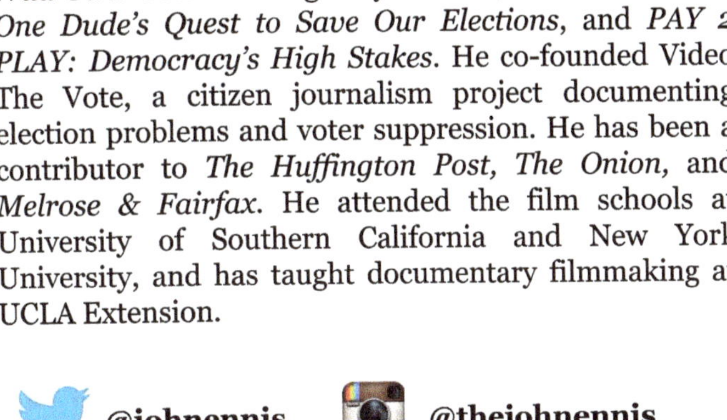

John Wellington Ennis is a filmmaker, activist, and father. His films include the Upright Citizens Brigade's *Wild Girls Gone* starring Amy Poehler, *FREE FOR ALL! One Dude's Quest to Save Our Elections*, and *PAY 2 PLAY: Democracy's High Stakes*. He co-founded Video The Vote, a citizen journalism project documenting election problems and voter suppression. He has been a contributor to *The Huffington Post, The Onion,* and *Melrose & Fairfax*. He attended the film schools at University of Southern California and New York University, and has taught documentary filmmaking at UCLA Extension.

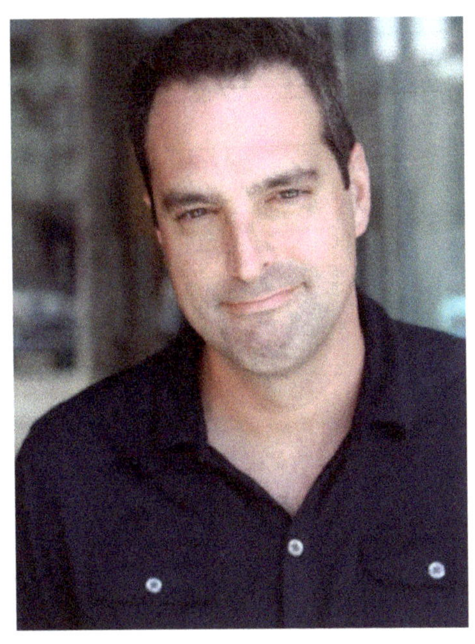

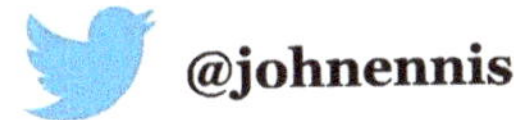

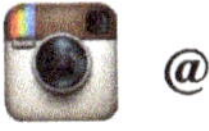

@thejohnennis

THANKS TO OUR PARTNERS

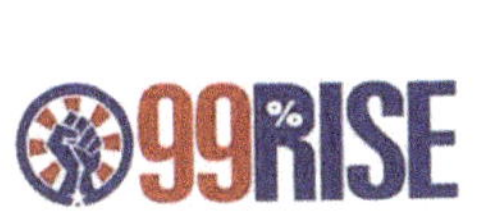

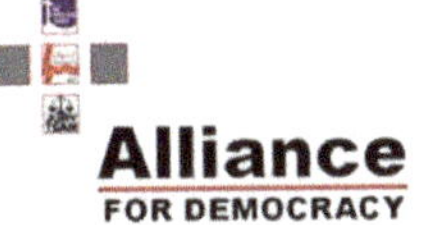

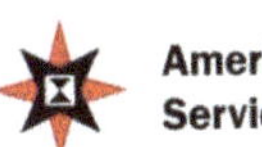

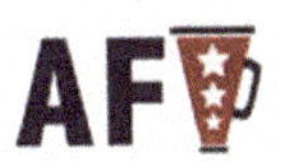

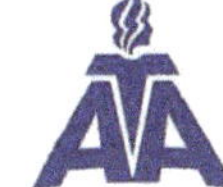

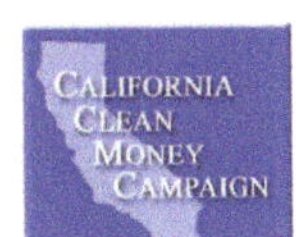

Center for Media & Democracy

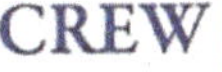

colorofchange.org

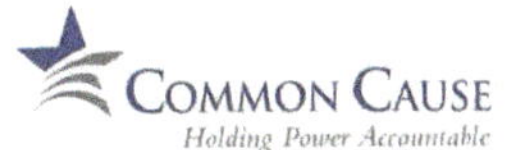

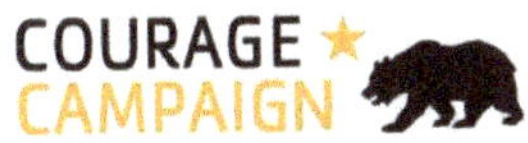

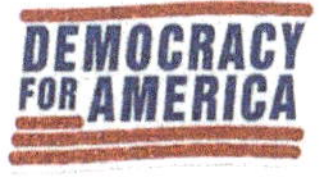

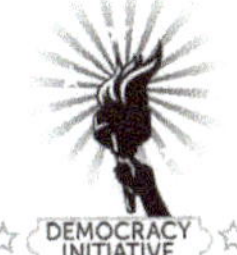

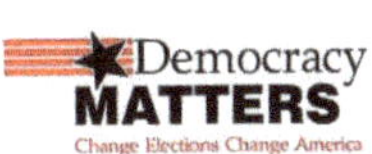

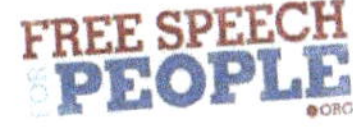

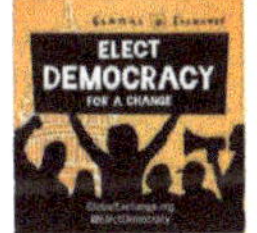

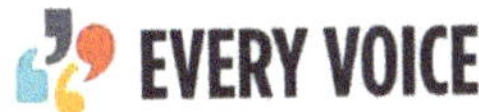

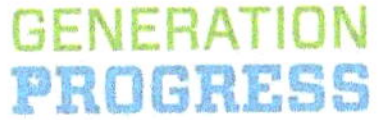

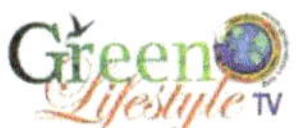

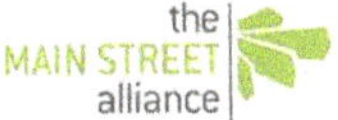

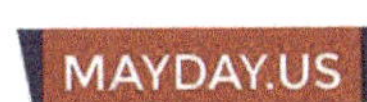

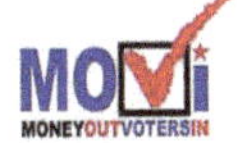

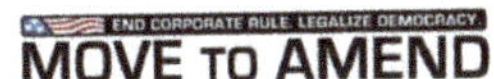

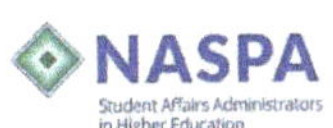

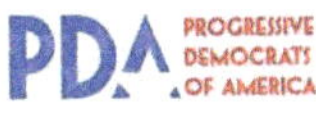

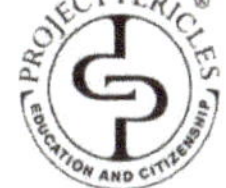

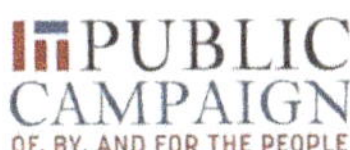

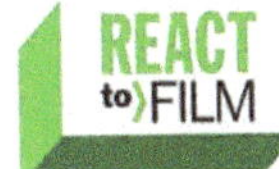

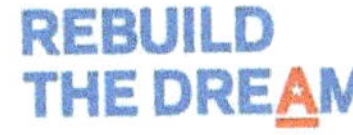

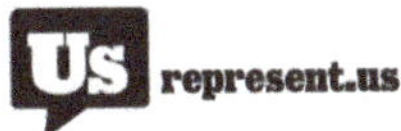

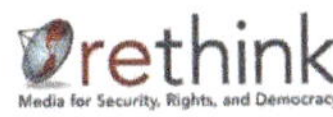

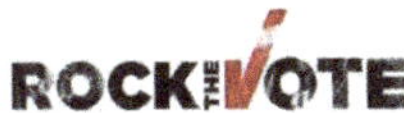

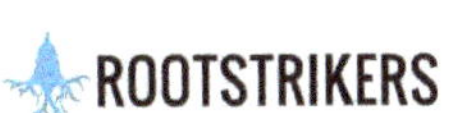

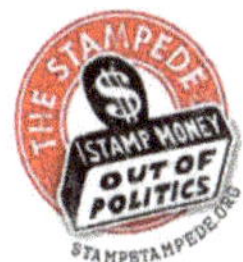

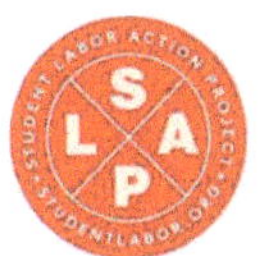

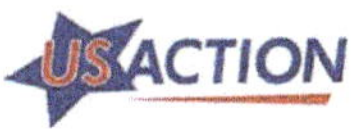

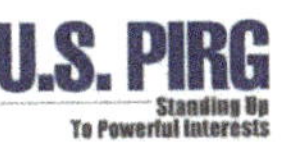

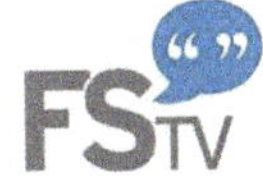

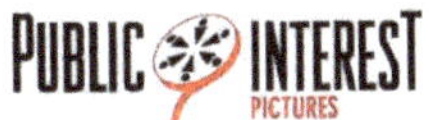

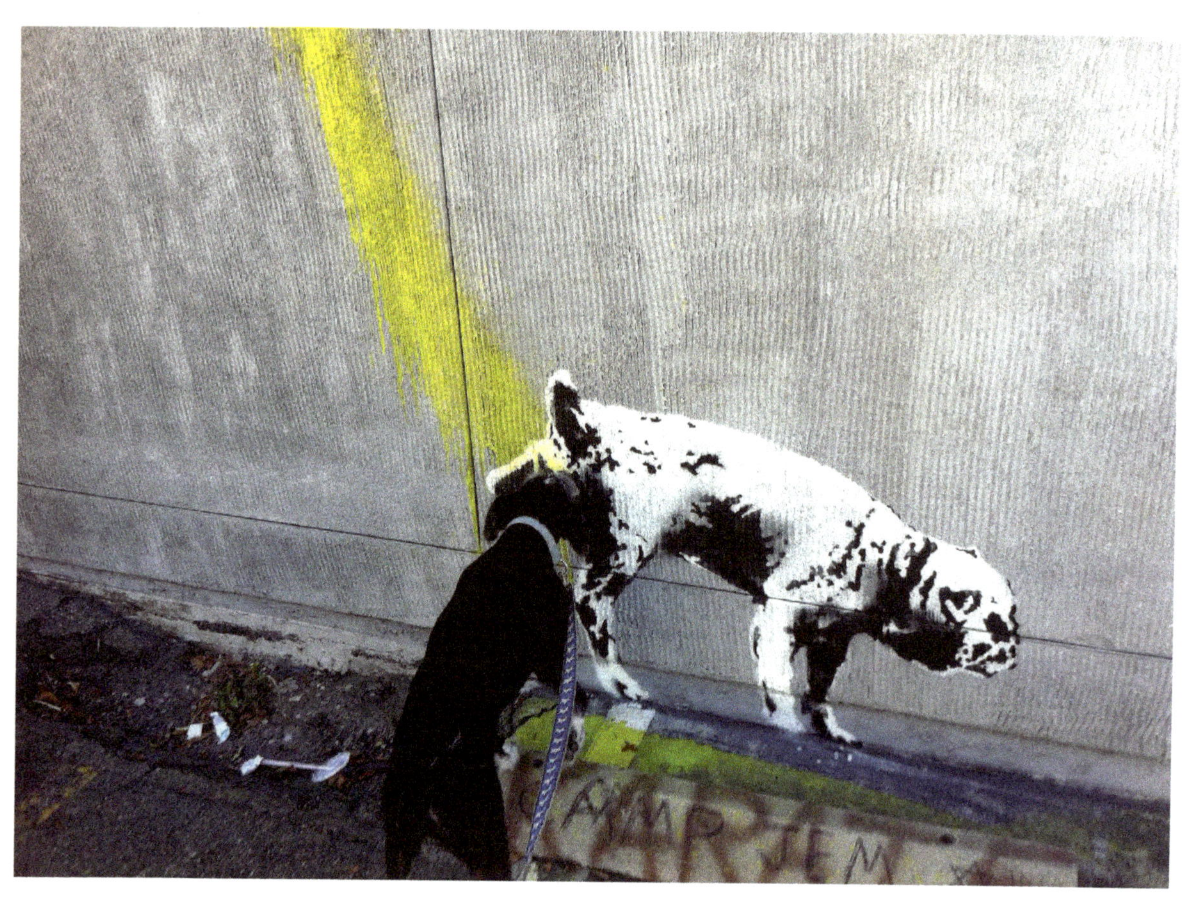

The End

www.ingramcontent.com/pod-product-compliance
Ingram Content Group UK Ltd.
Pitfield, Milton Keynes, MK11 3LW, UK
UKHW062007290726
14090UKWH00022B/1428

9 781941 519974